D1560619

COLOSSAL

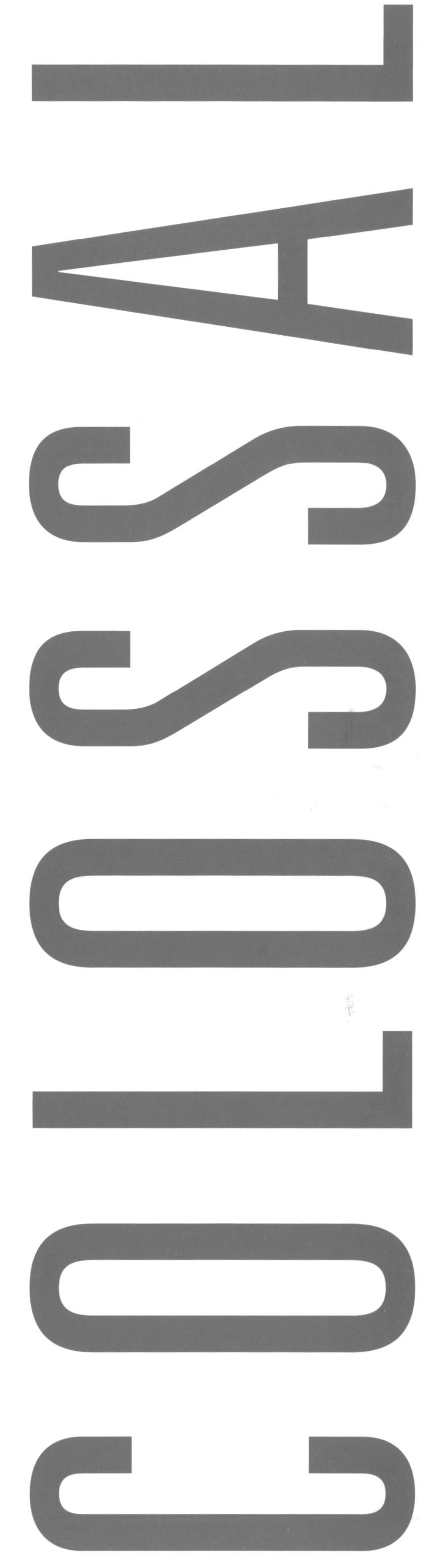


**Engineering the Suez Canal, Statue of Liberty, Eiffel Tower, and Panama Canal**

Transcontinental Ambition in France and the United States during the Long Nineteenth Century

**Darcy Grimaldo Grigsby**

In memory of
my Panamanian grandmother
GREGORIA ALMILLATEGUI
mother of five, seamstress, tamale-maker, and bruja
who sold aphrodisiacs to American women
she smoked rolled tobacco with the fire in her mouth,
had no formal education yet acted as a lawyer for the poor,
and when she lived with us pretended to speak no English
and
my American grandfather
LOUIS SINCLAIR GRIGSBY
father of three, Lieutenant in the U.S. Navy,
and a member of Philadelphia's Chamber of Commerce
though long unemployed he was always loyal, loving, and very funny

A generous grant from Furthermore Grants
in Publishing, A Program of the J. M. Kaplan Fund,
subsidized publication of this book.

Periscope Publishing, Ltd.
Pittsburgh and New York City

Distributed by Prestel Publishing
900 Broadway, Suite 603
New York, NY 10003


Printed and bound in China
First edition



Editors: Sara Lickey, Madelaine Dusseau,
Chelsea Weathers
Design: Diane Jaroch Design
Typeset in Univers Condensed and Rockwell

Cover image: Man Climbing Staircase
Eiffel Tower, Paris
Photo: Bruno Ehrs / CORBIS

ISBN 978-1-934772-76-8
Library of Congress Control Number 2011944521

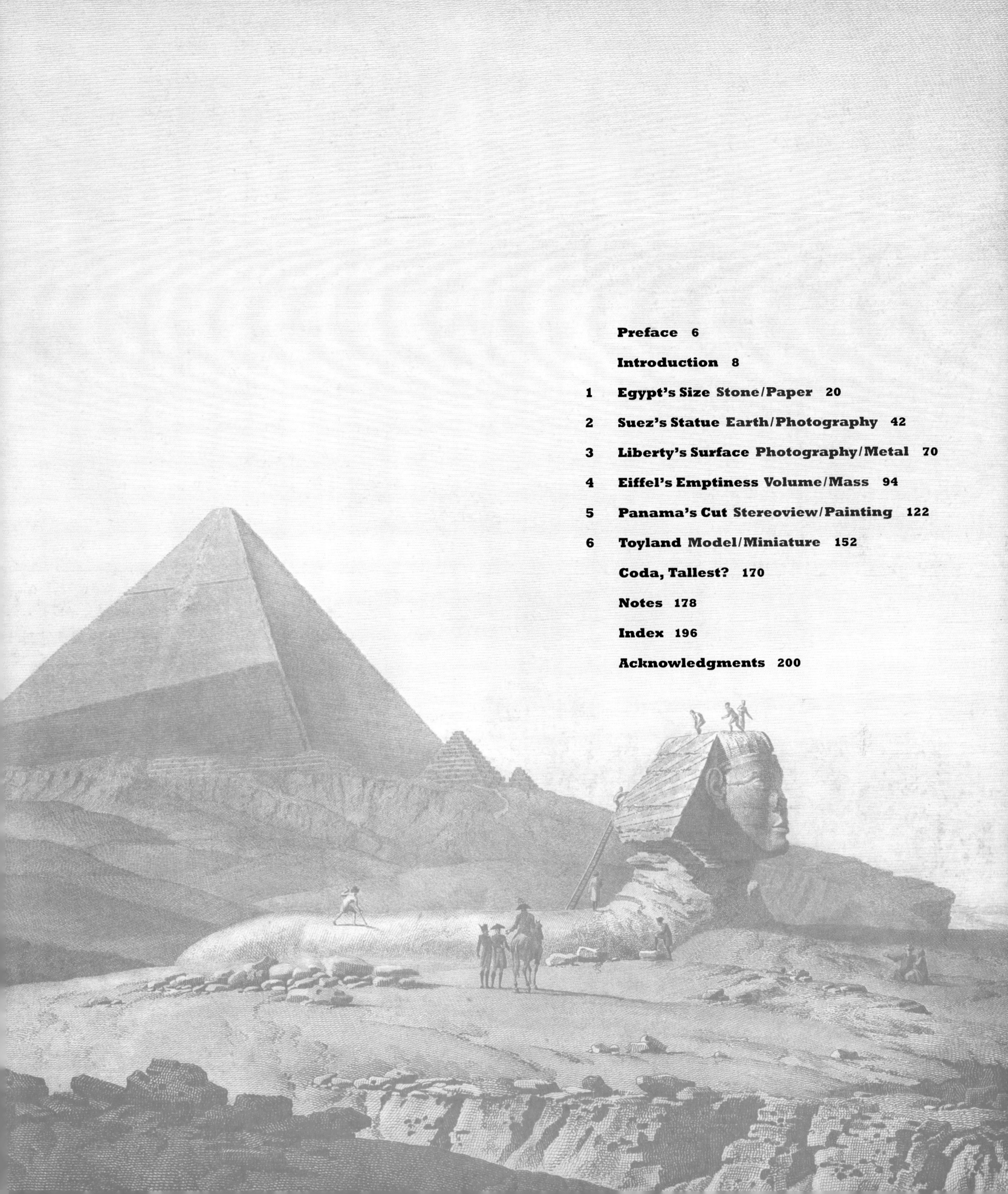

# Preface

*Colossal* reconstructs a history of engineering and Franco-American relations. It begins with Napoleonic engineers in Egypt and ends with the American attempt to trump the French, who failed to make a canal at Panama. The oddity of *Colossal*'s subject derives from my interest in a tale that is partly my own. Of course, every book tells us about its author, but this book contends with the geographic breadth of my own life.

As a scholar, I first concentrated on the Napoleonic Empire, yet my life began in the Panama Canal Zone in the hospital built by the French, where most American nurses treated my Panamanian mother rudely. In their view she was another of those native women who had trapped an American soldier. Only African American nurses were kind, my mother told me, and she never forgot that kindness. After my parents divorced when my father began graduate studies at the University of California, Berkeley in the late 1950s, my mother had to decide whether to return to Panama with her two daughters or to remain in the United States. She chose to stay because she wanted her daughters to have the opportunities so many immigrants have sought here. I was raised by my mother in a university community where she worked as a secretary most of her life.

Though this history is now long past, it remains relevant to my work. *Colossal*, like my first book, *Extremities*, concerns empire, and I have always perceived empire personally and bodily: as a matter of accents and skin color and pierced ears and "good" or "bad" hair, as the caress of my mother's beautiful hands and the anxiety she felt when we drove through the South. In *Colossal*, however, I have distanced myself from the intimacy of bodies. I was determined to continue to interrogate representation and French imperialism, still I could not face the ugliness of late nineteenth-century racism. I decided instead to shift the scale of my objects of study. I abandoned the paintings of life-size persons and turned to the building of things so big they were barely comprehensible in relation to the human body: a copper statue that transformed female personification into abstract shapes; a tower that turned the product of labor into a structure so large, so mathematical, and so prefabricated as to seem almost independent of human effort; two canals so enormous as to require the replacement of manual labor by immense, newly engineered machines that made human beings their ant-like attendants.

Quite consciously, I had chosen to distance myself from the corporeal. But after immersing myself in the oversized ambitions of my protagonists, I came to realize that focusing on colossal scale risked duplicating their sleight of hand. Increasingly I came to appreciate how effectively colossal scale obscures the criminality of human aggression and the ruthlessness of capitalism with a rhetoric of progress and the benevolent, indeed altruistic, engineering of global commerce. And repeatedly I was forced to acknowledge how complicit my book was with late nineteenth- and early twentieth-century imperialism. Colossal scale demands a bird's-eye view; it requires distance to be apprehended, and, at a distance, people and human suffering shrink from view. How is it possible, I asked myself, that I sometimes address workers from afar, as ciphers whose worth to engineers resided only in their labor, in their usefulness to the building of a capitalist future?

Partly, the answer lies in the fact that workers enter visual representation only sporadically and they rarely figure in the archives compiled by those wielding power. In this book, I examine how engineers, financiers and bankers, and governments in France and the United States came to work together to revolutionize international transport in the name of modern progress. Although I reconstruct the point of view of the powerful, I am also careful to bring into view the ways colossal undertakings foregrounded issues of labor. The nineteenth century preoccupation with the ancient pyramids, for example, led to debates about ancient and modern conditions of work. In my chapter on the Panama Canal, I introduce the voices of West Indian laborers. If this book is devoted to the visualization of the engineering feats of men wielding enormous power, I have tried to remain alert to the exploited and forgotten partly because of my own personal history as a Panamanian-American. I am, after all, as one reader pointed out, the progeny of Ferdinand de Lesseps's ambitions and also likely the great-grand-daughter of a West Indian worker. My grandmother Gregoria Almillategui was born during the American phase of building the Panama Canal. I exist because of this intersection of the powerful and the disempowered. I exist because of the failure of the French and the success of the Americans, as do so many Panamanians, including my beloved cousin, Jorge Newell, who maintains the garden of the French cemetery where thousands of the fallen were buried. Jorge and his brothers, Augusto (called Napo), Danilo, Henry, and Richard, are the grandsons of an American engineer whose photograph hangs in the Canal Zone and whose last name they bear. They are also the grandsons of Tomás Monasterios, a Venezuelan of mixed descent who designed parts of the inland Panamanian town of Penonomé, until one day he drank some water and died of malaria. My mother proudly showed me the city benches he designed when she took me to see the town of her birth. And although she had marched in protest against American control of a zone cutting her country in two, she was also proud of the canal. Throughout my childhood, Willis Abbot's large, red book, *The Panama Canal in Prose and Photographs*, was one of our precious possessions from the Panamanian past.

While writing this book, I have remembered many people, including the Haitian Pedro Prestan. In 1885 he led an uprising that, in turn, incited government troops to slaughter Jamaican canal workers in their company barracks. Riots on the part of black workers ensued; Prestan was captured and hanged; and the French found it far more difficult to recruit West Indians to dig the canal. Here is the thickness of a history remembered, if not discussed.

*Colossal* was written in the United States at the University of California, Berkeley, where Teddy Roosevelt, speaking in 1911 at the Greek Theater, proclaimed: "I took the Isthmus, started the canal and then left Congress—not to debate the canal but to debate me." In a theater financed by the yellow journalism of Randolph Hearst, Roosevelt was pretending to have initiated what Ferdinand de Lesseps had begun. Here are the larger than life, brutal, and powerful men of the nineteenth century. Because of my unlikely good fortune, I write at a university. But this public institution to which I have always been loyal is being compromised by the greed and mismanagement of capitalists. I also write at a time when the hubris of men's disregard for the fragility of the earth has finally become frighteningly clear. The University of California at Berkeley initiated the nation's first geography department in 1898, across the bay, not coincidentally, from the Panama-Pacific Exposition that celebrated the opening of the Panama Canal in 1915. The canal was partly responsible for the founding of a discipline; it was as well an extreme example of the overconfidence and shortsightedness that destroyed people and lands.

I write from this university, but my personal geography spans both here and there, the United States and Panama, and even, strangely enough, France and Haiti, where my daughter Gregoria and my son Pierre were born, respectively. I have produced a strange and singular book, but my history in its geographic and colonial complexity is similar to that of so many others.

# Introduction

The engineers have not yet spoken, but indisputably the tower haunts the spirit of our neighbors and troubles their sleep. The people who do not have their tower will not be a great people it seems.
**Paul Bluysen, *Paris en 1889 Souvenirs et croquis de l'Exposition,* 1890**

When the Egyptian student acquired a copy of Louis Hine's photograph (fig. 1), it was an emblem of modern New York—the dynamic city that built the world's tallest buildings. After the student led the 9/11 attack on the World Trade Center, the meaning of Hine's photograph of men at work on the Empire State Building was forever changed.

According to news reports, Mohammad Atta resented the spread of "Western" high-rise buildings in Cairo[1] of the sort where he and his family had lived for more than a decade. Upon completing a degree at Cairo University with a thesis on Islamic architecture, Atta moved to Germany to pursue graduate study in urban planning and architecture at the University of Hamburg. There is evidence, coming mostly from his teachers in Germany, that Atta saw the skyscraper as the supreme symbol of a political and economic system threatening Islam with imminent destruction. Tall can certainly be considered Western and modern. For some it is wrong.

Conflating size and modernity with Western dominance has become common practice. Champions and detractors of modern architecture have long posited as much. The 1889 Universal Exposition in Paris juxtaposed a reproduction of a Cairo street with the Eiffel Tower.[2] No effort was spared in making the "typical" Cairo buildings look old and decaying; the many cracks in the plaster walls were clearly visible because they had been filled with dirt (fig. 2). The triumph of the Eiffel Tower was thus cast as a step forward in a narrative of progress. One-thousand feet in height, the Tower was not only the tallest man-made structure ever built, it was also erected in just two years. In 1889 French superiority and the modern were identified with the engineering of an edifice of colossal height; the construction of humble, low-lying buildings with Egyptian backwardness.

Yet ancient Egyptian monuments were consistently admired. Even the Statue of Liberty does not outclass the Sphinx in a photograph that records an actual if unlikely event (fig. 3). In 1989 an eight-ton replica of the Sphinx was loaded onto a barge that circled New York Harbor to promote a production of *Aida*, Verdi's Orientalist opera about doomed lovers in Old Kingdom Egypt. The photographer must have known he had a great picture when he pointed his camera at the barge passing in front of the Statue of Liberty. But he was probably unaware he was witnessing a reenactment of an all but forgotten episode in nineteenth-century history.

Although now a U.S. landmark, the Statue of Liberty was first conceived when in 1855 Frédéric-Auguste Bartholdi visited Egypt and started to plan a gigantic statue. Based on drawings of Egyptian women, this statue was to be a draped female figure, one arm raised, placed at the entrance to the Suez Canal, where it would have served as a lighthouse and as a symbol of French expansion in the Middle East. The photograph of the Statue of Liberty and a replica of the Great Sphinx is not only *not* a product of photo montage, it evokes historical fact and can stand for a larger history. Even as contemporary Egypt was being denigrated as an impoverished backwater, Frenchmen were extolling its ancient monuments, studying them, and seeking to rival their grandeur. Indeed parallels between ancient Egypt and modern France no doubt increased support for the grandiose projects of Gustave Eiffel and likeminded engineers and financiers. But insofar as the Egyptian monuments helped to stir public debate on methods of construction and labor policies, the parallels had problematic consequences. Most people then assumed that the pyramids were the work of thousands of slaves. Did laborers fare better at the sites where modern colossi were being built, especially at Suez and Panama? The development of "labor-saving" machines did not end discussion of the ethical problems that reinvention of pharaonic monuments brought to the fore. In the century when slaves and serfs were freed, critics continued to ask if colossal monuments, modern or ancient, cost too much in human suffering.

Why did Mohammad Atta keep a photograph of workers at the Empire State Building? A photograph of a finished skyscraper would have offered a more faceless and alienating emblem of U.S.arrogance. Hine's photographs of the Empire State Building, much like Henri Rivière's 1889 photographs of the Eiffel Tower (fig. 4), place the worker at the center of modern achievement. Suspended high above the city, men are seen at work placing steel beams at angles engineers had calculated. Both Hine's and Rivière's photographs are difficult to interpret. Do they glorify the laborer or reveal his alienation? Is the worker astride the engineer's structure exalted or diminished by its inhuman scale? Was it right or wrong for engineers to put a worker there? Perhaps ambiguities of meaning were what attracted Atta to the famed photograph of workers

**1**
Lewis Hine, *Construction of the Empire State Building*, 1930–31. Photograph. New York, New York Public Library.

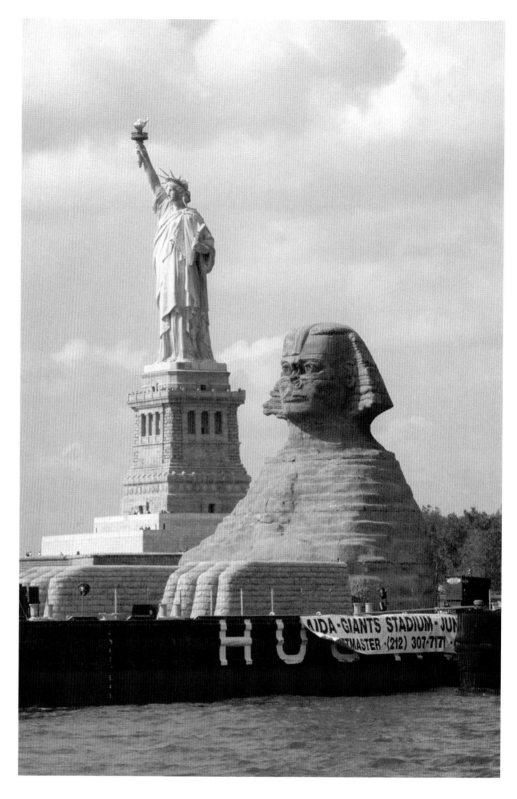

**2**
Street of Cairo, Universal Exhibition of 1889, Paris. In *L'Architecture à l'Exposition universelle de 1889. Principales constructions du Champ-de-Mars et de l'esplanade des Invalides* (Paris: E. Bigot, 1889). Berkeley, University of California. Photo: Julie Wolf.

**3**
Henny Abrams, *Great Sphinx Replica and the Statue of Liberty*, 1989. Photo: Bettmann/CORBIS.

**4**
Henri Rivière, *Eiffel Tower. Painter on a Rope*, 1889. Photograph. Paris, Musée d'Orsay, fonds Eiffel. Photo: Adoc-photos/Art Resource, NY.

on a skyrise in New York City. It encapsulates the quandary facing anyone assessing the aesthetics and ethics of building colossal edifices.

The polarity that opposes "humanistic" art to industrial technology is basic to the modern organization of knowledge. During the nineteenth century more and more prestige was accorded to engineers, men such as Eiffel and Isambard Kingdon Brunel, mastermind of British bridges and railways. Yet engineers also came to be regarded as men who doggedly turned all questions into material and economic equations, who thought in terms of the absolute truths of physical and economic laws as they considered the pros and cons of a decision. In this "humanistic" narrative, engineers understood there were choices; some cost more money and time than others, but human suffering or conditions of labor were seldom deemed critical variables in their ruthless calculations.

When I began *Colossal*, I knew it would implode if I failed to interrogate the stereotypes of the engineer, both the negative one and the positive image of the engineer as a bringer of beneficent change. My research soon led to a massive expansion in the scope of my book and an experiment in historical methodology. I decided to use my training as an art historian, particularly in close analysis of the implications of visual form and the impact of "pictures" on the collective imagination—and to branch out to the history of technology, economics, and politics. This approach had the very considerable advantage of enabling this book to study "the engineer" at the moment of his emergence as a double figure, hero and antihero, who made a crucial contribution to the imperial enterprises of France and the United States during the late nineteenth and early twentieth centuries. Along with their predecessor Brunel, engineers from both countries established what were hailed as new horizons of possibility for monuments and utilitarian structures; these, in turn, catalyzed radical shifts in aesthetic criteria and put the engineer at the center of public debate.

The controversy mounted to a new pitch in the wake of the Universal Exposition in Paris. An article in the *Revue des deux mondes* of 1889 announces that the word engineer was on everyone's lips; crowds had flocked to see the Eiffel Tower at the Exposition and come away with diverse, sometimes hostile opinions. "The engineer has become for us what the philistine was for our predecessors, by definition an anti-literary being." Stage set, he goes on the defend the engineer against negative criticims (fig. 5):

> This is a very rudimentary judgment against a profession, against an art that is characterized in the following terms in the statutes of the English society of Civil Engineers: "the art of directing great sources of nature's strength to the greatest profit of man." Such a profession does not belittle those who exercise it, nor does it close down their understanding of beauty.... Most of these men have undertaken a burdensome task, matter is rebellious, the problems are obscure, the resources are lacking; more than one man falls along the way. No matter, the pace of the others does not slow down; they do not get discouraged; they believe that nature cannot resist them forever, and that sooner or later they will achieve their goal. Their tranquil obstinacy can be explained; they have a faith in their work; they feel themselves transported by the spirit that blows where it wishes and which often passes across diverse forms of human activity through the epochs. This spirit animated men of war in the first years of our century; literary innovators in the last years of the Restoration, and politics have known it, during those beautiful hours of illusion when politics seemed to smile with promises. Today the engineer has captured it with other sources of strength. The name of this spirit is not difficult to determine; it is life beating in full arteries.[3]

The Napoleonic Empire had its soldiers; the Bourbon Restoration its innovative writers; some eras their great politicians, but, in 1889, the *Revue des deux mondes* proclaims, engineers have captured the animating spirit of their epoch. The "tranquil obstinacy" of the engineer in face of "rebellious matter" proves that they know they are right. More than that, it demonstrates that they will triumph. The bravado of this rhetoric is all the more remarkable for having been written in the year the French Panama Canal Company declared bankruptcy. Engineers had just failed to harness "rebellious" matter. Many more than one engineer had "fallen along the way." But the dream, whether expressed at the base or at the top of the Eiffel Tower, or in the Exposition's Gallery of Machines, could still have the ring of truth in 1889 France.

A photograph of the Suez Canal from the 1860s, when construction was still underway, shows that modern enterprise did, after all, sometimes accomplish feats of horizontal and vertical engineering (fig. 6). The photograph links French intervention to the stark, straight-edged cutting of land that was possible only through skilled use of up-to-date machinery. Egypt, by contrast, appears as the irregular land, the raw matter, that engineers are making more productive. Men with camels evoke the system of transport that Egyptians had relied on for centuries. The canal, slicing through the earth, represents a future, an engineered future with rectilinear forms that create a space of exceptional clarity.

Related to Renaissance perspective systems and today a familiar part of everyday life, this space is sometimes considered natural and universal. Quite the opposite is true. It is artificial and a hallmark of the West's modernizing process. A massive evacuation of a site is the first step in its creation; extraneous matter and signs of life are cleared away in order to provide a thoroughfare—canal, railroad or highway—for human commerce. Simple as the photograph of the Suez Canal surely seems, it deserves recognition as a complex historical document of how "development" mobilized the resources of industrialization: stronger, less expensive iron and steel; engineering; and such technological innovations as steam-powered machines and photography.

We all know this story. Bartholdi, best remembered for the Statue of Liberty, knew it as well. His wonderfully absurd oil painting *Nymphs and Fauns Frightened by a Train* combines a lovely wooded glade with an expanse of land bearing signs of recent industrialization (fig. 7). Cut diagonally across the picture's foreground, at far right, are four parallel lines, railway tracks for the oncoming train. At left, as if alarmed at the sound of the train, nymphs and fauns, denizens of the pastoral world of Theocritus and Virgil, flee into the woods. In the pastoral heritage Arcadia was understood to shelter and inspire poetry and, more broadly, to provide a mise en scène for a tradition of painting in which human and mythological protagonists appear to live in harmony with nature. In Bartholdi's pastoral the approach of a train disrupts that venerable system of art, even as it signals the existence of a new world with different rules and powers. Modern transport menaces an ideal of nature and the motifs constituting that ideal—picturesque landscapes, birch leaves shimmering in the sunset, mythological creatures from antiquity. Ever so playfully Bartholdi uses the orthogonals of the railway to open a conspicuously modern space alien to pastoral and hence to art itself.

**5**
Neurdein Frères, Panoramic Photograph, *Gallery of Machines*, Universal Exhibition of 1889. Paris, Bibliothèque Nationale.

**6**
Anonymous Photograph, *The Suez Canal*, n.d. Author's Collection. Photo: Julie Wolf.

**7**
Frédéric-Auguste Bartholdi, *Fauns and Nymphs Frightened by a Train*, n.d., 57 x 74cm. Colmar, Musée Bartholdi. Photo: Christian Kempf.

*Nymphs and Fauns Frightened by a Train* is undated but was probably painted in the late 1860s, the years when Jules Verne was also lacing irony with dire prophesies. In a recently discovered, previously unpublished novel *Paris in the Twentieth Century*, Verne predicts the end of art:

"So in the twentieth century, no more painting, no more painters."
"Are there sculptors, at least?"
"None whatsoever, ever since they planted the Muse of Industry right in the middle of the Louvre courtyard: a vigorous shrew crouching over some sort of cylinder, holding a viaduct on her knees, pumping with one hand, working a bellows with the other, a necklace of little locomotives around her neck, and a lightning rod in her chignon!"[4]

Most nineteenth-century statues of women idealized their beauty; Verne burlesques those ideals with a statue of a "vigorous shrew," brandishing emblems of industrialization: cylinders, viaducts, bellows, locomotives, and lightning rods. One of Verne's interlocutors asks, "What has killed art?"

*"[I]t's really machinery that's doing the mischief."*
*"Why is that?"*
"Because there's this one good thing about finance: at least it can pay for masterpieces, and a man must eat, even if he has genius!… But mechanics, engineers, technicians—devil take me if Raphael, Titian, Veronese, and Leonardo could ever have come into being! They'd have had to compete with mechanical procedures, and they'd have starved to death! Ah, machinery! It's enough to make you loathe inventors and inventions alike!"[5]

**8**
Photograph, *Bartholdi at His Easel*, 1887–91. 20.7 x 26.8 cm. Colmar, Musée Bartholdi. Photo: Christian Kempf.

**9**
Frédéric-Auguste Bartholdi, *Workshop Model with Plaster Maquette for the Head of the Statue*, 1879. Paris, Bibliothèque du Conservatoire National des Arts et Métiers.

During the twentieth century, Verne presumes, machines will supplant art because mechanics, engineers, and inventors will be the dominant patrons of culture. Still, Verne as much as Bartholdi was fascinated by the machines that were daily changing the future and making it into a realm where the artist could cross into science and technology to spin novel fantasies. Passing from the known to the unknown, this was the journey that enthralled Verne and Bartholdi, author and artist, throughout the 1860s.

Later, in a photograph of 1887–91, Bartholdi appears in his Colmar home with *Nymphs and Fauns Frightened by a Train* on his easel (fig. 8). The dark, ornamented interior features, among other furnishings, two easels, gilt-framed paintings, sculptures, books, porcelain vases, wall hangings, tapestries, rugs, plants, and, in the back, an obedient wife at the piano. Endowed with a surfeit of objects pertaining to art, the scene marks the beginnings of a divide that will grow ever wider as the nineteenth century drew to a close. Assigned to a separate sphere, art will be forced to coexist with, yet contest, science, technology, engineering, and industrialization. The dandified artist holds a palette in one hand and a brush in the other as if putting finishing touches on his painting, although it was completed some twenty years earlier and has a frame. Bartholdi's photograph is obviously retrospective, taken after the painting was done and, yet more significantly, after the Statue of Liberty had been erected in Paris, dismantled, and reconstructed on Bedloe's Island in New York Harbor. The only signs of this, his supreme achievement, are maquettes in two glass vitrines at the far right, behind the easel with *Nymphs and Fauns*. The maquettes, one slightly larger than the other, show the statue's head in the process of being made (fig. 9). Each is covered with scaffolding; at the far right, tiny figures dressed like ladies and gentlemen appear to be looking up at the work in progress; other tiny figures in workers' clothing are perched here and there on the scaffolding as if busy at their tasks .

Through drapery and similar classical motifs, the Statue of Liberty harkens back to the mythological beings at the left of Bartholdi's pastoral; whereas the railroad at the right of the painting is one of several developments in industrial technology that were essential to the statue's construction and transport. Further, as the maquettes demonstrate, a quasi-factory system was used in its construction; teams of workers built it piece-by-piece. And the era's leading engineer Eiffel designed the armature, hidden inside the statue, that gave it the resilience to withstand the powers of wind and water after installation on Bedloe's Island. If the statue of the shrew Verne envisaged pumping bellows in the courtyard of the Louvre merges art with industrial products, Bartholdi's statue and photograph are no less anomalous. Bartholdi staged himself as a traditional artist, a painter, palette in hand, within a scene, which, at first glance, seems tranquil, almost itself a kind of pastoral; everything and everyone is arranged in an order that seems impervious to time and change. But closer study of the photograph reveals that Bartholdi altered the role of the artist in response to the demands and opportunities of the industrial age. These included using a camera and realizing a fantasy about a colossal statue cum electric lighthouse.

The young Verne was equally alert to technological advances. *Paris in the Twentieth Century*, his most anti-industrial novel, has the art-loving protagonists stroll along the docks of a new canal, admiring the "magnificent spectacle" of immense ships from all over the world, which, because of the canal, could now be anchored at the very heart of Paris. The scene epitomizes the visions of accumulation dear to late nineteenth-century capitalists. They dreamed limitless wealth would be theirs if they increased industrial production, increased mass consumption, increased the number of colonies available for "development." No wonder they celebrated their successes with a tedious recital of numbers, most often, numbers about quantities. Their fixation on rapid growth prompted Verne to hazard several predictions:

> In less than fifteen years, a civil engineer named Montanet cut a canal which, starting on the Plaine de Grenelle, ended just above Rouen, measuring a hundred and forty kilometers in length, seventy meters in width, and twenty meters in depth;... Excavations in the bed of the lower part of the river opened the canal to the biggest ships. Thus navigation from Le Havre to Paris no longer raised any difficulties. It is easy to imagine how cutting through the isthmus of Suez and Panama had increased long-distance commercial navigation; maritime operations...enormously increased; ships multiplied in all forms. Certainly it was a magnificent spectacle, these steamers of all sizes and nationalities whose flags spread their thousand colors on the breeze; huge wharves; enormous warehouses protecting the merchandise which was unloaded by means of

the most ingenious machines…all the products of the four quarters of the world were heaped up in towering mountains of commerce;…a tide-signal tower stood at the entrance to the port, while at the rear an electric lighthouse, no longer much used, rose into the sky to a height of 152 meters. This was the highest monument in the world, and its lights could be seen, forty leagues away, from the towers of Rouen Cathedral. The entire spectacle deserved to be admired.[6]

Verne was writing in 1863 when neither the Suez nor the Panama Canal existed, although Ferdinand de Lesseps had begun work at Suez. Verne nonetheless imagined a future in which the Suez and Panama Canals already lay in the distant past. He envisaged as well the building of a third canal, from France's shores to its inland capital, designed to transport "the products of the four quarters of the world" to consumers in Paris. Canals and imported commodities belong to incompatible categories. Canals are huge and fixed in place, as are all the major structures considered in this book; commodities are small, easy to transport, and quickly consumed if markets are flourishing. But the desire to buy and sell "towering mountains of commerce" was what forced the constant enlargement of ships, wharves, lighthouses, and waterways, an expansion that continues at full throttle today.[7] And even if lighthouses, towers, and canals seem to be permanent structures, bound to the earth at specific sites, they required complex international negotiations and resources from around the world. Foreign investments, government backing, imported machines, imported parts, and laborers from around the world—all these were coordinated for the construction of modern colossi, whether sculpture, buildings, railroads, or canals.

As if the order were preordained, Verne's narrative shifts from the Paris Canal to "towering mountains of commerce" to the "highest monument in the world," which is identified as an electric lighthouse. The panorama presupposes that the energy driving the "twentieth-century world" comes from the capitalist-imperialist system. In this book I myself encompass roughly the same panorama in that I connect the histories of the Suez Canal, Statue of Liberty, Eiffel Tower, and Panama Canal to the capitalist-imperialist ambitions that underwrote them. Although the French initiated these engineering projects, the United States soon answered French exploits with their own. But by the 1890s that drive was less about the accumulation of territory than the expansion of markets for investment. The historian Neil Smith assesses the situation in this way:

The dilemma facing the U.S. ruling classes in the 1890s was not primarily one of space, however, for all that it came to be expressed that way. The real dilemma lay in the over-accumulation of capital and surplus value by a rapidly industrializing national economy and the shrinking opportunities for reinvestment domestically. This was not a uniquely American dilemma and had already been confronted in Europe where economic expansion had run up against the boundaries of nation-states even as these states themselves were still in formation. The solution lay in the expansion of national sovereignty over imperial possessions.[8]

Expansion was problematic for the United States of the late nineteenth century. Not only had Africa already been carved up and allocated to European nations, but the United States, though upholding the Monroe Doctrine, was disinclined to colonize the independent republics of Central and South America. The United States nonetheless decided to occupy Hawaii in 1893; Puerto Rico, Guam, and the Philippines in 1898; and Samoa in 1899. Then too reticence to colonize Central and South America "rarely hampered U.S. interference, up to and including the invention of a new country (Panama)."[9] Significantly, in the latter case, the United States was aiming to control a canal, not a colony. At this late stage of imperialism, canals, more than colonies, were desired "possessions" because they improved the flow of capital throughout the world (fig. 10).

*Colossal* turns the spotlight on the engineering of modernity, its representations as well as its material conditions. These engineering projects represent, more or less legibly, technology, the forces of production, the resistance of nature, and the mediation of labor. Yet the power of capital itself remains implicit if not suppressed in the history of modernity. The economic motives and ruthless exploitation of persons and countries in the engineering projects—all this is forgotten when historians take as their top priority celebration of the engineering of the modern world, its symbols, and channels of transport. Their narratives have a blind spot: the forces of capitalism, nationalism, and imperialism, which were all-pervasive. So much so engineers and industrialists became accustomed to calculating how many human lives a project might "cost" and how those costs would alter profits.

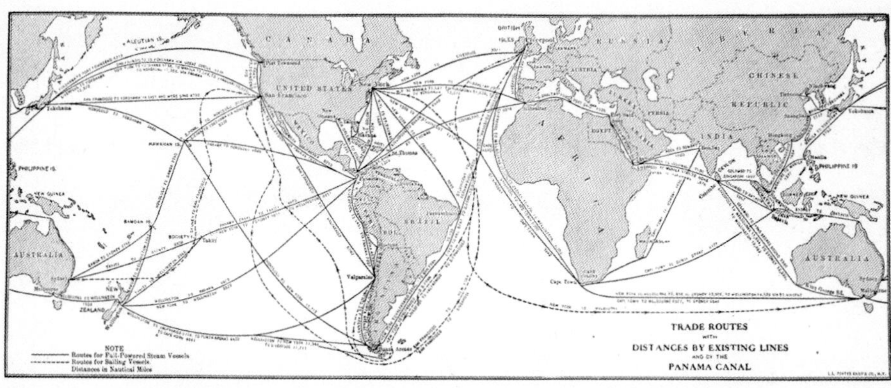


DISTANCES FROM NEW YORK, NEW ORLEANS, AND LIVERPOOL TO VARIOUS PORTS.

| To | FROM NEW YORK | | | FROM NEW ORLEANS | | | FROM LIVERPOOL | | |
|---|---|---|---|---|---|---|---|---|---|
| | Via Panama | Via Magellan | Via Suez | Via Panama | Via Magellan | Via Suez | Via Panama | Via Magellan | Via Suez |
| San Francisco | 5,262 | 13,135 | ........ | 4,683 | 13,551 | ........ | 7,836 | 13,502 | ........ |
| Port Townsend | 6,032 | 13,905 | ........ | 5,453 | 14,321 | ........ | 8,606 | 14,272 | ........ |
| Honolulu | 6,702 | 13,312 | ........ | 6,123 | 13,728 | ........ | 9,276 | 13,679 | ........ |
| Guayaquil | 2,810 | 10,215 | ........ | 2,231 | 10,631 | ........ | 5,384 | 10,582 | ........ |
| Callao | 3,363 | 9,613 | ........ | 2,784 | 10,029 | ........ | 5,937 | 9,980 | ........ |
| Valparaiso | 4,633 | 8,380 | ........ | 4,054 | 8,796 | ........ | 7,207 | 8,747 | ........ |
| Manila | 11,548 | ........ | 11,547 | 10,808 | ........ | 12,947 | 13,961 | ........ | 9,701 |
| Hongkong | 11,190 | ........ | 11,628 | 10,611 | ........ | 13,031 | 13,764 | ........ | 9,785 |
| Yokohama | 9,798 | ........ | 13,079 | 9,098 | ........ | 14,924 | 12,251 | ........ | 11,678 |
| Shanghai | 10,645 | ........ | 12,384 | 10,070 | ........ | 13,833 | 13,274 | ........ | 10,637 |
| Melbourne | 9,945 | ........ | 13,009 | 9,813 | ........ | ........ | 12,574 | 13,219 | 11,654 |
| Wellington | 8,851 | 12,852 | 14,387 | 8,272 | 11,760 | ........ | 11,425 | 11,711 | 12,989 |
| Bombay | 14,982 | ........ | 8,186 | ........ | ........ | ........ | 17,610 | ........ | 6,226 |
| Colombo | 14,112 | ........ | 8,629 | ........ | ........ | ........ | 16,740 | ........ | 6,736 |
| Singapore | 12,522 | ........ | 10,177 | ........ | ........ | ........ | 15,151 | ........ | 8,329 |

**10**
"Distances from New York, New Orleans, and Liverpool to Various Ports," in Ralph Emmett Avery, *Greatest Engineering Feat in the World.* Panama, 1915, p. 256. Photo: Julie Wolf.

The ironies were evident to the acerbic writer beloved by the Symbolists, Auguste Villiers de L'Isle-Adam, when he appraised the temper of the era in "Celestial Publicity." Published in *Cruel Tales* of 1883, Villiers' story subjects Ferdinand de Lesseps and his cohorts to humor far more scathing than any Verne deployed. Villiers knew "business is business," especially if great progress is being pledged.

Oddly enough, and at the risk of making a financier smile, this story is about Heaven. But let us make this clear: about Heaven considered from a serious, commercial point of view.... A learned southern engineer, Monsieur Grave...conceived the luminous plan of putting the vast spaces of the night to practical use, and, in short, of raising the sky to the level of the times. What use, in fact, is the azure canopy which serves no purpose except that of exciting the sickly imagination of the latest dreamers? Would not the man be entitled to expect the gratitude of the public and, let us add (why not?), the admiration of Posterity, who converted those sterile spaces into truly and profitably instructional spectacle, who turned those immense moors to account, and who finally obtained a good return from those vague, transparent steppes....

This is not a matter of sentiment. Business is business....

At first sight the very essence of the matter seems to border on the Impossible and even on Madness. Clearing the sky, putting a value on the stars, exploiting the twilight and the dawn, organizing the dusk, turning the hitherto unproductive firmament to account—what a dream! And what a thorny task, bristling with difficulties! But, fortified by the spirit of progress, what problems can Man not hope to solve?... The doubters will have a fine time until then, as in the days when Monsieur de Lesseps talked of linking two oceans—something which he has since done, in spite of the doubters. Here again, Science will have the last word, and Monsieur Excessively-Grave the last laugh. Thanks to him, Heaven will end up by being good for something and by acquiring at last an intrinsic value.[10]

Turning the sky into a profit-making machine, projecting advertisements for corsets and political candidates, Villiers' engineer parodies Lesseps, who had turned the water of Suez into a successful commercial venture. Nothing exceeds the reach of engineers collaborating with capitalists; they will turn the elements into profit; put "a value on the stars;" exploit "the twilight and dawn;" organize "the dusk;" and obtain "a good return" from the sky.

Villiers' glee is palpable. He relishes the absurd possibilities of the "cruel" modern world, no matter that he eventually condemns them. Villiers is a writer I will return to later in this book. His encounter with the large, hollow woman of metal eventually sent to Bedloe's Island, led to *The New Eve,* another mordant text on the engineering of modernity.

**Artists banded together to protest against the Eiffel Tower in the name of art. Didn't they know that immensity is also a form of beauty?... It is in this plain spread out under your feet that the past comes to its conclusion. It is here that the future will be accomplished.**

**Jules Simon, *Guide illustré de la Tour Eiffel*, 1893**

In the long nineteenth century, nationalism, imperialism, industrialization, and rapid technological change incited rivalries expressed in crude comparisons of size: the size of achievements, the size of machines, the size of profits. But size is not a straightforward matter.[11]

What is termed "actual size" promises fixed and verifiable truth yet "actual size" is relative. It derives from a comparison between things and units of measure. And the authority of numbers notwithstanding, units of measure are themselves neither unchanging nor universal.[12] They have varied from place to place and era to era. So-called standard measurement is a modern device developed during the Enlightenment and the Industrial Revolution. The advantages of international standards of measurement for industry and trade are incontestable. But it should not be forgotten that it is difficult to ascertain the size of material things, given that they exist in three dimensions and are usually complex and irregular in shape. To attempt to measure either immense or minute structures intensifies the problems.

Scale has always been understood to be comparative. Here is one architect's definition: "Whenever the word scale is used, something is being compared with something else.... Thus scale is not the same thing as size; scale is relative size, the size of something relative to something else."[13] Other authorities have argued that scale should be correlated to "apparent size," which, unlike either "relative size" or "actual size," is based on a viewer's perceptions of an object.[14] Albeit a key concept in measurement, scale is far from being a stable referent and is loosely and variously used.

But the ambiguities were forgotten in a type of representation, popular during the late nineteenth century, that helped teach the public to apprehend edifices through comparisons in which size and scale appear to be clear and certain. Images of this sort exploit the fact that juxtaposition of two or more things changes the viewer's sense of the "size" of each of them (see figs. 11, 12). Therefore any clarification the pictures offer is illusory; add another object, everything changes; and there is a price to pay. The images compress space and time. A monument that seems immense in its own setting can look diminutive if placed next to another taller monument. Or, a monument that looked huge in the year 1200 can appear small in 1900. What is more, these images standardize structures: though different in date, location, thickness, length, and mass, all buildings and monuments are turned into two-dimensional shapes meant to convey height—not depth, volume, weight, or even width. Such images are still common, which is unfortunate. They continue to confine modern colossi to an ahistorical sphere where they appear to be products of a linear progression in which the buildings of one era surpass those of another.

The complexity hidden within our apparently monolithic colossi has one more element that merits mention at this juncture of my book. Rather than being simple to understand, colossi have confounded the intellect in ways that for centuries have intrigued artists, writers, and philosophers. The apprehension of immensity is disorienting, its representation perplexing, and the concept difficult to formulate. Kant defined the colossal as "the mere presentation of a concept which is almost too great for presentation, that is, borders on the relatively monstrous."[15] His judgement rests on an argument in Aristotle's *Poetics*: "Nor, again, can [an organism or any whole composed of parts] of vast size be beautiful; for as the eye cannot take it all in at once, the unity and sense of the whole is lost for the spectator; as for instance if there were one [an entity] a thousand miles long."[16] Together these passages sum up the colossal's main challenges: first, it is "too great" or too "vast" to be represented and apprehended; second, it violates criteria for the beauty exemplified in a Greek temple. Several exceptionally ambitious responses to those challenges, responses above all to the challenges of conceiving and representing gigantic structures, are examined in this book.

From imperialist expansion to philosophic conundrum, *Colossal* addresses the histories hidden in plain sight in edifices so familiar—so seemingly simple—they are taken for granted as landmarks. I connect four feats of modern engineering to one another and to sources in Egyptian antiquity. I go on to appraise the web of social and political circumstances joining them. But my principal concern is the ways that they were devised to analyze and plan—represent and publicize—immense monuments in media, ranging from drawings and engravings to, stereoviews, paintings, and miniatures. In addition, I dwell at length on the shifting role of the engineer, his training, and his methods of design and construction.

## NOTABLE HIGH BUILDINGS OF THE WORLD.

| | | Feet High |
|---|---|---|
| | EIFFEL TOWER | 1000 |
| 1. | Washington Monument | 555 |
| 2. | City Hall, Philadelphia | 535 |
| 3. | Cathedral of Cologne, Germany | 511 |
| 4. | Cathedral of St. Stephen, Vienna | 470 |
| 5. | Cathedral at Strasburg | 468 |
| 6. | St. Martin's Church, Landshut, Germany | 463 |
| 7. | Chimney at Glasgow, Scotland | 460 |
| 8. | Pyramid of Cheops (Great Pyramid), Egypt | 450 |
| 9. | St. Peter's Cathedral, Rome | 448 |
| 10. | King Shafra's Pyramid, Egypt | 447½ |
| 11. | St. Paul's Cathedral, London | 404 |
| 12. | Torazzo Tower, Cremona, Italy | 396 |
| 13. | Florence Cathedral, Italy | 387 |
| 14. | Cathedral at Fribourg, Switzerland | 386 |
| 15. | Amiens Cathedral | 383 |
| 16. | Aqueduct delle Torre, Spoleto, Italy | 380 |
| 17. | Hotel de Ville, Brussels, Belgium | 364 |
| 18. | Cathedral at Milan, Italy | 360 |
| 19. | Victoria Tower, Westminster, London | 340 |
| 20. | Bartholdi Statue, New York | 329 |
| 21. | St. Patrick's Cathedral, New York | 328 |
| 22. | Dashoor Pyramid, Egypt | 326½ |
| 23. | St. Mark's, Venice, Italy | 323 |
| 24. | Norwich Cathedral, England | 315 |
| 26. | Lincoln Cathedral, England | 300 |
| 27. | Belfry Tower, Bruges, Belgium | 290 |
| 28. | Trinity Church, New York | 284 |
| 29. | St. Botolph's Church, Boston, England | 282 |
| 30. | Pantheon, Paris | 258 |
| 31. | Monument, London | 240 |
| 32. | Cathedral at Canterbury, England | 235 |
| 33. | Masonic Temple, Philadelphia, Pa. | 230 |
| 34. | Bunker Hill Monument, Boston | 221 |
| 35. | Pyramid of Mycerinus | 218 |
| 36. | Rankot dagoba, Pollanarrua, Ceylon | 200 |
| 37. | Mosque of St. Sophia, Constantinople | 182 |
| 38. | Albert Memorial, London | 180 |
| 39. | Leaning Tower of Pisa | 179 |
| 40. | Tower of Chicago Water Works | 175 |
| 41. | Pont du Gard, Nîmes, France | 170 |
| 42. | Arc de Triomphe, Paris | 162 |
| 43. | Column of July, Paris | 154 |
| 44. | Alexandria Column, St. Petersburg | 154 |
| 45. | Skerryvore Lighthouse, Scotland | 138 |
| 46. | Trajan's Column, Rome (exclusive of Figure) | 127½ |
| 47. | High Bridge, New York | 116 |
| 48. | Pompey's Pillar, Alexandria | 100 |
| 49. | Girard College, Philadelphia | 97 |
| 50. | Cleopatra's Needle, New York | 68 |

**11**
"Notable High Buildings of the World," Rand, McNally and Company, *Atlas of the World*, Chicago, Illinois, 1895. Author's Collection. Photo: Julie Wolf.

**12**
Medal of Eiffel Tower. *Souvenir de mon ascension au 1er étage de la Tour Eiffel 1889* (Souvenir of my ascent to the first floor of the Eiffel Tower, 1889). Reverse: *Les travaux ont commencé le 27 janvier 1887. Le monument a été inauguré le 6 mai* 1889 (Work was begun 27 January 1887. The monument was inaugurated 6 May 1889). Author's Collection. Photo: Julie Wolf.

Chapter 1 introduces the French engineers who, during the Egyptian campaign of 1798–1799, produced most of the drawings later reproduced in the *Description de l'Égypte*, a watershed publication that established the terms by which colossi would be revived and depicted. Chapter 2 examines the Egyptian origins of the Statue of Liberty and Bartholdi's unsuccessful attempt to design an electric lighthouse for the Suez Canal. The unorthodox procedures that Bartholdi employed in financing and making the Statue of Liberty are considered in chapter 3. In chapter 4 I turn attention to Gustave Eiffel, looking at the armature he designed for the Statue of Liberty and the tower he made to dwarf Bartholdi's colossus. Discussion of Eiffel's part in the collapse of French efforts to build a canal across Panama leads in chapter 5 to an account of how America completed the Panama Canal and how the victory was portrayed in stereoviews and a cycle of murals. I invert scale in chapter 6 to examine souvenirs and miniatures, including toys, based on the Eiffel Tower and Statue of Liberty. A coda brings the story up to date with a brief consideration of recent endeavors to raise the world's tallest building and the world's tallest statue.

It bears emphasis that Bartholdi, Lesseps, and Eiffel's projects share a substantive history not heretofore traced and evaluated. All four were unprecedented in scale; conceived in relationship to the colossi of ancient Egypt; and built by engineers with training in drawing and design that separated them from the beaux-arts tradition. Each project demanded the extraction of masses of material to create hollowed out structures. In each case halting construction occasioned a sequence of radical shifts, each related and conducive to the other: from manual to machine labor, from masonry to metal construction, from handcrafted parts to prefabricated ones, from the shaping of solids to the shaping of volumes, from drawing to photography.

Readers familiar with the modernist movement will not be surprised to find fundamental issues of art and architecture embedded in the construction of canals and of a tower and statue resembling skyscrapers.[16] To hazard a different perspective, to look at Western modernism in conjunction with capitalism is to see that immense size became a supercharged value at the peak of imperial expansion in Asia, Africa, and South America. "Big" often did mean power and dominance. Some artists kicked and screamed, of course; most accepted the imperatives of the new order and proceeded to come up with techniques and devices for representing colossal structures in virtually all available media—drawing, printmaking, painting, sculpture, photography, and stereography. A cycle of murals from 1914–15, depicting the construction of the Panama Canal and requiring almost 1,000 square feet of canvas, set a record. It is one of the largest groups of murals by an American artist on display outside the U.S. Virtually forgotten today, William Van Ingen's murals are reproduced in their entirety for the first time in chapter 5 where their commissioning and meaning are accorded long overdue consideration.

Triumph is only occasionally the outcome of colossal enterprises. As easily as they can demonstrate human capacity to harness technology, they can threaten human ability to control the consequences of technological advance. That the contradiction was recognized during the nineteenth century makes the mania for gigantic structures all the more compelling—and sometimes farcical, sometimes tragic. As they walk along a new canal, the characters in *Paris in the Twentieth Century* admire a new ship, Leviathan IV: thirty masts, fifteen chimneys, 30,000 horsepower—20,000 for the drive wheels and 10,000 for the propellers—and railway tracks from one end of the deck to the other. The sight leads Uncle Huguenin to exclaim, "Soon they'll manage to construct that fantastic Dutch ship whose bowsprit was already at Mauritius when its helm was still in the harbor at Brest!"[17] The ship Uncle Huguenin envisages, a ship spanning the thousands of miles between the southeast coast of Africa and the west coast of France, makes mockery of maritime transport. The ship would not move; goods would move across the ship as if it were a spit of land joining France to the Indian Ocean.

Verne was right to believe an era was fast approaching when man would no longer be the measure of all things. Leviathan IV is all but unimaginable and could never be built on the planet we inhabit. But the relationship between material limitations and limitless fantasies was completely redefined in the late nineteenth century. The emergence of science fiction as a popular genre of literature is but one manifestation of the new desire to look to the future with the expectation of exploring a world that engineers will have transformed. In this book I narrate a variant of science fiction in which the improbable proves to have been real and enduring.

# Egypt's Size

## Stone / Paper

**Monge, Monge, we are right in the canal. Bonaparte to the geometer Monge, according to Edmé-François Jomard, 1853**

Napoleon Bonaparte's campaign in Egypt had one unexpected consequence. It set the stage for the great engineering projects of the nineteenth and early twentieth centuries. Ancient Egypt was seen as a land of prodigious building that now, as never before, inspired monuments and canals in places as far apart as Paris, New York, and Panama, no matter the failure of the French offensive. Or did military defeat contribute to Egypt's tenacious hold over the French imaginary? Whatever the cause, the power of ancient Egypt would not dissipate for more than a century. Americans, too, could not forget this remote past. The pyramids, statues, and canals of ancient Egypt provided examples of colossal engineering to emulate, if not surpass.

The Egyptian monuments also forced French visitors to confront the limitations of the rational systems with which they expected to determine ancient methods of construction. But measurement proved surprisingly elusive. And the immense structures raised uncomfortable questions about labor: to what extent was the building of pyramids, colossi, and canals a function of the Egyptian exploitation of slaves? In modern times could equally impressive monuments be built in a humane way? Engineers were expected to find a solution. It turns out they needed to do so on paper.

The French relinquished possession of Egypt in 1801, but they brought home the remarkable research of the 151 savants whom Napoleon had had the foresight to recruit. Alongside soldiers, these men, most of them very young, attempted to compile encyclopedic knowledge about a land still dominated by the vestiges of its brilliant pharaonic past. They encountered a civilization, eroded, half covered in sand, whose scientific bases remained mysterious though retrievable because of the sheer abundance of material signs: rock carved, rock inscribed, rock made into sculpture and architecture. Yet the pharaonic past was not merely, or even primarily, a matter of antiquarian or archaeological interest to the French. The savants, much like Napoleon himself, sought in its ruins a precedent for modern engineering also as a modern empire. The land of the ancient pyramids, strewn by stone colossi, was also the land inscribed by mathematics and systems of measure, mapping, construction, and transport. Here, to cite the French chief cartographer Pierre Jacotin, was "where geometry had been invented and put into practice" in order to contend with the flooding of the Nile.[1]

Somewhere in the midst of the rubble of the desert were the vestiges of the Suez Canal, which had been cut more than 3,000 years earlier during the reign of Pharaoh Sesostris, extended by the Romans, and abandoned only after the eighth century.[2] When Charles-Maurice de Talleyrand first proposed the Egyptian campaign in 1798, he insisted that reconstructing the Suez Canal would be a cheap and easy way to extend French control across the Egyptian desert and simultaneously thwart British ambitions.[3] The Egyptian past would map the French Empire of the future.

Bonaparte discovered the ancient canal on his first Christmas in Egypt, according to the story told by one of the savants—Edmé-François Jomard, the engineer and geographer who after 1807 would oversee production of the *Description de l'Égypte*—in his biography of another of the savants, Gaspard Monge, the mathematician famed as the founder of descriptive geometry. In a "sea of sand," the general recognized the trace and supposedly called out, "Monge, Monge, we are right in the canal [nous sommes en plein canal]!"[4] Napoleon and Monge defied centuries of neglect and forgetting by making direct physical contact with the pharaonic legacy and claiming it as their own. The fortuitous turn of events and the stature of the protagonists led everyone to assume that the engineers on the expedition would face few obstacles in reopening the canal as an efficient, up-to-date means of transport. They were of course all wrong. Napoleon left Egypt in 1799; Egypt was returned to Ottoman control in 1802.

Of the 151 savants who accompanied Napoleon to Egypt, none were archaeologists.[5] Nor were they historians or antiquarians. There were scientists, mathematicians, and doctors and some interpreters; the majority were engineers (fig. 13). A dozen were engineering students from the École Polytechnique, several of whom took their exams while in Egypt. Only a few were artists or architects. The tense of these specializations was the present, even the future, not the past. Yet the savants' primary accomplishment in Egypt was the description of its ancient stones. Central to that description was drawing.

To depict Egypt's monuments was to assert mastery over them, Edward Said argued over thirty years ago.[6] But the drama of Egyptian antiquity resided in immensity that defied representation. For the scale of the Napoleonic achievement to be fully appreciated, the scale of Egypt's

**13**
Letterhead, *L'Ingénieur des Ponts et Chaussées [Louis Joseph] Favier*, 1823. Paris, Archives Nationales.

monumentality needed to be conveyed, not merely disciplined. To tame the ordinary was hardly as impressive as taming the object that verged on the unrepresentable. When the authors of the *Description de l'Égypte* chose to emphasize monumentality, they moved a descriptive quandary to center stage. Their desire to discipline Egypt was contradicted by their need to represent the extent to which it was overwhelming. Not surprisingly, engineers were less inclined than artists to embrace such a test to their control.

---

**I am becoming anxious about my purpose in Egypt, not understanding how a geometer could be useful in such an expedition.**
**Édouard Devilliers, *Journal et souvenirs sur l'expédition d'Égypte*, 1899**

Published between 1809 and 1822, the *Description de l'Égypte* is itself a colossal monument to the power of drawing and engraving.[7] Over nine square feet in size, the 924 plates include over 3,000 separate images. Five volumes of the large-scale plates, some measuring over 50 by 26 inches, were devoted to antiquities; three concerned natural history and two, the modern state. Add to this the immense, fifty-sheet topographical map published in 1825; if this atlas's pages were placed side by side, they would measure 29.5 by 16.5 square feet.[8] The accompanying texts, by contrast, are bound in small volumes and seem almost an afterthought. These reports on subjects ranging from botany to disease to ancient astrology appear disorganized. Individual specialists present hypotheses and air disagreements with rivals; personalities emerge. No comparable dissension appears in the plates.

The homogeneity is all the more impressive given that the young men had learned to draw in a variety of contexts, the majority as engineers. I am not, however, contending that the drawings in the *Description de l'Égypte* are consistent or even stylistically similar. They are not. Plate 20 (Antiquities,volume 2), a landscape dominated by the ruined Colossi of Memnon, bears little resemblance to the subsequent plate reconstructing the same sculptures (figs. 14–15). In the first of the two pictures, the two ruined statues loom over distant, low-lying hills as well as the diminutive viewers who serve as our surrogates. Against the casual Lilliputian visitors, the eroded statues acquire a severe, blind grandeur. They are immense and have survived time and change for eons; beside them human beings seem slight in every way.

By accommodating the imaginative traversal of space, perspectival views such as plate 20 inscribe the inexorable passing of time. But what they convey of age value—to use Alois Riegl's terminology—they sacrifice in information about what the statues originally were.[9] Frenchmen's beloved ruins can convey only so much about ancient Egyptian monuments. But the *Description de l'Égypte* combines multiple modes of representation. Its drawings do not look alike because they are called upon to do different things. Plates 21 and 22, for example, are immaculate orthographic reconstructions of the front, side, and back views of the Colossi of Memnon; the images propose to restore what the colossi once were. Here are drawings "from nowhere," to quote Lorraine Daston, drawings that emphatically renounce perspectival points of view.[10] Freed of surrounding space and thus of time, the statues are also oddly independent of dimension.[11] Visually, the colossi are located nowhere and have no properties of scale, no size. In plate 21 (fig. 14), the Colossi of Memnon are consummately engineered models, uncannily whole substitutes whose coherence exists only on paper. Their unity is achieved, however, only by disaggregation. The solitary sculpture becomes three views, which we must cognitively rather than optically reconcile. Note, too, that their displacement from Egypt onto paper also

**14**
André Dutertre, View of the Two Colossi, Thebes, Memnonium, *La Description de l'Égypte*, Antiquités, vol. II, plate 20, Paris, 1809–1822. Courtesy of the Bancroft Library, University of California Berkeley.

**15**
Jean-Baptiste-Prosper Jollois and Édouard Devilliers, Details of the Southern Colossus, Thebes, Memnonium, *La Description de l'Égypte*, Antiquités, vol. II, plate 21, Paris, 1809-1822. Courtesy of the Bancroft Library, University of California Berkeley.

**16**
Manufacture de Sèvres, Pylon of Edfu, Colossi of Memnos and Avenue of Ram-Headed Sphinxes for the Temple at Karnak. Detail of the Centerpiece from the Dessert Service with Egyptian Views. Based on plates from *La Description de 'l'Égypte*. Biscuit Porcelain, c.1805. Moscow, The State Museum of Ceramics and the 18th-Century Kuskovo Estate.

sacrifices their specific existence as a pair. Drawn by two young engineers, these plates purport to reconstruct what was, yet they speak in the future tense. The drawings function as a plan; they could have preceded the statues' making. And the template, like all templates, could be used to produce one statue or a thousand of any size. In fact, the Colossi of Memnon were fabricated in porcelain between 1804 and 1808 as part of a centerpiece for Napoleon's dessert service; they measure 9 1/2 inches in height (fig. 16).

Plate 20 is by André Dutertre, the most talented and productive of the draftsmen trained at the École des Beaux-Arts.[12] Plates 21 and 22 are by Jean-Baptiste-Prosper Jollois and Edouard Devilliers, both graduates of the École Polytechnique, who consistently worked as a team.[13] Along with Dutertre and Jomard, also a graduate of the École Polytechnique, Jollois and Devilliers were among the most prolific draftsmen to contribute to the *Description*.[14] In 1798, Jollois was twenty-two years old and Devilliers was eighteen. Surprisingly, given his authoritative role, Jomard was only twenty-one. Dutertre, by contrast, was thirty-five.

We know too little about the gifted Dutertre. Like Jacques-Louis David, he had studied with the painter Joseph-Marie Vien; and he won the drawing prize at the Salon of 1794.[15] In Egypt, he proposed a drawing course at the Institute of Egypt, founded by Napoleon.[16] A careful twentieth-century historian of Napoleonic cartography wrongly refers to him as an engineer, an understand-able mistake given the many roles he played in Egypt.[17] He was willing to measure monuments, and he may have done some mapping. A talented landscapist, Dutertre also drew the often-published, rapid and incisive portraits of his fellow savants. He was accustomed to drawing and to careful looking; he was quick to see the subtle specificity of a profile; his line could effortlessly lay down the curve of a nose. At the age of thirty-five, he brought years of practice to his work in Egypt.

The engineers brought not experience but skills learned with efficiency in engineering school. Engineering education had featured drawing since the ancien régime. The École Royale des Ponts et Chaussées (Royal School of Bridges and Roads) was first founded as the Bureau des Dessinateurs (Bureau of Draftsmen) in 1744; it was renamed only twelve years later.[18] Drawing, primarily cartography, was a prominent part of its curriculum, which included competitions in the drawing of maps, ornaments, human figures, and, after 1775, landscape. The rival institution of military engineering, the École Royale du Génie de Mézières, also emphasized drawing, as did the postrevolutionary École Polytechnique, founded in 1794. The professors at the new institution believed as much as their predecessors that the teaching of science required lessons in drawing. The engineer, who needed to "to represent objects of all kinds: buildings, machines, ornaments, the configuration of terrains," must be able promptly to make "le trace de ces objets."[19] In his 1799 instructions concerning the education of "students who wanted to become part of the service of engineers, geographers, artists," General Claude-Marie Meunier stressed that "it would be very useful for these engineers to know the principles of perspective and that they readily draw landscape, because there are numerous circumstances where the view of a siege, an attack, a battle, or even just a site interesting in some respect would greatly aid the understanding of a map, no matter how well it was made."[20] Besides calling for an archive of uniform "models" of maps made at the same scale, Meunier explained why studying landscape (la nature du pays) would help engineers see more consistently: "With this training one could accustom eyes to see almost all in the same way, because I knew an engineer who saw mountains everywhere, and another who saw solely plains and considered a mountain only those really difficult to climb."[21]

The general was well aware that consensus was needed to define a mountain, and drawing, he believed, would teach engineers "to see almost all in the same way." But drawing was not merely a means to see more accurately or a skill for its own sake; it was essential to building. Witness Chastillon in his 1763 *Traité des ombres dans le dessin géométral*:

> Since the beginning of the School of Military Engineering at Mézières, particular attention has been paid to giving young officers the principles of drawing and to do so with method. Facility of expression with a pencil and the understanding of drawing lead to good construction of fortresses, of the trace and relief of fortification, and, in general, everything related to them. [Drawing...] trains the power of observation [coup d'oeil] for the survey of fortresses. In a word, it is drawing, understood and applied to all objects, which in part characterizes engineers.[22]

Chastillon is unequivocal. Facility with a pencil leads to good construction; it enhances engineers' skills as designers and builders and strengthens their coup d'oeil, the power of observation formerly attributed to the highest-ranking military officers but now deemed teachable. Still, it would be misleading to identify engineering drawing primarily with observation or even construction. To do so would be to misrepresent how engineering students actually practiced drawing.

Although they depicted buildings, ornaments, bodies, and landscapes, students spent the great bulk of their time on drawing exercises in geometry, above all in descriptive geometry as formulated by Monge, the mathematician who later accompanied Napoleon in the rediscovery of the canal in Suez.[23] For Monge, descriptive geometry is nothing less than the language of precise representation.

Descriptive geometry has two goals in view: the first to determine methods for representing on a sheet of drawing paper that has only two dimensions, viz., length and breadth, the forms of solid bodies which have three, length, breadth, and thickness [*profondeur*], provided that these bodies can be rigorously defined. The second goal is to determine methods for recognizing from an exact construction, the forms of solid bodies, and thence to deduce all the truths resulting from both their forms and respective positions.[24]

Monge understood the goal of geometry to be the representation of three dimensions, the "thickness" of solid bodies, on a two dimensional sheet of paper, as well as their respective positions. Monge's reliance on the word "descriptive" is deceptive; his method is highly theoretical. Unlike Chastillon, he begins not with real objects, like lampposts, but with abstract forms. Descriptive geometry entails the rigorous interrelating of two projections of the same object(s) (fig. 17). Imagine projecting a cylinder onto perpendicular horizontal and vertical planes of a cube; a circle would inscribe both horizontal planes while two straight lines would project onto the verticals. Together, they describe the cylinder in its three-dimensions. Or inscribe a circle on one horizontal plane and a point on the other; on the vertical sides draw diagonals that meet at the top; you will have mapped a cone.

**17**
Gaspard Monge, *Géométrie Descriptive*, Plate IV, 1798. (Paris: Baudouin, an VII–1798). Photo: Julie Wolf

**18**
A. Frézier, "Escalier vis de Saint-Gilles suspendu," *La Théorie et la pratique de la coupe des pierres*, 1739.

Joel Sakarovitch and other scholars have pointed out that descriptive geometry is little more than the generalization of stonecutting techniques stemming from the Middle Ages.[25] Monge had made theoretical an artisanal practice of drawing on the perpendicular faces of a stone block to produce the specific, irregular blocks required in vaults or arches (fig. 18). Previously, in the early modern period, the practice of stonecutting had already led to the development of layout drawings (*traits*).[26] Monge was less concerned with the definition of the abstract form (in stonecutting, the individual block) than with the task of representing the spatial relationships between forms on a two-dimensional surface. In his definition quoted above, the phrase "their respective positions" conveys his abiding concern with spatial projection. The mathematician who would join Napoleon inside vestiges of the pharaohs' canal had long been preoccupied with the way the trace, or line, could define space and the relative position of forms.

Student exercises in descriptive geometry were tedious. And the drawings were so abstract as to be all but incomprehensible to the nonexpert. They were meant to teach engineers how to regulate objects in space (for example, a cone intersecting a sphere) and, by extension, how to discipline the workings of their own minds.[27] Champions of the system had long declared that geometry in an engineering curriculum served to harness the imagination, tempering the "freedoms" inherent in the "free sketch." Only geometry could "prevent the imagination from flying off, and contain it within the bounds of reason."[28] In his book on the engineering of firearms during the French Revolution, Ken Alder notes that mathematics and mechanical drawing played key roles in consolidating engineering into a profession. "The goal [was] to reduce the discretion of both the person drawing the plan and the person reading it... As a quasi-public and mathematicized language—what Theodore Porter calls a 'technology of distance'—mechanical drawing binds those who use it to a common vision of the object."[29] Both mathematics and mechanical drawing imposed a "uniformity of habit and thought," offered students common knowledge and skills, and also instilled a respect for "the virtues of uniformity and precision."[30] Alder points out that "These were virtues that made agreement matter."[31] Recall General Meunier's comment that studying landscape would "accustom eyes to see almost all in the same way."

In Egypt Jollois and Devilliers worked as a team; they shared a set of skills and assumptions about the goals of representation. Their drawings resemble drawings by other engineers,

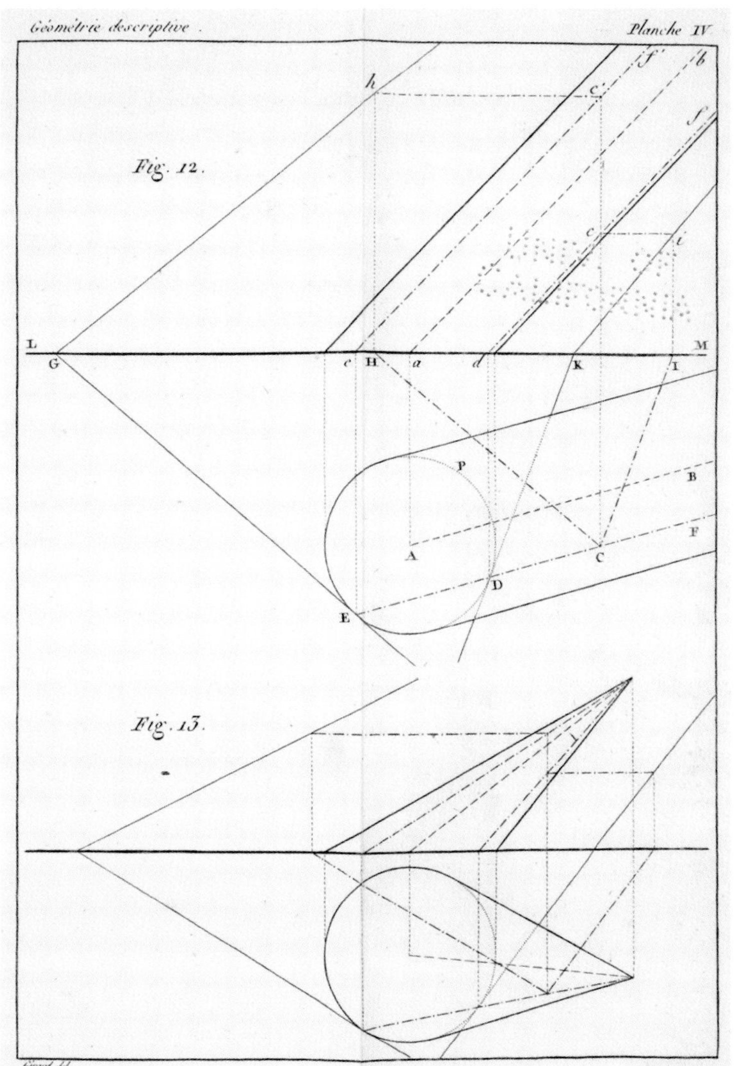


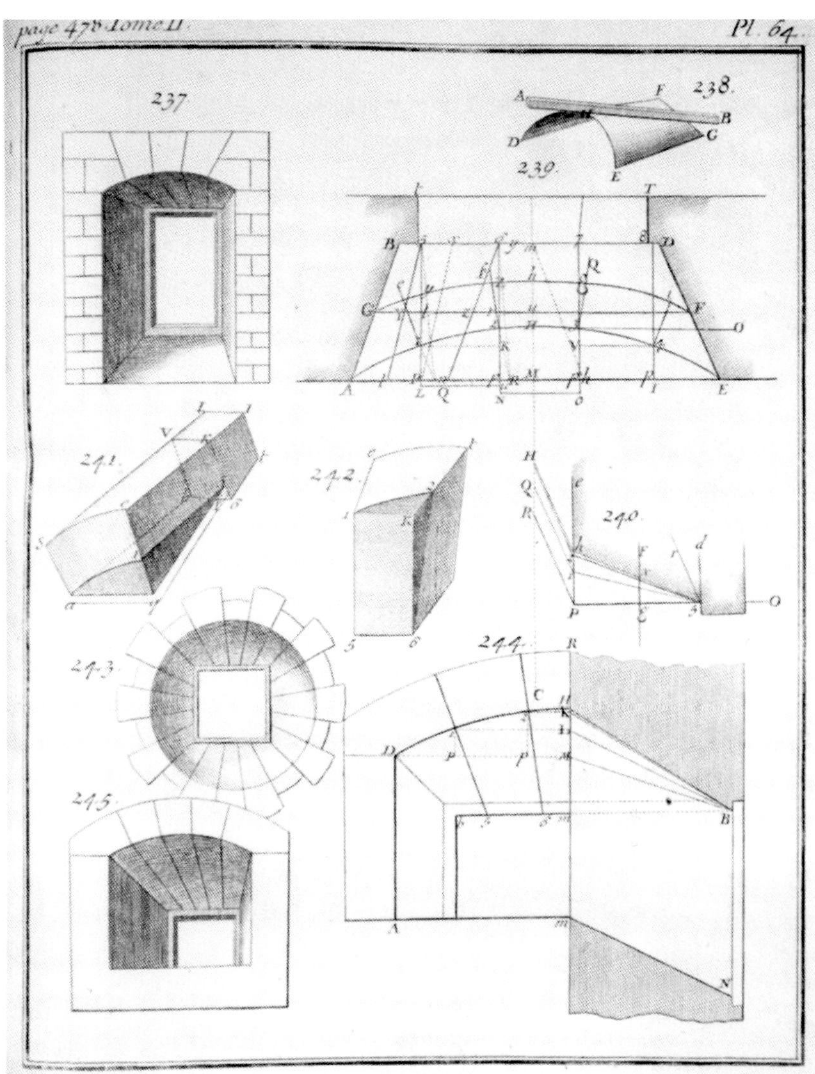


including Jomard. Monge had distinguished mechanical drawing from the art of painting. Not surprisingly, he defined art in terms of "feeling," "emotion," "impression," and "the habit of deepest contemplation." Painting moreover "is subject to no general rules." Against the individuated, free sphere of the art of painting, Monge emphasizes that "nothing is arbitrary" in a "systematic and exact" mechanical art: "everything can be foreseen by strict reasoning because everything is the necessary result of objects perfectly known, and of given conditions." But even Monge admits that "rapidity of execution, which is often necessary, would seldom allow the practice of a method that would deprive the mind of every material aid and would have it entirely dependent upon its reasoning powers alone...it is much easier for a painter to place the objects before him."[32] Sometimes it is easier to imitate things than to reason about them. Monge had been outraged to find that some of his students faked required geometry drawings simply by copying other drawings. To thwart the temptation of mere mimicry, Monge insisted on the policing of student work. Of course, even the students who plagiarized were learning the skills of precise draftsmanship; they simply did not understand the underlying logic of what they represented. One wonders how Monge's regimen might inadvertently have prepared them to copy forms they did not understand, hieroglyphs in Egypt, for example.

To have been selected to join the Egyptian expedition, Jollois and Devilliers must have been talented students; they certainly worked hard. But whether they practiced descriptive geometry's exercises or "faked" them (and surely they did the former), they had come to know that their drawings should look alike. Consensus was the goal. Consensus allowed the hasty recording of information on the ground of Egypt to accrue authority as objective knowledge. Every drawing in the *Description de l'Égypte*, like every written report, was discussed and approved by the commission in charge of its publication; the engineer Jomard was the senior editor.[33]

**When we wish to make a map of a country, we usually suppose that all the remarkable points on it are connected by straight lines which form triangles...** Gaspard Monge, ***Descriptive Geometry***, **Paris, 1798**

Plates 20 and 21 extracted the Colossi of Memnon from their location and reconstituted them anew. But engineers understood their job to be not only the description of things like statues but the mapping of space and how objects occupy it. After all, descriptive geometry was intended to represent the relationship between three dimensional things in space. Dutertre's drawing situates the colossi in a landscape and attempts to convey their immensity. On the preceding page, a map indicates scale but diminishes the colossi to spots on the map of a region (fig. 19).[34] This is a typical sequence. Mapping determines the structure of the *Description de l'Égypte*; the plates depict one region after another, moving from Upper Egypt in the south to Lower Egypt in the north.

Many engineers were also geographers. Jomard belonged to this hyphenated category, the ingénieur-géographe. In 1795 the École des Ingénieurs Géographes had been founded as an institution of further training for École Polytechnique graduates.[35] Initially withheld from publication because Bonaparte considered it a military resource, the atlas is one of the *Description de l'Égypte*'s most formidable achievements. When Napoleon's troops first landed in Egypt, they relied on an antiquated and incomplete map of 1765 by Jean-Baptisted'Anville. The cartographer Pierre Jacotin observed that the army of the Orient "had almost no knowledge of the region it had to travel through across the desert."[36] He understood that providing the army with maps was the chief job of the engineers. If size is made affective in the Dutertre plate and irrelevant in the plates by Jollois and Devilliers, its representation was the very goal of mapping. For French engineers, to map was to measure.

The minuscule numbers inscribed on every plate of the *Description de l'Égypte* promise to attach representation to the earth. Monge played a decisive role in the anchoring; he was the most powerful and stubborn advocate of the new standard of measure called the meter, a term derived from metron, the Greek word meaning measure.[37] A meter was defined as one ten-millionth of a meridian between the pole and the equator (from Barcelona to Dunkirk).[38] In France, the metric system was part and parcel of the French Revolution's rationalizing of time and space. The famous chemist Antoine Lavoisier exclaimed, "Never has anything more grand and simple, more coherent in all its parts, issued from the hand of man."[39] (He did not anticipate that ferocious disagreements about measure would later play a part in his execution at the guillotine).

Lavoisier was expressing a pervasive desire among the French to authorize their new measure, not merely as one language among many, but rather as an objective and universal truth. And though time could offer a unit of spatial measure—the distance traversed by a pendulum in a given period—the pendulum was deemed too subject to variables like gravity, temperature, and

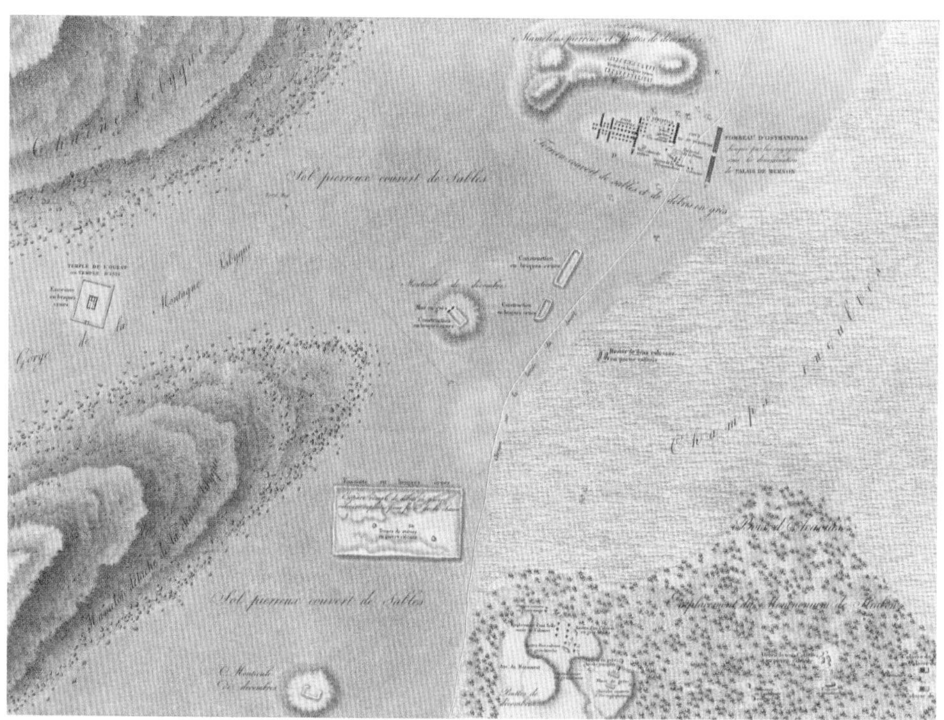

altitude to provide a universal unit of duration.[40] For the French eager to establish the authority of the metric system, mapping the earth became an enterprise of the utmost importance. The metric system would eliminate regional differences as well as the variety of units used for different kinds of things or activities. Most dramatically, the new scientific system would overturn the time-honored primacy of the human body as the basis of all systems of measurement.

Seen in this context, Dutertre's turn-of-the-century pictures of men contemplating towering statues become profoundly nostalgic (figs. 14, 20). French dandies with portfolios under their arms, determined the size and significance of the inanimate world merely by looking at it. One of Dutertre's plates suggests that he grasped the difference between the contemplative observer and the engineer (fig. 21).[41] At left, a military officer displays a colossal stone fist to the viewer; at right the lower-ranked engineer Gratien Le Père supervises his crouching assistant Jean-Marie-Joseph Coutelle in the act of measuring with a rod. Thus Dutertre depicts both a social hierarchy and the way that hierarchy was predicated on a division of labor. The engineer directs the mechanic, whose labor is manual and requires a tool. Like so many other members of professions in the process of consolidation, young Napoleonic engineers were sensitive to questions of status.[42] One École Polytechnique graduate resented the fact that, during the Egyptian campaign, scientists dined with upper military officers while engineers were required to eat with the subalterns. He pointed out that this meant that the younger Delille brother, who was a botanist, dined with officers while his more accomplished older brother, an engineer, did not. (And botany, the graduate protests, is not even a demanding science!)[43]

According to the caption, Dutertre's plate shows an engineer preparing to transport the colossal hand. The massive stone sculpture has been loaded onto the wooden platform formed from one of the huge date palms dominating the composition; at right, the gigantic stump is taller than the engineer. The text also explains that the colossal hand made it to Cairo and then to Alexandria; but the French ultimately lost the sculpture to the English, who displayed it at the British Museum (where it remains). Fortunately, the caption adds, a plaster cast would enable the French "to form an exact copy of the monument." War, not just site specificity, made the creation of various sorts of reproduction crucial. Whether the monuments were too large to move or too easily seized by the English, the French needed to manufacture substitutes on paper or as casts. They were constructing a virtual museum.

To judge from Dutertre's preparatory watercolor, he was as preoccupied with the disposition of the three foreground figures as he was with depicting the colossal fragment. In another drawing of the object, the architect Balzac lingered on the fist itself. His appealing yet strange preparatory drawing squeezes a date palm and a figure into the space left after he centered the fragment (fig. 22). Palm and man compete as foils to the fist; perception of its size changes according to which comparison is made. Technique as well as dimension contributes to the contrast between large and small; the expansive, broadly brushed palm is so bold as to diminish the more finely drawn sculpture. Because the drawing does not convey the size of the date palm, it cannot be used to determine the fragment's size. Whereas the lightly sketched male figure, partly pinned beneath the rock, restores its immensity. We presume that we know the size of the human body. But Balzac also offers numbers. The measurements that span the hand mediate between the conflicting impressions derived from comparing stone hand to tree and to man. Balzac provides the data compiled by the men in Dutertre's plate. Yet Balzac's own marvelous plate in the *Description*, surrounded by pictures drawn by Jomard, renders scale once again ambiguous because the human figure has been eliminated (fig. 23). Perhaps for this reason Balzac chose to inscribe the fist with (very small) numbers.

These two images of a sculpted hand, the one circumstantial, the other surreal, exemplify the cross referencing prominent in the *Description*.[44] The viewer is asked again and again to correlate plates; to realize, for example, that this view is from point A in a previous image. Viewers are meant to understand that the two pristine squares to the right of Balzac's eerie landscape show bird mummies seen from above and from the side; viewpoints specified with letters in the cross section of the tomb provided at left. Such interconnections between plates are meant to ensure the accuracy of the *Description*; its claims can be corroborated across plates, even across data compiled by different savants. In its scope and its concern for making observed data into verifiable, "scientific" facts, the *Description* continues the work of the Enlightenment

**19**
Jean-Baptiste-Prosper Jollois, Édouard Devilliers, Jean-Baptiste Coraboeuf, and Alexandre Saint-Genis, Topographic Map of the Tomb of Osymandyas, the Two Colossi of the Plain and the Surrounding Ruins, Thebes, Memnonium, *La Description de l'Égypte*, Antiquités, vol. II, plate 19, Paris, 1809–1822. Courtesy of the Bancroft Library, University of California, Berkeley.

**20**
André Dutertre, View of a Colossus Placed at the Entry of the *salle hypostyle* of the Palace, Thebes, Karnak, *La Description de l'Égypte*, Antiquités, vol. III, plate 20, Paris, 1809–1822. Courtesy of the Bancroft Library, University of California, Berkeley.

**21**
André Dutertre, View of the Ruins from the Southeast, Memphis and its Surroundings, *La Description de l'Égypte*, Antiquités, vol. V, plate 3, Paris, 1809-1822. Courtesy of the Bancroft Library, University of California, Berkeley.

towards compiling great encyclopedias of universal knowledge. According to the geographer Matthew Edney, the Enlightenment's "encyclopedic mentality" was "rooted in two convictions, first that 'every point of view, whatever its source, could be brought into rational debate with every other,' and second that 'such rational debate could always, if adequately conducted, have a conclusive outcome.' The implication of these convictions for geography was that accounts of the same phenomena from different sources could, in principle, always be reconciled, no matter the degree of difference between them ...eventually producing one definitive archive of knowledge."[45]

Though promising universal knowledge, accessible to all, in practice the enlightenment archive served an elite implicated in advancing French imperialism. All can be known, all can be measured, all can be made logical for those trained to manage the system. To be sure, the *Description* can reward the inexpert viewer, who derives pleasure from the (relatively few) correlations he or she can recognize: the colossal fist is being measured; here it is again with the measurements imposed.

The system of knowledge governing the *Description* is self-corroborating; therein lies its ideological efficacy.[46] Numbers are reassuringly specific, but they are arbitrary as representations of the world unless we know what units they stand for. Numbers can suggest proportion, but they cannot communicate absolute size independent of measure; and measure is a convention that requires consensus, even when derived from the size of the earth. (Why did the meter depend on the distance between Barcelona and Dunkirk?)

Balzac's pictures of the fist give much of this away. The numbers inscribed on the preliminary drawing are feet (pieds); the numbers on the final engraved plate are meters.[47] Andro Linklater has argued that measurement entails abstracting a quality from an object and giving it numerical value. "Originally, the unit used to make the measurement might have been personal—'your' foot; then it became social—'the' foot, an agreed average; now the foot had evolved into something scientific—a fraction of time" (or in the case of the meter, a fraction of the earth).[48] Such a progression had led the French Académie to attempt to regulate the definition of the toise (approximately two meters or 76.7 inches). Standardization required sending material copies of the toise to all eighty of France's provinces.[49] This meager attempt at standardization could not overcome local practices. In 1789 Arthur Young complained that "the unending proliferation of measures is quite beyond imagination. They differ not only in every province, but in every canton too, and in almost every town; the differences drive people to despair."[50] Commerce was frustrated by such variability, but it made perfect sense in daily practice. "The traditional measures had variety because they related to different activities. Cloth was measured by the ell or the aune because it was natural to hold it and stretch out the arm to full length. A journey was measured by the yard or the toise because the road was walked. Land was measured by the acre or the arpent because that represented work." Linklater, relying on Witold Kula, concludes that the metric system was long resisted because of its alienating abstraction from experience.[51]

Laypeople were accustomed to comparing things to their bodies and its movements. Such comparisons could lead to dissonance in representation; Balzac inscribed "feet" on a hand. Nor were measurements such as "3 *pieds*" precise. (A French engineer asked the obvious question: *Which* Englishman's "foot"?) In sum, measurement itself is problematic; in Balzac's drawing, it is unclear which span of the fist is purportedly measured. Balzac must rely on a dashed line to indicate the length to which it refers. But did he mean to stop just short of the thumb? And how should the limits of curvilinear things be determined? Monge called the perceived edges of things "apparent outlines"—visual phenomena, not objective limits.[52] Finally, and just as importantly, the convention of overlaying a line on the things of the world fails to take into account their irregular, undulating surfaces. Much as is the case in maps, measurement in Balzac's drawing seems to refer to a length as a straight shot; it does not register the undulating shape of the fist.[53]

Regularizing of terrain is often what we want from measurements. The distances in a map should indicate how far one site is from another, as well as how long a winding road over the intervening mountains might be. Does it come as a surprise that the French word for surveying, *nivellement*, is as well the word for leveling? But to get from one place to another, both kinds of information about distances are required; thus the illusionistic shading of terrain in the *Description's* maps; thus the subtle shading of the fist in Balzac's drawing. Monge was alert to the problem of representing irregular, curving structures:

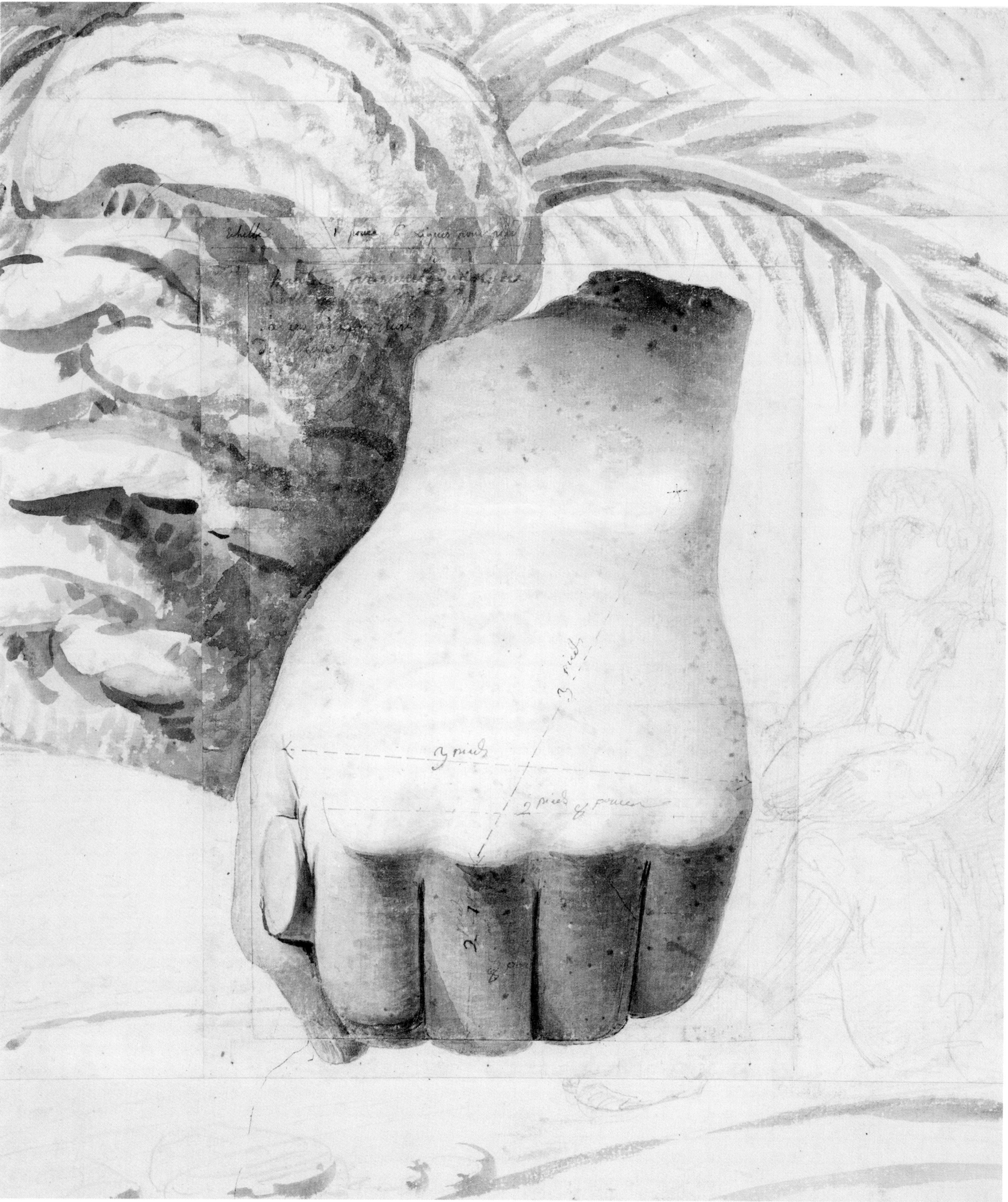

When we wish to make a map of a country, we usually suppose that all the remarkable points on it are connected by straight lines which form triangles, and similar triangles on a smaller scale, are to be described on the map in the same order as those they represent. The operations to be performed upon the ground consist chiefly in measuring the angles of these triangles.... [But] If the plane of the angle is oblique to the horizon, we have to construct the horizontal projection of it, and not the angle itself.... The operation for performing this is known by the name of the reduction of an angle to the horizon.[54]

Because the earth is spherical and maps are flat, mapmakers must always contend with the distortions inherent to any projection. "Each projection [of a sphere] is a compromise between correct shape and correct size or between what is preferable in the lower latitudes or closer to the poles."[55] Note the opposition here: every mapmaker must decide whether his priority is correct shape or correct size. Such distortions are less apparent in the large scale maps of small areas deployed in the *Description*, but they indicate how very vexed was the quest to represent the size and shape of Egypt.

No wonder Napoleonic engineers focused on the pyramids, which seemed to promise both measurable size and precise geometrical, three-dimensional shape. What is more, the Great Pyramid of Giza offered a fixed point of reference for the mapping of Egypt. Cartographers decided that the center of the large pyramid of Giza would function as "the point of intersection of the meridian and parallel and, thus, as the center point of the [entire] projection" (fig. 24).[56] It is disquieting if unsurprising to learn that the industrious and capable astronomer Nicolas-Antoine Nouet determined the longitude and latitude of the great pyramid "by calculating [its] distance from the Maison de l'Institut, which was the astronomically determined location for Cairo."The Maison de l'Institut in Cairo was the building that had been seized to house the savants. Could the mapmakers have bound their representation of Egypt any more tightly to French dominion?

The measurement and position of the Great Pyramid of Giza therefore determined the *Description*'s comprehensive map of Egypt Moreover, the height of the Great Pyramid would assist engineers in their calculation of the height of the Red Sea and the Mediterranean.[57] These figures were of the utmost importance because the assumption that the two bodies of water were unequal heights had long made a sea level canal at Suez seem impossible. Here, once again, there is a serious conflict between between so-called geographic mapping of horizontal surfaces (the trace) and the topographic mapping of relative heights (Balzac's arrows shooting across the curving fist). And it would be height, not horizontal expanse, which would eventually thwart French ambitions.

Working under dangerous conditions and pressed for time, the engineers took inaccurate measurements and concluded, wrongly, that the height of the two seas differed by more than thirty feet. They were forced to argue that the Suez Canal could not be built. Measurements, not material obstacles, ultimately thwarted the Napoleonic plans to engineer of a modern canal.

**22**
Charles-Louis Balzac, Preparatory Drawing for *La Description de l'Égypte*, Antiquités, vol. V, plate 4, Paris, 1809-1822. Paris, Bibliothèque Nationale.

**23**
Charles-Louis Balzac and Edme-François Jomard, Memphis and its Surroundings, *La Description de l'Égypte*, Antiquités, vol. V, plate 4, Paris, 1809-1822. Courtesy of the Bancroft Library, University of California, Berkeley.

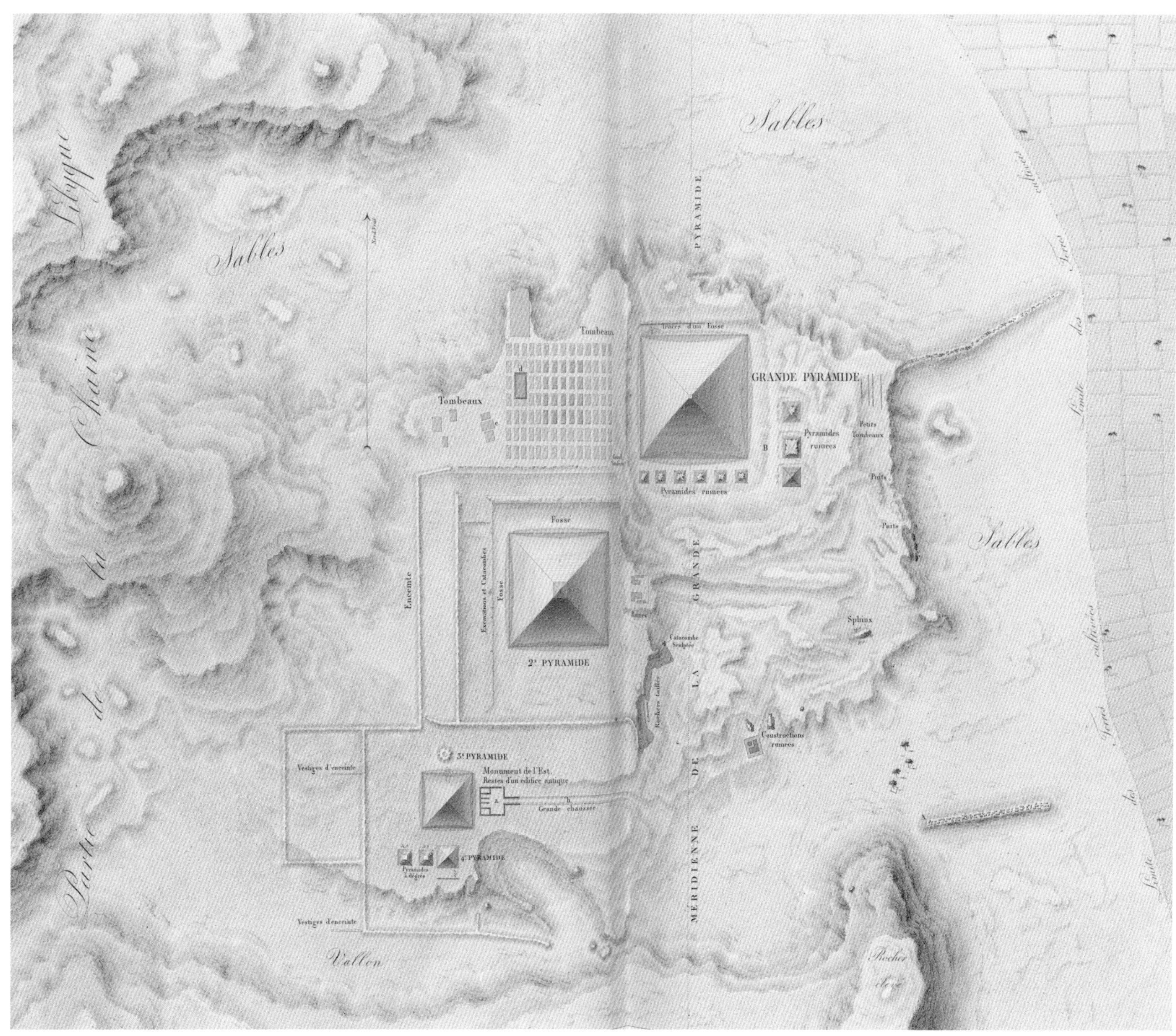


**24**

Topographic Plan of Pyramids and Surroundings, Pyramids of Memphis, *La Description de l'Égypte*, Antiquités, vol. V, plate 6, Paris, 1809–1822. Courtesy of the Bancroft Library, University of California, Berkeley.

**We do not know to what extent liberty and human dignity were respected in these long and painful works.** Edmé-François Jomard, "Remarques et recherches sur les Pyramides d'Égypte," *La Description de l'Égypte*, 1809–1822

Triangulation is the extrapolation of the lengths and position of the sides of a triangle from one side's length and the size of two of its angles. This simple procedure permitted the astronomer Nouet to determine the Great Pyramid's position and orientation. Triangulation was efficient; it also released him from the task of measuring the ground the pyramid occupied: "When you figure out the other sides of a triangle, you can use any one of them as the known line for the next triangle.... Only once, when the initial base line is laid out, is it absolutely necessary to measure every meter of any line."[58] But French engineers were still resolved to measure the height of the pyramid. This required time and men and a great deal of hard work.

During the 1801 campaign of measurement, Dutertre, Le Père, and Coutelle were accompanied by fifty Egyptian workers and an escort of one hundred soldiers.[59] Although climbing up the enormous blocks of stone was the closest the engineers came to experiencing the physical difficulties of building the monument, most of them understood the inordinate size of the monument as a testament to the inordinate efforts required to build it. To them the Great Pyramid was all but synonymous with coerced labor. The influential eighteenth-century traveler and political theorist Constantin-François Volney was one among many to move at breakneck speed from the rhetoric of admiration to criticism of the pharaohs' tyranny.

Finally one reaches [the pyramids], and nothing can express the variety of sensations you feel there: the height of their summit, the rapidity of their slope, the amplitude of their surface, the weight of their base, the memory of the times they recall, the calculation of the labor that they required, the idea that these immense rocks are the work of man, so small and so weak, who crawls at their feet: everything seizes the heart and the spirit at once with astonishment, terror, humiliation, wonder, respect: but, you must admit, another sentiment follows this first transport. After having had such a great opinion of the power of man, when one begins to reflect upon the aim of his employment, then one looks only with regret upon his work; one is distressed to think that in order to construct a worthless tomb, it was necessary to torment an entire nation for twenty years; one bemoans the host of injustices and humiliations that must have resulted from the onerous forced labor and the transport, cutting, and accumulation of so many materials. One is indignant at the extravagance of the despots who ordered these barbaric works.[60]

Volney confounds his reader with a vivid enumeration of the pyramids' physical mass. Their height, slope, surface, and weight are evoked with the certainty that they will seize "the heart and spirit at once" with sensations from "astonishment" to "respect." Confusion between the characteristics of an object with the experiences they cause in a beholder has received much analysis, especially in discussions of the sublime. But Volney's account of a visit to the pyramids makes consideration of labor integral to the effects of the outsized. This is unusual. From Aristotle to Burke to Kant and Derrida, philosophers have privileged the dyad of apprehending person and inanimate thing in their investigations of the colossal.[61] Volney does as well, but he is not content to assume that the relation between subject and object is merely aesthetic or, more broadly, philosophical. It is intertwined with an awareness of the labor that produced the monument. That awareness makes possible political criticism.

Jomard knew his Volney, which along with an earlier classic by Claude-Étienne Savary, was selected by Monge as reading for the French officers on the campaign in Egypt. Jomard's debt to Volney is evident in his own account of approaching the pyramids.

One sees, one touches some hundreds of courses [each] two hundred cubic feet and thirty thousand pounds in weight, with thousands of others [above] which yield nothing to them, and one searches to comprehend what force has removed, dragged, and raised so great a number of colossal stones and how many men have worked there, what time it took them and what means they have adopted. The less one is able to express all these things the more one admires the effort which has triumphed over such obstacles.[62]

Jomard goes on to observe that the building of the pyramids was an act of tyranny but tempers the criticism with counterarguments; for instance, that ancient Egyptian rulers "wanted to exercise a happy influence on the health of the people, by imposing on them regulated work and preventing the inhabitants from falling into idleness."[63] Skating on thin ice, he characteristically shifts his argument from politics to science, hoping to convince his readers that "there is too much care

**25**
Edmé-François Jomard, Pyramids of El Métanyeh and Saqqârah, Fayoum and its Surroundings. *La Description de l'Égypte*, Antiquités, vol. IV, plate 72, figs. 4 and 6, 1809–1822, Paris, 1809–1822. Art and Architecture Library, Stanford University.

**26**
Edmé-François Jomard, Illustration to "Exposition du système métrique des anciens Egyptiens," (Exposition of the metric system of the ancient Egyptians), *La Description de l'Égypte*, Mémoires VII, Paris, 1809, pp. 1–575, here p. 537. Courtesy of the Bancroft Library, University of California, Berkeley.

and art, at least in the construction of the greatest of [the pyramids], not to be made to recognize that it was science that presided over the work and not a mad ostentation or a blind despotism."[64]

Jomard is correct to call attention to the manual skill and theoretical knowledge that went into building the Great Pyramid. A depiction of other pyramids in the *Description de l'Égypte* assimilates monuments and landscape in a way that robs the monuments of all drama (fig. 25).[65] It is unclear whether the pyramid is a man-made object or a natural part of the terrain. After all, pyramids from a distance resemble mountains, as Jomard himself admitted.[66] The challenge was therefore to convey immense scale while preserving the pyramid's status as man-made artifact. Pyramids, unlike human bodies, are simple, indeed homogeneous, predictable shapes; they appear unified and uniform, singular rather than composite.

There are several ways to underscore the man-made character of pyramids, to make them visibly unlike mountains. One is to emphasize their mathematical precision; the other is to show the composite character of their seemingly unified form. The two possibilities defy reconciliation; mathematical precision is not compatible with the inherent irregularity of the man-made. For those—Jomard included—who valued the geometry—that is, the a priori ideality of mathematical concepts, the pyramids were best seen as outside time and as miracles of precise manufacture (fig. 26).[67] In addition, believing the pyramids to be eternal standards of measure, Jomard expected the measurements of the pyramids to prove that ancient Egyptian measure, like the French metric system, was not arbitrary but was instead based upon the size of the earth.[68] Although previous surveyors of the pyramids had never reached agreement, the French hoped against all likelihood to produce definitive measurements. Like so many before and after him, Jomard was intent upon making the Great Pyramid "a metric monument, designed to embody and to perpetuate a system of measures."[69] Working separately, several different engineers proceeded step by step to measure the pyramid's base and height. When they compared results, they were compellingly close. Elliott Colla has remarked that, "Quantifying the Pyramid served not only to describe it as a material object but also to stabilize the very units of quantity by which measure was obtained in the first place. In this sense, the quantified description of the object was guaranteed by the object itself."[70]

In Jomard's renditions, the pyramid becomes a mathematical proof, inscribed with measurements that transform its size into sizeless ratios. In his "Analytic of the Sublime" of 1790, Kant points out that any object can be made to seem infinitely big or infinitely small relative to others.[71] Size is fundamentally comparative, but flexibly so. Man is one measure but has no priority. In the mathematical land of measurements, scale becomes wildly relative. (Our sense of an object's size depends, of course, on whether we compare it to the minuscule or to the planet.) In such infinitely graded scales of measure, there is no such thing as the colossal. To see the pyramids as mathematical proofs might be to invest them with absolute authority, but to preserve the colossal grandeur of ancient Egypt, it was necessary to preserve the priority of the human body, to make the human body the measure. The geometric figure makes lived scale irrelevant. It may be impressive, but it will not be experienced as colossal. Colossi depend on us.

The other way of articulating the man-made nature of the pyramids is to show that they are cumulative, composite products rather than simple, natural, geometric (or metaphysical) phenomena. Writers, including Kant, have demonstrated, this is not so easily done. How, Kant asked, after reading the French traveler Savary's remarkable *Lettres sur l'Égypte*, can one simultaneously apprehend the Great Pyramid as over two hundred tiers of stone blocks and comprehend its colossal geometric form? The problem—for Kant, and Aristotle before him—is to experience at once constitutive parts and overwhelming whole.[72] Draftsmen struggled against all odds to convey the pyramids' immensity and their composite—that is, man-made—nature. In fact, Kant takes the need to apprehend the constructed character of the pyramids so much for granted that he does not even propose an argument:

> This explains Savary's observations in his account of Egypt, that in order to get the full emotional effect of the size of the Pyramids we must avoid coming too near just as much as remaining too far away. For in the latter case [being too far away] the representation of the apprehended parts (the tiers of stones) is but obscure, and produces no effect upon the aesthetic judgment of the subject. [However,] in the former [being too close],...it takes the eye some time to complete the apprehension from the base to the summit; but in this interval the first tiers always in part disappear before the imagination has taken in the last, and so the comprehension is never complete.[73]

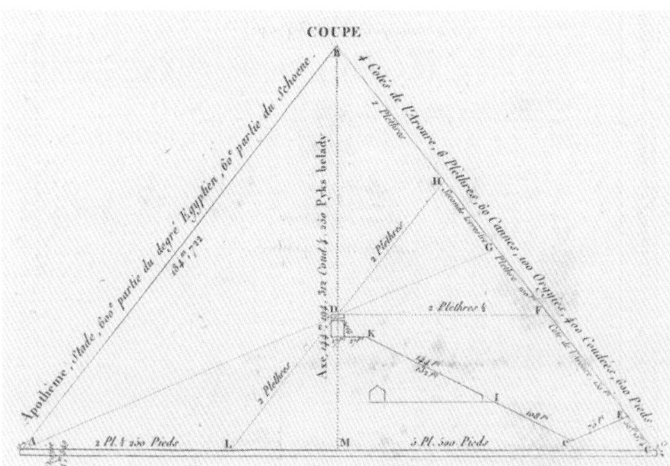


Kant assumes scale can only be appreciated if one is aware of the pyramid's parts, its making. For Kant, there can be no aesthetic judgment without seeing the layers of rocks; the pyramid must be seen as man-made. I am inverting Kant's emphasis. His concern, like Savary's, is the human incapacity to comprehend the whole overwhelming pyramid when visiting it up close for then it can appear to be a pile of rocks. Kant conjures a phenomenological amnesia; only so many rocks can be remembered at a time. One never arrives experientially at a summation of the parts.

But there is another possibility: that some effort must be exerted, especially in two-dimensional representation, to prevent the accumulation of discrete rocks from disappearing altogether, given the power of the simplified geometric form to subsume irregularity and formal complexity. Kant and Savary worried that pyramids disintegrated into heaps of rocks; I worry that tiers of rocks disappear into ideal form and with that disappearance, awareness of sustained labor also vanishes. Unless we can simultaneously understand both the colossal whole and the physical units out of which it was made, we cannot understand the man-made colossus, its manual achievement. Ideal form threatens to imply an a priori perfection. I take from Kant, however, an anxiety that we cannot hold together whole and part; an awareness of both colossal form and constituent material, colossal form and colossal making, what we know by seeing and what we know (and make) by moving our bodies.[74]

---

**But this edge is never sharp, never a mathematical straight line.** **Gaspard Monge, *Descriptive Geometry*, Paris, 1798**

There are numerous plates in the *Description de l'Égypte* devoted to the pyramids. And their effect, when taken together, is to emphasize these monuments' variable appearances according to time of day, point of view, and relative distance (figs. 27–28). Yet repetition of the pyramids across plates and within single images verifies the constancy of their form; it subjects their variety and complexity to the ruthless simplification of pure Euclidean shape. Repetition may make possible some heterogeneity or variability of effect, but it ultimately underscores these monuments' eternal, a priori geometry. Plate 10 by Dutertre is no exception (fig. 29). The quick recession of pyramids into the distance describes the progressive simplification from right to left of heterogeneous, irregular materials into unified, ideal geometric form. Distance turns the variable phenomena of the world into the view from nowhere of orthographic projection. Yet Dutertre's picture manages to imply another movement in the opposite direction from left to right, from distance to closeness. What makes his picture extraordinary is the view of a pyramid from very close (fig. 30). Proximity, Dutertre's representation suggests, disintegrates conceptual unities into a material irregularity that verges on the formless. It is striking on Dutertre 's part to have decided to represent the most eroded corner of the Great Pyramid so that it barely signifies geometric form, let alone a pyramid. Has there ever been a more subtly swelling, wayward contour, promising at one glance roundness, at another an S-curve, at another the ghost of the straight line of a triangle? This edge of tiered

**27**
François-Charles Cécile, View of Entry to the Great Pyramid taken at the Rising Sun, Pyramids of Memphis, *La Description de l'Égypte*, Antiquités, vol. V, plate 9, Paris, 1809–1822. Art and Architecture Library, Stanford University.

**28**
Charles-Louis Balzac, General View of Pyramids and of Sphinx, taken at Setting Sun, Pyramids of Memphis, *La Description de l'Égypte*, Antiquités, vol. V, plate 8, Paris, 1809–1822. New York Public Library. Photo: The New York Public Library/Art Resource, NY.

**29**
André Dutertre, View of the Second Pyramid, Pyramids of Memphis, *La Description de l'Égypte*, Antiquités, vol. V, plate 10, Paris, 1809–1822. Courtesy of the Bancroft Library, University of California, Berkeley.

**30**
Detail, André Dutertre, View of the Second Pyramid, Pyramids of Memphis, *La Description de l'Égypte*, Antiquités, vol. V, plate 10, Paris, 1809–1822. Courtesy of the Bancroft Library, University of California, Berkeley.

rocks is coy, flirting with geometry but continually withdrawing from its demands. Here are Savary's and Kant's rocks; apprehending them one at a time makes the pyramid as colossal form slip from comprehension.

Monge, the geometer sensitive to the undulations of the terrain, recognized the ambiguity of the edges of things and the difficulty they cause descriptive geometry. An edge is never sharp, never a mathematical straight line: the materials of which it is constructed are not absolutely free of porosity, the tools used in shaping them are not perfect; the hands of the workman fail to shape a strictly perfect edge. Afterwards, everything striking, or merely rubbing, against it, has blunted it; and really, instead of being a sharp edge it is nothing but a rounded surface that can be conceived as a portion of a cylinder of a very small radius.[75] Then too, Egypt's eroding colossi reminded French savants that things made by men are subject to material conditions, the absorbency of stone, the limitations of tools, and the passing of time.

As if responding to Monge's formulations and the experience of Egypt, Dutertre's picture captures the way specific things have become subject to erosion. Although the fragment of a colossal sculpture—the hand, the foot—gauges the gigantic body from which it fell, the fragment from the corner of the pyramid is not comparably synecdochical; it fails to suggest its original form or even its man-made status. In Dutertre's plate, the landscape is strewn with rocks; take a pyramid apart and, unlike a stone body, it rejoins the earth. Layered upon one another, the individual rocks are evidence of man's intervention. But they can easily become mere rubble so tenuous are the indices of labor and human intentionality imposed upon them; they must be assembled, layer by layer, into a form of some predictability. This—the remarkable balance required to make labor visible—is what the mound at the far right of Dutertre's plate evinces. To convey man-made monumentality, the image must counterpose contingency and order, randomness and coherence, formlessness and form, accident and intention.

In Dutertre's picture, line is called upon to perform that balancing act. Line is marshaled, on the one hand, to discipline chaos, that is, to articulate form, and, on the other, to register the mutability of form, its material specificity and its unpredictable variety. Dutertre accomplished this —as did the engraver who translated his drawing into a print—by succumbing to a kind of obsession, setting down lines to describe rock after eroded rock. Both artists reconcile continued alertness to changes in shape and texture with a determination to convey an impression of engineered even and regular layers of masonry. Extraordinary technical facility, discipline, and perseverance are required to give each stone its portrait and, at the same time, subordinate that portrait to an integrated composition. Of course, pictures generally do this, but Dutertre's picture of pyramids devotes more attention than most to the effort required to depict small and large, part and whole at once. His willingness to submit himself to tedious repetition (look at the layers of rocks in the central pyramid) comes as close as artistic work can to a reenactment of a pyramid's building, the effort to move irregular (and thus resistant) part after part into coherent order. Dutertre's drawing accomplishes a feat: it makes visible geometry and materiality, whole and part, and by so doing it conveys colossal scale more effectively than any other plate in the *Description*.

To apprehend the size of the pyramids, one must leap that gap between the irregular edge of the Great Pyramid and the silhouetted, simplified but subtly irregular edge of the Second Pyramid behind it. The heap of rocks at far right acts as the closest tile in the receding floors of perspective systems. Here is size and constituent part, they indicate; here is a cue to scale. And the distant pyramids offer the vanishing point that compresses things—rocks, in this case—into straight-edged geometric angles. To depict rock, whether recently quarried or long eroded, necessitates attention to material irregularity. Yet the accomplishment of the pyramid builders was to submit that heterogeneity to a disciplining order, to line up blocks of stone in ways that produce sharp, clean edges slanted so as to assume the shape of a pyramid. Where the laying down of stones stopped mattered greatly to the successful production of a geometric form, whether in Egypt's desert or on France's paper.

The *Description de l'Égypte*, itself a colossus, also required an uncommon disciplining of its disparate, constituent parts. Its 924 plates composed of some 3,000 separate images, had to be given a coherent structure, a task that demanded skills of organization and composition on the part of the engineer Jomard and other editors. Organizing the *Description* further required the suppression, as far as possible, of the individual draftsmen's hands. The project was never intended to be an album of artworks by individual artists. The authority of its compilations resided in its profound impersonality and purported objectivity, its application of principles of engineering, not the beaux arts. Its plates were intended to present views not only from nowhere but also by no one in particular. Any positing of subjectivity within the series was therefore deeply fraught as was representation of anything unusual or anomalous.

In reading Dutertre's engraving it is important to recognize the tension between the designation of various material qualities and the project's goal of regulating individual authorship. Drawn lines were asked to report the textures of the world without betraying the personality of the maker, even though the artist was working within a perspective system that posits a point of view and was using shadow to modulate distinctions in position, shape, and texture. Mastery of the fall of light over various substances notwithstanding, shadows change the status of an object; they place it in the sphere of mutability where it depends on human vision; shadows are fundamentally corollaries of the condition of being seen. There is no need for shadows in the engineer's orthographic projections, although they were often added to make it easier for viewers to discern structures. Ever changing, the interplay of light and shadow marks experience in the world. It signals human embodiment and whispers subjectivity.

Plate 10 by Dutertre, like all the other perspective views in the *Description*, reflects the conflicts in expectation and practice among the savants. Line by line, Dutertre was called upon to represent material appearances without suggesting his own subjectivity. Line would have made his endeavor harder rather than easier. Line is a fictional entity, a translation of edge (or force or direction) into thing, of a shadow into a mark. Duterte's commitment to engineering the rocks into a pyramidal form is evident in his handling of line, which appears even and controlled. The translation of drawing into engraving further disciplined the lines making up the image. In engraving, line is incised into a metal plate; there are no free marks, mistakes are not tolerated. But even engraving cannot guarantee a precise and neutral image, or at least, one that could meet the savants' standards. An etching by Giovanni Battista Piranesi shows how painterly, improvisational, and deeply subjective a print can be (fig. 31). In this print, the sky alone suggests an atmospheric and emotional universe. Skies, deserts, and other empty places may have posed the greatest problem for artists seeking to rein in their subjectivity. In these vast spaces handling cannot be subordinated to a minute rendering of shapes and surface textures. Sky and expanses of land: these were the most constantly shifting parts of Egypt that the savants encountered, and the ones that they most neglected.

The celebrated mechanic who invented a new gunpowder and other technical devices for Napoleon's army stepped in to alleviate the problem of erupting subjectivity, or, at the very least, signs of individuality. Nicolas Jacques Conté invented an engraving machine for

**31**
Giovanni Battista Piranesi, *The Temples at Paestum.* From "Différentes vues de quelques restes de trois édifices...Pesto...Posidonia...dans la Lucanie." Etching. Berlin: Kupferstichkabinett, Staatliche Museen zu Berlin. Photo: Bildarchiv Preussischer Kulturbesitz/Art Resource, NY.

**32**
Produits de la machine à graver (Products of the engraving machine [invented by Conté]), *La Description de l'Égypte*, État Moderne, vol. II, plate 245 (bis), Paris, 1809-1822. Courtesy of the Bancroft Library, University of California, Berkeley.

the production of the *Description de l'Égypte* (fig. 32).It could engrave plates with parallel lines, and these machine-incised lines had a strong impact on the look of the *Description*'s numerous engraved images, imbuing them with visual cohesion and a look of ordered regularity and objectivity. The lines cut with Conté's machine make hieroglyphs and relief carvings seem to float on smooth stone; cross sections appear machine-made; and skies are uneventful and always, on every plate, the same.

Conté's mechanical lines run parallel across the upper half of Dutertre's plate and meet the irregularity of the pyramid's edges. Dutertre's hand and then the hand of the engraver had drawn those edges. The point where parallel, horizontal, mechanical line meets hand-drawn, often perpendicular line strikes me as a site of concerted efforts of containment. The engineered, forever geometric parallels are meant to prevent the possibility of a contaminating irregularity and subjectivity. Plate 10 as a whole can be considered an experiment. Conté's mechanical lines contain and coexist with the man-made, thereby demonstrating control. These machine-made lines enact what Monge had proven. Any irregular shape, like the eroding edge of a pyramid, can be represented by a series of points.[76] The hard-edged ruler was too crude a tool to render that irregular contour, but math and machine could lay down the parallel lines whose endpoints define its variegated edge. The engineer Jomard's faith in precise measure thereby enters a picture whose emphasis on erosion and material irregularity would seem in every way its refutation.

The appearance of the engineer's faith is tenuously sustained in Dutertre's image. The irregular, swelling heap of stones at right may be contained by the impersonal, parallel lines, but the stones surely call into question one's capacity to determine immutable measurements. Although the numbers on the print's sides are explained in the textual key, their significance is undermined by the fact that they measure an incomplete monument; they remain hypothetical. Some of the numbers, according to the key, specify a point in the rubble in the middle ground where the small path curves as the former location of the cornerstone of the Great Pyramid. The rubble turns out to be all that is left of the corner, a devastation that leads the engineers and draftsmen to dwell obsessively on this, the missing northeast corner of the Great Pyramid, this corner that has been emptied. Indeed they attempt to recreate it in cross section and plan in another plate (fig. 33).

---

**Towards the bottom you must creep like serpents to get into the interior passage.**
**Claude-Étienne Savary, *Letters on Egypt*, 1787**

The dense mass—tons upon tons of rock—of the Great Pyramid posed innumerable problems to men such as Jomard, who attempted to dematerialize stone edifices into pure form and immutable standards. But the greatest trauma for the savants was not some Kantian crisis of comprehension before a colossal pile of rocks, but rather their surrender of optical control altogether when they entered the pile itself. Kant for his part concentrated on Savary's brief statement about the problem of seeing the pyramid's exterior; this is misleading inasmuch as Savary devoted the great bulk of his text to the pyramid's dark, unreadable interior. When Savary reaches the Great Pyramid, he says not a word about its appearance up close; he reports instead that he threw off his clothes and climbed inside, slithering "like a serpent." "The internal air of this edifice, never being renewed, is so hot, and mephitic, that one is almost suffocated. When we came out of it, we were dropping with sweat and pale as death."[77]

Jomard was even more traumatized when he crawled inside the pyramid. His account in the text of the *Description de l'Égypte* relates an experience of utter physical abjection:

> It is necessary to descend bent or crouched; one stops at each footstep on some notches worked into the floor of the passage. On descending, one perceives that the height decreases more and more, such that the knees approach the chin remorselessly; finally one comes to a place where it is necessary to stretch full length and to progress on one's abdomen, the head plunged into the sand, with the help of elbows and knees. The extreme heat produced by the lights and the thick and stifling air that one breathes, bathes one in perspiration and the fatigue is extreme. Fortunately, one does not remain for long in this punishing attitude.... On leaving this narrow place, one has traveled, as I have said, for a length of sixty-seven feet; then one finds oneself at a location where one is able to hold oneself upright and where one perspires liberally... Upon leaving this passage one is all in a sweat, the face and body are all red; and one is so tired—exhausted with fatigue.[78]

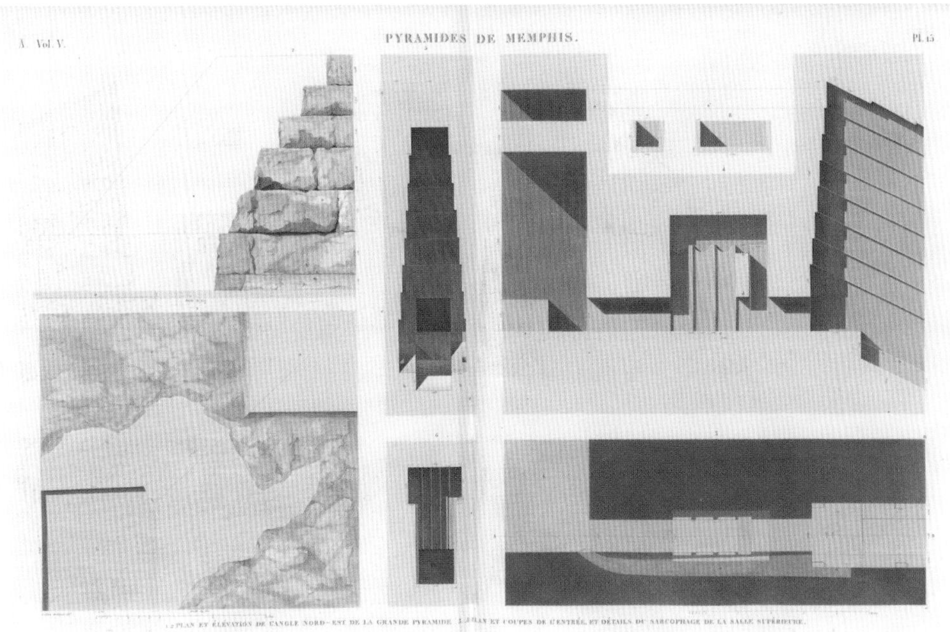


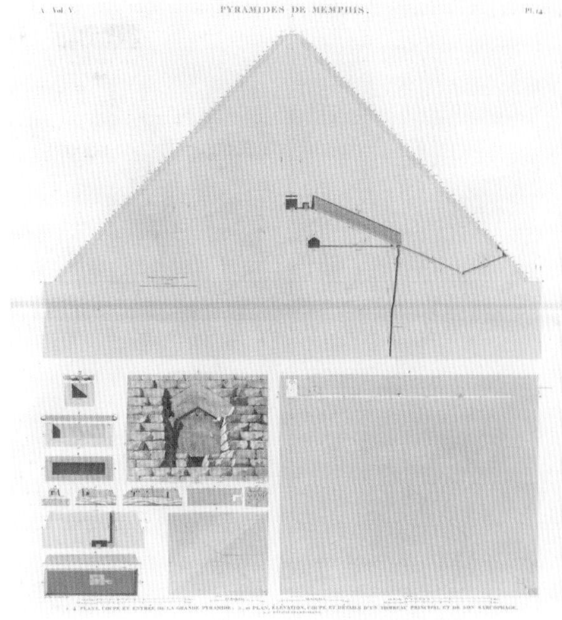


**33**
Jean-Baptiste Le Père, Pyramids of Memphis, *La Description de l'Égypte*, Antiquités, vol. V, plate 15, Paris, 1809–1822. Courtesy of the Bancroft Library, University of California, Berkeley.

**34**
Jean-Baptiste Le Père, Detail, Pyramids of Memphis, *La Description de l'Égypte*, Antiquités, vol. V, plate 14, Paris, 1809–1822. Courtesy of the Bancroft Library, University of California, Berkeley.

Inside the pyramid Jomard is reborn. He brings his abdomen, elbows, knees, and red face into visibility. Finally, he admits his body is a compass—that it determines the scope and nature of his knowledge. But blind physicality did not stop his mania for measurement; head plunged into the sand, he traversed a length of sixty-seven feet. These descriptions—and Jomard's is only one of many contemporary accounts—demonstrate that inside the Great Pyramid, geometer-engineers were forced to traverse with their bodies what they had measured and drawn. Cross sections of the interior of the pyramid in the *Description* (made, not incidentally, with Conté's engraving machine) offer maps of channels as straight lines through solid stone, but men inside solid stone cannot know what occurs in the uncharted mass above and below them; they know only the spaces into which their bodies bend and squeeze (fig. 34). They could not portray what they could not perceive. It is telling that the cross section fails to include a series of openings above the uppermost king's chamber that were discovered later.[79]

The difficulty of comprehending the totality of the pyramid became overwhelming when its pure and beautiful geometric structure was opened. No illuminating inner truth about its building or meaning were ever found within its once secret channels and chambers. Inside, in fact in striking contrast to today's open architecture, there is no possible experience of the whole structure. The placement of channels and chambers can only be determined by measurements of length and incline; lines and angles must be extrapolated from the experience of crawling because there is no possible optical knowing. Perspective requires some distance between subject and seen object. Whereas inside the Great Pyramid distance is collapsed, and knowledge is embodied; it is also more closely bound to labor. Not only does this kind of knowing require great physical exertion—leaving Jomard red and "exhausted with fatigue"—but the tunnels these men penetrated were the product of arduous physical effort. Savary's account includes some thirty pages by another Frenchman Benoît de Maillet, who attempted to reconstruct the stone-by-stone work of the pyramid's original builders.[80] Maillet proceeded by tracking the tomb robbers who removed the massive blocks that had been initially used to seal the pyramid. For him, the pyramid was a site of violence and vandalism and therefore an artifact that had undergone corruption. The idea that tomb robbers broke into the Great Pyramid never crossed Jomard's mind. He assumed that boundaries preexist and are inviolable; this is why they are measurable and why he believed he had found the system ancient engineers had put into place.

History was on Maillet's side. Entry into the Great Pyramid was possible only because tomb robbers had earlier removed stones to open channels into the depths of the monument, presumed to be a pharaoh's tomb. The lines in the diagrams in the *Description* record long prior acts of violence that displaced matter even as they marked it. Making lines requires physical effort; but lines also dematerialize both that effort and that which they inscribe.

# Suez's Statue

## Earth / Photography

For me it is not enough to have traced my gigantic programs on paper, rather I want to write my idea on the earth.
Émile Pereire, Saint-Simonian, 1835

Napoleon and his engineers had believed the Suez Canal would bring modernity to Egypt, yet a publication proved to be their most colossal achievement. The *Description de l'Égypte* is a multi-volume, oversize series, issued between 1809 and 1822, replete with detailed descriptions and thousands of illustrations of monuments the French had explored. Two decades after Napoleon's expedition and only a few years after the *Description*'s last volumes were published in 1822, the utopian thinker Claude-Henri de Saint-Simon revived the Napoleonic ambition to bring engineering to Egypt. At the center of Saint-Simon's thinking was the conviction that man is destined to progress; that industrialization would advance mankind; and that canals, beginning with Suez, would link the world. But progress demanded a change in government. Scientists, engineers, and industrialists, not representatives of church or crown, not aristocratic inheritors of privilege, should be in control. Saint-Simon had taken classes at the École Polytechnique and come away confident that at such schools "future leaders would learn how to manipulate nature and shape the earth to suit the needs of mankind."[1] Work would change the world.

Many of Saint-Simon's followers were École Polytechnique graduates as had been the case with a number of the savants who accompanied Bonaparte to Egypt. Far and away the most famous and influential among them is Auguste Comte; but Comte's later formulation of "positivism" is a great deal more coherent and systematic than any of his teacher's doctrines. Though Saint-Simon ventured a materialist vision of an engineered world of work, he became increasingly preoccupied with spiritual dichotomies and propounded a structure of archetypes. To him the Suez Canal acquired ever broader significance as a means of conjoining West and East, Father and Mother, Intellect and Earth. This vein of mythography reappears in the work of another of Saint-Simon's eminent, if controversial, followers, Barthélemy-Prosper Enfantin, who led a mission of engineers (and a few women) to Egypt in 1832:

> Captains, our old comrades from the École Polytechnique, .... At its birth the École visited and described Egypt with Napoleon; today it is necessary to enrich the Egypt of Mohammed [Ali]; we will not decipher the old hieroglyphs of Egypt's past grandeur, but we will engrave on its earth the signs of its future prosperity. Fourteen armies will come forth from the womb of the MOTHER of the world and will spread over the globe to found the universal republic and to defend it against barbarism. Remember Napoleon, who also trained his general staff and his institute under the hot sun of the pyramids. Remember the women who want to see you build the great, the colossal, so that they may say that they love us.[2]

Enfantin's statement is characteristic in proffering wild, gendered imagery and connecting the Napoleonic campaign with the École Polytechnique. Although Saint-Simonians criticized Bonaparte for sacrificing industrial progress to the acquisition of political power, they shared many ideas with the authors of *The Description de l'Égypte*.[3] Enfantin nonetheless criticized Jomard and Napoleonic engineers for merely describing the past and engraving it on paper. Their successors, the Saint-Simonians, were more enlightened and forward looking; they would inscribe the promise of wealth onto the land of Egypt: "We will engrave on its earth the signs of its future prosperity."[4] In the 1830s, in the wake of Saint-Simon's utopian teachings, French engineers redefined their mission. No longer would they simply record Egypt, they would rebuild it. Seeing themselves as the engineers of modernity, the Saint-Simonians believed "the next phase of world history" would be realized in Egypt because of its isthmus.[5] "Later, we will pierce the other at Panama."[6]

Enfantin wrote his letter from Egypt in 1834, the year the Saint-Simonians hosted a party in Egypt to celebrate both Bonaparte's birthday and the ongoing construction of a dam at the Nile. Egypt's ruler Mohammad Ali was committed to modernization and had started the dam, although he opposed the Suez Canal because he feared it would permit European powers to bypass territories under his control. For the Saint-Simonians the dam was a provisional compromise; they hoped its engineering would persuade Mohammad Ali to change his mind. They had every reason to assume that when the Suez Canal was built, they would be in charge.

The 1834 party marking Napoleon's birthday was meant to draw attention to the Saint-Simonian engineers' expertise and progress. Workers were given the day off; an official delegation with Mohammad Ali and representatives from France toured the site; and, after luncheon with wine and champagne, they lay the foundation stone for an engineering school to be modeled after the École Polytechnique.[7] "Remember Monge and Carnot; it is necessary to introduce science here and ORGANIZE industrial VICTORY."[8] In important ways the Saint-Simonian vision was also Mohammad Ali's. The Egyptian ruler supported the technical education of Egyptians in the hope that they would eventually build roads, waterways, and weapons to usher in a modern Egypt.

Work on the dam advanced quickly through corvée (forced) labor by tens of thousands of workers, but only two years after the grand festivities for Napoleon, the project was abandoned. Writing to a fellow Saint-Simonian, Enfantin reported the recent death of the Egyptian administrator of dams and went on to explain Mohammad Ali's thwarted plan to demolish one of the Great Pyramids in order to use its massive stone blocks to dam the Nile.

As for the dams, the pasha contemplates something that will rouse against him all the European jokesters and idlers, the tourists above all. Three days ago he sent Mouktar-Bey, Artyn-Effendy, and Linant to visit the pyramids to see which to throw into the Nile at the dam. You see that he does not pull his punches. This is a great and political idea, like so many of the ideas of the prince, but it will not easily be understood by our writers and prattlers.

Mohammad Ali will not demolish this pyramid now that he is not going to make the dam [of the Nile], because the destiny of this man is a bit like that of Saint-Simon, to make projects, but his projects are grandiose, pyramidal. To dam the Nile and fertilize the earth of Egypt, by laying down one of these old ruins in the river, this is certainly the most beautiful transformation of the power of the past and it is beautiful that for such a work, man destroys that which time alone could not destroy...that he gives life again, a new and useful and greater life, to that which centuries could not kill or respect, this is even better; it is progress replacing immobility. I would be very surprised if your newspapers, in announcing this news, do not hasten to put this pyramid on the back of the Saint-Simonians, and accuse [them of being] vandals, barbarians...; besides they would not be completely mistaken.[9]

Enfantin contrasts the immobility of ancient Egypt's stone monuments to the "new and useful and greater life" created by engineering. To destroy the past—to throw a pyramid's mass of stone into the waters of the Nile—this was to "give life again [redonne la vie]" by fertilizing Egypt's soil. Destruction, as well as construction, was needed to introduce progress to Egypt.

Enfantin reverses Dutertre's image. He knew how far-fetched the idea would seem to Parisian "jokesters and idlers" who, in the press, would put "the pyramid on the back of Saint-Simonians." They would be accused of the barbarism Napoleon's engineers had associated with Arabs. Under Bonaparte's leadership École Polytechnique graduates such as Jomard, Jollois, and Devilliers had conceived their task as the conservation of an eroding, neglected ancient Egyptian past so that the knowledge thereby attained could revolutionize measurement and produce a rational future. Enfantin proclaims a remarkable about-face: one must destroy the ancient monument to make a modern one. But the "destiny" of Mohammad Ali, "like that of Saint-Simon," was to have his "grandiose, pyramidal" projects remain unrealized."Pyramidal," the word is meant to signal the impossibility of such schemes.

---

**The moment has arrived to carry out the prediction of Napoleon.** Ferdinand de Lesseps, *Souvenirs de quarante ans dédiés à mes enfants*, 1887

The Suez Canal had been all but forgotten by the 1840s, except among Saint-Simonians. Enfantin insisted "We must be *the only ones* to undertake this great work."[10] By 1845 Enfantin was declaring that the Suez Canal "is no longer a philosophical theory or a political question, it is a business."[11] To advance the business in Egypt and to claim their rights to it, they founded the Société d'Études pour le Canal de Suez, an organization purportedly dedicated to scientific research of the terrain. Enfantin's concern with rights—his insistence that they be "the only ones"—was a desperate response to the growing power of the diplomat Ferdinand de Lesseps, who would ultimately win the rights to build the canal and realized its completion in 1869. From the point of view of Enfantin, Lesseps stole their canal. Dubbed "le grand français" Lesseps had ties to Egypt stretching back to his youth and was ever "excited" by scale.[12] That said, it is clear he adopted the Saint-Simonian belief that realizing Napoleon's unrealized canal would inaugurate a new age of progress, industry, and peace. Although he would never borrow Enfantin's fantastic images nor attribute his ambitions to a desire for women's love, he did assume that monumental

**35**
Carte-de-visite with photograph of Ferdinand de Lesseps and his family, c.1885. Collection de l'Association du Souvenir de Ferdinand de Lesseps et du Canal de Suez

scale was evidence of virility. And as if to prove it, at the age of sixty-four, immediately after the inauguration of the Suez Canal, he married a twenty-year-old. Louise-Hélène Autard de Bragard of Mauritius bore him twelve children, the youngest of whom was born when he was eighty and another, his son, Charles, would be his partner in business. His first wife, Agathe Delamalle, had already given birth to five children before she died of scarlet fever in 1853. Thus "le grand français" sired seventeen children. An oft-reproduced photograph shows the patriarch with his brood in a formation that resembles the Great Pyramid seen in the distance (fig. 35).

But the great man did not want to share; collectivity was not Lesseps' dream. By 1846, when the Saint-Simonians founded the Société d'Études pour le Canal de Suez, Lesseps was as determined as Enfantin to be the canal's sole promoter. For his part Enfantin claimed Lesseps feared being "eclipsed, subordinated, evaded, even robbed."[13] The rivalry was personal and entrepreneurial, a matter of glory and also of money.

The Saint-Simonians and Lesseps shared many assumptions. Each resorted to the rhetoric of universal progress. Each assumed the canal would be masterminded and executed by French engineers—industrialists, in Saint-Simonian language—with the help of Egyptian corvée labor. Each believed the canal would "benefit mankind." But the disagreements between the Saint- Simonians and Lesseps were substantive. The Saint-Simonians imagined a canal of "planetary importance" dependent upon France, whereas Lesseps more shrewdly argued that the project should be defined as Egyptian, not French.[14]

Nor did they agree about the canal's design. Lesseps supported the "direct trace" that originated with Linant de Bellefonds, a Navy officer in Egypt since 1818 whom Mohammad Ali had appointed as an hydraulic engineer.[15] A very different plan for an "indirect trace," which Paulin Talabot proposed in 1849, won the Saint-Simonians' commitment and for good reason.[16] Linant was considered an autodidact, whereas Talabot enjoyed impressive credentials; he was a graduate of the École Polytechnique and, along with his brothers, an engineer for the Saint-Simonian Société d'Études. His plan resuscitated the canal of antiquity; it cut the Nile but not the isthmus.[17] His competitors, Linant and Lesseps, were advocating a shorter, straight canal across the desert that would extend the entire length of the isthmus to connect the Mediterranean and Red Seas. Linant's "direct trace" had the support of Egypt's leader, now Saïd Pasha, who ruled from 1854 to 1863. Saïd Pasha preferred that the canal cut through the desert rather than through the Nile basin, Egypt's richest area. Contrary to his predecessor, Mohammad Ali, he thought this "direct" canal would make foreign powers less likely to attempt to seize Egypt. Furthermore Saïd Pasha had in Linant de Bellefonds and Lesseps men well acquainted with Egypt and its ruling family. By contrast Talabot had never traveled to Egypt; his plans issued from Paris.

Among Lesseps' other advantages over the Saint-Simonians were his many family ties in France and in Egypt. Empress Eugénie, wife of Napoleon III, was his cousin, but his connections in Egypt were more decisive. In 1804 Napoleon I had appointed Ferdinand's father, Mathieu de Lesseps, consul in Egypt. Mathieu's main responsibility was blocking British efforts in the area, something he managed by befriending Mohammad Ali and supporting his rule.[18] Although Ferdinand grew up in Pisa, returning to Paris only after the Hundred Days, he followed his father and uncle (also a diplomat) in their careers. He represented the French in Lisbon and later in Rome, and throughout the 1830s he was consul to Egypt. There he too befriended Mohammad Ali as well as Mohammad's overweight son, Prince Saïd Pasha. Asked to help the son lose weight, Lesseps rode horses with him daily but did not try to control his diet. On the contrary he catered to the prince's cravings for pasta (no doubt a consequence of his Pisan childhood). Shared daily activity and evasion of strictures on food secured a long-standing friendship between the two men.

Once Saïd finally came to power in 1854, Lesseps went into action, canal plan in his pocket. Always the opportunist, he knew he needed to wait until the most advantageous moment and, before then, he intended to win the support of everyone who mattered.

As I take leave of the viceroy, I decide to show him that his horse, whose powerful legs I had already tested on the first day, is a top quality jumper; turning to wave to my host, I urge my steed over the tall stone parapet and gallop on up the hill toward my tent. You will soon see that this act of rashness may have been one of the causes for the approval the viceroy's entourage gave to my project, which was absolutely necessary for my success. The generals who came to lunch with me complimented me on it, and I saw that my boldness had considerably raised me in their esteem.[19]

The man who had gone horseback riding with Saïd was convinced daring horsemanship gained him the approval of the military men surrounding the Egyptian viceroy. He believed too that a rainbow spanning east and west was a sign that his time had come: "I swear, I felt my heart beat faster, and I had to stop my imagination from seeing this as a sign of the alliance spoken of in the Scriptures, of the true union between the West and the East, and as a message that today would see the success of my project." He lost no time in approaching Saïd, and using the grand abstractions that he shared with the Saint-Simonians, he spoke of destiny, progress, and wealth. Finally he turned to glory. The canal would eclipse the ancient pyramids: "The names of the Egyptian sovereigns who erected the pyramids, those useless monuments of human pride, will be ignored. The name of the prince who opened the grand canal through Suez will be blessed century after century for posterity."[20] On 15 November 1854, the day he saw the rainbow, Lesseps won the rights to build the canal.

The Saint-Simonians were in disarray; their Société had only lasted two years, and they had no inside track to the powers of Egypt and France. Lesseps gradually distanced himself from them. When he founded his canal company, the names of Saint-Simonians, much to their dismay, were buried in a long list of members. The building of the canal required further diplomacy and more than ten years of continual digging. Its inauguration did not occur until November1869, and even then it was not finished. In 1869 no Saint-Simonians were invited to the festivities.[21]

---

**You seem indifferent to the population that lives and dies in this country, the bronzed fellaheen, the women with floating clothes, with forms so slender and so noble.... Far from it. I only want to say that the character of landscape prevails over every figure.** Narcisse Berchère, *Le désert de Suez: Cinq mois dans l'isthme*, 1863

In 1855 Bartholdi, creator of the Statue of Liberty, visited Egypt for eight months with the painter Jean-Léon Gérôme, ten years his senior (fig. 36).[22] The sculptor, alongside other artists, traveled on board the ship transporting Lesseps and his official, fifteen-man International Scientific Commission charged with the execution of the Suez Canal.[23] We do not know if Bartholdi and Lesseps spoke, but certainly the sculptor was aware of Lesseps and his mission. Lesseps had likely seen the sculptor's colossal statue of General Rapp at the Universal Exhibition in Paris that year. And Bartholdi and Gérôme had an official mission of their own: the French government had financed their "study of the antiquities of Egypt, Nubia, and Palestine as well as the photographic reproduction of the most remarkable human types of these various countries."[24] In 1855 two groups of men traveled from France to Egypt: one to modernize Egypt by engineering a canal; the other to continue the Napoleonic project of recording its monuments and people, partly by using the modern technology of photography.

Yet neither Bartholdi nor Gérôme were professional photographers. The sculptor had learned the rudiments of photography in France, but he was still a novice. Taking his commission seriously, Bartholdi proceeded to apply himself to drawing, following the example the Napoleonic draftsmen had established, even drawing many of the same subjects. He stood alongside Gérôme as he drew, but his sketches appear crabbed and clumsy, demonstrating neither the skill of Dutertre and the Napoleonic engineers nor the fluency of his talented friend (figs. 37-39).

Bartholdi was incessantly mocked for his efforts wrote the French painter Léon Belly in a letter to his mother. But the teasing did not stop an artist whose career attests, if nothing else, to the perseverance Belly noted and admired even as he reported the mockery.

> I see you have judged Bartholdi as I have judged him and I believe of all the Egyptian artists [meaning the French artists in Egypt, that is, Gérôme, Narcisse Berchère, Édouard Imer], he is the best. His good character has a certain naive side, in the good sense; his youth...has made him the butt of all jokes. During the voyage to Upper Egypt his painting and his drawings were continually mocked. Nevertheless, it was he alone who worked; he made a quantity of photographs and a considerable number of studies and drawings, because although a sculptor, he does not lack interest in color, and his studies, a bit unformed like those of a beginner, seem to me much better than those of Gérôme, who made so much fun of him.[25]

**36**
Frédéric-Auguste Bartholdi, *Bartholdi and Gérôme in Oriental Costume*, n.d. Albumen print. Colmar, Musée Bartholdi. Photo: Christian Kempf.

This letter, as Régis Hueber has noted, betrays Belly's animosity towards Gérôme, a rival possessed of affluence and the easy confidence so often its corollary.[26] Bartholdi had Gérôme's bourgeois privilege, but his youth and lack of skill allowed Belly to express generosity albeit laced with condescension. Still Belly was right in one regard. Bartholdi was productive in Egypt, far exceeding Gérôme in output. Not only did he produce 211 drawings and 28 oil studies, but in the very early taxing days of photography, he made 103 calotypes.

Besides youth, inexperience, and a lack of facility in drawing, Bartholdi suffered yet another disadvantage. He was the only one among his companions that the circumstances of travel forced to work in media other than his own primary art. He was the sole sculptor. Though Anne Wagner has taught us that drawing was fundamental to a nineteenth-century French sculptor's training, drawing was nonetheless a medium that was ancillary, preparatory, and radically unlike the three-dimensional products ultimately displayed to an audience.[27] For sculptors of bronzes like Bartholdi, drawing represented but one step in a series of translations from the three-dimensional referent (often a live model), through two-dimensional experiments in drawing, to a series of three-dimensional studies, eventually made into a negative mold from which were derived plasters and finally bronzes.[28]

Translation was therefore a problem at the center of the sculptor's art; translation between media and thus between two and three dimensions; between sizes, small and very large; between materials with different effects such as clay, plaster and metal; and finally between negative imprints and positive things. In the process of making sculpture, provisional and discrepant things and ideas were coaxed into a discrete form (which could, of course, be endlessly repeated and modified in scale). The ultimate fixing of referent and ideas as artistic form was long delayed and a matter of sustained work, patience, and postponed gratification. In comparison to sculptors, painters seem to arrive far more quickly at their final figuration.

How then would a sculptor try to make art during a journey to Egypt? By definition transient journeys impede the execution and transport of sculpture. Everything about the situation is provisional, but the same could be said about the artist's situation anywhere. She or he shapes the ephemeral into figuration or some other form. From November 1855 to June 1856 Bartholdi exerted great effort to turn the foreign into form. With the diligence of a young, ambitious student, he understood his efforts to be his job. Bartholdi had been commissioned, along with Gérôme, to produce "studies," generally understood to be drawings, and also to take photographs. He made no sculptures.

If Bartholdi was exceptionally productive in Egypt, he was equally determined to transform the bulging portfolio from his travels into art that he could display in Paris. The sculptor exhibited five paintings of Egyptian scenes at Salons between 1857 and 1865.[29] Around 1857–58 he created five Orientalist lithographs, inspired by his on-site drawings and photographs; and in 1858 he also made some preliminary plans for an *Album de dessins orientalistes*, which never

**37**
Frédéric-Auguste Bartholdi, *Untitled [Fellaheen carrying water]*, 1855-56. Graphite on paper. Colmar, Musée Bartholdi. Photo: Christian Kempf.

**38**
Frédéric-Auguste Bartholdi, *Untitled [Fellaheen carrying water]*, 1855-56. Graphite on paper. Colmar, Musée Bartholdi. Photo: Christian Kempf.

**39**
Frédéric-Auguste Bartholdi, *Untitled [Fellaheen carrying water]*, 1855-56. Graphite on paper. Colmar, Musée Bartholdi. Photo: Christian Kempf.

appeared. Bartholdi seems to have been uncertain whether his works as a draftsman and painter would help or hinder his career as a sculptor. He exhibited his remarkable paintings under the astounding pseudonym Amilcar Hasenfratz, but he signed his lithographs "Aug. Bartholdi." Among the few sculptures based on his Egyptian voyage was a statue of the famous French Egyptologist Champollion standing on the head of a sphinx, exhibited as a plaster in the Egyptian section of the 1867 Universal Exhibition.[30]

To this we must add the Statue of Liberty, the design of which originated in the drawings and clay models of an "Egyptian woman" or "female fellah" executed between 1867 and 1869 (figs. 40–43). The names are Bartholdi's, but he would not have agreed with my claim of lineage from fellah to Liberty, which the visual evidence verifies and scholars now accept.[31] The resemblance between Bartholdi's Statue of Liberty and his earlier project for a monumental lighthouse at the Suez Canal was noted and made public as early as the 1880s. In print Bartholdi contested what he took to be an accusation of a clandestine and opportunistic recycling of a failed Egyptian project into an American success. The following passage was originally in English.

> At this period I was expecting to execute a statue of Egypt for the Suez Lighthouse. I even laid before Ismaïl Pasha a project. It was this that made an evilly disposed newspaper say, and others repeat that I had executed a colossal statue for Egypt, which had not been used, and that I had resold it to the Society of the French-American Union in order that from it might be made the Statue of Liberty. Now I never executed anything for the Khedive except a little sketch which has remained in his palace, and represents Egypt under the features of a female Fellah.[32]

He replied as follows to charges in the *New York Times*:

> [A] colossal statue of an Egyptian woman holding a light aloft...was declined on account of the expense. At the time my Statue of Liberty did not even exist, even in my imagination, and the only resemblance between the drawing that I submitted to the Khedive and the statue now in New York's beautiful harbor is that both hold a light aloft. Now, I ask you, sir, how is a sculptor to make a statue which is to serve the purpose of a lighthouse without making it hold the light in the air? My Statue of Liberty was a pure work of love, costing me the sacrifice of ten years and of twenty thousand dollars—little perhaps for Americans, but a great deal for me. The Egyptian affair would have been purely a business transaction. I declare most emphatically, and I defy anyone in the world to contradict me, that the Statue of Liberty was ever offered to any other government.[33]

The defensive tone is unmistakable; so is the desperate reaching for counterclaims. Bartholdi seems to believe that the issue hinges on what he actually "executed" for Ismaïl Pasha (who ruled from 1863 to 1879, following Saïd): not a colossal statue but only a "drawing,"

**40**
Frédéric-Auguste Bartholdi, *Maquettes de Suez et de la Liberté*, n.d. Terra Cotta. Colmar, Musée Bartholdi. Photo: Christian Kempf.

**41**
Frédéric-Auguste Bartholdi, *Maquette for Egypt Bringing Light to Asia*, 1869. Terra Cotta, 29.5 cm high. Colmar, Musée Bartholdi. Photo: Christian Kempf.

**42**
Frédéric-Auguste Bartholdi, *Egypt Enlightening Asia*, 1869. Watercolor glued on paper. Colmar, Musée Bartholdi. Photo: Christian Kempf.

**43**
Frédéric-Auguste Bartholdi, *Statue of Liberty as Lighthouse,* undated. Watercolor on paper. Colmar, Musée Bartholdi. Photo: Christian Kempf

"a little sketch." Bartholdi assumes that Liberty could not be "purely a business transaction," partly because it cost him so much money and time. Liberty is thereby associated with the artist's self-sacrifice, a self-sacrifice that removes the sculpture from economies of money and time, all the while drawing attention to their expenditure.

The fellah, however, is defined as a matter of money and its exchange (Ismaïl merely failed to meet the necessary costs). Bartholdi's argument is odd and incoherent, but it does expose his anxiety. This was one transformation whose recognition he wanted to abort. Liberty and fellah were not, he claims, continuous despite their formal and functional resemblances. But, as Bartholdi knew, the five extant clay models and two watercolor drawings of a female fellah were easily confused with the other small clay models which metamorphosed into the female figure that would become the colossal Statue of Liberty. The translations are apparent. Moreover, all of these clay models began in on-site drawings, three of them to be exact, which included no less than five female fellaheen at the edge of the Nile (see figs. 37–39). The Statue of Liberty, so remote, abstract and chastened, began in actual encounters with Egyptian peasant women.

Bartholdi's decision to focus on a fellah in a proposal submitted to Ismaïl Pasha in 1869 is not surprising. The fellah was a key "type" for the French, encountered in ancient Egyptian art, in travel accounts, and also throughout Egypt, particularly its countryside.[34] During this period, Orientalist art had shifted to a georgic mode wherein peasants replaced warriors.[35] When Bartholdi included fellaheen in his later painted genre scenes such as *Café on the Banks of the Nile*, shown (under a pseudonym) at the Salon of 1861, he was not alone. In the 1860s, fellaheen proliferated in the sculptures and paintings exhibited by other artists, including Gérôme, at the official Salons.[36] They also figured prominently at the Universal Exhibition of 1867, both as the subjects of four of Charles Cordier's ten "mannequins" of ethnographic types in the Egyptian pavilion, where Ismaïl Pasha himself held court, and in several French paintings, one by Charles Landelle and another by an unidentified artist, which were mounted high on the walls of the Suez Canal Company's exhibition (fig. 44).[37]

In Egypt Ismaïl Pasha assumed the title "prince of fellaheen" in a bid for closer identification with his peasant subjects.[38] The fellaheen's cultivation of cotton had become pivotal to Europe during the American Civil War, much to the (temporary) benefit of Egypt's economy. Ismaïl seized one-fifth of Egypt's cultivated lands in the belief that agricultural productivity would become a great source of wealth.[39] By the time Bartholdi presented a fellah lighthouse to the viceroy in April 1869, fourteen years after his first visit to Egypt, Ismaïl had commissioned a novel entitled *Le fellah* from Bartholdi's friend Edmond About.[40] *Le fellah* had started to appear in serial form in Paris in February 1869. Bartholdi certainly would have been acquainted with it as well as with its origins in a commission from Ismaïl. Then too About had invited sculptors to find their models among the fellaheen. "The poor people who work on the two rivers seem brutalized by fatigue; they are not even curious; most do not lift their head to see a boat pass…. We were amazed by their plastic beauty: so many men, so many statues. European sculptors complain they can no longer find models; why don't they search the Nile?"[41] About's assertion merits a special place in the annals of the aesthetics of colonialism: the degradation of the peasants does not undermine their "plastic beauty." On the contrary their fatigue and lethargy may be the reason he thinks of them as sculptures: "so many men, so many statues." When Bartholdi twice traveled to Egypt he was following his friend's advice.

About was not alone. In the late 1860s the French had come to associate the fellah with the land of Egypt itself. Théophile Gautier wrote in the same year:

> An observation that arises in the mind of the least attentive traveler, from his first steps in this lower Egypt…is the profound intimacy of the fellah with the earth. The name of earth-bound native [autochthone] is that which truly suits him: [the fellah] comes from this clay that he treads; he is molded by it and barely extricates himself from it. Like a child at the breast of his wet nurse, he massages it, he squeezes it, in order to make spurt from this brown breast the milk of fecundity…. [The fellah] works [the earth] almost without tools, with his hands…. Nowhere is this harmony of man and soil more visible; nowhere does the earth have greater importance. It spreads its color over everything.[42]

Gautier connects the fellaheen and the earth so closely he questions the distinction between them. Here are dark-skinned people who barely attain human status, so "molded" and "barely extricated" are they from the clay out of which they are made. Yet they are human in a primitive infantile way, grasping with their hands the great breast of the Egyptian earth in order to make it give forth.

Such associations also inform Alfred Assollant's review of Charles Landelle's *Woman Fellah* at the Universal Exhibition of 1867, a picture whose cloying prettiness would seem far from Gautier's primitive clay dwellers . Assollant nonetheless treats it as a point d'appui for interpreting fellaheen as a thoughtless, inactive people and faulting Gautier for valuing attributes that ultimately destine these Egyptians to extinction:

> One recognizes [in this picture] another race of women, modest and strong at once…. What is lacking in this woman, otherwise so beautiful, is thought. From this characteristic one recognizes a race that will die.
>
> Certain painters and poets of this century have much admired the fatalistic immobility of the figures of the Orient. This is the typical theme of M. Théophile Gautier. For him, nothing is more beautiful than a dervish, crouching in a contemplative attitude, smoking his pipe and thinking of nothing. But grass also thinks of nothing and yet is not more admirable for it; and rock is not superior to man. To move, even by chance, is to live. He who remains immobile is already dead and wants little more. This is why the Orient which nothing disturbs has been for such a long time prey to the first comer… An entire destiny of a people is traced in a few brushstrokes on this woman.[43]

Assollant and Gautier share many of the same familiar Orientalist assumptions; they differ primarily in how they evaluate the torpor they associate with the Orient.[44] Assollant casts Gautier's primordial primitivism as a mindless inertness. For him immobility signifies death and the end of a people who in the most fundamental way cannot move with history. This pervasive sense of Egypt's petrification was compounded by the stasis associated with pharaonic art, those stone persons frozen in time and scattered across Egypt's landscape.

For Bartholdi too, the modern machine accentuated Egypt's unchanging primitivism. While he was far from sure how to explain Egypt's failure to change, he was certain that technological progress was as an index not only of modernity but also of "civilization." In a letter of 1856 Bartholdi referred back to the earlier promises of the Viceroy Mohammad Ali, the ruler Ferdinand de Lesseps' father had befriended at the beginning of the century.

> How adorable a thing is Egypt in all regards, for art, for customs, for nation and its civilization which I had forgotten. She certainly has her charm.
>
> To write to you, for example, I am obliged to confide my letter to couriers who with a bell on their foot will carry it from village to village until Cairo. This is very pretty, but it does not offer very much security. Whatever one can say about Mohammad-Ali [the modernizing ruler of Egypt from 1805 to 1848], it was he alone who searched to make something of Egypt. He made Egyptians respect Europeans who hardly had been. He organized some departments, some schools, and a little

**44**
Engraving of Charles Landelle, *La Femme fellah,* in *L'Exposition Universelle de 1867 Illustrée. Publication Internationale autorisée par la Commission Impériale*, Paris, 1867, II, p. 116. Photo: Julie Wolf.

industry and he bought some machines etc. Since then, the administrations have tended to return to their original state as have the schools. Industry goes similarly because the Arabs are too dazed and lazy to occupy themselves with it. The machines bought by Mohammad-Ali were magnificent. They all rust in the Arsenal, in a frightening disorder. The cavalry trumpets on top of the weaving looms, the boilers, the cannonballs, the gears, the cannons, the keys of pianos, old windows, astronomical instruments with the butts of rifles...here is the ensemble of the Arsenal. This is a visible metaphor laid bare of the history of all things in Egypt. One has at hand all the perfect instruments to use, but one makes gears out of wood. They have all the hydraulic machines to furnish water for miles around, they construct chadoufs. They appear to concern themselves with civilization only in order to make clear that they prefer not to make use of it. If Europeans could possess the land, they could probably make something of it, but they could not get it except by a feat of skill and then it would be necessary for them to be married. You can understand how in these conditions, this would be almost impossible.[45]

Aesthetic pleasures were to be found in Egypt's traditions, yet Bartholdi ends by championing modernization over the picturesque, whether couriers with bells on their feet or a vast still life of rusting machinery. If, in this 1856 letter, art and modernization wage war for Bartholdi's loyalties, it is clear that the modern ultimately wins out. Bartholdi writes as an incipient imperialist (like other colonists even pondering the problem of wives).

Gautier's own description of Egypt's timelessness was written "while traversing this vast brown plain with the gallop of the locomotive" to attend the inauguration of the Suez Canal.[46] To discuss Egypt as a space outside time, change, and modernization, particularly in the late 1860s, was to harken back to earlier Orientalist rhetoric and to ignore the present. The locomotive transporting Gautier furnishes a glimpse of a key moment in technological modernization, and it happened in Egypt. Gautier was traveling to the Suez Canal's inauguration even as he conjured a people "petrified" by the "clay" out of which they had been "molded." When twenty-one-year-old Bartholdi traveled in Egypt from 1855 to 1856, he visited a country just prior to sweeping changes that he anticipated and wished to exploit.

The sculptor knew that he shared this hope with Lesseps and the Saint-Simonians. In Egypt he had met a famous Saint-Simonian, Joseph Machereau, a history painter who had studied with Jacques-Louis David and who had arrived in Egypt in 1833. By the time Bartholdi met him in the 1850s, Machereau was "a quasi-legendary figure of Egyptian Saint-Simonism." He had converted to Islam, married an Egyptian woman, and was named professor of drawing at the École de Cavalerie de Gizeh as well as director of the theater of Mohammad Saïd.[47] Machereau, Linant, and the latter's Egyptian disciples were the main representatives of Saint-Simonian thought in Egypt.[48] A number of unpublished letters provide evidence of Bartholdi's acquaintance with Machereau. In one undated letter, the painter refers to the very amiable young friends of Gérôme.[49] Another, dated 15 May 1856, recounts the progress of the Suez Canal and thereafter refers to "Bartholdy" by name; in this letter, Machereau mentions how "comforting" were "the very sweet joys" he found "among these gentlemen."[50] A month earlier Bartholdi wrote a letter referring to a history painter whom the scholar Régis Hueber identifies as Machereau.[51]

In Machereau, Bartholdi knew a Saint-Simonian who, decades earlier, had made several drawings of a colossal woman-temple, holding a scepter before a pyramid (fig. 45). Another image shows staircases rising from her feet and entering her skirt. Machereau was illustrating the prose poem "La Ville nouvelle, ou le Paris de Saint-Simoniens" by the Saint-Simonian Charles Duvéyrier.[52] Published in 1832, the poem opened, as do so many celebrations of the colossal, by humbling earlier monuments from all over the world (demanding "Lift your heads and bend your knees!"). The poem continues: "MY TEMPLE IS A WOMAN!" A spiral climbs "around her vast body up to her belt:" the body of the woman-temple is ornamented with stained-glass and spiraling galleries "spaced like the garlands on a ball dress." Duvéyrier's imagery is baroque. His colossus is the elaborately ornamented wife of the colossal city of Paris and her body incorporates a plethora of urban functions, not the least of which is a school of engineering. But the best is saved for last: a flame that is both pyramid and lighthouse. "I placed in the left hand of the wife of my colossus a scepter of blue and silver that touches the earth.... From the enlarged summit of this scepter rises, in a sharp pyramid, a flame, an immense lighthouse whose light illuminates

the distances and makes visible in the heart of night the smile of her face."[53] Machereau's quick drawings simplify Duvéyrier's imagery and link the colossal woman-lighthouse to Egypt.[54] There is no way of knowing whether Bartholdi was aware of Machereau's drawings or Duvéyrier's poem created two decades earlier. All that can be said is that Bartholdi and Lesseps knew Saint-Simonians in Egypt who had already imagined engineering both the colossal canal and the colossal female lighthouse. Neither sculptor nor entrepreneur ever admitted the debt.

---

**Industry will kill art.**
**Edmond and Jules Goncourt, *La révolution dans les moeurs*, 1854**

When Bartholdi returned to Egypt fourteen years later to sell his woman-lighthouse, the canal was almost complete, and Cairo had been, in his words, "Haussmannized" and "Europeanized" beyond recognition.[55] Like many Frenchmen, Bartholdi had already been partly prepared for the changes he would find in Egypt by the Universal Exhibition of 1867, where he had exhibited his statue of Champollion in the Egyptian section. There Ismaïl Pasha, ruler from 1863, had held court for Napoleon III and the Empress Eugénie, and Lesseps had delivered educational lectures on the Suez Canal in the company pavilion (figs. 46–47).[56] Ismaïl Pasha was determined to continue his father's efforts to modernize Egypt. Two decades earlier, he had studied engineering in Paris.[57] In 1864, the year after he became ruler, he founded a Ministry of Public Works.[58] The 1867 exhibition in Paris was intended to demonstrate, in the words of a contemporary publication, that "Egypt had visibly chosen to introduce the rest of the Orient to modern civilization."[59] In opposition to Orientalists such as Gautier and Assollant, Ismaïl was endeavoring to identify Egypt with modernity, not unchanging primitivism.

In the Suez Canal Company gallery at the Universal Exhibition, the painting of a female fellah with child and urn looked down from its elevated position onto two relief maps that celebrated modern man's capacity to transform Egypt's geography by cutting through an isthmus with the assistance of newly designed French machines.[60] But the painting of a woman fellah managed at once to glorify and to mask the traditional labor of Egyptian men, the way fellaheen moved earth in baskets, water in vessels, held on their heads. Effaced from the Company Pavilion was the forced labor of as many as 40,000 male fellaheen. They dug the Suez Canal until 1863 and were rarely accompanied by wives (fig. 48).

Lesseps gloated that the building of the Suez Canal would require more labor than the building of the pyramids but would cost much less. He recounts that "Mister MacClean made another calculation; he says that to elevate in Europe a monument resembling the greatest pyramid of Gizah would require twenty-five million francs, and that the Suez Canal will represent a work (in displacement of earth and movement of materials) thirty times superior to that of the pyramid and it will cost only eight times what it would cost to build [the pyramid] today, that is, two

**45**

Joseph Machereau, Untitled drawing in his sketchbook, Album Machereau, Paris, Bibliothèque de l'Arsenal, 33 verso.

**46**

Suez Canal Company Pavilion, 1867. From *L'Exposition Universelle de 1867 Illustrée. Publication Internationale autorisée par la Commission Impériale*, Paris, 1867, I, p. 113. Photo: Julie Wolf.

**47**

Engraving after D. Lancelot, *Relief plan of the Canal and Model of the Works*, Suez Canal Company Pavilion, 1867. From *L'Exposition Universelle de 1867 Illustrée. Publication Internationale autorisée par la Commission Impériale*, Paris, 1867, I, p. 116. Photo: Julie Wolf.

**48**

*Travaux du canal maritime de Suez—vue du Seuil D'El-Guirs*, Wood engraving, from *L'Illustration Journal Universel* 39, January-June 1862, Paris. Author's Collection. Photo: Julie Wolf.

hundred millions."[61] Thirty times the work, thirty times the matter that needed to be moved, but only eight times the cost of erecting the Giza pyramid in Europe today. The equation of two colossal projects of mass-moving in Egypt, pyramids and canal, attests to the grand scale of Lesseps' ambition. It also points up a willingness to preserve the ancient system of forced labor. Lesseps was relying, after all, on Egyptian serfs.

The machinery that formed the company exhibition's centerpiece had been devised only after Ismaïl Pasha's abolition in 1863 of the corvée labor that Egypt's ruler had agreed to provide Lesseps in his original contract. In 1863, with more than half of the distance left to dig, the British, who had hoped to thwart the French canal from its inception, suddenly persuaded the Egyptian government to withdraw what Britain called "slave laborers" from the project. When Prime Minister Palmerston defined corvée labor as a form of slavery, he ignored the fact that England had used it to build the Alexandria-Cairo-Suez railway and the trans-India railway, both with a great loss of life.[62] Meanwhile the Suez Canal Company collected a medal at the London Exhibition of 1862 for its humanitarian treatment of workers. Slavery was nonetheless connoted because of the precedent of the pyramids.

The reliance on thousands of fellaheen was inefficient. In his 1863 publication concerning the canal, Bartholdi's fellow artist Narcisse Berchère had emphasized that the transport of provisions for the huge fellaheen work force was labor-intensive and slow.

It was necessary to bring everything, from water to wood and to stone, from the tools of the worker to the bread and meat that nourish him... If you add that a camel carries no more than two hundred kilograms, and that it takes him three days on average to reach the center of the works, you easily appreciate the enormous amount of groundwork that was necessary before being ready to remove one mere cubic meter of earth from the route [trace] of the canal."[63]

Cumbersome it was, but corvée labor had been just as essential to the realization of the Suez Canal as it had been to the railways in Egypt and India. This point was reinforced in a review discussing the models of machines at the far end of the Suez Company's room at the Universal Exposition of 1867:

It is known that at the beginning, the Company counted on the labor of the indigenous to remove this enormous quantity of earth. The unskilled Egyptian road worker is an expeditious laborer. He has almost no need of tools. With his hands he digs out the earth; he [then] fills pans that he carries on his head.... This process of extraction is only as rapid as the workers are numerous, and in all other countries the expense would be exorbitant. But in the ancient land of the pharaohs in which the immemorial custom is to make populations pay part of their taxes in labor, the employment of men in grand public works has nothing that can offend sincere philanthropy.... [After the abolition of the corvée] it was necessary to improvise new means of execution; to substitute the machine for man.[64]

Fellaheen were agricultural workers, nursing the "brown breast" of Egypt's soil; they were also indentured laborers descended from indentured laborers who had been executing public works from time immemorial. Berchère wrote of them as "Poor devils, subject at will to exploitation and corvées since the invention of the pyramids," and most others followed suit.[65] Here, according to European observers, were the very people who had built colossal ancient Egypt, its pyramids, its monuments, its canals.[66] In Gautier's view fellaheen were "molded" and barely "extricated" from the earth. Because of their skin color and because of their work, fellaheen were coupled with the earth that they transported after removing it with rudimentary tools. Writing before the machines' replacement of men, Berchère bears witness to the spectacle at Suez when throngs of fellaheen were moving earth:

Most certainly, a man, shovel in hand or carrying a basket on the back,...holds no interest in and of himself, but multiply this unit, increase it to the number of 20,000, look at the profile of one of these trenches that we follow [all the way] to the horizon, the human hive of activity that moves and rushes about; beyond El-Guisr, this worksite no. 4, whose throng of small black dots in motion points to [their] occupation, and you will have right in front of you a scene made to strike the most unfeeling and most biased minds. What shows the extent of the work is the magnitude of the means employed to carry it out, and this army of workers, this multitude, creates a truly awe-inspiring and most moving scene.[67]

**49**
"Dry Excavator" at the Suez Canal in Louis Figuier, *Les Nouvelles Conquêtes de la Science*, Paris, 1883-5, IV, p.185. Photo: Julie Wolf.

Far from being immobile, fellaheen endlessly toiled. Far from being molded by the earth, they were molding it. But together the ceaseless repetitiveness of their labor and their absorption within a multitude created the impression of an inextricable binding of persons and soil, an activity that paradoxically appeared unchanging, like bees at a hive. After Ismaïl Pasha abolished the corvée, machines emptied the isthmus's landscape of men. In 1863 the French company's manpower abruptly dropped from 40,000 to fewer than 6,000 men. In another show of European force the Egyptian government was forced to pay the Suez Canal Company eighty-four million francs in compensation for the loss of labor.[68]

Enter modernization. The Suez Canal might have been aborted had not Lesseps and his engineers turned to machines that extracted earth and sand, bucket by bucket (fig. 49). Lesseps had, in a sense, sold "slaves" back to their original owner and bought machines with the income. Only the abolition of what the British called "slavery" led to modern mechanization.

The abolition made the machines signify powerfully in the company's pavilion. A few (heroic) French protagonists moved center stage and replaced the anonymous collectivity. In his 1869 novel *Le fellah*, Bartholdi's friend Edmond About has an Englishman acknowledge the brilliance of France's engineers:

> The edict which forbade corvées constrained the genius of men to make miracles. The large dredge and the conveyor of Mr. Lavalley and Mr. Borel are the highest expressions of modern industry. You will see machines as grandiose as cathedrals and as precise as Greenwich marine watches. I visited one which did the work of 300 workers with only fifteen men; it extracted 80,000 cubic meters of earth in a month."[69]

After 1863 the spectacle at Suez no longer resided in the unimaginable number of dirt-cheap men, men whose numbers and subjection evoked the building of the pyramids. Instead the marvel of man's prowess was seen in modern monuments, those precision machines the size of cathedrals. The female fellah who supports both child and clay urn on the wall of the Suez Canal Company pavilion of 1867 thus suppresses the labor of her 40,000 male counterparts, the men who before 1863 had left their wives and children to work for five years altering Egypt's geography, those men who had dredged straight-edge, modern lines of transport with their hands, pickets, and baskets.

Modernization had exploited the fellaheen's labor but it had also moved beyond it. To be fully realized technologically, the remapping of Egypt required the loss of its "slaves" and the return of the fellaheen to their "timeless" role as agricultural workers. After excavating the soil, they needed to be returned to it in order that machines designed by French engineers could take their place. And Ismaïl hoped to profit from cotton.

"Egypt is destined to become the salvation of Europe, sometimes for its wheat, sometimes for its cotton, and soon for its transit. He who rules the confluence of three worlds, in such a position and with such resources, will always be a powerful prince well-cherished everywhere."[70] This passage evokes an Egypt that Assollant had entirely denied, though both he and this author attended, and responded to, the Universal Exhibition of 1867. Was Egypt a land of a dying race or Europe's salvation, or both? Was the fellah a sign of Egypt's past or a builder of its future? Were Egypt's people petrified by their land or were they the active agents of its reinvention? Was it possible to imagine Egypt without the endlessly exploited labor of its poorest class? In the late 1860s the French remained undecided; but how one interpreted the relationship among fellaheen, machines, and Egypt's land determined whatever provisional answers were put on offer.

---

**Listen to Photography...I will master nature and place it in your hands!** Maxime Du Camp, "Songs of Matter," 1855

In stating in 1885 that his earlier project represented "Egypt under the features of a female Fellah," Bartholdi left little doubt that he believed somatic, even racial, differences distinguished the Suez statue from its American counterpart. Such a suggestion returns us to his original mission: to undertake "study of the antiquities of Egypt, Nubia, and Palestine and the photographic reproduction of the most remarkable types of the diverse races in those countries."[71] "Study" is an ambiguous term connoting drawing, but in the wording of the commission it applies solely to "antiquities." Photography is called upon to "reproduce" "types of the diverse races." Yet Bartholdi's efforts to turn both "monuments" and "types" into representation were tentative, experimental, and, in the end, utterly different from one another.

Bartholdi's plan was not original. From its inception in France, photography had been imagined as a tool to record the richness of Egypt. When François Arago, permanent secretary to the Academy of Sciences, publicly introduced photography to the French Chamber of Deputies in 1839, he seized the opportunity to contrast the new technology with the efforts of Napoleonic draftsmen in Egypt.

> [E]veryone will imagine the extraordinary advantages which could have been derived from so exact and rapid a means of reproduction during the expedition to Egypt; everybody will realize that had we had this process in 1798 we would possess today faithful pictorial records of that which the learned world is forever deprived of by the greed of the Arabs and the vandalism of certain travelers.
>
> To copy the millions and millions of hieroglyphs which cover even the exterior of the great monuments of Thebes, Memphis, Karnak and others would require decades of time and legions of draftsmen. By daguerreotype, one person would suffice to accomplish this immense work successfully.... [I]nnumerable hieroglyphics as they are in reality will replace those which now are invented or designed by approximation.[72]

For Arago, Daguerre's invention competed with the *Description de l'Égypte* and, because of its speed and "fidelity of detail," it won.[73] Just as the French engineer with his newly invented dredging machine replaced thousands of fellaheen, one man wielding the camera could replace twenty years of work by "legions of draftsmen."

It is no surprise then that the French government started to commission photographers to work in Egypt. In 1849, six years before Bartholdi's journey, Maxime Du Camp had obtained a commission from the Ministry of Public Education for himself and a friend, the then unknown writer Gustave Flaubert, to photograph and record the monuments of Egypt. Du Camp, like Bartholdi, had probably learned photography in order to obtain such a commission. Du Camp knew Arago's argument; he justified his embrace of the new medium in exactly the terms Arago had proposed a decade earlier.

In my prior travels, I had noticed that I lost precious time in drawing the monuments or views that I wanted to remember; I drew slowly and in an incorrect manner; furthermore, the notes I took to describe an edifice or landscape seemed confused to me when I reread them later, and I understood that I needed a precision instrument to bring back images that would allow me to make exact reconstructions.... I wanted to be in a position to gather as many documents as possible. Therefore, I entered into an apprenticeship with a photographer and started manipulating chemicals.[74]

To Du Camp's way of thinking, drawing and writing were too slow and too imprecise even if the draftsman was expert. His statement implies he had a long-term commitment to recording foreign lands, but at the end of his trip Du Camp traded his camera for oriental fabric to ornament his Parisian apartment. He would never take another photograph. Still his project in Egypt became a great success. Working obsessively he had produced 214 negatives and in 1852 published a book of ninety-four plates, *Égypte, Nubie, Palestine et Syrie*. Most were photographs of archaeological sites, even though he had taken many pictures of Arab villages. Du Camp was basing his book on the precedent of the *Description*. For his efforts he won membership in the Legion of Honor. Unsure of his purpose while in Egypt and disappointed, Flaubert railed against this "admirable epoch in which photographers are decorated and poets are exiled."[75]

According to Arago in 1839 and Du Camp in 1849 and again in 1855 when he wrote "Songs of Matter," photography surpassed draftsmanship in speed and precision. In Du Camp's poem, photography taunts draftsmen:

I defy all pencils.
My only master is the light of day
The most difficult outlines
Drawings, a man would not attempt
Are, for me, always docile;
I need but look upon them.[76]

The claim is debatable on several counts. Given the unwieldy nature of photograph equipment in the 1850s, it was hardly a speedy process. A gifted and experienced draftsman like Dutertre could probably have created finished drawings faster than DuCamp was able to prepare his plates, set up his shot, and process the plates once they had been exposed. Nonetheless, if the speed of the medium was questionable, the claim for its possessing greater precision was convincing to most. Arago showed a photograph of a large stone with hieroglyphs accurately recorded all at once that impressed those who saw it. Still it is worth emphasizing that an optical process registering tonal gradations of light fails to capture crucial qualities such as the precise edges of a carved shape. Instead the play of shadow and light often obscures the contours of a form. A case in point being a photograph by Du Camp of the inscriptions on the Colossus' throne at the Temple of Gurnah: it provides abundant though in some places unclear information (fig. 50). Imagine trying to determine the exact shapes of the hieroglyphs in the lowest portion of the stele where shadow robs them of distinctness.

Du Camp's photograph seems yet more problematic when compared to the plate of another relief from the *Description de l'Égypte*. The artist and the engraver attempted to treat the whole surface as if evenly lit; the emphasis throughout is on line even as slight depth and concomitant shading are added to convey relief, even erosion (fig. 51). Although the engraving cannot secure our full confidence in the draftsman's accuracy, if we value information of this sort, lines and shapes rather than haptic qualities like textured, uneven surfaces and eroded stone, the engraving better answers our needs. It restitutes the pristine surface of the original design, that is, the engineer's template. Thus if one were to copy or to study a given relief, the engraved plate would provide more relevant information. Du Camp, in his "Songs of Matter," had simplified a

**50**
Maxime Du Camp, *Inscriptions on the colossus' throne. Temple of Gurnah. West Thebes, Egypt,* 1851. Photo: Adoc-photos/Art Resource, NY.

**51**
"Slaughtering Geese," *La Description de l'Égypte,* Antiquités Vol. IV, Plate 68, Paris, 1809-1822. Private Collection, Cairo, Egypt. Photo Credit: © François Guenet/ Art Resource, NY.

**52**
Frédéric-Auguste Bartholdi, *The Colossi of Memnos,* 1855-6. Salt Print. Colmar, Musée Bartholdi. Photo: Christian Kempf.

**53**
Friedrich Finsch, Mold from nature of the bust of a Diggani, Oriental Africa (*Diggani, Afrique orientale*) 1880. Dresden, Staatliches Musuem für Völkerkunde.

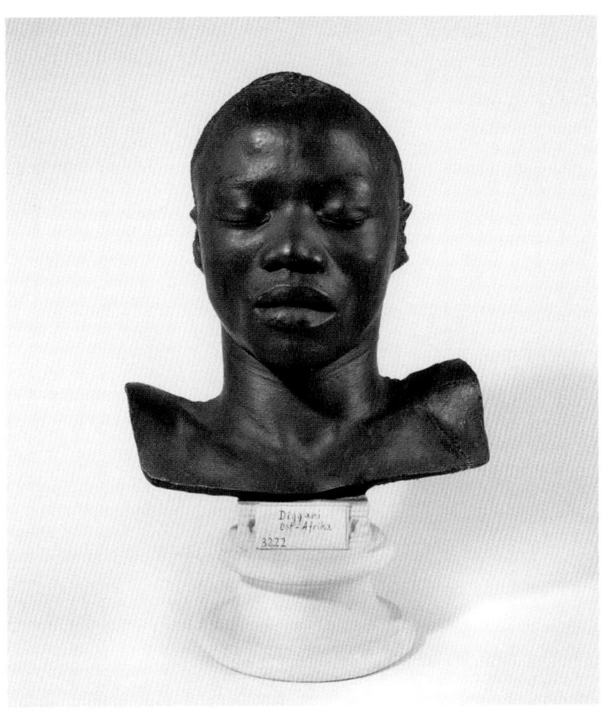

representational complexity. Photography was not equivalent to seeing, not least because the viewer can compensate for any given lighting effect by shifting attention or position. Nor is or was photography able to capture "more" than the draftsman's hand.

Bartholdi was a clumsy draftsman, but the photographic machine he wielded in Egypt had its own profound limitations. One of the more famous and striking of his photographs, the *Colossi of Memnon*, can elucidate the problem (fig. 52). The gravity, majesty, and silent immobility that Bartholdi would later celebrate in textual manifestos on colossal ancient Egyptian art are here beautifully expressed.[77] The photograph's vertical composition, tight cropping, extremely low horizon, and formal severity successfully exploit the eerie doubling and syncopated rhythm of difference in the two colossi, the far statue more eroded than the other, the two bluntly, blindly, gravely staring off stage left.

But as a rule early photography diminishes all things to human scale. This was considered one of its wondrous achievements. In 1849 David Brewster declared that the sculptor now "may virtually carry in his portfolio...the gigantic sphinxes of Egypt."[78] Conversely, among photography's many losses was scale. Like printmakers and photographers before him, including most famously Du Camp, Bartholdi resorted to the inclusion of human beings to signal the colossal size that he admired. At the lower left corner of the foreground statue of Memnon appear two standing, presumably Egyptian men, but they are barely visible. Not only are they diminutive (as intended), they are subject to the same lighting as the statue itself. They precisely repeat in tone the corner's harsh divide between light and shadow. One man is bleached into the whiteness of light; the other darkened into the shade's obscurity. Photography seems to absorb the men into a black-and-white system that swallows their difference from their environment; it assimilates them. To focus on the monument is to lose the type.

In an unpublished letter written in Egypt in 1856, Bartholdi himself assesses the challenge: "As for the types, I am working on them.... Everything is fine except that people do not want to let themselves be molded [*mouler*], in photography some are afraid, the others move without stop."[79] Bartholdi's friend Edmond About had misled him: the fellaheen were not so tired as to resemble statues. The photograph of the Colossi of Memnon may seem to turn men into stone, but in fact the medium struggles to do so, because men, unlike stone, may refuse to be photographed or they may move. The minimum two-minute exposure time required for calotypes in the 1850s demanded that human subjects mimic stone's stillness; but they seldom were able to do so.[80] Looking again at Bartholdi's photograph, the doubling of men appears ambiguous. Did the two men really look so alike or does the photograph register one person's occupation of two different positions? Is the blurred figure at right swallowed by the shadow or by a temporal incommensurability with a self at left? Is it darkness or time or failed self-discipline that makes the man at right a ghost compared to his double at left?

Bartholdi's comment, "people do not want to let themselves be molded, in photography some are afraid, the others move without stopping," is significant in its identification of "molding" and photography. It is probable that Bartholdi imagined photography as a form of molding, because life casts and photography played similar roles in the early days of anthropological classification. Consider a cast made in 1847 by staff members at the Musée de l'Homme. It shows a man who could hold himself still (fig. 53). In the 1840s and 1850s casts were a preferred form of documentation, at once accurate, informative, and life size. Compared to photography, however, casting is a much more time-consuming and cumbersome process. Even in the 1850s, when photographic exposure times were long, sitters at the Musée de l'Homme were paid four times as much to sit for a cast as for a photograph. For this reason people were often solicited to sit for the camera, at times in an armature that ensured their stillness. Scientists prized both casts and photographs for their authority as indexical forms of representation produced through direct physical contact. As late as 1889 the sculptor Rodin could speak of photography as a form of casting in order to distinguish it from art: "Many cast from nature, that is to say, replace an art work with a photograph. It is quick but it is not art."[81]

There is no evidence that Bartholdi planned to cast sitters in Egypt, although casts were occasionally made during trips.[82] By the late 1840s and 50s, the new medium of photography had increasingly replaced cast making in the "reproduction" of foreign peoples. Arago's photographic machine had wrongly or rightly made both drawing and casting seem slower and less efficient.

Not coincidentally Bartholdi's commission had specified the "*photographic* reproduction and the most remarkable types of the diverse races," not merely their "reproduction" in any medium.[83] This inclined Bartholdi, trained as a sculptor, to approach the recording of human types through photography and life casts as analogous processes. His training sensitized him to the truth that both indexical modes of representation required more, not less, cooperation on the part of sitters.

Bartholdi ascribes volition to the persons who do not allow themselves to be fixed in place. The word "mold" (*moulage*) is inherently ambiguous. In both French and English it connotes the mold and the molded: the term can apply to the hollow form or to the cast object made from that form.[84] It is clear that Bartholdi asked the Egyptian people to still themselves, to resemble statues in order to become types in the medium of photography. I am reminded of Roland Barthes' oft-cited resistance to the imperatives of photography: "Now, once I feel myself in the process of 'posing,' I instantaneously make another body for myself, I transform myself in advance into an image. This transformation is an active one: I feel that the Photograph creates my body or mortifies it . . ."[85] Barthes imagines that posing imposes photography's mortification of the self as "image," whereas Bartholdi assumes that sitters must fix themselves—must behave like statues. In his comment the sculptor focuses not on the photographic operation or product, but on the earlier step in which persons must stop moving in order to be made into two-dimensional representation. In this way he shifts the emphasis from photography's indexicality as an imprint of light to a prior stilling of movement--photography's precondition.[86] To be photographed the world first must be made static, but persons, annoyingly, must do this themselves. Bartholdi never worried over the dilemma Barthes brought to the fore. Familiar with several arts, Bartholdi came to believe that models exercised more power in photography than in either sculpture or painting. Unless the person held still while the photographer was working, he or she could not be transformed into a work of art.

Du Camp had responded to this challenge by convincing his model, the one-eyed Nubian sailor Ishmael-Hadj, that the camera was a cannon which would fire at him if he moved.[87] If Ishmael-Hadj ever considered this to be true, it is hard to imagine that he continued to do so after posing for Du Camp for more than a year. Time and time again Flaubert saw a strange sight: Du Camp, hidden beneath the black cloth draping his one-eyed camera, staring down the one-eyed sailor. The aggression of photography troubled Flaubert; the camera assaulted like "the bullet leaves a rifle, like the arrow leaves the bow." But he also recognized that this machine's violence "imprisoned" and "decapitated" Du Camp. The words are Flaubert's, put into the mouth of a harem woman who felt herself more free than the camera's operator.[88]

Other photographers devised equally strange solutions to the problems that the long exposure times caused. In their 1862 publication *La vallée du Nil: Impressions et photographies*, Henry Cammas and André Lefèvre explained how they had solved the problem in order to convey monumentality:

> Our cameras had notably reduced the size of the temples, and at a certain point we felt the need to rectify this by providing an indication of their colossal proportions. The lengthy exposure times did not allow us even to dream of posing a living human being so we fabricated a dummy of medium height, dressed in European garb and topped off by a hat onto which we inscribed a name (Abou-Simbel). . . . [E]specially for we who made him, Abou-Simbel exists; always ready to hold the most awkward poses on the knees of the colossi or at the foot of obelisks, he was eminently useful in a number of portraits. He is now a man like any other; he lives in photography.[89]

Abou-Simbel, the "dummy of medium height," recalls the mannequins that the photographer Nadar was propping up as workers in the catacombs of Paris (1861). Only one of Nadar's catacomb photographs contains a living person, and it is the photographer himself, the man who could mimic a dummy for the eighteen-minute exposure time required underground.[90]

The incessant movement of models unfailingly defeated the photographer; but it was also annoying to the draftsman. Bartholdi said as much to fellow artists in another letter from Egypt: "I work as much as I can; as you told me, the models are not easy to make pose. . . . What is absurd is that all these people when they pose, do not pose; this is even more absurd because: when individuals (especially of the female sex) decide to pose for you, they laugh and do not remain for an instant in the same pose."[91] Surely Bartholdi was comparing these foreign persons to paid Parisian working-class models. While the movement of sitters in photography led to invisibility, in other arts it led to extra sessions or to exercises of memory or to improvisations and often to anatomical inaccuracies or deformations.[92] Narcisse Berchère also expressed frustration with models in Egypt, and the painter Léon Belly wrote at length about the difficulties of drawing fellah women at the river: "I can hardly make them pose and it is necessary entirely to remember them. Once I am sure of a *living movement*, I use models for the arms and hands, but for the movement, one no longer has it truthfully once it is posed. A figure drawn thus and found is worth a hundred made in the studio."[93] Movement frustrated draftsmen and painters, but they could compensate for the ways it deprived them of significant information by exercising their art (and memory). Not so for photographers, according to Bartholdi. In this medium, models, not camera operators, decided the outcome.

Indexical representations can seem merely a medium's (active) registration of a (passive) object. We are prone to look at a cast and see it as the marvelous product of an act of molding. We may take for granted that the object, in this case the person, was simply there. C. S. Peirce argued that photographs were "physically forced to correspond point by point to nature;" he thereby described photography in the terms of casting, wherein plaster, wax, or clay are forced to conform to bodies.[94] What Bartholdi's example makes clear, however, is the extent to which the object determines whether indexical representation can be realized. Especially in the early days of photography, it was the sitter who had to choose "to correspond point by point" to the requirements of the medium. In Paris the museum could authorize such reproductive procedures, paying sitters to be photographed or cast, but travelers abroad had far less control. In foreign lands, there may have been a greater number of potential sitters, but in general they appear to have been disinclined to stay still.

It is no surprise then that most of Bartholdi's calotypes are entirely devoid of people. With some notable exceptions, often involving himself, fellow artists, and the sailing crew with whom he lived for months (persons whom he could evidently influence), the few photographs to include people show them "half-consumed in blurs of emulsion" (fig. 54).[95] Thus the most modern of European technologies of representation returned the world to the stasis associated with the primitive in Orientalist rhetoric, but it also evacuated it. Without casting or photography as options, the one way to capture the ethnographic type—people's characteristic look and dress, was to wield the rudimentary pencil just as the "types" themselves wielded urns, baskets, and pickaxes. People were not docile. It is no coincidence that Du Camp's list of subjects in his "Songs of Matter" does not include them. Early photography in Egypt disproved the stereotype: the Egyptian fellah was animated, not inanimate. Most vividly, and most disruptively, women laughed. That detail in Bartholdi's letter is powerful.

If Bartholdi were to fix Egypt's timeless primitivism in photography, he had to point the machine at the inert. Instead of fellah women getting water, Bartholdi's calotypes, at least three, depict Egyptian water machines, the wooden *chadoufs* that he had denounced for their inefficiency and compared unfavorably to the hydraulic machines rusting at the Arsenal. Inert (water) machine may have better suited inert (photographic) machine, but many of Bartholdi's photographs, while formally satisfying, suffer when set alongside his oil paintings.

Bartholdi's calotype of a row of three *chadoufs* is less informative than his landscape painting of the same subject exhibited at the Salon of 1864 (figs. 55–56). Bartholdi's proximate, narrow view in the photograph shows neither the river from which water is being extracted, nor the farmland that is being irrigated, nor the people who make the machines work. The calotype does not narrate as does his painting; instead we are offered the unpredictable arrangement of bright light and deep shadows across an irregular rocky bank and its rubble; three vertical lines punctuating a white sky, and a boat at left that orients us but also occludes our view. As viewers, we feel ourselves to be blocked by clumsy, irrelevant things from acquiring the information to situate what we see. Nor does this series of *chadoufs* look age-old, as it does in the painting; instead we see a technology that remains opaque, even trivial, to those who do not already know its mechanism, its purpose, and its significance since antiquity to Egyptian life.

In Egypt Bartholdi was forced to contend with the technical limitations of his media and his skills. Regardless of his mission to produce "the photographic reproduction of the most remarkable types of the diverse races," he could not fix persons in photography. "Types" could

**54**
Frédéric-Auguste Bartholdi, *Environs of Edfu*, 1855-6. Salt Print. Colmar, Musée Bartholdi. Photo: Christian Kempf.

**55**
Frédéric-Auguste Bartholdi, *Chadoufs*, 1855-6. Calotype. Colmar, Musée Bartholdi. Photo: Christian Kempf.

**56**
Amilcar Hasenfratz (Bartholdi), *On the Bank of the Nile*, 1863 (Salon of 1864). Oil on canvas, 46 x 24 cm. Colmar, Musée Bartholdi. Photo: Christian Kempf.

only be "molded" provisionally in the (iconic) medium of drawing. Doggedly Bartholdi made drawing after drawing that attempted to do just that. Most of his sketches show people, seen from either the front or the back, standing against a blank ground—standing, that is, like statues.

But Bartholdi's drawings of female fellaheen are distinctive because of their persistent interest in the women's activity of moving water (see figs. 37–39). One woman awkwardly bends down to fill an urn at the river; another crouches, resting meditatively at a riverbank; one passes a vessel to another's head; another walks away from us with an urn balanced on her head. We see, in the five figures, the operation, or we might say the mechanism, of their labor. We see how they lift and move things (their song of matter). The photograph of the *chadoufs* shows no such thing. Rodin was right when he later denounced photographs for arresting the body's movement while sculpture and painting could seek to evoke its progressive movement within a single figure.[96] But Bartholdi had not yet summarized motion within a single figure. During his trip, his drawings were serial—they captured a sequence of frozen moments. Against all likelihood, he was trying again and again in both drawing and photography to arrest action and to mold persons. When he returned home, he could no longer avoid deciding how to make sculpture out of them.

---

**We can judge Egyptian colossal art with our own eyes. To all those who have studied it, Egyptian art has been the object of profound admiration, not only in view of the masses, the millions of kilograms moved by the Egyptian people, but on account of its concrete and majestic character, in design and in form.** **Bartholdi, *The Statue of Liberty Enlightening the World*, 1885**

Between 1867 and 1869, more than a decade after his first journey to Egypt, Bartholdi devised a way to integrate the two goals of his official commission. Finally (colossal) monument became type and type became (colossal) monument. He returned the female fellah to the timeless immobility that the fellah women themselves had resisted: laughing, moving, refusing, running away, working. In France, Bartholdi molded them as he had not been able to arrest them in Egypt. And he did this in the consummate material for such molding, clay (*terre*, literally "earth"). The clay models show that Bartholdi was seeking a figure that was broad, stable, and simple, just the qualities he praised in the Colossi of Memnon and similar ancient Egyptian sculpture (see figs. 40–42). He experimented with the incorporation of the slightest suggestion of movement, using *contrapposto*, the convention of animation fundamental to the European (and ancient Greco-Roman) tradition, a shift in weight onto one leg, the slight asymmetry of hips. And he threw her arm up to hold a torch rather than an urn. In profile some of the clay models closely follow Bartholdi's drawing of a fellah lifting a vessel onto her companion's head.

But his proposed statue was intended to be eighty-six feet tall and to stand upon a forty-six-foot-high pedestal. Such a colossus could afford only so much asymmetry. Bartholdi understood that the stability and majesty of Egyptian monumental sculpture resided in its grave simplicity, equilibrium, and immobility. He therefore tried to create a compromise: a sculpture that emulated and rivaled immobile Egyptian colossi and simultaneously displayed his skill as a modern French sculptor. Movement, even if subtle, would signal his difference as a French artist of the nineteenth century.

"Egypt Enlightening Asia," he grandiosely called his statue and imagined it serving as a lighthouse for the Suez Canal's harbor, a sculptural monument to welcome ships to an engineering monument. Bartholdi was well aware of one of the Wonders of the Ancient World, the Colossus of Rhodes, a statue over a hundred feet tall, which had stood on an island in Rhodes harbor, bearing aloft a flame; he would later mention it as a precedent for the Statue of Liberty.[97] He certainly planned to fashion his own "Wonder of the World."[98] Nonetheless he chose not to emphasize classical and Italian antecedents, and he never travelled to Rome, perhaps because of his Protestantism.[99] He instead visited Egypt and the United States.

Bartholdi's statue was designed with an eye on classical precedents, but his real inspiration was the memory of his experience in Egypt. His proposed fellah-lighthouse recollects that land's colossi as well as its fellaheen. It was meant to function, moreover, much like the painting of a fellah woman standing guard, or perhaps playing hostess, high on the wall of the Suez Canal Company pavilion at the 1867 Universal Exhibition, a timeless Egyptian water carrier sanctioning the machine-made water carrier that was the canal (see fig. 47). And like the painted fellah, Bartholdi's colossus would connote a past and a present that suppressed the recent history of fellah labor on the canal itself. Or rather this is the question: would she conjure or erase traditional labor put to new purposes? And which of the two would appeal to the man who

**57**
Frédéric-Auguste Bartholdi, Sketch in Journal, Tuesday, 13 April 1869. Colmar, Musée Bartholdi. Photo: Christian Kempf.

**58**
D. Lancelot, *Drague a Longue Couloir*, n.d. From *L'Exposition Universelle 1867 Illustrée*, Paris, 1867, 1, p. 117. Photo: Julie Wolf.

**59**
Frédéric-Auguste Bartholdi, Sketch in Journal, Tuesday, 13 April 1869. Colmar, Musée Bartholdi. Photo: Christian Kempf.

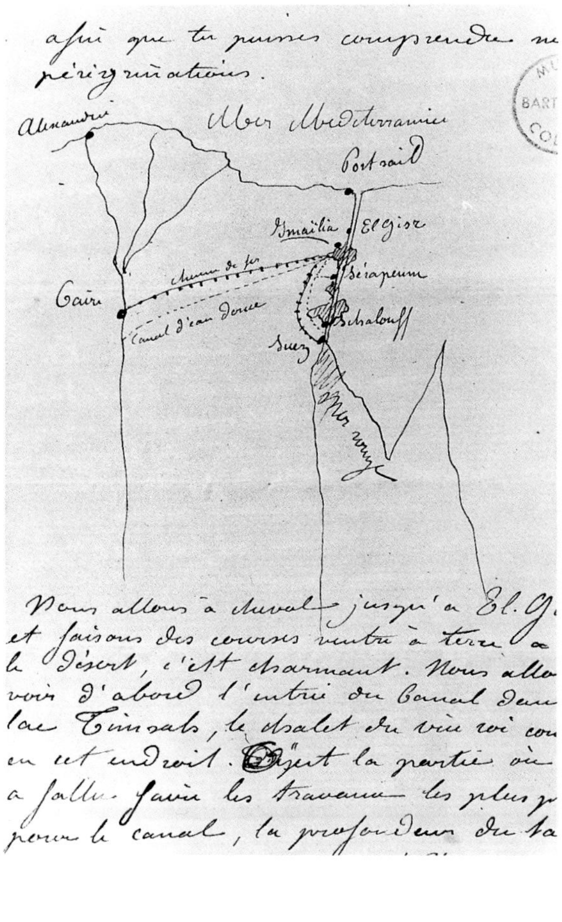

would commission the lighthouse? Not Lesseps, not Napoleon III, but Ismaïl Pasha, viceroy of Egypt, landowner, "prince of fellaheen," but also Europeanizer, Haussmannizer, engineering student, and fluent speaker of French and English.

Bartholdi's correspondence and journal reveal that he had invested great hope and effort in the project but knew it was a gamble. He returned to Egypt in April of 1869 in the hopes of selling his statue-lighthouse. Before leaving he wrote to his mother from Paris:

> I am going to devote myself entirely to my Egypt business, it has the advantage of frankly showing its impossible side; but at least…I am seizing all possible [means of] support, I have excellent ones, but with this there is an aspect of the lottery and a play of luck is needed…. I will do all that can…and if I fail it will be because there is not a ghost of a chance.
>
> I had my project shown to the Emperor and Empress. It seems that all the world was enchanted with it; but they limit themselves to wishing for my success…. As little as this is, it will allow me to say that they have [such] wishes, without having to lie.
>
> I will equally have the support of Mr. de Nieuwerkerke [the French Superintendent of the Arts]. By the end of the week, I will have collected all [the support] that I can get. After that, I will go seize the bull by the horns.[100]

Once arrived Bartholdi devoted himself to the diplomacy required to realize his ambitions. The middle-aged sculptor made none of the prolonged studies or photographs he had done in his youth. Only two images survive from this later trip. In his journal, Bartholdi sketched the new modern dredging machines that had been invented since his trip thirteen years earlier, the very machines that he had seen as models at the Universal Exhibition of 1867 (figs. 57-58). Unlike those rusting in disuse in Mohammad Ali's Arsenal, these machines were changing the world by inscribing a canal on the earth of Egypt. Bartholdi noted this recently fashioned channel, in his careful if schematic map of the isthmus (fig. 59). Bartholdi's thumbnail sketches were drawn while he was abroad; they were supposed to function as traditional eyewitness notations. Nonetheless it is notable that his two pictures reproduced the information already displayed in the Suez Canal Company pavilion two years earlier. Both the machines and the maps were on view in Paris in 1867; the sculptor did not need to have traveled to make them. The fellaheen, who had earlier preoccupied him, are absent.

In 1869 Bartholdi believed Lesseps' lack of support for his Suez lighthouse was decisive. His judgement was probably astute. Well-positioned to influence both Empress Eugénie and Ismaïl Pasha, Lesseps clearly chose not to exercise his power on Bartholdi's behalf. He was not present when the sculptor presented his idea to the emperor and empress. In Egypt when Bartholdi joined him in his train compartment, Lesseps slept all the way to Cairo. In Bartholdi's view, he made only "a diplomatic welcome to my project;" he "dampened my enthusiasm;" he continually offered an "amiable but superficial welcome."[101] Lesseps was again pointedly absent when Bartholdi finally made his proposal to Ismaïl himself.[102] On 11 April 1869, the sculptor wrote an exceptionally revealing letter:

> At the moment I am with Mr. Lesseps at Ismaïlia in the middle of the Isthmus. I acted as if he had been very devoted to my projects; he is very amiable with me, his hospitality is most gracious. I can only reproach him for one thing, that is for hardly supporting me in my endeavor. I [pardon him] though generally one prefers one's affairs to those of others, but one needs to consider how much he is occupied by his great work. My project being only a very accessory detail, he does not wish to work hard on its behalf. Nevertheless he shows me much pleasantness and sympathy like someone who would say: Try to succeed and I will be delighted by it.[103]

Bartholdi pretends that the diplomat of Herculean ambition was irreproachable, even well-wishing, although he offered no support whatsoever. The sculptor, now thirty-five years old, had the makings of a courtier: "I acted as if he was devoted to my projects." "Acting" was essential; a mere three weeks earlier Bartholdi had expressed his resentment of Lesseps' self-interest. Referring to himself in the third person, Bartholdi wrote: "Ferdinand de Lesseps, friend of the Court, is very likely responsible for the imperial lack of enthusiasm. Bartholdi's plan can only annoy him. On the eve of inaugurating 'his' canal, he does not intend that anyone be able to divert

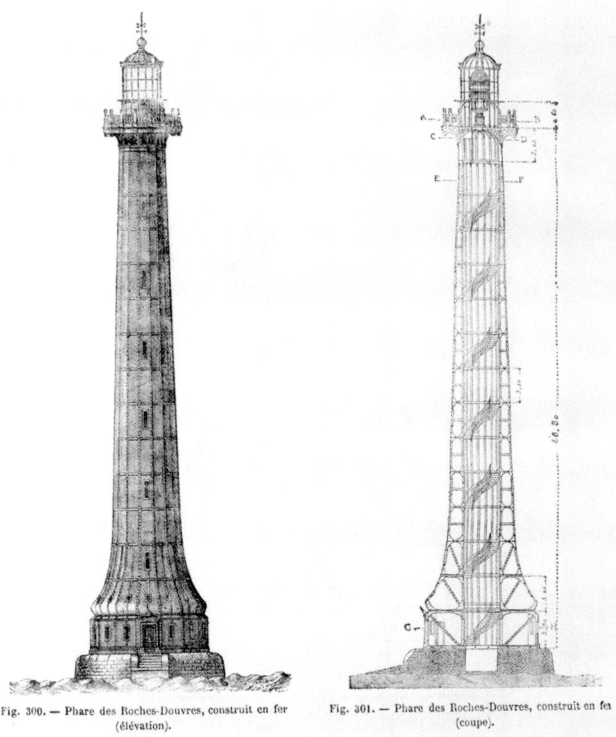


**60**
Phare des Roches-Douvres in Louis Figuier, *Les Nouvelles Conquêtes de la Science*, Paris, 1883-5, IV, p. 483. Photo: Julie Wolf.

Ismaïl's attention (and money), towards anything that he, de Lesseps, did not plan, choose, carry out. I wager that he devoted himself, in France as well as in Egypt, to undermining the insolent project."[104]

Bartholdi's anger is palpable. Lesseps would not support anything that he did not "plan, choose, carry out." Note Bartholdi's use of quotation marks around the word "his" in reference to the canal; Lesseps, he implies, had wrongfully appropriated the canal as his own. This recalls Enfantin's remark that Lesseps was a man who feared being "eclipsed, subordinated, evaded, even robbed."[105] Decades later Lesseps offered Bartholdi the gift of his five-volume *Lettres, journal et documents pour server à l'histoire du canal de Suez* (1875–1881) that he inscribed "Regards to my old friend Auguste Bartholdi." Bartholdi never cut the pages.[106]

Lesseps may have been an instrumental, perhaps necessary ally, but Bartholdi knew that the man he had to convince was Ismaïl Pasha. Here is Bartholdi's account of their long-awaited encounter, a meeting arranged with some strategic behind-the-scenes pulling of strings.

After having waited two hours the Viceroy's doctor arrives and he introduces me. I enter apartments with an entirely European appearance, the only distinctive characteristic consists of a divan that [goes around] half of the room. In the sitting room were M. Mariette, the doctor Burguières, and some servants. After some generalities, I present my drawings and the statuette to the Viceroy. He looks with interest, I give him explanations, he says to me that he would prefer to see the luminous apparatus held on the head in the manner of women fellaheen. I reply to him that this would be easier, in order not to annoy him (however this would not be as good). I ask him permission to leave him my drawings and to see him again during his voyage [to Paris] in a month, and with a small salute retire.[107]

Our limited evidence suggests that Ismaïl did not dislike Bartholdi's decision to represent Egypt as a female fellah. He seems to have wanted the statue to be more, not less characteristic of that "type." The problem could have been that Bartholdi's watercolor drawing and clay statuette did not look artful enough to him. It is likely that Bartholdi intended the statue to be made out of cast metal and its light to be electric like the tall metal lighthouse admired in the French section of the Universal Exhibition of 1867 (fig. 60). But to Ismaïl Bartholdi's monument may have appeared neither a modern engineering triumph like the canal nor a valuable French artwork. I conjecture here. Certainly financial reasons may have played a decisive role; Ismaïl and Lesseps were struggling to finance the completion of the canal as well as the transformations of Cairo.Yet during his reign Ismaïl managed to pay for both lighthouses and sculptures.[108] Regardless of ancient precedents like the Colossus of Rhodes, it is conceivable Ismaïl did not appreciate Bartholdi's combination of engineering and artistic functions. And I think it wise to question the sincerity of the khedive's suggestion that the statue should look more like a fellah. Though Ismaïl understood himself to be the "prince of the fellaheen," the identification of modern Egypt with its uneducated peasantry would not occur until the twentieth century.[109]

The viceroy may also have been responding negatively to *how* Bartholdi designed his sculpture, how he imagined the female fellah. The key piece of evidence to support such a hypothesis is Ismaïl's sustained patronage of Charles Cordier. Cordier had won renown for ethnographic statuary of imposing naturalism, often embellished with lush polychromy, and had met Ismaïl and his father Ibrahim Pasha through his own brother, a military officer. He thus had a family connection to Ismaïl as had Lesseps to Ismaïl's predecessor, Saïd Pasha.[110] In 1865 Cordier had received a commission to travel to Egypt; he stayed there from February to June 1866. Afterwards he produced plaster figures that may have served as seven of the ten statues in the Egyptian pavilion of the Universal Exhibition of 1867. As a token of gratitude, Ismaïl gave Cordier the extraordinary gift of his Egyptian palace at the Universal Exhibition of 1867, which Cordier moved and rebuilt in Orsay between 1868 and 1870.[111]

Clearly Muslim injunctions against figural art, which vary greatly according to region, did not impinge on Ismaïl's support of Cordier. Cordier's portrait bust of Ismaïl presided over the "Egyptian corner" at the Universal Exhibition of 1867, and Ismaïl did not hesitate to commission Cordier to make an equestrian statue of his father, Ibrahim Pasha, to embellish Cairo.[112] The sculptor exhibited the statue at the Salon of 1872, and it still stands outside Cairo's Opera House, attesting to Ismaïl's willingness to commission European figurative sculpture in the late 1860s. It is notable, however, that the khedive chose to erect a highly conventional statue to honor his family lineage and right to rule, not a symbolic personification such as "Egypt enlightening Asia."

Ismaïl favored a sculptor other than Bartholdi. Knowing this, one of Cordier's sculptures of a woman fellah may afford a glimpse of the mannequins shown at the 1867 Exhibition (fig. 61). Looking at Cordier's statue, the words sensuality and facility come immediately to mind, as do erotic, slick, serpentine, young, and relaxed. What the sculpture does not connote is labor or peasantry or the earth. This woman reaches up not to hold her vessel but as a pretext to display her body in a swelling curve. Her arms do not hold weight or move water; instead they enhance her supple elegance and intimate her receptivity to pleasure. She lifts her arms to permit us to glimpse not only her breasts beneath the low-cut opening of her robe but also the contours of her hips and the swell of her belly and abdomen, enhanced by the lapping waves of her clinging drapery. The sheen of the bronze statue heightens the effect of its sinuosity. In a review of Cordier's ten mannequins at the Universal Exhibition of 1867, Charles Edmond noted the seductive qualities of some of the figures. After praising the "precision" and "striking truth" of Cordier's sculpture, which "fixes ethnographic traits in sculpture," Edmond characterized the male fellah carrying pickaxe and bundle as a placid, naive and honest type who divides his time between work and prayer.[113] The female fellah, by contrast, attracts closer attention to her appearance: "The fellah woman, ravishingly beautiful in her innate elegance, demeanor, and clever vivacity, returns from the bank of the Nile, carrying on her head a large vase coquettishly tilted towards her ear, and, in the palm of her hand drawn up to her shoulder, a smaller vase." If this was what Ismaïl wanted in a sculpture of a woman (and why not? it was also what Napoleon III wanted), then Bartholdi had no chance.[114]

Cordier's coy statue helps us appreciate the placid sturdiness of Bartholdi's clay figures (fig. 62). Their heaviness and androgyny, once so banal and ordinary, now appear a not insignificant achievement. Colossal scale and an admiration of sculptures such as the Colossi of Memnon, a comparative lack of facility and a dependence on improvised clumsy drawing,

**61**
Charles-Henri-Joseph Cordier. *Woman Fellah taking water from the Nile*, 1866. Bronze, 76 cm. high. Location unknown.

**62**
Frédéric-Auguste Batholdi, *Maquette for Egypt Bringing Light to Asia*, 1869. Terra Cotta, 29.5 cm high. Colmar, Musée Bartholdi. Photo: Christian Kempf.

a return to clay but an imagining of stone's immensity, even a heightened awareness of the play of light across architectural mass because of his photographic practice: these ambitions, sensitivities, and limitations had led Bartholdi to produce small clay figures with a gravity and monumentality that better resembled the strength and exertion of women bearing water in Egypt.[115]

Clumsiness can convey effort, both the fellah's and Bartholdi's. Here are awkward, blunt, and stalwart little clay sculptures that convey a sense of mass; the weight of the earth and the weight of bodies. Here are solids; small masses of clay rapidly pinched into a schematic form. Measuring nine inches tall, these terra cotta figures are exercises in the balancing of weight. Bartholdi was determining how the body could support the extension of the upheld arm, and he did not take many risks. All the figures are thick and heavy, although some offset the upward thrust of the torch bearing arm with the sway of the body. The sculptor seldom attends closely to the faces in marked contrast to the casts made from foreign persons. Instead the headdress and drapery offer a means to simplify the body's contours. The figures are not deprived of all movement, but their movement is broad and abrupt, especially compared to Cordier's *Woman Fellah*, a matter of balancing masses rather than providing pleasure. The effort is tangible and produces an effect of concentration and a certain remoteness.

Bartholdi had sought to immobilize the women who laughed and would not be molded. Ultimately a statue did succeed in capturing them. Despite her name and the chains of slavery lying broken at her feet, the American colossus stands fixed in the harbor of New York City. Turning the living into the inanimate was not, after all, solely the purview of photography. Gautier had described not only the fellah as petrified. If casts suggested death masks, Gautier also called sculpture "a dead art… Nothing is more dismal to look upon than this kind of sculptural morgue, where under one pale damp ray of light are laid out the marble cadavers of former gods which their heavenly relatives have failed to collect."[116] For Gautier the death knoll of sculpture was modernization. "In our industrial and civilized world, who gives a thought to the purity and whiteness of marble? In this age of hydrogen gas and steam engines, who is still thinking of the day when Venus came naked from the sea?"[117]

This was the long-standing anxiety of the nineteenth-century and the trap into which Bartholdi fell.[118] As a twenty-one year-old Bartholdi had absorbed all the arrogance and commitment to technological innovation of his contemporaries such as Lesseps. He had condemned rusting metal machinery and adherence to traditional methods and materials like wood. He had drawn picturesque types and photographed picturesque machines in order to make art out of them, but he had been certain that Egypt's future necessarily lay in modernization and technological progress. In 1869 he expressed greater ambivalence, because suddenly, not only Egyptian artisanal traditions seemed to be at risk, but so too did their French counterparts, including art. In 1869 Bartholdi admitted that his sculpture would have been only "a very accessory detail" to the Suez Canal. And a few days later, he lamented: "It is unfortunate that with modern ideas, art and poetry seem superfluities; because truly I [believe] that few works of art in these conditions would appear more striking than this one. We will see, one need not despair of it yet."[119] The sculptor was rehearsing a lament that had recently been incited by the Universal Exhibition of 1867 where the fine arts had been radically reduced in importance and where artists had protested exhibiting alongside industry to no avail.[120] Two years before Bartholdi the art critic Charles Blanc had asked: "Is it appropriate that art, whose mission is to manifest the Beautiful and to recall the Ideal, is presented in this event as a pleasant accessory, as an additional graciousness?"[121]

Bartholdi believed his lighthouse was a "work of art," and yet like so many entrepreneurs of the period he tried to exploit Egypt's modernization. To succeed he felt he needed, like Egypt, to update his product, to modernize sculpture by enlarging it and giving it a function. But to compete with engineering on its own terms was to lose. By contrast Cordier's elegant ornament fulfilled a traditional function in French art, and for this Ismaïl Pasha was willing to pay.

"It was he alone who worked:" so spoke Belly about Bartholdi. And work hard Bartholdi did, twice in Egypt and throughout much of his career in France and the United States. The sculptor's work was manual and social, a matter of making and of continual negotiations as he sought commissions and attempted to control artisans' production of his work. In sum he acted not only as a manual laborer but also as a diplomat, businessman, and foreman. He identified himself, how-ever, primarily as an artist who made his art with his hands. But his specialty, sculpture, especially colossal sculpture, and his moment in history were between the hand-made and the engineered, between clay and the machine, between the primitive and the modern. So too was Egypt.

During his travel in Egypt Bartholdi wielded the rudimentary pencil and the modern photographic machine. And although it is true that only the primitive tool could represent the primitive fellaheen who carried urns and pickaxes, while the machine could record machines like *chadoufs*, the difference between what a pencil and a machine could each do hinges on other distinctions, not primitive versus modern, not tool versus machine, but rather animate versus inanimate, active versus static, living versus inert. The camera returned man to an immobile world of stone things yet at the same time prophesied an engineered future in which machines evacuated people from the landscape. It pointed in two directions.

The draftsman survived but as a virtual anachronism, tied to the economy of manual labor that the fellah knew on far more onerous terms. Bartholdi the draftsman and sculptor of clay was able to create that effort's analogue or representation. When, however, Bartholdi turned the female fellah into a lighthouse, he projected turning her not merely into a cast (rather than hand-molded) metal sculpture but also into a hollow, static machine, a machine that inverted the camera's absorption of light so as to send light out from its empty core.

Valued "a little less than an animal and a little more than a plant," the fellah, according to Maxime Du Camp in 1854, was no more than a mechanism of labor, "something which is born, lives and dies like a man, but is not one; ... [the fellah] is not even a slave because a slave represents capital; this is an animated machine."[122] Fundamentally the question in nineteenth-century France was whether the fellah, or to be more specific, the fellah's labor, was deemed human or not. Inertness, after all, describes both Gautier's clay fellah and Du Camp's machine fellah, both the molded and the mold, both the primordial earthen past and the industrial future. The dehumanized fellah could be identified with either. It was the laughing, restless, hardworking women in Egypt who proved that fellaheen were animate, human, and resistant to the machine's propensity to render the world inanimate and inert.

Bartholdi's colossal Suez statue began in the frustrating encounter of draftsman and photographer with these animate, ever-moving persons. The failure of his proposed lighthouse stemmed from its paradoxical goals; to fix the living as the inert, to rival ancient achievement, and to promote an industrial future. Eclipsed was the present. But in the limbo between a stone past and an industrial future, a portrait of nineteenth-century Egypt remains visible.

# Liberty's Surface

## Photography / Metal

The sensation of vacancy!
Villiers de L'Isle-Adam,
*Tomorrow's Eve*,
1886

When Bartholdi first traveled to Egypt, he was twenty-one and already dreaming of colossi. Back home in Colmar he had just completed the model for a giant statue to honor the Napoleonic general Jean Rapp; the statue can be seen in a photograph from the 1870s (fig. 63). Bartholdi had started to study photography in 1854, the year before his arrival in Egypt; and he seems to have done so to win a commission to Egypt and to promote his sculpture. One of Bartholdi's very earliest calotypes depicts the full-scale clay model of his statue of Rapp (fig. 64). An example of the new negative-positive paper photograph, this 1854 calotype was made two months after the sculptor began using a camera.[1] It shows the almost thirteen-foot-tall clay sculpture that Bartholdi (seated at right) had made with the help of his model, who holds his upper body in the statue's pose. The setting is Bartholdi's studio in Paris: the statue's destination was his distant home in Alsace; Bartholdi carried the photograph to Colmar and presented it to the mayor. His calotype was intended to make an argument—an argument about the sculptor's competence but also an argument about scale.

To persuade the mayor that the statue should be big was not easy. Bartholdi's exasperated mother kept her son abreast of the drawn-out proceedings: "The [most] idiotic opinion, the very stupidest [le plus stupidissuum], is [that of] the Mayor…who would like to scale down the statue by half to lessen the expenditure. One could not imagine an opinion more lacking in all common sense."[2] Stupid the mayor may have been, but he won the game. The statue was made twice life-size because Bartholdi's wealthy mother paid the additional cost. Many aspects of the history of the Statue of Liberty are anticipated here: the role of photography in the promotion of sculpture in advance of its existence; the deployment of photography to overcome the difficulties of transporting colossal statues; the reliance on photography to convey scale; the skeptical audience, incapable of imagining the impact of scale; the difficulty of raising funds without a community's commitment to the cost of colossal size; the stubborn conviction of the Bartholdis, son and mother alike, that immensity mattered so much it was worth their own financial loss.

The problems facing Bartholdi were themselves mammoth. How could he convince audiences of the desirability of colossal size in advance of the completion of a sculpture such as the Statue of Liberty? Few sculptures in our cultural imaginary have had their status as objects so throughly preempted by their status as symbols. As a symbol the Statue of Liberty has all but lost its material and visual character. We need to take the Statue of Liberty apart in order to focus on how Bartholdi staged its coming into being.

Bartholdi's calotype demonstrates the fragility of the photograph in 1854 especially in the hands of a novice. Covering its surface is a vivid scrim formed by applying volatile chemicals to paper: granular dots, puddles of darkness, stains, and seemingly suspended areas of bright white paper. Bartholdi's calotype has a complex, delicate surface, but it threatens to dissolve physical objects into the blur of its emulsion. The three-dimensional comes into focus in fragments, then evaporates into the fog, the thin residue left behind by a liquid process upon a two-dimensional surface. Most sharply delineated are the upper body of the statue with its epaulets and braids, the top of the ladder and scaffolding, places where inert substances offer emphatic, sustained, and familiar alternations of light and darkness.

Most blurred are the living men who had trouble maintaining the absolute stillness required for the two-minute exposure. The professional working-class model, a man named Galali, proves better at holding still than Bartholdi, who turned his head and consequently lost his profile which stutters across the calotype's surface as clouded pools of light. In the mid-1850s the three-dimensionality of the inert better survived translation into the photographic. Intended to sell his statue, this calotype shows viewers that sculpture exceeds the living body; it enjoys a greater duration and a greater material intensity. The outcome is paradoxical. In the medium of photography, sculpture can appear more distinct, more massive, more solid, and more like the world we inhabit than the ghostlike surfaces of breathing men.

Bartholdi's photograph succeeds in conveying Rapp's enormity. Men and little things, jugs and tiny sculptures draw attention to the discrepancy between small and large. The scaffolding and the plunging diagonal of the ladder upon which Galali rests his foot mark out how many measured intervals would have to be crossed to arrive at his thighs. The statue's head threatens to rise above the calotype's upper edge; he seems barely to fit. By contrast Galali appears puny, even vulnerable, in his half-nakedness. How, the calotype proposes, could life-size ever be considered adequate for monumental statuary? What was the mayor of Colmar thinking?

**63**
Frédéric-Auguste Bartholdi, *Statue of General Rapp in situ*, 1865. Albumen print mounted on cardboard. Colmar, Municipal Archives. Photo: Jean-Baptiste Gerst.

**64**
Frédéric-Auguste Bartholdi, *Statue of General Rapp in Bartholdi's Studio, Rue Vavin, Paris*, 1855, Calotype. Colmar, Musée Bartholdi. Photo: Christian Kempf.

**Nothing beside remains.**
**Round the decay**
**Of that colossal wreck,**
**boundless and bare**
**The lone and level sands**
**stretch far away.**
**Percy Bysshe Shelley**
**"Ozymandias," 1818**

Galali's presence in the calotype of the statue of General Rapp may have made Bartholdi overly confident. A year later he took his camera to Egypt, assuming it would help him on his official mission. Bartholdi knew that the camera was quite capable of recording the grandeur and stasis of stone sculpture, but he appears to have been surprised that it did not help him to fix—"to mold"—Egyptian people.[3] Most of Bartholdi's calotypes have no human figures.

One notable exception is an image that is striking yet confusing because of its double exposure (fig. 65). At left is the blankness of sky against which a minaret hangs upside down. At right two men squat on the deck of a boat. Bartholdi has his back to us; a turbaned, faceless assistant turns toward us. The two men are crouched in their efforts to unwrap a mummy whose stripped, darkened torso and head are visible at right against the whiteness of the deck. Again Bartholdi's head has moved and is difficult to decipher; again certain inert substances come into startling focus, for instance the seams of Bartholdi's jacket and the white canvas curtain. The calotype offers another reason Bartholdi was predisposed to imagine the molding of Egyptian persons. Preserved like stone this ancient body was perfectly suited to recording in photographs. The mummy could be molded by photography because the sculptor and his Egyptian assistant had freed its form from the mold that for centuries had prevented its disintegration into dust.

Egyptomania had a dark side in the license it gave for the abduction and confusion of statues and petrified bodies. An immaculate arm torn off a mummy has an uncanny resemblance to Balzac's colossal stone hand depicted in the *Description de l'Égypte* (figs. 66, 23). Vivant Denon's foot of a mummified "princess" mirrors a colossal stone foot also from the *Description* (figs. 67–68).[4] Like many other Frenchmen of the era, Bartholdi seems to have thought about ancient Egyptian colossal sculpture and mummies in relation to one another, though he also contrasted them in important ways.

Scholars believe Bartholdi was responsible for much, if not all, of an 1876 publication entitled *Les Colosses anciens et modernes* (Ancient and Modern Colossi). Although Eugène Lesbazeilles is listed as author, this unabashed celebration of colossal sculpture was devised to

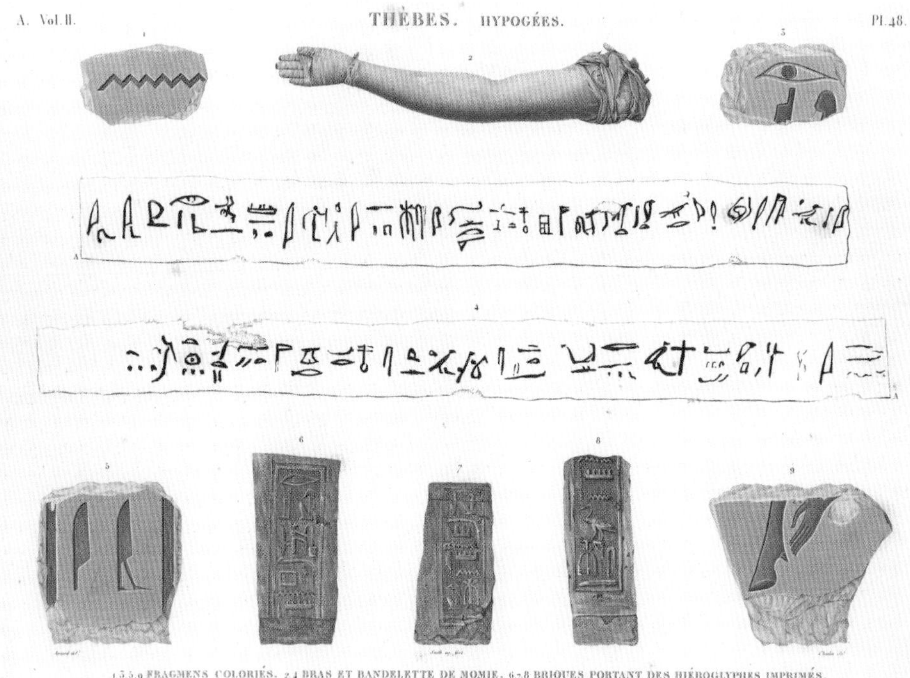
A. Vol. II.
THÈBES. HYPOGÉES.
Pl. 48.
1.3.5.9 FRAGMENS COLORIÉS. 2.4 BRAS ET BANDELETTE DE MOMIE. 6.7.8 BRIQUES PORTANT DES HIÉROGLYPHES IMPRIMÉS.

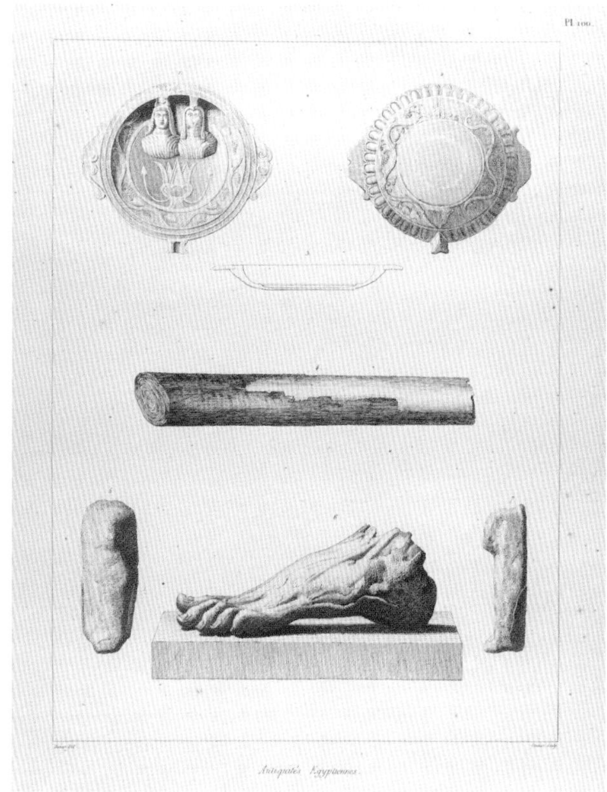
Antiquités Égyptiennes.

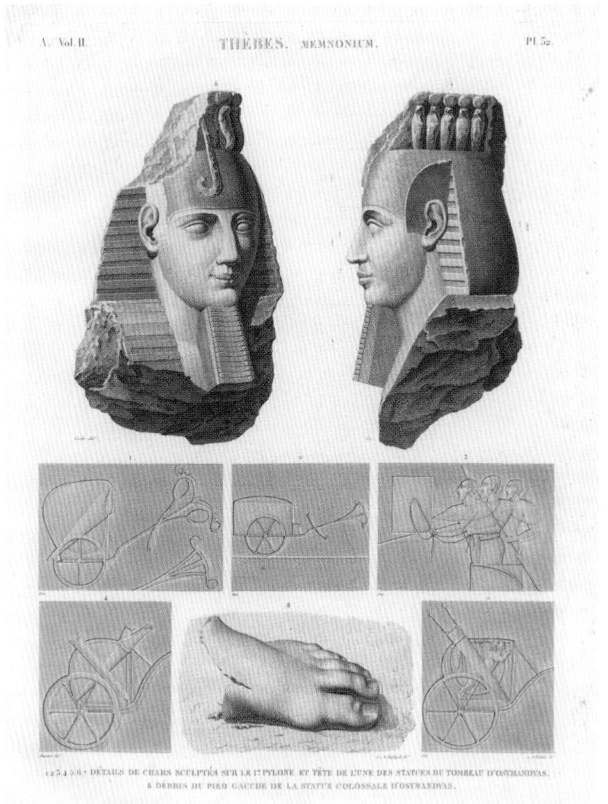
A. Vol. II.
THÈBES. MEMNONIUM.
Pl. 52.

**65**

Frédéric-Auguste Bartholdi, *Unwrapping mummy*, Calotype. Colmar, Musée Bartholdi, 1855–56. Photo: Christian Kempf.

**66**

Thèbes, Hypogées, *La Description de l'Égypte*, Antiquités, vol. II, plate 48, Paris, 1809. Courtesy of the Bancroft Library, University of California, Berkeley.

**67**

Fr. L. Gounod after Vivant Denon, in Vivant Denon, *Voyages dans la Basse et la Haute Égypte, pendant les campagnes de Bonaparte, en 1798 et 1799 Voyage en Egypt*, London, 1807, pl. 100. Stanford University Library, Special Collections.

**68**

Thebes, Memnonium, *La Description de l'Égypte*, Antiquités, Vol. II, plate 32, Paris, 1809. Courtesy of the Bancroft Library, University of California, Berkeley.

**69**

Frédéric-Auguste Bartholdi, *Le Ramesseum*, [1855–56]. Calotype. Colmar, Musée Bartholdi. Photo: Christian Kempf.

promote the Statue of Liberty during its fund-raising campaign; Bartholdi certainly wrote extensive parts of the book.[5] As might be expected, *Les Colosses anciens et modernes* focuses on ancient Egyptian precedent and even reproduces images from the *Description de l'Égypte*. The author concedes that colossi have often been criticized as an "infantile" art of "monstrous" proportions:

> The legitimacy of colossal sculpture has been contested. It has been claimed that these representations of the human form in unnatural proportions were monstrous; one has seen here the naive process of an infantile art that, not having intellectual means at its disposal, such as drawing and expression, to speak to the mind, has recourse to material means that strike the senses—mass, weight, size. Wanting to represent a great man [un grand homme], it has been said, the primitive artisan or the unskilled artist represents a large man [un homme grand].[6]

Yet Egyptian sculpture proves otherwise: "No traveler has been able to see these colossi of granite in Egypt...without experiencing a profound shock. Restore these gigantic figures to the ordinary dimensions of the human body, and you rob them of their terrible solemnity; they will be no more... than insignificant deathlike images, no more than petrified cadavers."[7]

Immensity saves sculpture from the predatory actions of those who dismembered mummies and treated body parts as souvenirs. A nineteenth-century biographer of Gérôme claims that Bartholdi and the older painter saved only the head and foot of one mummy; they threw the rest, like the linen wrapping that had molded it, into the waters of the Nile.[8] The "terrible solemnity" of stone colossi partly resides in their resistance to such outrageous human-scale interventions.

Any human gesture could seem inconsequential in Egypt where time the omnipotent had brought down countless monuments. The Colossi of Memnon were unusual in that they were still standing. Most of the immense statues Bartholdi encountered in Egypt were scattered pell-mell across the rubble. *Les Colosses anciens et modernes* claims that no fewer than seventeen other collapsed colossi surrounded the Colossi of Memnon. Why the author was sure of this remains a question. Fragments of rock are not easy to read. If the Colossi of Memnon had fallen, they would probably have lost their identity; many of their constituent parts are stone blocks. Another case in point is Bartholdi's calotype of the Ramesseum temple not far from the Colossi of Memnon (fig. 69). Unlike his calotype of Memnon with its tight cropping and low horizon, this long view fails to register that the four standing sculptures in the central middle ground are each thirty-two feet tall. Nor is it clear that, at the far right of this calotype, we are looking at fragments of an even more colossal statue of Ramses II rising incoherently from the ground. Bartholdi's photograph renders the stumps all but unintelligible. These parts prompt neither recognition nor, significantly, appreciation of colossal size. Such an image needs the supplement of text: "While exploring the scattered debris, we found the left hand and one of the feet. One would not correctly imagine the enormity of this colossus, if we did not give the exact measurement, with numbers, of its different parts: the ear is more than a meter long [3.28 feet]... The index finger is a meter long, and the nail of the big finger is nineteen centimeters [7.48 inches]."[9] My emphasis for the moment is the sheer force of recognition and comprehension of scale that feet, hands, and other body parts galvanize.

Illustrations to Bartholdi's publication often exploit the dissonance between the familiarity of anatomical fragments and the strangeness of their inordinate size; the sculptor was recycling images from the *Description de l'Égypte* (figs. 70–71). Amid the ancient debris in Egypt's vast spaces, gigantic body parts erupt as fully legible signs. Whereas the fragments at the right of Bartholdi's calotype of the Ramasseum palace fail to compel us because they do not appear to be parts of the human body; they lapse into an inert landscape of broken stone.

When Bartholdi remarked "people do not want to let themselves be molded," and "when they pose, [they] do not pose," he was surely comparing Egyptian subjects to studio models like Galali, whose self-disciplined capacity for stillness was proven in the calotype with which this chapter began.[10] But Bartholdi's calotype of a mummy also demonstrates that there were other ways of turning people into statues in mid-nineteenth-century France (figs. 72–73). It is likely that Bartholdi understood photography as a type of molding because life casts and photography had parallel functions in the process of reproduction often termed indexical. Sitters must stay motionless if photographs and casting are to succeed. And they have variable relations to scale. Indices—such as footprints, bullet holes, and casts—strictly correspond to the dimension of the

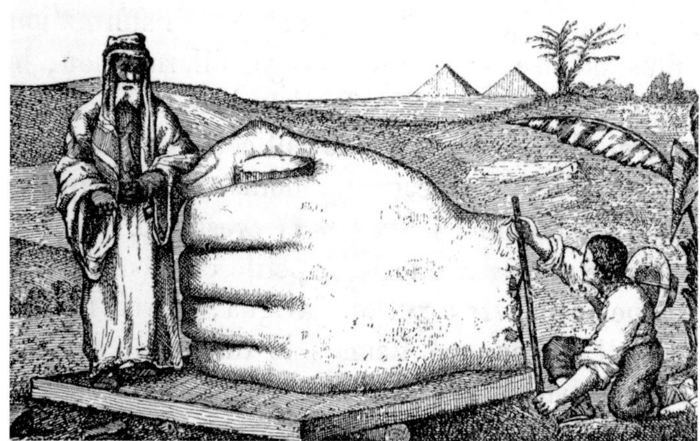

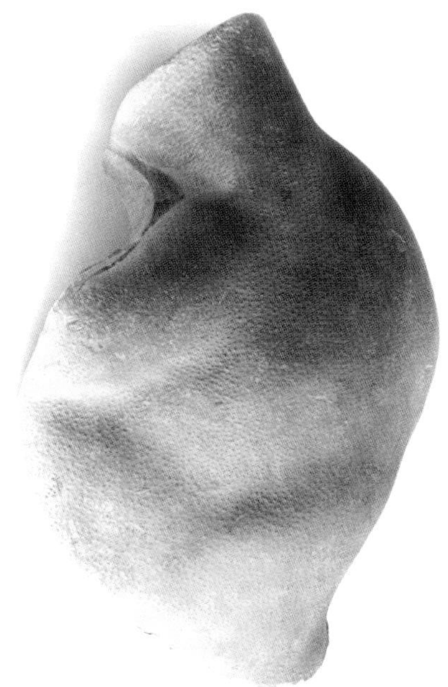

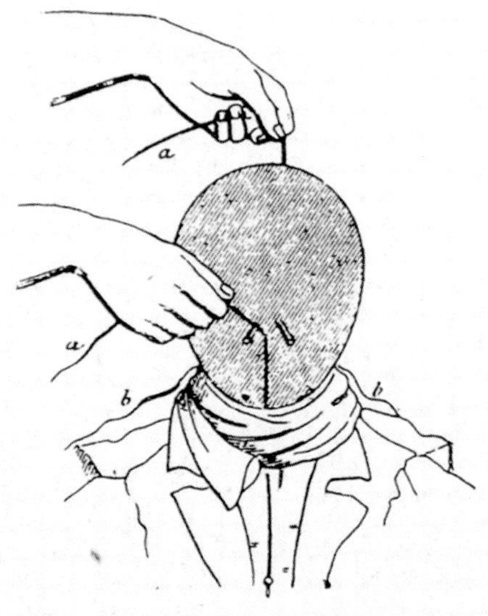

Fig. 24. Moulage de la tête, pose des fils.

object that brought them into being; solids inscribe themselves upon other solids on a one-to-one scale. As indices of the optical, not the material, photographs are different; they can contain and manage the colossal. When C. S. Peirce refers to the ways photographs are "physically forced to correspond point by point to nature," he implies a one-to-one correspondence in size that photography in fact eludes.[11]

But Peirce is accurate if his argument is applied to casts or rubbings which always correspond to their referent's dimensions. Life casts are actual size, but they are and were seldom whole bodies. Instead their power derives from their isolation as fragments and from the disparity between their vivid corporeal specificity and their material inertness, an inertness that their status as abruptly truncated fragments intensified. These are body parts that Georges Didi-Hubermann has aptly characterized as suffocated; the pronounced pores of the flesh register the reaction of living skin to the cold plaster.[12] Molding deprives the body of air or turns ambient air into a solid and hides the body from view. Body casts are not the negative molds, not the gloves, but the "dead" medium poured into them. To make a cast from life, the living body is forced to act like a mummy; it has to be still and hidden from view.[13] We can neither see the body when it is molded, nor can we see into the mold when it is cut off the body and sutured back together as an empty volume. To produce a fully volumetric sculpture, the mold must become a dark unseen space. The cast, that twice-removed substitute, returns the body to sight but is predicated on a condition of blindness.

---

## How Substance Changes with Form

**Villiers de L'Isle-Adam, *Tomorrow's Eve*, 1886**

Bartholdi associated casting with photography, anxious as he was that Egyptians failed to fix themselves.[14] A decade later, when the photograph's exposure time had been reduced to seconds, the fantasy that sitters could become statues photographically—that is, optically, indexically, and mechanically, without mediation—was briefly realized. The late 1860s witnessed a fascination with "photosculpture," a photographic process through which sculpture could be modeled. In his review of the process, Théophile Gautier extolled "the sun sculptor!"[15] The very man who had identified the fellah with the earth ("he is molded by it") was intrigued by human bodies rendered inanimate. Gautier's writings persistently feature men infatuated with statues, life casts, and mummies. Denon's mummified foot of a princess, for instance, inspired Gautier's famous 1857 novel, *Roman de la momie.*[16] This proponent of art for art's sake was also obsessed with external

**70**
"Colossal Hand found at Memphis," Eugène Lesbazeilles [co-author Bartholdi], *Les Colosses anciens et modernes* [Ancient and Modern Colossi]. Paris, 1876, p. 22. Illustrations based on *La Description de l'Égypte*. Photo: Julie Wolf.

**71**
"Fragment of a colossus found at Karnak." Eugène Lesbazeilles [co-author Bartholdi], *Les Colosses anciens et modernes* [Ancient and Modern Colossi], Paris, 1876, p. 30. Illustrations based on *La Description de l'Égypte*. Photo: Julie Wolf.

**72**
Adolphe Victor Geoffroy-Dechaume, *Mold after nature of the left shoulder of a man*, c. 1840. Paris, Musée des monuments français.

**73**
Casting procedure. M. Lebrun et M.D. Magnier, *Manuels Roret. Nouveau manuel complet du mouleur*, 1850. Bibliothèque Forney, Ville de Paris.

**74**
*Photosculpture of the Poet Théophile Gautier*, 1863. Chantilly, Bibliothèque Spoelberch de Lovenjoul. Photo: Pierre Fauré, Chantilly.

**75**
E. Morin, *Willème's Studio*, Wood engraving. From *Le Monde Illustré*, 31 December 1864.

surfaces: "I seek only the exterior…By a kind of instinctive reaction, I am always desperately clinging to material substance, to the external silhouette of things."[17]

The man in love with surfaces and exteriors could not resist the temptation of having himself made into a statue through an optical process (fig. 74).[18] To have his photosculpture produced, Gautier stood on a platform at the center of a rotunda equipped with twenty-four shelves holding photosculptures that hid the lenses of twenty-four cameras (fig. 75). Gautier recounted the process:

> You there take the pose that is the most natural and the most familiar to you; the operator counts ten seconds and asks you to come down. He no longer has need of you. Already you are seized in all of your profiles and perfected by invisible sculptor's assistants. In effect, below the shadow of the consoles shine twenty-four eyes, twenty-four lenses that you have not seen… A marvelous eye surrounds and envelops you. A statue is born from an image or to put it another way, from [twenty-four] images condensed and brought close to one another by an art that seems like magic. Without a template, without a clay model, a mechanical sculptor's assistant has perfected for you with an impeccable exactitude a statue whose original does not exist. In the past, who could have suspected that one could manage to mold a sunbeam?[19]

Each transparent image was subsequently projected and magnified by means of a magic lantern; a pantograph was then used to "disengage [a profile] from the clay." This process was repeated twenty-four times as the clay was rotated fifteen degrees at a time. Each view, in Gautier's words, "brings (forward) its essential line, its characteristic delay; the mass of [carved] clay forms a cavity, grows lighter, takes form; the features of the face stand out, the folds of the clothing are accentuated: the reflected light is transformed into a body."[20]

Bartholdi trusted the term *mouler* to indicate what sitters had to do to become statues and in turn become photographs. Photosculpture adds a sequel. Once persons have become still enough to appear like statues in photographs, the photographs are used to recreate the three-dimensional statues the sitters had become. We witness in photosculpture the return of the repressed third dimension. And photographic projections, unlike casts, also made the resulting sculpture's size entirely flexible.

The ray of light, Gautier explains, is sculpted. The image gives birth, mechanically yet magically, to a body "whose original does not exist." Or, to put it another way, the living model is absent and has not yet been sculpted. There is every reason to assume that photosculpture is the paradigmatic translation of two-dimensional surfaces, or optical effects, into three-dimensional sculpture. But this would be wrong. Photosculpture is a compilation of silhouettes. Its process privileges not surface but line, the edges of things. To describe the process as the compilation of twenty-four contour lines is to describe it graphically. To describe this process in

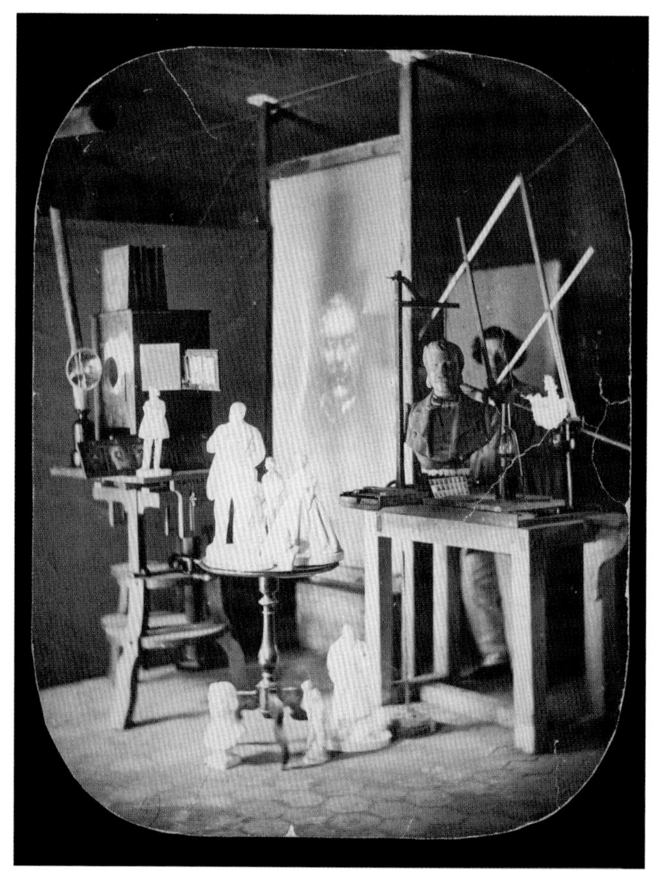

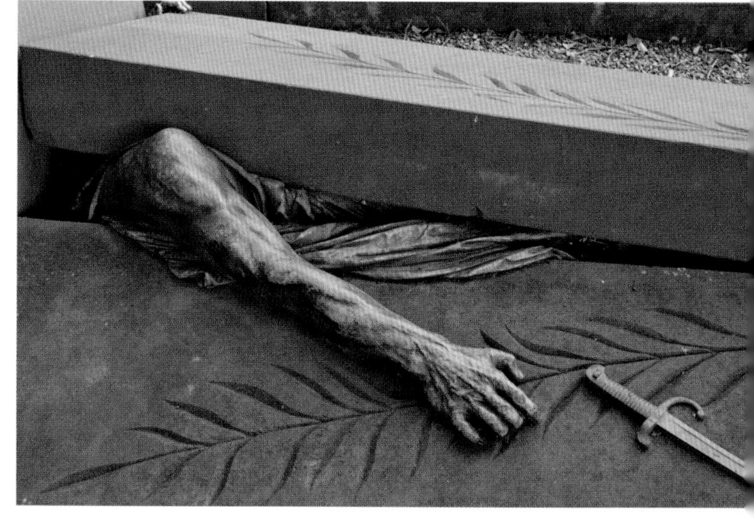

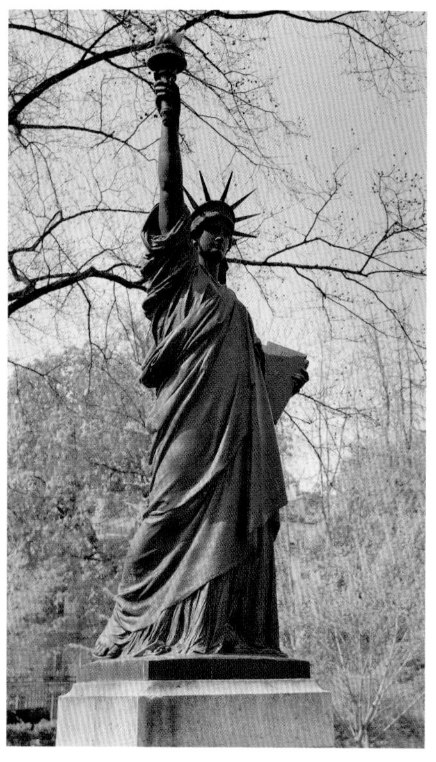

terms of sculpture is to say that the pantograph's operator depends on the photograph to measure extension; each of the twenty-four photographs shows how far the form extends from the very center of a mass at a given fifteen-degree interval.

The photograph was being used in a peculiar way, indeed in a way that is inappropriate to the medium. An engraving and a photograph both document photosculpture's operation, but they offer strikingly different versions of the image projected on the screen crucial to the sculpting process (figs. 76–77). Volumes in photographs are produced optically through the play of light and shadow. Photographs are accordingly unreliable sources of information about contours. Optical understanding of the volume of things is at sharp variance with the way three-dimensional things, sculpture included, are made. In photosculpture trained operators of pantographs were coerced into pretending to a certainty of outline that was seldom provided by photographic projections. Subsequently these technicians were required to approximate the surface extension between each of the twenty-four silhouettes, to fill in the fifteen-degree intervals between the photographs. And finally, and perhaps most problematically, they had to pretend to derive sufficient information from photographs to find form for interior details like eye sockets, nostrils, and the shapes of mouths. In actuality the technicians were sculpting, interpreting, making numerous decisions, and, of course, the pantographic process was generally used to reproduce a three-dimensional model. When such a model existed, the technician could depend on the model's continuous surface to furnish, in Peirce's vocabulary, "a point by point physical correspondence." Photosculpture technicians however were given only photographic projections to map the swelling form. It is to be expected then that photosculptures, objects championed for their indexical truthfulness, appear disturbingly generalized, particularly in the representation of facial features.

Photosculpture was supposed to be an indexical translation of a specific person into a statue. Its premise was that photographs and pantographs together made a product that bypassed the exercises of discrimination required by makers of resemblance such as sculptors and painters. Yet portraiture is particularly subject to the imperatives of resemblance; in Peirce's terms, portraits are paradigmatic examples of the icon. But the dream here was of an indexical production of the iconic. The dream seemed attainable because of the special status of photography as an indexical medium capable of transmitting resemblance. Oddly photographs can be an index and an icon at once. Yet photographs provided decidedly ambiguous and partial information: at fifteen-degree intervals, twenty-four views not of the edges of things but of their appearance under certain lighting conditions. In the photosculpture process, Gautier's "invisible assistants" needed to produce resemblances, and to do so, they had to compensate for the ways indexical signs typically fail to resemble their referent. They had to make three-dimensional icons even as they advertised that they were making three-dimensional indices from two-dimensional ones.

Casts are detailed, isolated fragments, whereas photosculptures are strangely generalized, variably dimensioned, often full-length bodies. When Bartholdi worked on the realization of the Statue of Liberty over a sixteen-year period, he exploited both effects.[21] Many large and small models of the whole statue proliferated in advance of the finished sculpture (as did two-dimensional images) (fig. 78). We can think of this as serial reproduction before production, or as souvenirs not of a past but of a projected future. Bartholdi wanted the statue to be so simple, so memorable, that it seemed already to exist. He capitalized on the fact that serial reproductions generally followed rather than preceded the completion of the original sculpture.[22] He knew that souvenirs and photographs implied a past tense and thereby implied that the statue of Rapp and the Statue of Liberty existed long before they had actually been finished. The art critic Lawrence Alloway notes that "Image-making has to supplement form-giving in public sculptures." Alloway points to the Statue of Liberty as an example of the "legible and learnable" form.[23]

Bartholdi was also conscious of the power of isolated sculptures of body parts. In 1872 he exploited their impact in his Tomb for the National Guard (fig. 79). During the 1870s he frequently used body parts to promote his colossal Statue of Liberty in advance of its completion. A finger more than six and a half feet long was displayed outside a fund-raising diorama (fig. 80). Just as he specified the measurements of the stone body fragments in Egypt, Bartholdi stated the measurements of the finger in order to suggest the enormous scale of the future statue: "the forefinger is 2.45 meters [8 feet] in length, and 1.44 meters [almost 4 feet 8 inches] in circumference."[24] In 1876 the sculptor exhibited the arm holding the torch ("46 meters high [150.9 feet] from

**76**
*Willème's Studio [Photosculpture sculpting process].* Prospectus de la Société Générale de Photosculpture, Paris, 1864. Getty Research Library.

**77**
Willème, *Studio still life with assistant,* 1863-67. Albumen print. Rochester, New York.

**78**
Frédéric-Auguste Bartholdi, *Bronze model for the construction of the Statue of Liberty;* given by Bartholdi to the city of Paris during the Universal Exhibition of 1900. Paris, Jardin du Luxembourg.

**79**
Frédéric-Auguste Bartholdi, *Tomb for the National Guards Voulminot and Linck,* 1872. Cemetery in Colmar. Photo: Christian Kempf.

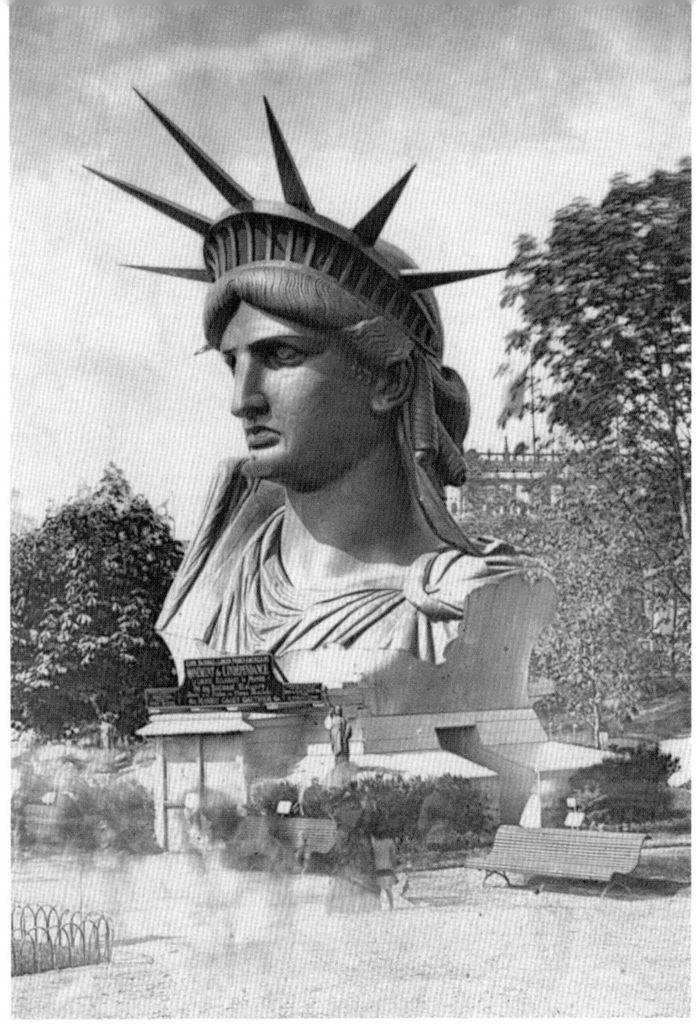

**80**
Photograph. *Finger of the Statue*, 1876–78. Hammered copper. Bibliothèque du Conservatoire National des Arts et Métiers, Paris, Musée des Techniques. Gift of Mme. Bartholdi in 1907.

**81**
Photograph. *The arm and the torch of the Statue of Liberty exhibited in Philadelphia*, 1876. Colmar, Musée Bartholdi. Photo: Christian Kempf.

**82**
Photograph. *The Head at the Exposition of 1878*. Albumen print. Colmar, Musée Bartholdi. Photo: Christian Kempf.

base to torch") at a Universal Exhibition in Philadelphia (fig. 81). Two years later he exhibited the head and the finger at the Universal Exhibition of 1878 in Paris (fig. 82). The transport of the head on a cart to the exhibition grounds was reported and illustrated in the press. At each event Bartholdi sold photographs and miniature sculptural reproductions.

The circulation of body parts thus preceded the finished Statue of Liberty. Unlike the thousands of the small, simple, and quite generalized models of the whole statue circulating in various media since 1870, the fragments of the Statue of Liberty were intended to communicate the projected sculpture's startling, unprecedented colossal scale. In addition Bartholdi knowingly exploited the nonsensical dislocation that had imbued the cast body parts as well as the Egyptian colossal anatomical fragments with some of their startling force. One critic in Paris recalled "the piecemeal exhibition of parts, here a head and there an arm, dropped in public parks and thoroughfares like the traces of some Titanic crime."[25]

The cluttered photographs of the Gaget and Gauthier atelier document the piecemeal construction of the Statue of Liberty (figs. 83–87). Bartholdi thought not like an engineer but a sculptor determined to create the unprecedented. His goal was idiosyncratic: he sought not just to make a colossal sculpture—he had already made his huge, solid stone Lion of Belfort (fig. 88) —but a portable (and affordable) 150-foot-tall colossus. To realize this goal, he conceived of the sculpture as a lightweight, thin outer surface of a volume rather than as a mass. As we have seen, he began with solid clay models, but he planned to enlarge the model not as a thing, but as a surface. The statue's very form was therefore no more than a patchwork compilation of sections of its molded copper surface hanging from Gustave Eiffel's metal armature.

The sculpture was fabricated through a series of magnifications of solid plaster models that Bartholdi designed.[26] The first was a little over three feet tall, the second almost ten feet tall, and the last reached about thirty-six feet tall. Each magnification entailed the traditional, laborious gridding of measurements, or points, which mapped the complex, swelling, irregular shape. It was a system that depended on geometry but remained three-dimensional, tactile, and physical. Objects became bigger objects. No calculation other than multiplication was demanded.

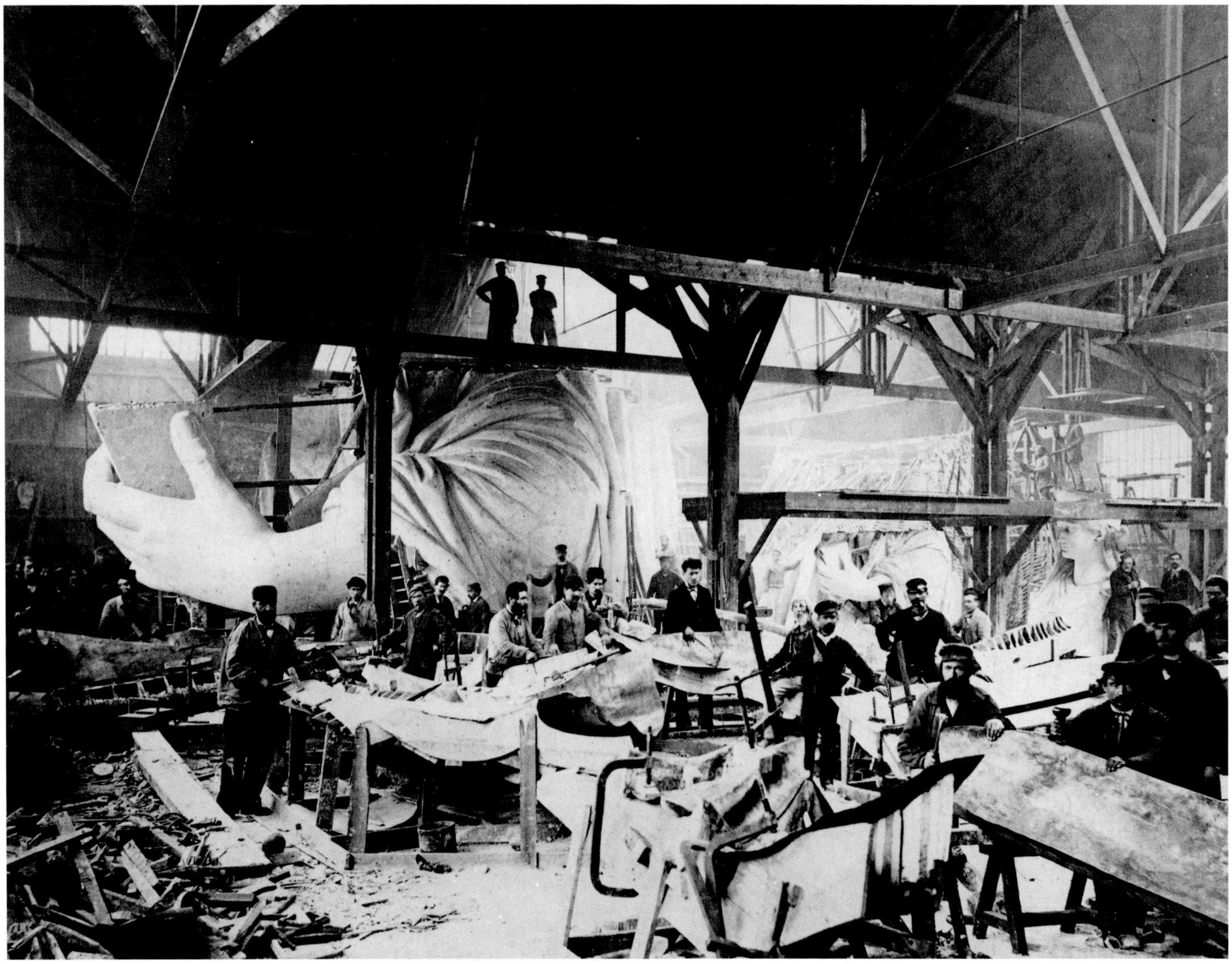

**83**
Photograph. *Hammering the Drapery*, 1881–84. Albumen print. Printed by P. Petit. Colmar, Musée Bartholdi. Photo: Christian Kempf.

**84**
Photograph. *The Plaster Arm and Hand*, 1881–84. Albumen print. Colmar, Musée Bartholdi. Photo: Christian Kempf.

**85**
Photograph. *Hammering: Mold Making*, 1881–84. Albumen print. Printed by P. Petit. Colmar, Musée Bartholdi. Photo: Christian Kempf.

**86**
Photograph. *Construction of the Drapery and the Hand*, 1881–84. Albumen print. Printed by P. Petit. Colmar, Musée Bartholdi. Photo: Christian Kempf.

**87**
Photograph. *Construction of the Head of "Liberty,"* 3 January, 1878. Colmar, Musée Bartholdi. Photo: Christian Kempf.

**88**
Frédéric-Auguste Bartholdi, *The Lion of Belfort*, 1880.
Photo: Christian Kempf.

**89**
Photograph. *The Plaster Arm and Hand of the Statue of Liberty in the Gaget and Gauthier Workshop, Paris*, 1878–84.
Albumen print. Colmar, Musée Bartholdi.
Photo: Christian Kempf.

Carpenters built the boxlike frame, and men proceeded to measure. If the distance from tip of head to elbow was a given measure, this needed to be multiplied so many times. The biggest thirty-six-foot model was then divided into fragments that were enlarged about four times to create the 150-foot-high final work.[27] Afterwards carpenters constructed broadly accurate, hollow wood enlargements of each section, which plasterers covered and refined by precisely matching a series of measured points (fig. 89). The foundry's report emphasized the workers' physical enactment of geometry: "One makes thereby the definitive form by the principles of geometry in space by locating a considerable number of points determining the lines and surfaces. On the contours thus established, marked by the heads of nails more or less driven into the plaster, the artist finished the work…by bringing into line and making flush all the marks, as is done with the *mise au point* of sculpture."[28]

Point after point, swelling planes were thereby defined. Each section required some 9,000 measurements. Once the immense plastered section was completed, carpenters returned to build a wooden mold resembling a grid that corresponded at every point to the plaster. Thus an inverse of the entire statue, a mold or template, was constructed out of wood. Gaget and Gauthier rightly attempted to reveal how laborious and impressive this process was: "Layer by layer, one has, one could say, sculpted in wood the statue itself in all its parts, and if, by some means, one could have reunited these pieces by placing them in their respective positions, one would have in the interior the spectacle of a statue sculpted negatively like a mold, a gigantic mold representing thousands of pieces of wood sawed, cut, tried, sized and hammered…adjusted, nailed without an appreciable mistake, without an error."[29]

The crowded photographs of the sculpture's construction indicate that the hollowing out of Bartholdi's solid plaster models necessitated the appearance and disappearance of vast amounts of different kinds of material: wood, nails, cords, rulers, wires, weights, plaster, trowels, wood and nails again, copper, hammers, chisels. The process of hollowing also required the impressive expertise of numerous artisans who specialized not in excavation but in specific kinds of construction. However"hollowing" is an inaccurate word here. Only Bartholdi's small demonstration models were solid plasters. As soon as the process of amplification and magnification began, the engineer and the laborer dispensed with solidity. To make skins, all they needed was an outer surface upon which to hammer. The final-size wooden frames, which were subsequently plastered, did not need to be solid. For practical reasons magnification, in this procedure, leads automatically to hollowness.

Spread across the crowded spaces of Gaget and Gauthier's atelier lie parts of different sizes and in various stages of work. Repeated enlargement of the original three-foot model ultimately divided the whole into parts, colossal fragments rising to the very roof of the place. One photograph includes no less than three such enlarged plaster models across its middle ground: beginning at far right, a head; at center a relatively small model of the arm holding the tablet; and at left the colossal full-scale plaster model of the arm (see fig. 83).

To build a colossal sculpture as a skin is a strange thing to do. It is to conceive of one's job as making a provisional colossal sculpture in fragments in order to mold those parts. But here the wrapping or molding is not, as in mummies, a matter of enclosing form with a pliant surface like cloth. Nor is it like the making of bronze sculptures wherein solid wax forms permit the making of a bronze cast whose empty interior always remains hidden from view.[29] Instead the provisional colossal model of wood and plaster was molded by equally temporary wooden grids in order that the sculpture's copper skin could be hammered from the inside against its outer limit. The final sculpture was being hammered from its interior, negatively. Workers were making the giant woman as if they were inside her.

The final sculpture was hammered onto molds. It was therefore a molded statue, but it was never a whole cast (like many bronze statues). Rather its wholeness derived from the slow aggregation of arbitrary portions of its surface, so many unique jigsaw pieces. In striking contrast to the photograph of Rapp, the photographs of the building of the Statue of Liberty linger on the illegibility of the elaborate process of the sculpture's making. In these photographs of the late 1870s, as opposed to the earlier calotype, the living men have come into prominence, but the sculpture itself has been dispersed and refracted into parts, doubles, and endless debris. Translation of small into colossal entailed many translations from positive to negative to positive forms and many different kinds of material turned into form and then destroyed. Here were enacted both construction and destruction. Optical discrimination shifted to tactile making.

If Liberty is a symbol, a collective sign, the initial full-length models were icons, that is, resemblances.[30] Their magnification entailed a series of multiplied measurements, but the sculptor also made adjustments to maintain the resemblance of each reproduction to its original model. Bartholdi was still sculpting on the basis of looking. Yet once the statue was blown up to its final colossal size, the process of its fabrication necessarily became not only a matter of delegated labor but also of indexical reproduction. Peirce usefully, if ambiguously, characterizes indexical signs as bearing "no significant resemblance to their objects," as referring to "single units," and as "direct[ing] attention to their objects by blind compulsion." Peirce's last attribute, "blind compulsion," is elusive yet suggestive in this context. The construction of the colossal disallows a dependence on sight to gauge resemblance.

At the Gaget and Gauthier atelier the men working on the colossus could not adopt the methods that the photosculpture technicians used for small or life-size figures. And even if they had entertained the idea of implementing visual discriminations, the atelier space was too small to gain sufficient distance to see the statue as a whole. Photographs of the giant inserted into an interior of human scale recall scenes from *Alice in Wonderland*. More fundamentally once a sculpture was blown up so very large, the distortions inherent to vision could no longer be ignored: look at the Statue of Liberty as one might actually see it up close (fig. 90). Colossal scale magnifies our awareness of the distortions intrinsic to sight, the way we see things from below or above, from the front or the side or the back, eclipsed and overlapped, foreshortened and compressed. All these distortions of seeing are exaggerated so acutely in colossal sculpture that even a nineteenth-century champion of photosculpture, Gautier himself, could not sustain the fiction that the optical seamlessly and mechanically produces the three-dimensional.

Instead fabricating the Statue of Liberty meant accepting a condition of blindness; hammering metal onto wooden molds was to accept that the mold, not the maker, necessarily dictated form. The workmen's job was to hammer one thing against another thing, not to judge or adjust it. Here was a sculptural process involving a real reliance on indexicality, but contrary to photosculpture, this indexicality was haptic, not optic; it was as well a collective act of delegated

**90**
Photograph. *View of the Statue of Liberty as seen from below*, 2004. Photo: author.

**91**
Frédéric-Auguste Bartholdi, *Guards, Old Cairo*, Calotype, 1855–56. Colmar, Musée Bartholdi. Photo: Christian Kempf.

**92**
Photograph. *The Statue of Liberty under construction*, 1881–84. Albumen print. Colmar, Musée Bartholdi. Photo: Christian Kempf.

labor. Workmen hammered copper onto wooden molds that they trusted to correspond exactly to the plaster colossus fashioned from a series of enlarged models. They worked blindly, especially when no figural cues could be ascertained. They produced shaped pieces of metal surface which drift away from reference. Most of the Statue of Liberty's sections are beautifully abstract; a landscape of folds that, part by part, seem all but arbitrary. Yet the sections needed to coalesce into figuration, into the icon that functions as the symbol. The process entailed moving figuration to abstraction and back again.

In several photographs of the Gaget and Gauthier atelier, body fragments appear amid the undulating, swelling copper sheets. In some cases careful scrutiny is required to discern them. In one photograph a finger lies on a table in the center middle ground (see fig. 85). In another the largest sheet of folds is so riveting in its complexity that it diverts attention from the overexposed sheet at right that represents four fingers clasping the edge of the tablet (see fig. 86). On the floor, between the two suspended sheets, is a bent finger, knuckle prominent, with workmen at either side. A photograph like this one resembles less Bartholdi's calotype of the Colossi of Memnon, a sufficiently distant view of colossi set in a landscape, than another calotype that Bartholdi took in Egypt in 1855 (fig. 91). This early photograph does what calotypes can do so well; it dwells on surfaces, most strikingly mounds of cloth from which emerge, front center, suddenly recognizable, two bare feet. If the blanket molds the human bodies that much like mummies, come into photographic visibility, the feet reveal what we are seeing. They reveal what shapes the drapery's form, that it enshrouds men—night guards, sleeping outdoors in the full light of day. At right lies more drapery. Did a man put it on the ground before walking away, out of the picture? It forms a miniature landscape barely recognizable as the surface residue of a human gesture. This drapery could not be read as an index of human withdrawal without those feet.

In the photographs of the Gaget and Gauther atelier when work on the Statue of Liberty was underway, the colossal body parts appear small, distinct, and identifiable when compared to the expanses of drapery. The body parts encourage visual discrimination: this thing looks like a finger; it looks stubby or long or elegant. Seen alongside the workmen, the body fragments function as both intelligible signs and units of measure. Fingers, hands, arms, and head signal that a statue of the human body somehow grown colossal is being assembled. And the fragments, unlike the undulating sheets of copper, forecast the size of the statue once finished. Bartholdi knew that the sight of body parts in and of themselves could generate mental images of towering figures. Littered with fragments, Egypt's landscape had taught him that lesson about the human imagination.

ÉCHET
AUX

Commissioned by Bartholdi, presented as gifts to dignitaries, the photographs of the Gaget and Gauthier atelier were intended to record and publicize the arduous labor and technical expertise that went into building the Statue of Liberty.[31] They also were meant to enhance the surprise of recognition when, suddenly, later, contiguous fragments locked into place, now intelligible as components of a colossus—and when, just as surprising, hovering surfaces adhered to the viewer's preconceived schematic sense of the statue's final form. This drama of work and delayed legibility is utterly at odds with the staging of photosculpture. Photosculpture was shown to erase as if by magic its means of production—twenty-four hidden cameras, the statue's almost overnight completion, the hidden magic lanterns and pantographs, the invisible technicians. Bartholdi went in the opposite direction. The photographs maximize our awareness of the man-hours expended on the colossus, while simultaneously intensifying our wonder at its final coalescence as a figure (fig. 92). Completing the statue demanded both a slow accretion over time—the statue rising piece by piece over the suburbs of Paris—and a staccato production of the parts of the figure: voilà the foot, the knee, the hand, the neck, the head, the arm, the torch.

The arm and torch were finished first, the head next, the feet later. The Statue of Liberty's parts resembled the ruins of Egypt in being scrambled. Bartholdi, always in the midst of fund-raising, found it advantageous to talk up the record-breaking size that the Statue of Liberty would one day assume and, in virtually the same breath, to manipulate the suspense that its incompleteness could create. Herein lay the tactical usefulness of the fragments of the Statue of Liberty strewn across the world: they were meant to elicit a desire to experience the heretofore unknowable, the statue so immense it could not be apprehended as a whole, a statue that verged, in Kant's terms, on the "monstrous."[32] If Egypt's fragmented monuments summon a distant past, the body parts of the Statue of Liberty functioned as glimpses of a future. Bartholdi exploited photography to heighten anticipation of the revelation of something never before seen.

---

**Such a work is really too good to have an "interior"; but, as it has one, we must do as the tourists do.** ***The Morning News*, Paris, 11 May 1884**

Fragmentation was required to transport the colossal statue across great distances. Bartholdi's calotype of Rapp had magically transformed colossal mass into a photographic surface and thereby made it seem easily transportable. The Statue of Liberty might be described as a material analogue to this process, the radical redefinition of mass as thin surface. But in the case of the Statue of Liberty, the copper surfaces, so different from photographic images, were indices that corresponded, like rubbings, one-to-one to the colossal, finished sculpture: they were true size and therefore immense. For this reason only small sections could be boxed and transported from Paris to New York City in order to be rebuilt.

Bartholdi was exercising control over vast spaces and size, but he was also demonstrating a mastery over time. Ancient Egypt's erosion into scattered ruins is, in its modern manifestation, made reversible. The Statue of Liberty was brought up, brought down, and brought up again. During that process, feet and hands and a head rested on the ground (fig. 93). The spectacle of the Statue of Liberty hinged as well on its hollowness, its cavernous emptiness. The sculpture, composed of copper sheets less than an inch thick, was really a mold that could have been filled and made solid if not for its scale. To see either a sculpture or its mold from the inside was an unprecedented experience, necessitating both colossal scale and emptiness to permit the viewer's movement within. As life casts make clear, assembled molds were usually the negative volumes of darkness, unknown to sight, at least in their wholeness. The Statue of Liberty offered the transgressive invitation of entry into the mold; in a number of images, we are invited into her foot (fig. 94). Bartholdi noted that "about forty persons were accommodated in the head at the Universal Exposition of 1878" (fig. 95).[33]

Some colossal sculptures of antiquity had been hollow: the Colossus of Rhodes consisted of thin metal plates attached to iron tie bars, although it was filled with stone blocks. Quatremère de Quincy's (incorrect) reconstruction of Phidias's Athena at the Parthenon dramatizes the hollowness of the almost forty-foot-high statue, destroyed early on presumably to plunder the ivory and gold from which it had been made.[34] In a diagram worthy of Giorgio de Chirico, Quatremère de Quincy presents a startling sight: a gold-plated, impenetrable, and idealized woman and an abstract wooden structure seen in cross section (fig. 96). Even in this image, knowledge of Athena's interior was not imagined to have been available to the spectator at the Parthenon.

The "cut away view" seems illicit, even compromising. The Statue of Liberty is different—it never harbored inner mystery. Bartholdi invited visitors to explore his colossus as if it were a building. And indeed the lighthouse with a circular staircase from the Universal Exposition influenced its design as surely as did the statuary of ancient Greece.[35] From the beginning access to the interior of the statue was essential to its construction and to its strangeness. For those enamored of surfaces, entry into the empty interior was disconcerting. What Bartholdi's contemporaries imagined hovering inside the Statue of Liberty varied, but its hollowness gripped their imaginations.

Thomas Alva Edison, the American inventor, immediately appropriated Bartholdi's statue to house his brand new invention, the disturbingly mechanical, non-anthropomorphic phonograph.[36] In 1878 the *Scientific American* reported: "He says that he can in time make the machine talk so loudly that it can be used on vessels to warn off other ships during fogs, and his last astonishing proposal is that he shall construct a huge phonograph to go in the great bronze *statue of Liberty* which is to be erected in New York harbor, so that the metal giant can make a speech audible over the entire bay."[37]

In an article ten days earlier, Edison had already claimed that his "aerophone" would amplify at great distances: "This thing will utter words which can be distinctly heard four miles away" and could thereby serve "in lighthouses on stormy coasts."[38] In 1878—the year Liberty's head was displayed, along with the newly invented phonograph, at the Universal Exhibition in Paris—the *Daily Graphic* also featured a cartoon on its cover (fig. 97). The image repeats Edison's boast, "I can make that statue speak so that it can be heard ten miles!" In the cartoon, the Statue of Liberty announces, in advance of its actual completion, "Welcome to our shores." Thus, if Edison got his way, the colossal statue's void would be filled not only with light emanating from its diadem but also with sound projected from its lips.

Invisible energies were beginning to circulate inside the statue. The Statue of Liberty was functioning as a human body in which new technologies, electric light and phonographic sound, could both be anchored and symbolically amplified.[39] The impulse to link phonograph and statue derived from the mechanical character of Edison's invention (fig. 98). "Here is really nothing but a revolving cylinder covered with a sheet of tinfoil, and a speaking tube; no levers, no springs, no keyboards, no artificial lips or larynx, no bellows."[40] No lips, no larynx. Bartholdi's statue could compensate for the disturbing self-sufficiency of the cylinder by linking sound to human volition and voice. But the conjoining of a mechanically generated human voice and a giant, inert receptacle masquerading as a woman was no less strange. In 1878 Edison patented his own anthropomorphic container for his phonograph, a speaking doll with cast limbs and a hollow torso (fig. 99). Edison's doll was a financial failure because of his inattention to dimension; the dolls were far too heavy and large for children to play with them.[41]

**93**
Photograph. *Toes and Torch of the Statue near the Parapets*, 1885–86. Photograph. Library of Congress, Washington, D.C.

**94**
Frédéric-Auguste Bartholdi, *Entrance to the Statue through the Foot*, 1881–84. Glass positive, gelatin-silver process. Paris, Bibliothèque du Conservatoire National des Arts et Métiers.

**95**
Muller SC, *Inside the Head of the Statue of Liberty*, from *Le Monde Illustré*, 21 September 1878. Collection Debuisson, Paris. Photo: Julie Wolf.

**96**
Minerva du Parthénon, in (Antoine-Chrysostome) Quatremère de Quincy, *Monuments et ouvrages d'art antiques, restitués d'après les descriptions des écrivains Grecs et Latins, et accompagnés de dissertations archéologiques, 1755-1849*, Paris, 1829, I, plate II. Photo: Julie Wolf.

**97**
Weldon, detail of "The Awful Possibilities of the New Speaking Phonograph," Cover illustration to *The Daily Graphic. An Illustrated Evening Newspaper*, New York, 21 March 1878. The caption to this detail reads "Liberty saluting the World. 'I can make that statue speak so that it can be heard ten miles!' Edison." Photo: Julie Wolf.

**98**
Thomas Edison, *Original Drawing, First Sketch of the Phonograph*, 12 August 1877. Reproduced in *The Life and Inventions of Thomas Alva Edison*, New York, 1894, p. 123. Photo: Julie Wolf.

**99**
Thomas Edison, *Talking Doll*, 1890. U.S. Department of the Interior, National Park Service, Edison National Historic Site.

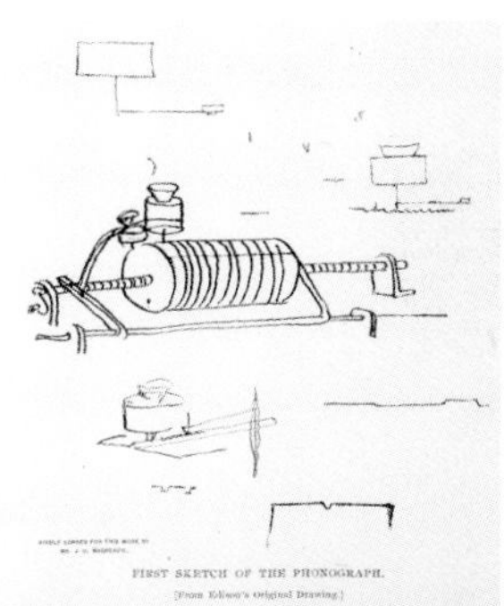

**Ask any good Frenchman who reads his paper every day...what he means by progress, he will respond that it is steam, electricity and gas lighting, miracles unknown to the Romans.... The poor man has been so Americanized...that he has quite lost sight of the differences that characterize the phenomena of the physical and moral world, the natural and the supernatural.** **Baudelaire on the 1855 Exhibition, 1855**

In the 1870s the French novelist Villiers de L'Isle-Adam, a great admirer and close friend of Gautier, contributed money to the subscription for the Statue of Liberty. In 1878 the theater debuting his play *Le nouveau monde* displayed a thirty-two-foot-high Statue of Liberty with an oxyhydric torch projecting light.[42] The reproduction was provided by Bartholdi's Franco-American Committee. Remember that 1878 was the year the Universal Exhibition in Paris featured Liberty's head and Edison's phonograph. It was also the year Edison imagined the Statue of Liberty speaking and that Villiers began writing his greatest novel, *L'Eve future*, known in English translation as *Tomorrow's Eve*. Versions of the novel appeared serially in the press more than once between 1880 and 1886, but the book was not published until 1886 after the colossal Statue of Liberty had finally been erected in the United States.[43]

Written while Bartholdi's statue was under construction, *L'Eve future* opens with the haunting image of a woman's arm lying alone on a purple silk cushion in the home of none other than Thomas Alva Edison (see fig. 100 for a life cast that evokes that strangeness). Throughout the novel Villiers identifies Edison as the American "engineer." This mysterious arm, blood clotted at its shoulder, suggesting villainy, immediately raises a question about Edison's character. The suspense is heightened on the following page with an anecdote:

Some years ago, according to the American newspapers, Edison had found the secret of stopping short, without the least inconvenience, two trains headed toward one another on a collision course under a full head of steam.

One fine moonlit night, the switchmen therefore set two trains packed with passengers on the same line, heading for one another at thirty leagues per hour. But the engineers lost their nerve at the last minute, in the face of imminent danger, and went quite counter to the instructions of Edison who was standing on a nearby hillside to watch the experiment and chewing on a cigar.

The two trains collided with a terrible crash. Within an instant, several hundred victims were scattered across the landscape, helter-skelter and in every direction. People were crushed, burned, and ground to bits, men, women and children, both the engineers and the firemen, of whom it wasn't possible to discover even a trace.

The great experimenter murmured simply, —Clumsy idiots!...Any visitor who remembered such experiments from the past—experiments many times renewed—might have had reason to suspect a similar trial in pursuit of some new form of knowledge, at the sight of this radiant arm so rudely torn from its socket.[44]

In Villier's novel Edison ruthlessly, knowingly risks lives; he interprets human bodies strewn across the landscape as merely a failure on the part of the train engineers. Train accidents were a constant threat throughout the nineteenth century, dominating the press and preoccupying the public. A drawing entitled "The Engineer E. making the test of an inexplosable [*sic*] locomotive of his invention, February 3, 1856" is telling evidence of those fears (fig. 101). In this case the "Engineer E.," who nonchalantly hops over the tragic explosion below his feet, is Gustave Eiffel, not Edison.

The arm in *L'Eve future* proves not to be the residue of a ghoulish experiment; the inert arm's remarkably lifelike skin derives neither from mummification nor from life casting but from various technologies that include a "photochromic" process. The detail, linked to a technology that may or may not exist, is typical of Villiers. His novel gives a painstaking technical account of the fabrication of a hollow, metal figure that simulates the appearance of a woman whose beauty is explicitly likened to a classical statue. Resembling stone, inspiring metal reproduction, this living woman knew how to mold herself, à la Bartholdi. But her metallic reproduction was done without her knowledge.

Even as she posed for what she believed would be a traditional sculpture, the invisible processes of photosculpture worked their wizardry. Terra-cotta, that earth out of which Bartholdi modeled the fellah woman, was used to deceive her: "a dozen sittings, in the presence of a terra-cotta model...will disarm her suspicions."[45] Later the insertion of a phonograph made the metal sculpture speak; electricity and mechanics made it move. Life-size, not colossal, this metal woman was fabricated as a photosculpture, but her stunning mimetic appearance approaches

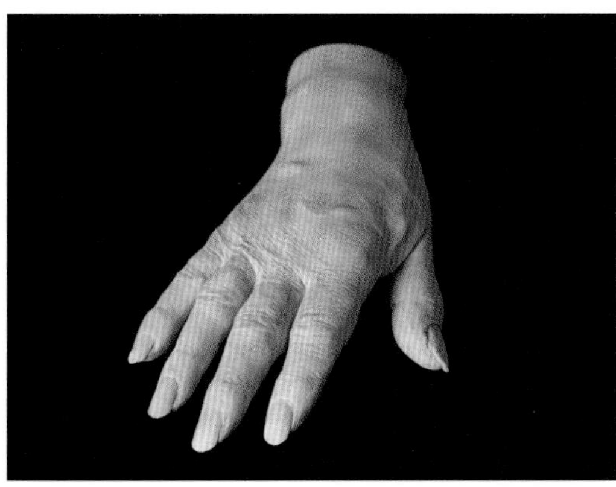

**100**
Girolami, *Mold from nature of the right hand of Victor Hugo*, 1877. Paris, Musée Carnavalet.

**101**
Chanmoit?, *The Engineer E. attempting to make an inexplosive locomotive of his design, February 3, 1856* ("L'ingénieur E. faisant l'essai d'une locomotive inexplosible de son invention, 3 février 1856 ). Crayon and pastel. Paris, Musée d'Orsay, fonds Eiffel.

the life-cast. Indeed casting was deployed. After the real woman is made "quite unconscious," Edison "takes an exact print of her teeth, as well as of her tongue." Villiers' metal woman was a mimetic double, a deceptive and disturbing and erotic object.[46] "I will also record on the Cylinder of Gestures that magnificent toss of the hair that you mentioned as typical of your beloved."[47]

Villiers' Eve helps us appreciate the extent to which Bartholdi relied on colossal scale to chasten his metal woman. She replaces the optical and overwhelming impact of Bartholdi's statue with the uncanniness of an animated life cast. Villiers' novel ultimately condemns nineteenth-century materialism as sterile. At the novel's end a soul comes to inhabit the interior of the metal sculpture without Edison's knowledge. Villiers foregrounds the immateriality of the spirit, yet he also celebrates the immateriality of late nineteenth-century technology. He reveled in the fact that invisible rays of light, waves of sound, and currents of electricity leave traces and (magically) inscribe matter.

But those traces could not be mistaken for life. When the lover Lord Ewald first sees the android's interior he is sickened: "The outer integument slowly drew open. Lord Ewald shuddered and grew very pale. Until that point doubts had still lingered in his mind. In spite of everything his learned guide had said, he had found it impossible to admit that the Being which had given him up to now the illusion of a living woman enclosed in a suit of armor was in fact a fictive being created by Science, patience, and genius."[48] Significantly it is the hollow interior filled with mechanical devices that proves the lifelessness of the metal woman; the mimetic exterior is a successful illusion.

That void at the statue's center is the terrifying proof of her status as machine. Villiers wraps that void or "original emptiness" or "fundamental nothingness" with multiple "concentric envelopes," to cite Jacques Noiray, "the metallic armor first,...around the armor, the complexion, skin, and clothing...; then a symbolic case, a heavy casket, and a vast square crate."[49] Noiray observes as well that these envelopes partly dissimulate and protect her empty interior, but they also invite desire.

Villiers' metal Eve is boxed and transported in a ship's hold when she accompanies her aristocratic lover to England. This is how the Statue of Liberty was transported to the United States; but Bartholdi's sculpture was disassembled into over two hundred fragments boxed in their numbered crates. By contrast Villiers' metal woman travels below deck in a coffin evocative of Egyptian ritual. Eve had always resembled a mummy; she returned nightly to her elaborate coffin, which was, Villiers makes explicit, "a modern improvement on an Egyptian coffin, suitable for the burial of a Cleopatra."[50] Predictably a shipwreck leads to Eve's demise just as it doomed Virginie and so many other French literary heroines.[51] But the loss of Eve, unlike the loss of her many virtuous tragic counterparts, is caused by her inertness. The statue descends to the bottom of the sea because no one thinks to rescue the nonliving. Villiers' novel makes tragic the limitations of science's mimicry of the human.

Time and again Villiers betrays his own intentions. His obsessive account of the android's creation lingers over each and every detail; he writes as an inventor, a fine craftsman, and a connoisseur. He writes too as a maker of the finished product that none of the specialists he employs could predict; those makers of wigs, false teeth, and glass eyes did not know what the figure would finally become. And he writes as an Edison or as a Bartholdi overseeing the material production of never before experienced things. The Statue of Liberty attracted the Symbolist Villiers, not as a Peircean symbol, nor as a hackneyed personification of Liberty. To this critic of his century's materialism, the Statue of Liberty was a strange and marvelous, mimetic and immobile made thing.

One of the French visitors to the Universal Exhibition of 1889 was the wheelchair-bound Villiers de L'Isle-Adam.[52] His friends had hoped Edison would meet the author; they had sent him a copy of *L'Eve future* in advance. Their correspondence exudes the excitement with which they approached the meeting. At the end of June Villiers reminded his loyal friend Stéphane Mallarmé, "Dear friend, do not forget the Edison business: that would be very felicitous."[53] Mallarmé responded that a mutual friend had "something in mind for Edison and is going to tell you [about] it."[54] Villiers died of cancer on 18 August having named Mallarmé and Joris-Karl Huysmans his literary executors. On 7 September 1889, a week before the *Scientific American* article praising Edison, Paul Verlaine wrote a letter to a friend:

**102**

Maurice Koechlin, "Pylon of 300 meters in height for the city of Paris, 1889. Advanced project of M. E. Nougueir and M. Koechlin," June 1884. Blueprint and pencil on paper. Photo: Zurich, ETH-Bibliothek.

**103**

Photograph. *View of the Face of the Statue of Liberty Hung in Wooden Frame*, 1885–86. Collection of Andrew J. Spano.

**104**

Photograph. *Interior View of the Face Hung in Wooden Frame*, 1885–86. Collection of Andrew J. Spano.

**105**

"New York. Preparing the Statue of 'Liberty' on Bedloe's Island for the Formal Unvailing [sic] on October 28. The Present State of the Work," Frank Leslie's *Illustrated Newspaper*, 9 October 1886, p. 120; also published as cover to *L'Illustration* 23 October 1886. Washington, D.C., Library of Congress.

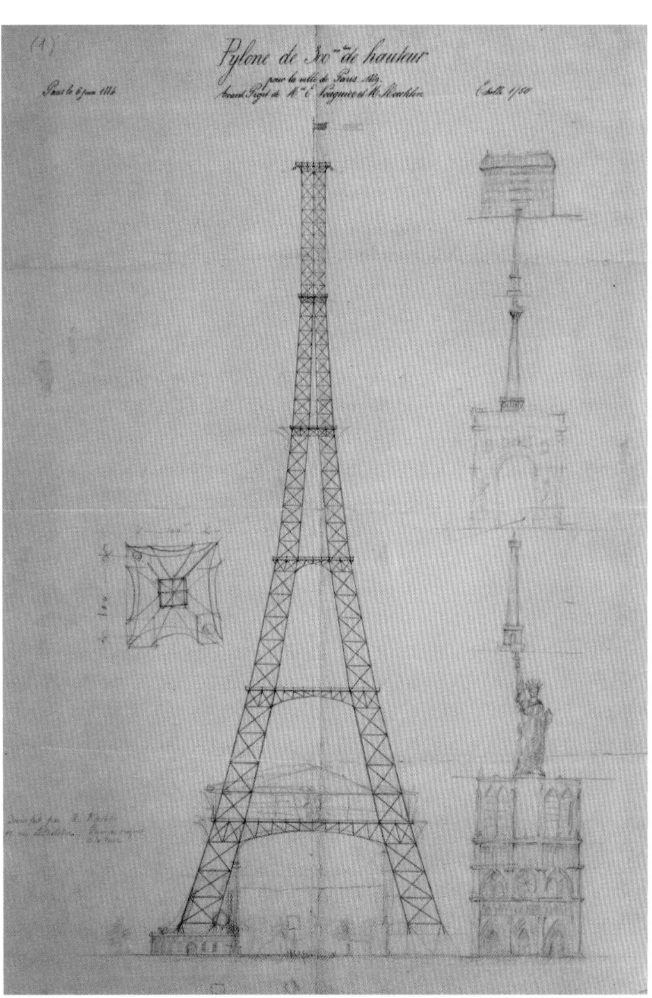

Have you noticed that Edison was in Paris at the time of Villier's death? This Edison who is perhaps intelligent, as they say, and doubtlessly a brute of an engineer. Does he know that L'Eve future has him as a hero and that this hero is a marvel of symbolism, modern science ending in an enormous catastrophe: the literal death of a soul,...[and] the ruin of the machine invented by him (small pity). The novel ends with the moral annihilation of the fictitious Edison.[55]

Had Edison read Villiers' novel in 1889? Did he ever read it? All we know is that he donated twenty-five dollars in 1910 to the Villiers de L'Isle-Adam "committee" in Paris for a commemorative statue.[56] Despite Villiers' ambivalent description of his cruelty and hubris (in Verlaine's words, his "moral annihilation"), Edison seems to have been flattered rather than insulted by *L'Eve future.* After all "the wizard of Menlo Park" was well-accustomed to fantastic accounts of his secret, possibly occult powers.[57] Villiers would have relished the incongruity of Edison's contribution to his own petrification as sculpture.

When Gustave Eiffel decided to build a 1,000-foot tower for the Universal Exhibition of 1889, his ambition was simply to raise a structure of record-breaking height. He knew his tower would make the Statue of Liberty appear old-fashioned and small. A diminutive, sculpted female personification teeters on the cathedral of Notre Dame in a drawing by one of Eiffel's employees (fig. 102). Eiffel's tower was almost seven times the size of Bartholdi's giant and twice as high as any extant structure.[58] In the crude calculus of nineteenth-century technological competition, the tower dwarfed the Statue of Liberty and sent it hurtling back in time.

The Statue of Liberty is, as Bartholdi intended, an unfamiliar manual achievement, the hovering surface that a confounding series of negative-positive translations produces (figs. 103–104). The statue thematizes such translations because it offers visitors access to both an exterior and an interior, or, alternatively, to a positive and negative surface. It is remarkable how much the exterior and interior of Liberty's face resemble photographic positives and negatives. And inside the empty spaces of the Statue of Liberty's interior stood the logic of Eiffel's engineered, prefabricated armature—structure's future (fig. 105). Because it is both colossal and empty, both a sculpture and a building, the Statue of Liberty straddles the Egyptian and beaux-arts past and the modernist architectural future. It is precisely its betwixt and between status that made it so compelling to late nineteenth-century modernist writers such as Villiers. The Statue of Liberty is at once metal and human, inert shell and projector of energy, engineered and handcrafted, arbitrarily subdivided and magically unified, abstract and mimetic, disorienting and traditional, rational and yet somehow extraordinarily irrational.

# Eiffel's Emptiness

Volume / Mass

How can you be enclosed within emptiness, how can you visit a line?
**Roland Barthes, *The Eiffel Tower and Other Mythologies*, 1979**

By the end of the nineteenth century most French politicians were engineers.[1] Charles de Freycinet, an engineer with a degree from the École Polytechnique, was a senator for over forty-three years and prime minister four times between 1879 and 1892. As minister of public works he took a leading role in equipping France with some 11,000 miles of railway.[2] And he wrote books, one on modern Egypt and, in 1903, a small, elegant treatise, *De l'expérience en géométrie* (Of Experience in Geometry).[3] Albeit direct and simple Freycinet's title poses a question fundamental to an engineer: does "experience" yield new truths about geometry? In the next 178 pages Freycinet expounds a geometry—post-Euclid, post-Descartes, post-Leibniz—peculiarly suited to the age of canals and colossi. Freycinet begins with the body and subtracts its matter to achieve abstract, emptied space. This is radical because he inverts the Euclidean procedure still used in teaching elementary geometry. Euclid starts with the point as a self-evident entity and builds progressively to line, plane, surface, and body, even space, as various relations among points. Monge's descriptive geometry follows Euclid in its premise that all possible projections, and thus space itself, are established through points.[4] Freycinet's very different materialist conception of geometry is rooted in Aristotelian principles that France's positivist philosopher Auguste Comte had also adopted.[5]

Freycinet's book is an important yet largely overlooked source for the history of modern thought. By way of introduction, here is a generous sample:

> The bodies of Nature, particularly solid bodies, are the origin of the fundamental concepts of Geometry. First we distinguish volume, that is to say the portion of space or the extension occupied by the body. To give it a concrete representation, one can imagine that the body is replaced by a very thin envelope which exactly reproduces the exterior form.... The first abstraction made by Geometry consists therefore of retiring from the body its own material and leaving only the place it occupies in space. Contrary to Mechanics which...neglects the form of the body and retains only the mass, Geometry ignores the mass and only retains the form, which it supposes to be invariable after the disappearance of the matter. This abstraction seems to us very simple because we have been habituated to it.... But this is one of the boldest [abstractions] one can make and it requires a very great effort of imagination. We need to withdraw from a body that which constitutes it, that by which it exists, and speculate on a sort of phantom....
>
> The body being thus led to a state of simple volume or geometric form, we envision its exterior contour, the ideal envelope which contains the volume, and we give the name of *surface* to this infinitely thin skin, or, better, to this appearance of skin under which it seems to us that the body still subsists. The surface has nothing of the material, it is...a 'being of reason.' It is the separation between the body and the space which everywhere surrounds it.... It is like the imprint that the body leaves in the space after it has been removed from it....
>
> The suture of two [surfaces] to one another has received the name *line*. It is by an even larger effort...that one comes to conceive the existence of line, to isolate it from the surfaces which give it birth. It is the abstraction in the abstraction.... This ideal object...is figured to our eyes as an extremely thin thread whose thickness tends to disappear. But however far we go down this path of attenuation, our mind goes further still and perceives a line whose fineness defies all realization.
>
> One degree further in abstraction and we create the *point*, the place of the encounter of two lines, as the line is the place of the encounter of two surfaces. We accomplish this wonder of seeing a being there where all elements of being have disappeared.... To make a concept rest on nothing, on the successive suppression of all conditions of reality, and at the same time to have such a need for this concept that it imposes itself on us at the most decisive occasions! We would not know how, without it, to mark the place, the position; it responds to our desire for precision and unity; it summarizes the object whose placement alone interests us...
>
> Consequently, the idea of matter must henceforth be excluded from these different concepts. They are beings of reason, but invincibly linked to the body itself.[6]

Freycinet starts with the world of bodies and describes the excavation of an ideal space as an act requiring great effort, or "labor." He underscores the fact that mechanics and transport are preoccupied with mass, with matter's weight and substance, while geometry focuses on points, lines, surfaces, and abstract volumes--on spaces designated by paper-thin, vanishing skins, threads, and grains, which the imagination alone is capable of conjuring and ever further attenuating. Writing as an engineer Freycinet was fully cognizant of geometry's "bold," "wondrous," "surprising" elimination of matter. Using the imagination, he claims, can become habitual, but geometry's immateriality requires effort nonetheless. For Freycinet geometry means work: the eradication of mass in order to produce an ideal space outside time. But it also effaces labor altogether. Once you have slipped into the massless, timeless space of geometry, mass and time are no longer at issue.

Nineteenth-century Frenchmen were enamored of geometry; they associated modernity with its beautiful clarity. What varied was the extent to which they understood the difference between volume and mass. The four major French engineering undertakings of the era, from Suez to Panama, required the elimination of mass; contemporaries tied their modernity to their emptied spaces. And the relative success of the projects can be correlated with the alertness of their makers to the difference between geometry's abstraction and the world's matter. In this regard engineers had certain advantages over those who mistook imagination—geometry—for the world itself.

Engineers also understood something Freycinet does not admit in his book. Geometry and abstractions like line can contain mass within their immaterial structures, at least for those trained to see it. Geometry does not always leave physicality as far behind as Freycinet implies, but it certainly translates it. Many key players in French public life remained blind to the ways geometry's lines could represent material constraints.

---

**Inside [the Statue of Liberty] we seem to be looking up to the lantern of a gothic cathedral into dim distance. It is rather dark, but the gloom is pierced by thousands of little eyelets of light marking the holes left for the rivets.**

***The Morning News: The Latest Telegrams of the Day*, Paris, 14 May 1884**

People were quick to compare the labor and cost of building the pyramids to that of building the Suez Canal. Pyramid and canal: it is strange to liken positive and negative things—matter and emptiness. But French engineers were prone to think of construction and excavation as similar acts: both entailed moving mass. And the transport of mass required calculable amounts of labor, as it was the business of the engineer to point out. Whether making roads, fortifications, or canals, the engineer's basic calculus aimed to discover how much labor was required to excavate and move matter: success hinged on the efficient "transport of enormous masses of earth."[7]

From the eighteenth century on, engineering exercises, including competitions, required the estimation of labor and transport. Of particular interest is the "problem of excavation and embankment [problème des déblais et des remblais]." To paraphrase Monge's treatise of 1776, this demands calculating the minimum amount of labor needed to transport mass from one place to another.[8] As usual Monge made the practical problem theoretical, treating it successively in two and three dimensions, "in the plane and in space, and referring to the minimum space traversed by molecules."[9]

In reality the problem was far more complex, but Monge himself was very modest about the limitations of his theorization.

> The solution to this problem, which was very difficult to find by ordinary methods of maximum and minimum, is very far from being applicable to practice, as much because of the difficulties that analysis can present as because we are not conforming to nature: in effect, in the transport of earth, each molecule cannot follow the line drawn from the point of departure to the point of arrival; one can only drag it across the surface of the terrain; [and] because of its weight it must follow the undulations [of the earth], especially in the vertical sense.[10]

Monge was right. In practice one cannot displace materials along the straight lines that he had proposed. Even deserts are not without their ups and downs. When mechanization replaced what the British called "slavery" at the Suez Canal, it was mechanization of a remarkably simple sort.[11] An engineer in charge would admit, "One of the advantages of the type of work we do lies in its utter sameness. Cubic yards follow one another, always the same."[12] Nonetheless the dredging of the canal was by no means an effortless proceedure. Cubic yards are not always the same. Cubic measures are volumes, not measures of mass. They indicate the size of containers, not what they hold. Cubic yards can be light or heavy, airy or dense, wet or dry, slippery or sticky. At Suez some kinds of silted sand adhered to the buckets and were extracted with difficulty.[13]

Everywhere on the canal, working out the ratio of water to sand was difficult and slowed the progress of the excavation. The chief engineer Alexandre Théodore Lavalley failed to "realize that mechanization was radically different from a quantitative increase in manual labor and that it demanded an organizational concept."[14] Yet machines operated by fewer men eventually did the job in ways that minimized the difference between geometry and matter. The completed Suez Canal replaces a sand mass with an emptied volume.

Egypt taught Bartholdi the role sculpture could play in the vast engineered spaces of modernity. And modernization was the way Bartholdi would trump the colossal monuments of ancient Egypt.[15] In 1875, after he had visited the United States, another country associated with gigantism, he recycled his Egyptian lighthouse as the Statue of Liberty. He and his ever-present assistant and friend Simon (known only by his first name) had visited the United States for five months in 1871 (fig. 106). Bartholdi traveled by train from the east coast to the west, admiring the sheer size of everything in the vast nation. He was astonished by California's redwood "colossi," Niagara Falls, Pullman cars, technologically daring bridges, and the huge steamboats, which he called veritable hotels on water (fig. 107).[16] "Everything is big here, even the petits pois are larger than those that I like. Everything is practical, but in a collective manner; the entire society marches like rail cars on tracks, but the isolated vehicle is obliged to stay on the rails if it is to move smoothly."[17]

The extent of industrialization in the U.S. oppressed Bartholdi almost as much it excited him. In a letter to his mother about Chicago, "the most American city," he confesses to strong feelings of isolation and something close to fear. "Today you see telegraph wires like enormous spider webs, churches, a hundred newspapers—the whistles of locomotives and steamers make a continuous sound like that of an Aeolian harp, smoke blackens the sky; a vast population rushes about, prey to what might be called business colic."[18] Though upset by "business colic," Bartholdi was himself visiting as an entrepreneur seeking support for his woman-lighthouse. He was also looking for possible sites where it could stand. His worried letters to his mother resemble those he had written to her from Egypt two years earlier when he was seeking to build his colossal lighthouse at the Suez Canal: "Each site presents some difficulty. But the greatest difficulty, I believe, will be the American character, which is hardly open to things of the imagination.... I believe the realization of my project will be a matter of luck. I do not intend to attach myself to the project absolutely if its realization is too difficult ... The important thing is to find a few people who have a little enthusiasm for something other than themselves and the Mighty Dollar."[19]

Once again Bartholdi speaks of luck. He knew his project was as unlikely to be embraced in the United States as it had been in Egypt. In 1876, in his official report on the decorative arts displayed at the International Exhibition of Philadelphia, Bartholdi castigates the American indifference to art.

> The American was compelled, in the beginning, to be tough for his own sake and for that of his things. Hence, a certain coarseness lingers in his tastes and his works: his drawing is angular, he does not like the curved line much. Concerned above all with the useful, he does not make things for the pleasure of making them; he makes them solely for the intended purpose.[20]

Bartholdi jumps from "hard" pragmatism to a national predilection for angular forms. The connection has no basis in fact, but his opposition of straight and curved lines pertains to his own sense of his colossal statue and the obstacles he faced. It could not have helped matters that Bartholdi saw the Washington Monument standing unfinished in the capital (fig. 108). Neglected for fourteen years, the squat block of a building appeared unlikely to reach its intended height.Thirty-seven years after its beginning in 1848, the Washington Monument was finally inaugurated in 1885, only months before the Statue of Liberty in New York City, and it would open to the public later than Bartholdi's statue.[21] The French artist grew convinced that the future of sculpture in the United States was blighted and that this raw country had to be taught to appreciate the arts.[22] His classical statue of a draped female figure would educate Americans; it would even be "of very great moral significance."[23]

Construction was another matter. Bartholdi designed the undulating sculpture, but he entrusted the architect Eugène Viollet-le-Duc to make his colossus stand. The architect had planned to pack the statue with sand-filled metal coffers, thereby updating the ballasting of the Colossus of Rhodes, which contained stone blocks inside its metal form, or the solid core of early modern colossal sculptures (such as the sixty-foot-high statue of St. Charles Borromeo in Arona). But Viollet-le-Duc's death forced Bartholdi to turn to the accomplished young engineer Gustave Eiffel, a Protestant like himself.

Eiffel replaced the sand-filled interior with an inexpensive, simple iron armature upon which the thin sheets of copper would hang (figs. 109–111). He turned Bartholdi's metal woman into a skin covering a structural skeleton. The change was key to the statue's realization. After all, the scale, financial viability, and transportability of the statue depended on the hollowing out of the sculpture's interior and the use of strong, flexible, and relatively lightweight metal. Eiffel made the Statue of Liberty more like the electric lighthouse at the Universal Exhibition of 1867 than the colossal statue of Athena as imagined by Quatremère de Quincy (see fig. 60). The 1867 electric lighthouse and the Statue of Liberty attached thin sheets of metal to an inner iron armature.[24]

Although the ancient Egyptian colossi and pyramids had offered Bartholdi an inspiring precedent, they were outmoded in their reliance on stone and mass as the means to achieve immense scale. For Eiffel modernity meant the excision of mass, as in the Suez Canal, not the accumulation of mass. The pyramid seen in a photograph of the canal represents the achievement of engineered emptiness, an emptiness that permitted transport and commerce as well as empire (fig. 112). Lesseps' feat in Egypt was to have removed earth, not to have amassed it. In contrast to the ancient Egyptian use of stone mass, the Statue of Liberty, with the help of Eiffel, became a hollow giant that could be built in Paris, dismantled, shipped across the world, and reassembled. Engineering's redefinition of Bartholdi's sculpture made it more like a canal, more like a passageway. The visitor to the Statue of Liberty was invited to ascend her colossal height by entering the sole of her foot or to wander inside her head. Emptied volumes permit movement. Empty statues can be sent across the world in labeled crates just as commodities circle the globe.

**106**
Samuel J. Mason, *A. Bartholdi and Simon at Niagara Falls*, 1 August 1871. Albumen print. Colmar, Musée Bartholdi. Photo: Christian Kempf.

**107**
Frédéric-Auguste Bartholdi, drawing of a train's sleeping car in a letter dated August 22, 1871 to his mother from Salt Lake City, Utah: "The space between the beds not being large, one dresses and undresses on one's bed behind curtains, somewhat difficult gymanastics for the women, but they do fine." Frédéric-Auguste Bartholdi papers 1871, Special Collections Office, New York Public Library.

**108**
Matthew Brady, *Washington Monument as It Stood for 25 Years*, glass, wet collodion, c. 1860. Washington, D.C., Library of Congress.

Bartholdi never publicized the statue's radical freedom from mass. Equally puzzling was Bartholdi's blithe confidence that his three-foot promotional model blown up some forty times would be structurally feasible. Bartholdi simply did not think in terms of structure. He did not worry about how the thing could stand. He thought in terms of form, surface, and aesthetic impact; he spoke of the need to simplify drapery and to keep planar surfaces broad.[25] He was responding to imperatives set out long ago for classical statues of any size, especially for colossi.[26]

*Colosses anciens et modernes*, the celebratory text intended to promote and raise funds for the Statue of Liberty, states what Bartholdi deemed to be the lessons learned from Egyptian precedents: "To express grandeur, they did not rely solely on amplitude of dimensions, on the volume of material…[T]hey sought with a prejudice that can appear extreme, the simplicity of lines, the extension of surfaces…. They sacrificed the parts to the whole, variety to unity; they feared diminishing the impression by dividing it. The simplest attitude, the calmest, the furthest from movement and action, are what they gave their colossi."[27] These were Bartholdi's goals, and he would repeat the same criteria in his publication of 1885, *The Statue of Liberty Enlightening the World*.[28]

Above all else a sculptor, Bartholdi adhered to traditional methods of making and enlarging sculpture. He turned for surface to a foundry, Gaget and Gauthier. For structure, he turned to an architect and then to an engineer.[29] His presumption was that artisan-experts with the assistance of construction specialists could make his statue erect, transportable, beautiful, colossal, and permanent. In his geometry treatise Freycinet emphasizes that surface, the ideal envelope that contains the volume, can be conceived as an "infinitely thin skin," an "imprint that the body leaves in the space after it has been removed from it."[30] The photographs of the Gaget and Gauthier workshop dramatize that the manufacture of this sort of a skin is laborious. They also demonstrate that it is possible to imagine the surfaces of volumes from both inside and out. Wooden molds were an "imprint" and offered a view of the sculpture's surface only as seen from its interior. Whereas the copper sheets, which were subsequently hammered onto the wooden molds, at last attained the thinness required to serve as a skin containing volume. The copper sheets cladding the Statue of Liberty are only 3/32 of an inch thick or the equivalent of the thickness of two U.S. pennies. Relative to the statue's size, they are a very thin surface indeed.

And yet none of this accomplishment either addressed or answered the problem of the statue's erection. In the real world of things, not the abstract (invariably drawn) space of geometry, the skins of hollowed solids will not necessarily stand. Hence the humor of Claes Oldenburg's soft sculptures. Surfaces are not self-supporting.

**109**
Photograph. *Eiffel's Armature and the Head*, n.d. Albumen print. Colmar, Musée Bartholdi. Photo: Christian Kempf.

**110**
Photograph. *Interior details of the Statue of Liberty: Drapery clasp at the left shoulder.* Jeannette Griffith, Photographic Studies of the Bartholdi Statue of Liberty, c. 1938, pl. IV, 4. Washington, D.C., Library of Congress.

**111** (right)
Photograph. *Statue of Liberty up to the Waist*, 1881–84. Albumen print. Colmar, Musée Bartholdi. Photo: Christian Kempf.

**112**
Photograph of the Suez Canal, published in Compagnie Universelle de Canal Maritime de Suez, *The Suez Canal. Notes and Statistics* (London: 1952), p. 61. Photo: Julie Wolf.

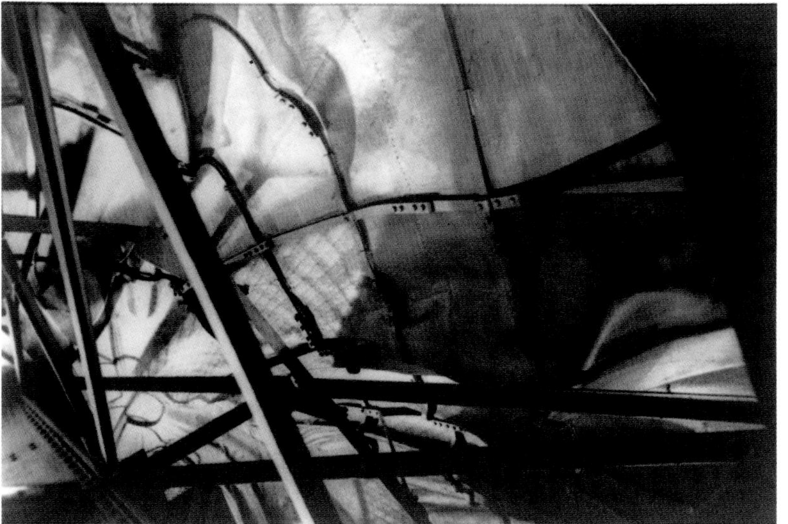

**There can no longer be any question that [the Statue of Liberty] is one of the finest as well as the largest works in the world—a "big thing" in every way, in art as well as in house building.** ***The Morning News: The Latest Telegrams of the Day*, Paris, 14 May 1884**

Enter the engineer. And enter geometry and calculation, not in the workshop, not in space, but on paper (fig. 113). This is the paradox that most interests me. Geometry, as Freycinet points out, typically excludes the notion of matter, despite the fundamental relation it bears to bodies in space. When the artisans making the Statue of Liberty restricted their uses of geometry to our three-dimensional space and moved and managed actual matter in that space, even to constitute surfaces through points, they would seem to have materialized the dangerously immaterial methods of geometry. Here was geometry returned to mechanics, to problems of mass and gravity. Yes, but not quite. The Gaget and Gauthier workshop was littered with immense sheets that were only fragments of the body Bartholdi had designed. The question was how to reassemble the whole. The workers' physical manipulation of parts may ultimately have led to a structural solution, but not necessarily and certainly not quickly.[31] Eiffel was both remarkably efficient and successful, in each case because of the key role of drawing as a site of experimentation and calculation for engineers.

Drawing was the means by which engineers designed, even when they disliked drawing exercises as much as young Eiffel. Not a brilliant student, Eiffel had failed to gain admission to the École Polytechnique, much to his family's sorrow and chagrin. (His sisters were crestfallen that they would not be able to walk arm in arm with a brother dressed in a handsome uniform.) Eiffel attended the less prestigious École Centrale, a school inspired by Saint-Simon's teachings and nicknamed the "Sorbonne industrielle."[32] Drawing exercises were key to the École Centrale just as they were to the École Polytechnique. But Eiffel was not a talented draftsman; his beginnings starkly contrast with those of the exceptionally talented, young École Polytechnique graduates such as Jollois and Devilliers who had accompanied Napoleon to Egypt. Some of his school exercises show that he struggled to control charcoal and ink, particularly when shading objects (figs. 114–115). His most competent drawing is a neoclassical "Head of a Helmeted Warrior," certainly copied in pencil, line by line, from an engraving (fig. 116). Eiffel expressed his mounting frustration with "ce diable de dessin" in letters to his parents: "Drawing," he wrote, "is my sole nightmare."[33] He was wrong of course. Drawing was every engineer's medium, and like every engineer, Eiffel would have to rely on it for computations and experimentation though not to create illusions of things. His drawings, unlike those of the engineers for the *Description de l'Égypte*, were used to build structures, often open trusses, not as artworks in and of themselves; he did not make elaborate presentation drawings.

Innovative, entrepreneurial, and opportunistic, Eiffel had a pragmatic intelligence.[34] Perhaps for this reason he excelled not in school but on the job, where he rose quickly and soon could employ draftsmen to make those "dessins de diable." Working first for a forward-thinking industrialist who made steam engines and train parts and subsequently for railway companies, Eiffel applied himself with energy and determination to commissions gigantic in size on building sites larger than ever before seen.[35] Essential to his success were experimentation, organizational skills, and a willingness to oversee operations that were physically gigantic. Drawing, no matter how resented, remained the primary means by which to experiment, communicate, and calculate. Eiffel could not have done without it, but he was also physically present at the construction sites. During the making of his first bridge, for example, he dove into the water to save a worker.[36] Responsible and resourceful, Eiffel came to be known as a man who met the challenges at hand.

Bartholdi had made several sketches when he initially conceived his sculpture, but once execution began, all drawing stopped. It stopped because Gaget and Gauthier were able, even inclined, to work from three-dimensional, not two-dimensional models (fig. 117). Sculptors had been doing so for centuries. The problem with three-dimensional models, however, is that they do not predict or control the effects of dimension.[37] A two-inch-tall Statue of Liberty is subject to different forces and strains than a two-mile-high Statue of Liberty. To enlarge the skin of Bartholdi's thirty-six-foot model was not to know whether it would stand or how to ensure that it would. Physical translation from one size to another seems to ensure the realism of the product; one is likely to believe it guarantees a material solution. The engineering problem has been there from the beginning: even the ancients were confounded to find that the behavior of catapults could not be predicted from small-scale models. Matter's behavior changes according to size.[38]

**113**
Gustave Eiffel, detail of *Drawing of the Armature for the Statue of Liberty*. Published as Plate 1 in *Le Génie Civil*, 1 August 1883. New York, New York Public Library.

**114**
Gustave Eiffel, "Study of Cube; Study of Cylinder," n.d. Pencil and ink on paper. Paris, Musée d'Orsay, fonds Eiffel.

**115**
Gustave Eiffel, "Study of Sculpted Head, in profile," 30 August 1847. Charcoal on paper. Paris, Musée d'Orsay, fonds Eiffel.

**116**
Gustave Eiffel, "Head of Helmeted Warrior, in profile," 16 May 1846. Pencil on paper. Paris, Musée d'Orsay, fonds Eiffel.

**117**
"France. The Colossal Statue of 'Liberty', to be erected in New York Harbour," c. 1884. Author's Collection. Photo: Julie Wolf.

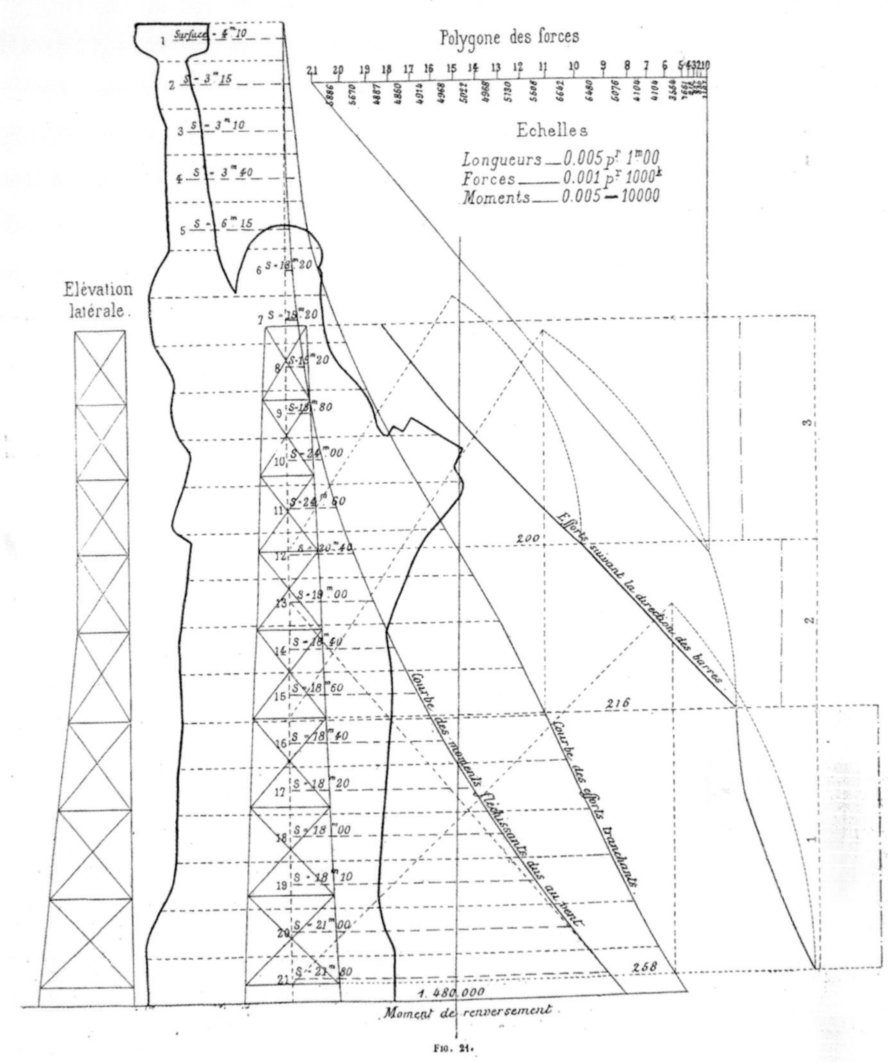


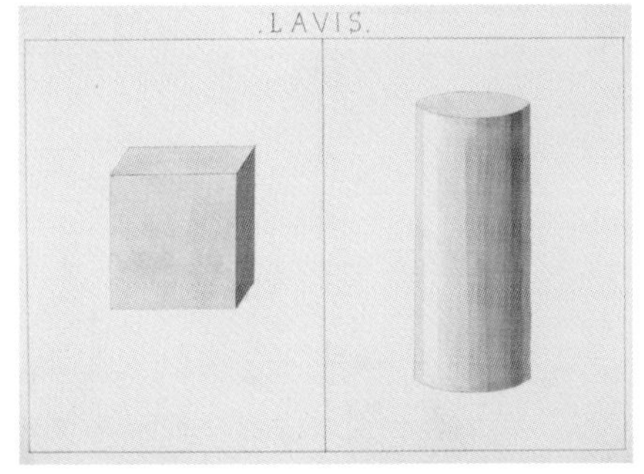


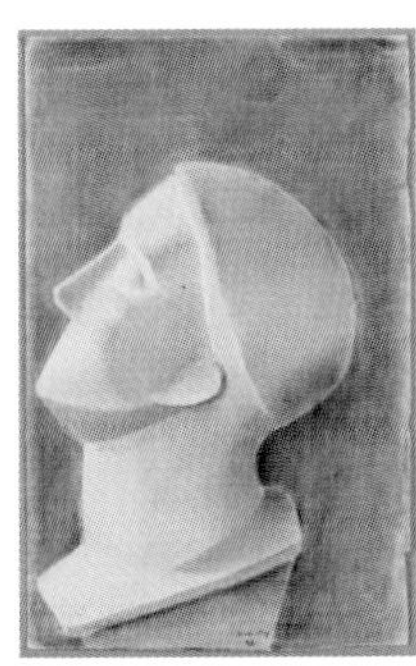

As one engineer explains to the layman:

> The difficulty is that models are all very well if one just wants to see what the thing will look like, but they can be dangerously misleading if they are used to predict strength. This is because as we scale up, the weight of the structure will increase as the cube of the dimensions; that is, if we double the size, the weight will increase eightfold. The cross-sectional areas of the various parts which have to carry this load will, however, increase only as the square of the dimensions, so that, in a structure of twice the size, such parts will have only four times the area. Thus the stress will go up linearly with the dimensions, and, if we double the size, we double the stress and we shall soon be in serious trouble.[39]

The phrase "if one just wants to see what the thing will look like" summarizes Bartholdi's naive perspective on the immense sculpture he hoped to build. What engineers knew, and sculptors like Bartholdi did not, was how to predict the variable effects of dimension (the "square-cube law" stated above, for example), and they did this in drawings that analyzed not only weight and gravity but also force, loads, stress, shear, fatigue, air resistance, and temperature changes. Their job was to combine geometry with physical conditions, to take into account not just shape or volume but also mass and the physical force of invisible powers: wind and heat or cold. The only drawings that I have found pertaining to the execution phase of the Statue of Liberty are Eiffel's, and they show a structure radiated by lines of force. Eiffel realized that the winds would pummel the colossal statue and that its metal skin would expand and contract with changes of temperature. Eiffel—but not Bartholdi—knew that he needed to allow the statue to breathe in order to make it stable.

The engineer knew all this because he was a scientist and an experienced maker of bridges and viaducts, one of which collapsed in 1884; he learned from that failure.[40] Eiffel straddled paper and things, geometry and making, volume and mass. An 1889 poster portrayed him as a manual laborer who also drew (fig. 118).[41] This was not the case. He was an engineer who drew, even if without facility, and who told other engineers, draftsmen, and manual laborers what to do. From what these workers made, he learned whether his drawings had predicted how matter of a specific sort and shape behaves at a certain scale under certain conditions.

**118**
*Homage to Mr. Gustave Eiffel. Souvenir of the Universal Exhibition of Paris in 1889. To the Workers* [Hommage à M. Gustave Eiffel. Souvenir l'Exposition Universelle de Paris en 1889. Aux Travailleurs] Paris, Musée d'Orsay, fonds Eiffel.

Eiffel's preparatory drawing for the armature signals a radical departure from the process by which Bartholdi had conceived the sculpture [see fig. 113]. Here, instead of a three-dimensional model, we confront an emptied two-dimensional contour drawing of the sculpture's shape. That shape is divided evenly into cross sections that provide the basis for calculating the impact of the wind on the statue and ensuring the armature's stability. The statue's contour, its swelling variable shape, matters here only in so far as it determines the amount of surface area exposed to the wind. These variable surface areas are indicated by the numbers straddling the armature's crossbeams; for example, section 21 at the bottom is labeled "s = 21m80". The emphatic black line tracing the contour of Bartholdi's statue thus counts neither as image nor as body but as a sequence of two-dimensional areas (square meters) subject to the impact of force (wind stopped and turned into pressure). The beautiful, most continuous, arcing curve plotted closest to the statue and labeled "Curve of the bending moments due to wind [Courbe des moments flechissants dus au vent]" shows the increasing burden borne at the statue's base to keep it from flipping over. Although wind exerts progressively more force on the structure as it rises, its pressure is borne by the structure's base, which must prevent it from turning over. In engineering terms, "the bending moment" is the pressure exerted on the structure, in this case by the wind; it is necessarily largest at the statue's base, because only there does the structure bear the wind's cumulative force.

Eiffel's drawing does not reveal how he will solve the problem, but it indicates the extent to which his calculations for the armature take into account the statue's envelope as exposed surface area but fully disregard the surface's physical objecthood. There is no notation of the weight of all of those hammered copper sheets. Rather the armature must answer a structural problem in which surface as a thing matters not at all. In this drawing, surface is only an exposed square area subjected to force.

Eiffel's computation relies on static graphical analysis. In the drawing's right half, the three sloping lines graph different kinds of force determined geometrically. The ghost of that process is recorded in the many dashed lines subdividing the drawing. Static graphic analysis refutes the elementary model of geometry proposed by Freycinet. As Freycinet well knew, engineers and geometers from mid-century had come to appreciate that calculations of force could be determined geometrically, not simply arithmetically. Geometry was often far more efficient than numerical calculation.[42] It was also consummately visual. At a glance an engineer could understand the forces with which he needed to contend. In static analysis, a line represents not the intersection of surfaces, as Freycinet would have it, but forces, pressures like wind or gravity or someone pushing.

If this still seems strange, try drawing several vectors pointing different ways (fig.119). Then if you want to achieve equilibrium, let us say, in a structure so that it remains standing, connect the vectors to one another (so that each vector's point meets the next vector's end) and supply the missing line that connects one side of the polygon to another. Point this arrow in the opposite direction of the other vectors. You have determined the size and direction of the countervailing force required to balance the vectors of force with which you began.[43] Overall shape in polygons of force is entirely arbitrary; you can arrange the given vectors, point to end, in whatever order you choose and the answering vector will be the same. In polygons of force, shape encloses nothing, no core, whether full or empty.

The game is to offset angled lines (understood as force or action) by closing them into a shape. The last line that turns a series of vectors into a closed shape is the answer. It shows how to make a structure conform to Newton's law; stasis means that for every force there is a counterforce. Stasis is essential in all buildings and most sculptures, especially colossal ones, and stasis in the engineer's model of proliferating forces must be carefully achieved. It is not the place to start from, as in Freycinet's body, but the place at which to end after the hard work of determining a counterforce to every force, or more likely, to a series of forces. For engineers stasis—the body at rest, the standing structure—is a profound accomplishment. The chair is being pushed up by the floor.

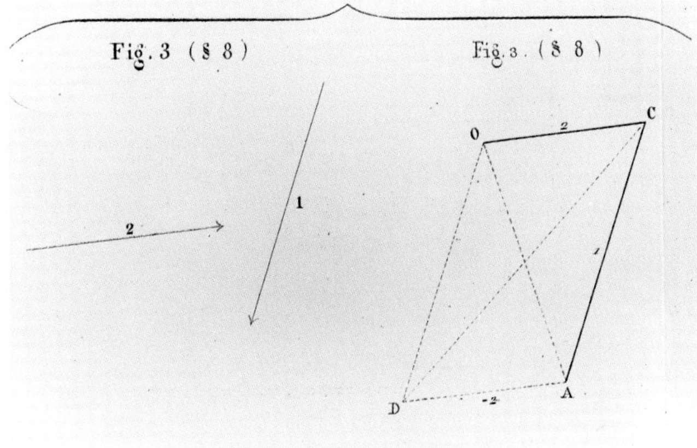


**119**
Polygon of force. Plate 1 in Maurice Lévy, *La statique graphique et ses applications aux constructions*, Paris, 1874. Vectors 1 and 2 are assembled point to tail as OC and CA. The closing vector is OA with A as the point; that is, OA opposes the direction of vectors OC and CA and thus represents the countervailing force that establishes equilibrium. Photo: Julie Wolf

Does Eiffel's drawing of the Statue of Liberty in cross section disregard mass as thoroughly as Bartholdi had disregarded its weight? (see fig. 113) No, not precisely. Instead, mass is translated into force. All forces, whether wind or gravity, are measures of accelerated mass. Force in this drawing is the means by which mass is reintroduced to an evacuated Statue of Liberty, but the force in this particular drawing is the force of the wind. Thus mass is hidden in that which we most associate with immateriality: not only the abstraction "force" but wind's elusive surge (rather than gravity's ponderous weight, for example). In other drawings the weight of those copper sheets and the iron crossbars were surely taken into account. This design only assesses the demand that the wind places on the structure, not the required answering forces, which would include the force of gravity, mass's weight.

Bartholdi's Statue of Liberty and Eiffel's Statue of Liberty are not easily reconciled. Bartholdi began with mass, the solid sculpted model, and then excised its core, leaving an atelier crowded with fragments of surface, those thin but nonetheless substantial copper sheets that weigh over 160,000 pounds.[44] Eiffel began with surface conceived as a series of computed areas, so many square meters—21m80, 21m00, 18m10, 18m20, 18m40, 18m60, 18m40, and so on. In his geometry treatise Freycinet maximally attenuates surface. Eiffel does the same by turning surface into surface area which has none of the materiality of the outer limit of a thing (as does a surface). Surface area is a size, not a substance. And the continuous transition between the discrete sections of surface area (say between 21m00 and 18m10) is marked in Eiffel's drawing by simply the black outline of the statue. The continuity of the sculpture's surface is of no significance to his computation.

The structural engineers with whom I have consulted all concur that they would not have expected Eiffel to make much of the statue's shape; a column would offer an adequate approximation for these calculations. This disregard for the colossal sculpture's shape, and in this drawing even for its mass, is stunning to me, especially given its dramatic contrast to Bartholdi's process, which privileged shape and surface above all else, and also to the onerous procedure by which the surface was constructed. Eiffel assumed an emptiness that he would fill with structure. The container of that emptiness was of slight importance to him. What mattered most in this context was the container's size, its height and surface area. The forces on that size and area would be received and answered by the armature's crossbeams, by Eiffel's structure which concentrated and answered their force. The outer envelope in such a model almost seems transparent; it is certainly useless. And as the envelope approaches transparency, the accomplishment and labor of all those artisans in the Gaget and Gauthier atelier disappear.

**Until now, Paris was lacking in the arrogance that comes with being the possessor of something colossal that attracts universal attention. The ancient Egyptians had it, with their pyramids.... To each his empire. It was time for the industrial genius to assert its growing power, with this Eiffel Tower, which stands proudly as a symbol of the mechanical arts.**

**Hippolyte Gautier, *Les Curiosités de l'Exposition de 1889*, 1889**

The Eiffel Tower was intended to dwarf Bartholdi's creation. This much is evident in Eiffel's drawing of a skyline in which his tower—still in its earliest phase—looms over the Statue of Liberty and all the other buildings of Paris (see fig. 102). Eiffel aimed to free engineering from its role as hidden helpmate to the Statue of Liberty. If Bartholdi revived ancient Egyptian gigantism, Eiffel would erect what he repeatedly called a modern "pyramid" of such enormous proportions that Bartholdi's colossal statue would appear to be of mere human scale. In his drawing of future triumph in Paris, Eiffel treats Bartholdi's colossus like a piece of architectural sculpture from the medieval past, positioning it on top of the cathedral of Notre Dame.

Conceiving of his tower as a modern pyramid was all but inevitable for Eiffel. In 1865 his employer had sent him to Egypt to sell thirty-three locomotives to the government.[45] Though the deal fell through, he wrote his father: "I made a very good and interesting voyage whether in the isthmus or in Cairo where I remained for several days and saw...most notably the pyramids...of Memphis. I have collected some notes on the Canal which I will probably publish upon my return."[46]

Always the good engineer Eiffel spoke in his notes of the cube of *déblais* (excavation rubble), its cost, and the cubic meters extracted by each laborer (one to two).[47] His experience of managing construction is no less evident. He found manual labor by the fellaheen to be both cheap and efficient and preferable to the new and untested machines that the British had forced on the French.[48] "No matter our habitual confidence concerning the superiority of machines relative to the labor of men, one cannot help, upon seeing these great works so rapidly and so economically made, but regret that they could not continue to be made in the way that they were so well started."[49] Corvée labor appealed to Eiffel; it was the way the pyramids had been built. But he would not build his tower in an ancient labor-intensive way; Eiffel's "pyramid" would be modern in its materials and construction and far taller than its Egyptian precursors.

Neither Eiffel's inspiration nor his ambition was lost on his contemporaries. Laudatory poems and prints from 1889 pair the tower and an Egyptian pyramid.[50] That same year, the cover of the journal *Centrale* featured a swaggering Eiffel, standing tall between his tower and a pyramid; a diminished Notre Dame Cathedral hangs like a fob from the pocket of his waistcoat (fig. 120). The dwarfed pyramid is inscribed "From the largeness of the work is measured the greatness of the man [À la grandeur de l'oeuvre, on mesure la grandeur de l'homme]." Eiffel pretended to disagree. When his young son lovingly inserted a photograph of the tower into a scrapbook, he admonished him for confusing great men with great monuments, a paternal affectation of humility if ever there was one (fig. 121).[51] But his son had been on target. Size was the point. Size was what engineers could do and sculptors could not.

If size could be attacked for artlessness and exhibitionism, Eiffel realized that ancient Egypt offered his structure a legitimating precedent, just as it had Bartholdi's colossus. When a contingent of outraged artists attacked the tower, he rephrased Bartholdi to defend its raw and visible technology.

> There is in the colossal an attraction, a charm of its own, to which theories of art are hardly applicable. Does one believe that it is because of artistic value that the pyramids have so powerfully struck the imagination of men?... And what is the source of this admiration if not the immensity of the effort and the grandeur of the result? The tower will be the highest edifice ever elevated by men. Is it not grandiose in its fashion? And why does that which is admirable in Egypt become hideous and ridiculous in Paris? I try to understand this, but I admit I do not find it so.[52]

According to Eiffel the colossal rendered artistic criteria moot. Building the highest edifice in the world was accomplishment enough.

Michel Serres has called the Eiffel Tower an anti-monument. Echoing Rodin, Roland Barthes pronounced it a monument in which there is nothing to see. Inasmuch as the tower was built to break records, Serres, Barthes, and Rodin are all correct.[53] The Eiffel Tower showed the world that modern engineering could produce a structure larger than any of the monuments of ancient Egypt. Its open structure—the unprecedented visibility of an iron skeleton no longer hidden within a figural sculpture—was no less spectacular. From the first, it was a monument to climb to attain a view and, yet more strange and new, a monument to climb to experience its construction, its vertical surge, its accomplishment. The tower was at one and the same time

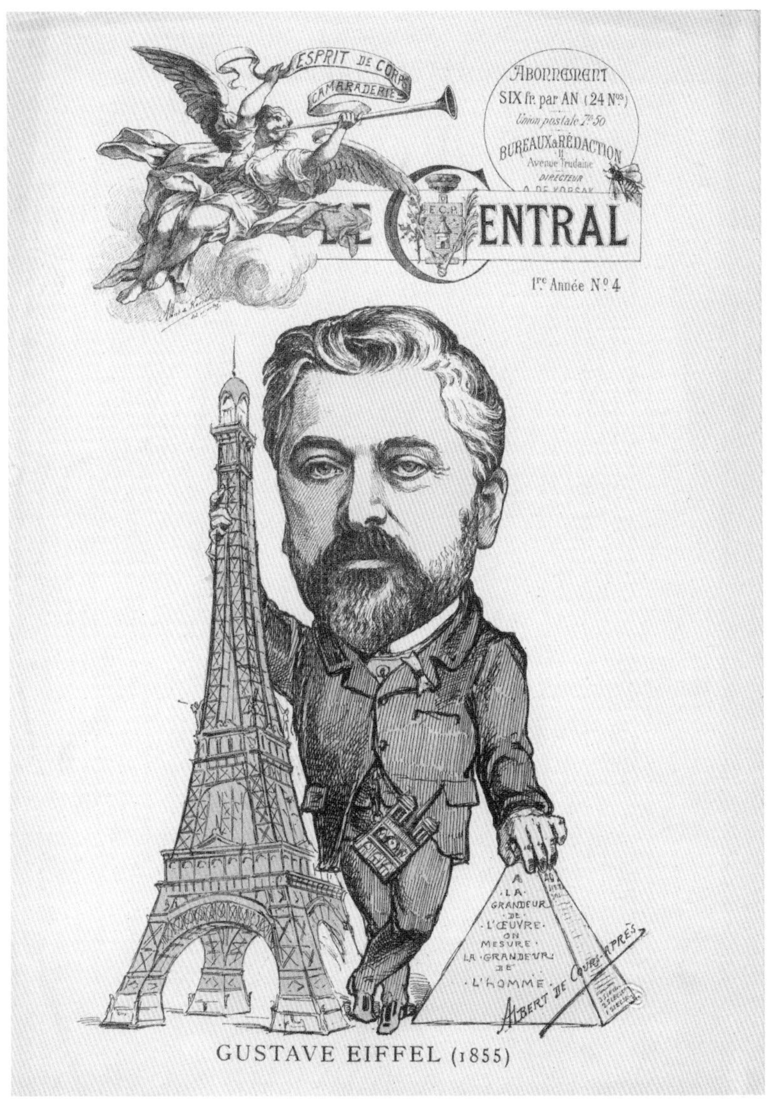


**120**

*From the grandeur of the work is measured the grandeur of the man* [A la grandeur de l'oeuvre, on mesure la grandeur de l'homme], *Le Centrale*, 1889. Paris, Musée d'Orsay, fonds Eiffel.

**121**

Photograph placed in scrapbook by Eiffel's son; published in the album by J. M. Dufrénoy, *Dans l'intimité de personnages illustres, 1850-1900*, Paris, Editions M.D. 1935.

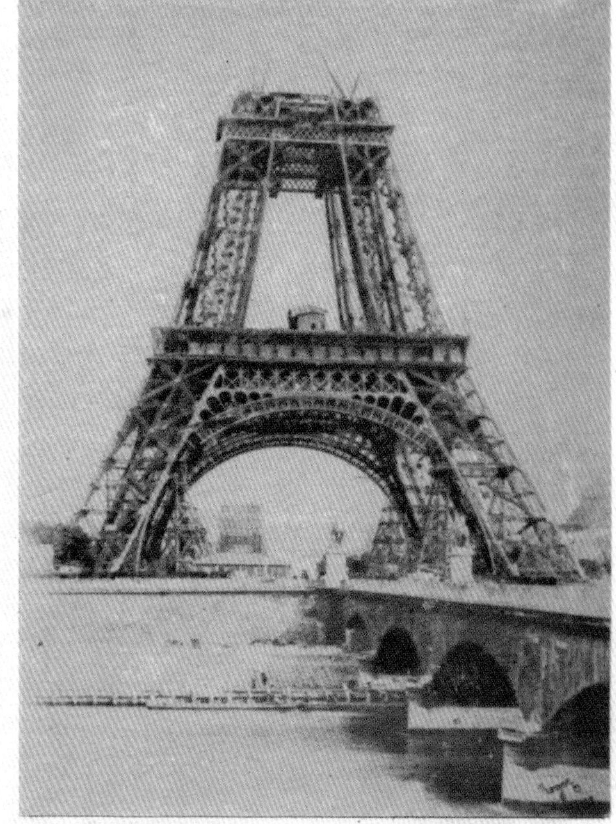

Photo de la Tour
au 2ème étage
pour faire une surprise à papa
moi je colle dans cet albome la
fotografie de la Tour Efel
caura 300 mètres ou papa ma
promis de me faire monter pendant
lesposiction

Mon petit garçon a confondu les grands hommes avec les grands monuments.

a colossus dominating Paris as no other monument had ever done—and a monument celebrating the art and science of engineering. One girder at a time, it introduces visitors to the materials and processes that determined its final form. Eiffel was initiating one and all into the aesthetic of the Machine Age.[54] The job of the Eiffel Tower was to make visible the engineering needed to erect a structure more colossal in size than any in the world.

---

**The effect is in the grandeur and the simplicity of the forms, and in the contrast and disproportion that exists between the stature of man and the immensity of the work which derived from his hand.** **Edmé-François Jomard, engineer, *La Description de l'Égypte*, 1809-22**

Taking a lesson from Bartholdi, Eiffel commissioned a photographer, in this case Louis-Émile Durandelle, to document the construction of the tower; Durandelle had earlier documented the building of Charles Garnier's Opera House (fig. 122).[55] Called "The State of Advancement on the Works of the Eiffel Tower," the series of fifty-eight photographs proves that the camera could be a means to track the workers' shifting roles. They come in and out of the initial pictures of building the stone masonry. They are lined up with shovels in several photographs. In others workers direct their gaze at the photographer. Points of view vary greatly. The photographs record the heterogeneous materials employed to make the iron tower: stone masonry, wooden scaffolding, and rope pulleys. As the tower begins to rise, the views become increasingly distant.[56] Eventually the wooden scaffolding is removed.[57] The workers disappear. Crowds of frock-coated, top-hatted dignitaries and engineers pose for five group portraits against the intersecting girders of the first platform (fig. 123).[58]

The most famous photographs of the building of the tower sustain a distant view of the site from beginning to end (fig. 124)[59] (The horizon is slightly lower in the initial pictures, revealing that the photographer had not anticipated how very high the tower would rise.) In this series of long views, workers are never visible. The photographic machine seems to capture a self-generating machine. Between January 1887 and May 1889, Eiffel's modern pyramid was erected so efficiently, it seemed to rise miraculously, even inevitably, without the hand of man. The medium of photography perfectly suited this technological feat. Indeed many argued that engineered iron and photography were well-matched affronts to architecture and painting. In a statement of 1857 Charles Garnier, architect of the lavish Opéra, joined the critics decrying the demise of art: "Thus does photography, destined to provide invaluable services, constantly attempt to replace art with science, feeling with exactness; thus does iron, whose use is far preferable to that of wood in almost all areas of construction, encroach on architecture, change its characteristic forms, and finally replace art with industry."[60]

But Garnier was disingenuous in his assessment of the materials reserved for art as opposed to industry. Not only did the Opéra depend on iron construction, but for over a decade iron had been incorporated into architectural design, most famously by Henri Labrouste. Still the Eiffel Tower exposed what had been veiled. At Labrouste's Bibliothèque Sainte-Geneviève, to cite Sigfried Giedion,"the iron construction [was] enclosed in the stonework of the exterior like the works of a watch in its case."[61]

Iron and photography became even more explicitly linked when industry was banished to the outskirts of Paris in 1860.[62] Thereafter numerous engineering projects came to be known primarily through photography. When the Eiffel Tower was erected at the center of Paris in 1889, it represented, said Jules Simon, the triumphant return of industry to Paris. Not everyone approved. A group of artists signed a petition protesting the "smokestack."

> One need only imagine for a moment a giddily ridiculous tower, dominating Paris, and the barbaric mass of a gigantic black factory smokestack crushing Notre Dame, the Sainte-Chapelle, the Tour Saint-Jacques, the Louvre, the dome of Les Invalides, and the Arc de Triomphe.... You who have such a love for Paris, you who have...so often protected her against the devastation by governments and against the vandalism of industrial enterprises, you now have the honor to defend her yet again.[63]

The poets, architects, and painters hostile to the Eiffel Tower saw it as industrial vandalism "crushing" their beloved city. Photographers came running, the critics charged, for all the wrong reasons. Photographs replaced "art with science, feeling with exactness" but also excised the makers—whether laborers or artists—from view, thereby condoning the self-sufficiency of machines, which had so depressed Delacroix in 1855: "The view of all these machines profoundly saddens me. I do not love this medium which appears to make, all alone and abandoned to itself, things worthy of admiration."[64]

The astute diplomat and critic Eugène-Melchior de Vogüé wrote in 1889 of the tower's inexorable rise:

> From the second platform…the work of the construction escaped our view.… We [only] saw the sky redden from the fire of a forge, we barely heard the hammers which riveted the iron fittings.… We almost never saw the workers on the tower; [it] rose alone, by the incantation of genii. We associate the great works of other ages, like those of the pyramids, for example, with the idea of human multitudes, pressing hard on crowbars and groaning under cables; [but this] modern pyramid was raised by a spiritual command, by the power of calculation requiring a very small number of hands; all the force needed for its elevation seemed to have been drawn in a mind which operated directly on the material. It required few people and there was hardly any action at the work site because there never was a stroke of a file or a strike of a chisel; every one of these ribs of iron—numbering 12,000—arrived perfect from the factory and came to be added to the prescribed place in the skeleton without any welding. Over many years, the tower had been assembled in the head of the geometer and realized on paper; all that was needed was to prepare the infallible drawing in cast iron. Here, at least, was what mathematicians call an "elegant demonstration."… One admires above all the visible logic of this construction, the accordance of the parts with the result to be attained. In every logic which has been translated to the eyes, there is an abstract, algebraic beauty.[65]

That same year, 1889, the French engineer Émile Cheysson had also marveled at the achievement of the Eiffel Tower, but he too fell prey to anxieties concerning conditions of labor. Thinking about labor hurtles him back in time, once again, to the building of the pyramids.

> When [the visitor] admires this audacious tower, the highest pedestal that man up to this point has known how to erect by his hands…, a thought arises that…can no longer be ignored: of the men to whom is owed all this magnificence, of their material condition, of their state of morale. Here is a new world which comes into view, that of iron and of grand industry. What does it do to these actors? The fellaheen once sacrificed by the pharaohs have spoiled the pyramids for us. If it is true, as claimed by the manifesto of the Socialist Congress that will open in a few days, if it is true that "the workers of which the Exhibition is the product are condemned to misery in the midst of the most colossal riches that human society has ever possessed," this image will ruin our admiration and we will find that industry has certainly made us pay too much for its services.[66]

Cheysson, famous for the invention of social engineering—the expansion of engineering to include conditions of labor—asked readers if the Eiffel Tower would be ruined for posterity as had the pyramids.[67] Colossal size, to his mind, did not divide West from East, nor present from past. Immensity was not new. What may have been new were the means of manufacture, the labor conditions that either spoil a monument or make it worthy of celebration. Was the price of erecting the Eiffel Tower too high in terms of human suffering?

Vogüé offered one answer to Cheysson's queries. If the Egyptian pyramids had been spoiled for the contemporary public by the thought of the peasants who had groaned under the cables, the modern pyramid did not require the oppression of multitudes. To Vogüé the tower was a demonstration of the mathematician's calculations on paper and required little physical exertion. All the measurements realized physically in the Gaget and Gauthier foundry were outlined on paper before work began. In the construction of the Eiffel Tower, experienced artisans did not devise solutions; men with pencils in hand were in charge.

Among the effects of engineering's "separation of thinking from making" is the splitting of the process of production, the increase in scale made possible by directing workers from above, and the speed of production.[68] A twentieth-century engineer put the point this way: "The effect of concentrating the geometric aspects of manufacture in a drawing is to give the designer a much greater 'perceptual span' than the craftsman had. The designer can [thereby] see and manipulate the design as a whole.… Using his ruler and compasses he can rapidly…predict the repercussions that changing the shape of one part will have upon the design as a whole."[69]

Vogüé underestimated the number of the Eiffel Tower's "iron ribs"—there were 18,000, not 12,000—and each type of rib had been drawn over a period of two years by fifty of Eiffel's calculators and draftsmen. Those 5,300 drawings, each of which measures almost one square

**122**
Édouard Durandelle, *Album sur les travaux de construction de la tour Eiffel*, 16 June, 1888. Paris, Musée d'Orsay, fonds Eiffel.

**123**
Édouard Durandelle, *Album sur les travaux de construction de la tour Eiffel*, 16 June, 1888. Paris, Musée d'Orsay, fonds Eiffel.

**124**
Photograph. *Construction of the Eiffel Tower as seen from one of the towers of Trocadero Palace*, seventeen photographs, 1887-1889. Paris, Musée d'Orsay, fonds Eiffel.

yard, indicated the dimension and shape of each piece as well as the position of every one of the tower's 2,500,000 rivet holes to one tenth of a millimeter (fig. 125).[70]

These are the kinds of drawings usually discussed when considering the role of drawing in engineering: "views from nowhere," orthographic projections that serve as templates for making things, since they do not distort form to accommodate a particular point of view.[71] They are shapes par excellence. At an off-site factory, over one hundred workers prefabricated each piece according to these drawings' specifications; the pieces were then inspected and, if necessary, remade at the factory. Other engineering projects of the nineteenth-century—most notably the Forth Railway Bridge in Scotland, built of steel in 1890—required constant improvisation, changes in design, and manufacturing and welding on-site. To avoid all this Eiffel seized control of his tower's construction through the medium of drawing that he had once resented.[72]

But he used drawing in a newfangled way inasmuch it helped him design the prefabricated parts of which the tower would be made. In short Eiffel conceived the tower as an object, a colossal object to be sure, but one to be manufactured. Historian of engineering Tom Peters considers Eiffel's process as a "construction kit of parts," the inspiration, in fact, of the Meccano set (sold as the Erector Set in the United States), an open-ended construction toy created in England in 1904 (fig. 126). Peters explains that Eiffel made "member cross sections and connections constant in his system, and he varied component length to produce similar, rather than congruent, elements. This enabled him to build complex objects without using the special components his predecessor had needed.... [H]is tower uses only nine basic gussets.... These are the generator of his construction system."[73] The interchangeable parts are fundamentally different from the unique jigsaw-like pieces of the Statue of Liberty, of which no two were alike, no two the same size.

Eiffel's draftsmen did not need to define each and every one of the tower's 18,000 parts. The 5,300 drawings represent constituent parts of differing lengths that were used over and over again. In sharp contrast to the templates that Napoleon's engineers drew almost a century earlier, these designs were done, not as records of the past, but as patterns for future manufacture in off-site factories where workers produced thousands of a limited number of iron shapes to exact specifications; each piece was numbered. On the Champ-de-Mars the job of the laborers would be the correct placement of parts and the subsequent insertion of rivets into holes already made at precise intervals in the iron. But first stone foundations for the tower's four piers would be excavated and built. Next wooden scaffolding for the first stage of building would be assembled; after the first platform the tower became self-supporting, and scaffolding was no longer necessary. Vogüé saw the process much as had the photographer Durandelle. Both noticed that the higher the tower rose, the less it seemed a matter of men's labor; the number of workers dwindled until there were none.

To look at the Eiffel Tower and see a drawing remade in iron is entirely justified. The tower is a structure whose height was made possible by its radical reduction of mass, the maximal attenuation of iron matter into line. And Vogüé made an important point when he declared the tower an elegant mathematical demonstration. Eiffel was designing a structure in which the bending moment—risk of overturn—produced by the force of the wind was exactly offset by the opposing bending moment produced by the force of gravity in the structure's weight.[74] The balance can be expressed as a calculus equation wherein one bending moment must equal the other:

$$0 \int h \; 4Df2 (x)f0 (x) = 0 \int h \; 2Pf (x) \; xdx.$$

But such an equation is useless unless I define its terms, and it was not how Eiffel and most French engineers approached engineering problems and their mathematical expression. In 1889 Eiffel and his employees would have performed analyses through graphs based on the efficient visualizations of geometry.[75] In the instance of Eiffel's design for the armature for the Statue of Liberty, the diagrammed curve indicates the demand exerted by "the bending moments due to the wind," the pressure, in other words, exerted on the structure by the wind's capacity to flip the entire structure over. That curve would appear again in the shape of the Eiffel Tower.

The bending moment translated into an iron graph, that is the Eiffel Tower. It demonstrates how structural form follows the equilibrium of forces.[76] Besides maximizing the weight at

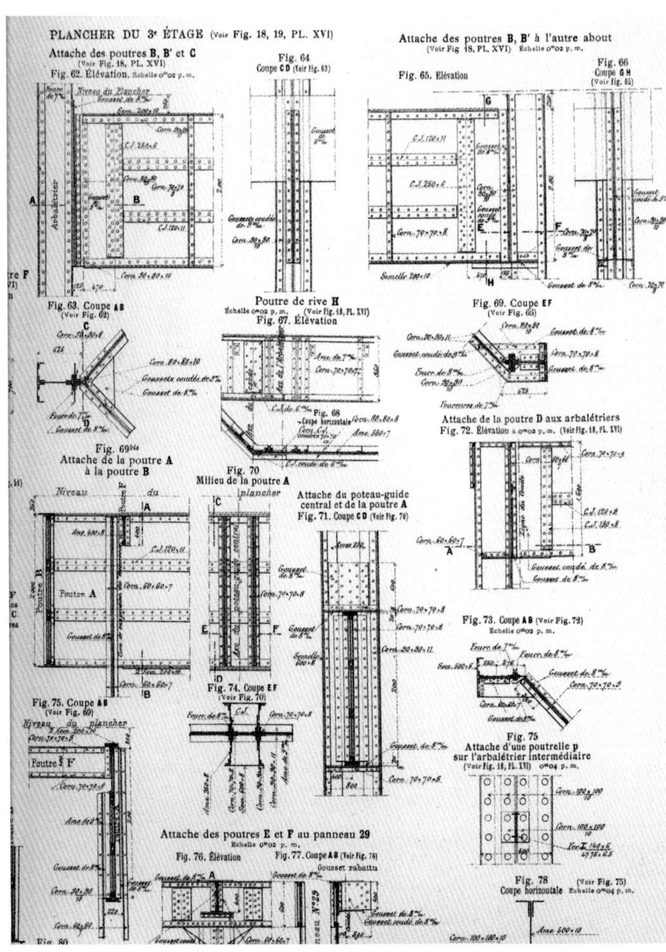

**125**
Gustave Eiffel, Detail of "Planchers des divers étages–Détails d'assemblages," Plate XVII, *La tour à trois cents mètres*, Paris, 1900. Special Collections, Stanford University Library.

**126**
Advertisement for Meccano Construction Toy, 1913. Author's Collection. Photo: Julie Wolf.

its base where exposure of surface area to wind is negligible, but where the risk of rotation from the cumulative impact of the wind across the structure's entire height is most acute, Eiffel also needed to minimize the surface area at the tower's top where the force of the wind is greatest. Hence the tower's tapering shape, which demonstrates the equilibrium of forces in an optimally designed structure (like a suspension bridge where the curve of the flexible cables responds at every point to the required load, no more, no less). Every section thus establishes the optimal equilibrium between the bending moment due to wind and the bending moment due to weight. Colossal verticality represents an equilibrium.

In the terminology of engineers the structure of the Eiffel Tower is funicular; every one of its sections bears and answers precisely the same load. Funicular structures are optimally lean and strong. No part of the structure is stronger or more massive than needed, nor is any part weaker. In the Eiffel Tower lines of iron are not just the means by which the structure is built; they dictate its very form. Eiffel himself articulated the tower's structural answer to forces in language that seems to move between drawn and physical lines: "Lines drawn tangential to each upright with the point of each tangent at the same height will always intersect at a second point, which is exactly the point through which passes the flow resultant from the action of the wind on that part of the tower situated above the two points in question."[77]

It is significant that this mathematical demonstration was conceived geometrically, not algebraically (as lines, not equations). Engineers were trained to see forces and structure's answer to those forces in geometric terms, and it was consummately easy, perhaps inevitable, that this visualization would come to be regarded as a template, a model for physical structure itself. Stare at those graphed curves long enough, they might transmute into form.

Lightness is the achievement of funicular structures. Eiffel continually boasted that the tower put little pressure on its foundation, no more, in fact, than a person sitting on a chair. One writer has pointed out that the air inside a cylinder of the same breadth and height would weigh almost as much as the iron structure.[78] This is hard to grasp but true and shows how much contemporaries admired the emptiness of Eiffel's structure—his radical transformation of iron mass into empty volume. Yet it is wrong to speak of an "empty" volume; this implies, à la Freycinet, that the mass was extracted to leave a volume within defining surfaces. The tower's form is light, efficient, and visible because it is not clad by surfacing. It has no copper sheets, no beaux-arts woman, not even a circumscribing container like a cylinder or box. Remove the container and the spread of the tower's base can be determined by the desired height rather than by the stride of a sculpted woman. Eiffel was able to elevate his structure ten times the height of the Statue of Liberty because he could greatly widen the distance between its piers and, equally importantly, he could also deprive the wind of surface area against which to push. Gone are those sheets of copper that Bartholdi's artisans hammered into place.

The tower was conceived as the configuration of vectors of force. Freycinet's empty volumes are inadequate structures; they will not stand at a colossal scale. Solid masses of masonry can attain remarkable size, as the Egyptian pyramids make clear, but hollowed shapes cannot. They require structure, and structure is not surface. Eiffel recognized that it was precisely the sacrifice of surface, not mass, that enabled his tower's achievement of unprecedented heights. Indeed the tower undoes Freycinet's notion of mass, volume, and surface altogether; there is no outside versus inside. Exterior and interior are collapsed, and yet mass, even if minimized, remains. Despite its lightness, the Eiffel Tower depends on the exact offsetting of wind and gravity, lateral and vertical forces, the pressure of air and the pressure of weight. Mass was excised from the tower's core, but it was also exactly calibrated, because mass alone provides the countervailing force to that of the wind. Thus surface, not mass, was redefined by Eiffel's Tower, becoming line, not plane—networks of iron bars, not enclosing walls or sheets, and punctured by emptiness at every point where no carrying of force was required.

Vogüé referred to the geometer's "infallible drawing." That propensity to visualize forces and structure's capacity to bear them would have made the Eiffel Tower seem to many a physical realization of drawing and a proof of drawing's irrefutable logic, its capacity to speak force through line. Vogüé gave voice to a characteristically nineteenth-century fascination: a one-thousand foot tower born and assembled in the geometer's head.

Great works accomplished without manual labor or material impediment? Vogüé's conception of a one-thousand-foot tower born and assembled in the head of a geometer was a fantasy, a dream that all material limits could be transcended and labor could disappear. But two strikes stopped the building of the Eiffel Tower. This was a decade of agitation by laborers, union organizers, socialists, and anarchists, among others. Construction and metal workers were some of the most active pro-testers.[79] But Eiffel had engineered his colossal monument with great skill. He had diverted labor to drafting tables and to off-site factories. He had made the spectacle of erection seem inevitable, unstoppable, and fast, the geometer's inspiration realized when in fact it was the engineer's. Vogüé had said that the Eiffel Tower was an incantation of "génie." Is it any surprise that civil engineers called themselves *Génie civil*? Magic workers.

And yet Eiffel was opposed to substituting drawing for the tower itself. When upholders of high culture—artists, poets, architects, write rs—first attacked him, he had turned to the Egyptian pyramids, directing attention to the colossal thing in and of itself. With palpable frustration Eiffel found himself obliged to caution that drawing and monument were fundamentally unlike.

> I would like to know on what [the protesting artists] have based their judgment. Because, note this, Sir, no one has seen this tower and no one, before it is built, can say what it will become. Until now it has been known only by a simple geometric drawing; and although it has been reproduced in hundreds of examples, can one appreciate with competence the general artistic effect of a monument from a simple drawing when this monument truly exceeds [all] dimensions previously constructed and [all] forms previously known?[80]

Drawing, Eiffel well knew, had made possible the calculation and thus the realization of a structure of unprecedented size. Similarly the design of a funicular structure like his tower would have been out of the question without drawing. And because the tower's structure was made funicular, optimally efficient, it soared higher, indeed twice higher, than any extant building of the era. But no drawing, Eiffel insists, could transmit the impact of that size; nor could any of the hundreds of reproductions of the tower. Further because it had not yet been completed, not even its makers could anticipate its final effect. Eiffel has it two ways then. The colossal tower required the engineer's expertise in drawing on paper to predict the interaction of all forces. Yet the tower promised to surpass all models, whether paper or souvenir miniatures; the total impact of a tower exceeding "all dimensions previously constructed" was beyond calculation. Eiffel intimates that the tower will be sublime.

---

**They will climb my Tower as they climb the Bastille Column. What was to be no more than a pastime for the worker may perhaps become a subject for study.** Auguste Rodin, as cited by his secretary Marcelle Tirel, *The Last Years of Auguste Rodin*, 1925

One of the last projects of the sculptor Auguste Rodin was begun in defiance of Eiffel's tower. Rodin had denounced his era "as one of engineers and manufacturers, not artists."[81] In a deeply felt reiteration of other critics of Eiffel's engineered monument, he regretted that "science" and "mechanics" had replaced "the work of the human mind with the work of a machine," thereby ushering in "the death of art."[82] His unfinished Tower of Labor was both to champion Art and replace Eiffel's offensive tower: "Erected in some spacious square—the Champ-de-Mars, for instance—where it might with advantage replace the Eiffel Tower, an elevation of a hundred yards would be possible."[83]

Rodin was competing with Eiffel; he imagined a tower that would be instructive, not merely spectacular. A small plaster model of 1898 shows that the tower would have had a staircase spiraling around its entire height. Standing on this platform visitors would have been able to peruse the relief sculptures depicting scenes of heroic labor (fig. 127). No mere rivets here. Rodin's secretary summarized his intentions:

"The Tower of Labour," he said, "will be a column...covered with bas-reliefs; but these, instead of recording historical events, will take us simply through the stages of the work of the human race. On the coping will be my Blessings, the reward merited by a life of labour accomplished. The worker will climb one by one the steps of the great stairway, pausing, thinking, before each bas-relief; and when he is at the summit, on the platform, the wings of the angel in blessing will cast a restful shade on his weary head."[84]

Visitors were intended to circle the tower with their backs turned to the view in order to examine the sculptures on its inner core. The climb mapped a progression from the labor of the body to the labor of the mind; Rodin's inscription states that the spiral would serve as an "emblem of man's evolution and growth."

In the basement of the tower is a crypt...showing the subterranean and subaqueous labors of the miner and diver. From here, the ascent in the industrial order is methodic: masons, carpenters, blacksmiths, joiners, potters, etc., clad in costumes indicative of the occupation rather than of a particular epoch. Each higher stage shows processes more and more freed from primitive material bondage, and attaining their results more and more through the activities of the mind.[85]

Although Rodin placed the arts at the tower's top, he regarded sculpture as a manual form of work that spanned and unified the breadth of man's labor. Thus the entire tower drew attention to the manual craft of the sculptor even as its ascent mapped an elevation from body to mind. Ultimately Rodin imagined the colossal tower as a monument to himself: "In the crypt below the ground will repose my remains when I am no more—the remains of one who was a great worker."[86]

The Tower of Labor would have been a funerary monument, but it also would have memorialized the death of the figurative and allegorical language Rodin had inherited and revitalized. After the Eiffel Tower, Rodin's Tower of Labor could only appear anachronistic. How idiotic, remarked a 1905 critic, was the idea that Paris would tear down the Eiffel Tower in order to replace it with a "hastily invented series of workmen niched in a ridiculous tower."[87] Engineered iron made sculpture appended to architecture appear old-fashioned and rife with condescension: imagine the workers, at each bas-relief, receiving the great man's blessing. Rodin wanted the monument to be artful and unique; an aggregation of individually crafted, original artworks (despite his own famous reliance on reproduction). The gulf between him and Eiffel cannot be bridged. Eiffel had turned work into an abstraction; labor was anonymous in a modern tower assembled from interchangeable engineered parts.

**We will engrave on the earth the signs of its future prosperity.** Enfantin, *Œuvres de Saint-Simon et d'Enfantin*, 1834

Thomas Alva Edison was already an international celebrity when he arrived at the Universal Exposition in 1889. His own exhibition filled almost an acre of the Gallery of Machines and featured the phonograph as well as a forty-foot-high incandescent light on a twenty-foot pedestal and, to augment the spectacle, thousands of small electric light bulbs.[88] The phonograph drew crowds and was second in popularity only to the Eiffel Tower.[89] Edison, the farm boy turned inventor, was awarded a medal of the Legion of Honor; in embarrassment he hid the medal under his lapel, or so the story goes.[90] The French Society of Engineers gave a banquet in Edison's honor. Guests were invited to take coffee in Eiffel's private salon at the top of the tower. Music was provided by Charles Gounod, the composer who, thirteen years earlier, had performed at a fund-raiser for the Statue of Liberty.[91] Both the French and the Americans understood the significance of the meeting between Edison and Eiffel—the American and French giants of invention. Even today wax figures of the two men simulate casual chat in Eiffel's office at the top of his tower (another absurd detail I can imagine Villiers de L'Isle-Adam relishing) (fig. 128). In 1889 the French tried to be gracious; the dinner hosted by the French Society of Engineers makes this clear. Edison responded in kind. He wrote a note to Eiffel, now in Eiffel's papers at the Musée d'Orsay: "The tower of M. Eiffel I consider one of the bravest and most gigantic undertaking [*sic*] of modern engineering. Thomas A. Edison."[92]

When a *Scientific American* reporter asked him what he thought of the Eiffel Tower, another guest retorted "the work of a bridge builder." To which Edison purportedly replied: "No, it is a great idea. The glory of Eiffel is in the magnitude of the conception and the nerve in the execution. That admitted, and the money found, the rest is, if you like mere bridge building. I like the French. They have big conceptions. The English ought to take a leaf out of their books. What Englishman would have had this idea? What Englishman could have conceived of the Statue of Liberty?"[93] When the reporter baited Edison with the query, "Will you beat the tower in New York?" Edison responded, "We'll build one of 2,000 feet. We'll go Eiffel 100 per cent better, without discount." In the rivalry of scale, Americans would win. The boast was risky, given that the 555-foot-tall Washington Monument, half the height of the Eiffel Tower, had only been completed five years earlier, thirty-six years after its construction began. The Eiffel Tower had been built in just two years.

Still Americans attempted to diminish Eiffel's achievement. *Scientific American* published a cartoon that turns Eiffel into a talking version of his tower. "How are you, mon ami?" he calls up to Edison, another, much taller tower, with his head encased in a light bulb at its top (fig. 129). The cartoon features two inventions associated with Edison, the telephone and the light bulb, both of which invisibly traverse space. Although Alexander Graham Bell had invented the telephone in 1876, it was all but unknown in France until Edison introduced his improved version

**127**
Auguste Rodin, *Tower of Labor*, 1898–99. Plaster model, 151 cm. high. Paris, Musée Rodin.

**128**
Wax figures of Edison and Eiffel at top of the Eiffel Tower. Photograph, 2009. Photo: Maud Chazeau.

**129**
"How are you, mon ami?" Illustration to "With Mr. Edison on the Eiffel Tower," *Scientific American*, 14 September 1889. Photo: Julie Wolf.

**130**
"Projet de transport d'un vaisseau sur un chemin de fer, dans l'isthme de Téhuantépec," in Louis Figuier, *Les Nouvelles Conquêtes de la Science*, Paris, 1883-5, IV, p.185. Photo: Julie Wolf.

France at the end of 1877.[94] The cartoon shrinks the Eiffel Tower not only by comparing it to one twice its size but also by showing that the structure is repeatable in ways that technological inventions (telephone and light bulb) are not. To replicate Eiffel's "idea"—an idea that, according to Edison, the English were incapable of conceiving—is not to innovate. Replication demands nothing more than reconstruction.

Uncomfortable with the official honors being bestowed upon him, Edison said he wished that he "had come over in [his] laboratory blouse, and could have gone about unknown and have seen something."[95] He noticed the apparent idleness of the French, and the man famous for sleeping only four hours a night had no hesitation about voicing his disdain: "What has struck me so far chiefly is the absolute laziness of everybody over here. When do these people work? What do they work at? I have not seen an earth load of goods since I came to Paris. People here seem to have established an elaborate system of loafing. Some of these engineers who come to see me, fashionably dressed, walking stick in hand—when do they work?" The reporter added "Edison pronounces the words 'work' and 'working' as some do 'prayer,' 'religion.'"[96] Though Edison conceded that the French possessed "magnitude of conception," he was confident Americans back home were superior to the French because they worked harder. They could realize their ideas. Edison would be proven right in Panama, at tremendous cost to the French.

When Bartholdi was constructing the Statue of Liberty at the Gaget and Gauthier workshop and attracting crowds of visitors at the outskirts of Paris, Lesseps was orchestrating an international meeting to sanction his second sea-level canal across an isthmus. Suez and Panama had long been linked, first by the Saint-Simonians and then by Lesseps. Europeans and Americans wanted to save themselves the time and cost of navigating around South America, even entertaining, à la Verne, the idea of moving immense ships by railway across an isthmus. More than one illustration of the 1880s demonstrate how gigantic steamships could be moved from the sea onto tracks (fig. 130). A decade later the Peruvian rubber baron Carlos Fermin Fitzcarrald hauled a dismantled thirty-ton steamship across land. In a 1982 film based on the story, Werner Herzog was truer to the nineteenth century: he decided to dramatize the absurdity of trying to transport an intact ship, not a dismantled one, over a mountain.

At the congress of 1879, Lesseps overrode protests on the part of many engineers, especially Americans (and Eiffel), who argued that Panama required locks. Lesseps insisted on "a canal of seawater at a constant level." After all "the experience of the Suez Canal has already demonstrated that a great transit of navigation requires a maritime canal as free as a

**131**
"Canal on Paper" in Walter B. Stevens, *A Trip to Panama*, St. Louis, Missouri, 1907, p. 120. Photo: Julie Wolf.

**132**
Jeannet, *Reception de M. Ferdinand de Lesseps sur la place de la cathédrale, février 1886*. Paris, Bibliothèque Nationale, Cabinet des Estampes.

natural Bosphorus."[97] A sea-level canal stood for freedom and financial advantage, particularly for the capitalist seeking to exploit a foreign isthmus. A canal "subjected to stops," he warned, was "even sometimes [subjected] to work stoppages" and was "profitable only to interior navigation."[98] International freedom versus internal profits and worker unrest: Lesseps knew how to manipulate rhetoric.

No engineer, Lesseps claimed that the Panama Canal was "an operation the exact mathematics of which is perfectly well-known." Only "two things need to be done: to remove a mass of earth and stones, and to control the river Chagres."[99] Lesseps' faith led him, criminally, to mistake paper and matter, geometry and mass. In 1886 he told a journalist, "We have changed the whole course of the river and made it run on the other side of the mountains altogether."[100] He meant they had moved the river around the mountains on paper, and for Lesseps paper was a place subject to few limitations (fig. 131). His sin was the geometer's and the imperialist's. He was convinced that "everywhere" was subject to his control or his abstraction and that "everywhere" was the same. What worked at Suez would work in Panama. He ignored the fact that he had never moved rivers or mountains in Egypt's desert. A photograph of Panama during the French phase nicely gauges the extent to which Lesseps imagined the construction of the Panama Canal as an extension of his personality (fig. 132). Another Wizard of Oz, his disembodied head presides over the scene in an illusion of power.

The Panama Canal was begun in 1882. As workers were raising high a hollow sculpture in Paris, tens of thousands of other laborers, including 50,000 men from the West Indies, were removing the earth of Panama, even attempting to level a 330-foot mountain at the Culebra Pass.[101] If finishing the Suez Canal had required the replacement of "slaves" by machines, the Panama Canal witnessed the return of dirt-cheap laborers who worked with shovels as well as machines, but machines ill-suited, at least initially, to Panama's very different terrain.

The Panama Canal was in every way an excision, "a cut," of the continent's dense interior, the endless disemboweling of earth by way of men and cranes, dredges, and railways. But the mountainous, geologically unusual, wet terrain of Panama, its mass, would not be emptied.[102]

Mudslides constantly refilled the space that men and machines had struggled to open (fig. 133). It was difficult for the engineer even to imagine the endlessness of Panama's mass, a mass that twisted, overturned, and swallowed pristine lines like those of railway tracks glimpsed in photographs (fig. 134). One historian resorts to the myth of Sisyphus in an effort to assess the work.

> The amount of digging involved was always greater than one might imagine, for the reason that the canal was being dug through a saddle between steep hills. So as the Culebra Cut was made steadily broader at the top, its sides, against the bordering hills, rose steadily higher.... This meant that the volume of excavation, the total cube, was being compounded steadily and enormously. The deeper the Cut was dug, the worse the slides were, and so the more the slopes had to be carved back. The more digging done, the more digging there was to do. It was a work of Sisyphus on a scale such as engineers had never before faced.[103]

Although some sixty-five million cubic yards of dirt had been removed, by 1887 even Lesseps had come to recognize that wet earth had engulfed his vision of clean, unhindered lines—the channels to be cut at sea level across the isthmus. The relentless entropy, which Barbara Johnson calls the "revenge of the referent," coerced a man prone to simplification to concede that he needed the help of more pragmatically minded engineers.[104] In 1887, a year after the inauguration ceremony of the Statue of Liberty in New York, where he had proclaimed "Good-bye until we meet at Panama," Lesseps finally and reluctantly approached Eiffel to design locks for the canal and to supervise their construction and the removal of earth required to install them (once again déblais and remblais).[105] To realize his colossal ambition Lesseps needed Eiffel's colossal engineering. If anyone in this story of dreams, triumphs, and disasters was forced to eat his own words, it was Lesseps. At the 1879 international meeting, where he had overwhelmed considerable dissenting opinion through the sheer force of his personality, Eiffel had argued that the Panama Canal required locks that could move ships up and across the mountains of the isthmus (fig. 135). His was one of the few votes opposing Lesseps' plan.

Eiffel's contract with Lesseps is dated 10 December 1887. The entrepreneur paid dearly for the engineer's expertise and prestige, raising the cost of digging, as one lawyer later put it, from seven francs to thirty-three francs per cubic yard.[106] Eiffel undoubtedly enjoyed the opportunity of proving Lesseps wrong and succeeding where he had failed. He also appreciated the advance of eighteen million francs, which would help fund the construction of his tower. In 1887, the year of the contract, he had just begun to build the structure to which he had committed his fortune. In January 1888 Eiffel ordered the construction in Nantes of enormous locks for the Panama Canal, some seventy-nine feet high, sixty-nine feet wide, and thirteen feet thick. In 1888 he began to supervise two labor crews, one removing water-soaked earth in Panama and the other in Paris building with iron, earth's gift to engineers. The trains and cranes brought iron to the tower to be raised on high, and at the same time hundreds of carloads of earth were being removed daily at the Panama Canal.

Eiffel was alone in grasping the special demands of Panama's geography. The lock system would provide vertical as well as horizontal solutions to the task of transporting goods and persons across a mountainous isthmus. Ships would be raised up and over the mountains. It is easy to understand why Lesseps could not accept the proposal of a lock-based rather than sea-level canal. Locks chop up space into small units; they enclose the ships, sometimes hiding them. They impede the view; there can be none of the endless vistas to the horizon so dear to Lesseps (fig. 136). Locks serve immediate mechanical purposes rather than figure the sublimely abstract truths that geometry promises.

Eiffel's locks could have completed the Panama Canal, but Lesseps had turned to him too late. The Panama Canal Company declared bankruptcy on 14 December 1888. At the Universal Exposition the Suez Canal Company hastily removed the Meso-American half of the pavilion that had been intended to publicize the two canals as twin achievements. But believing the Panama project could still be saved, Eiffel devoted half of his pavilion at the foot of his tower to the lock system. His pavilion was the only place where the debacle of Lesseps' work was recognized and corrected. Eiffel's model presented and promoted the locks that Lesseps had cavalierly rejected (figs. 137–138).[107]

**133**
"Official Photographer of the Isthmian Canal Commission," (Ernest Hallen or unknown predecessor), *Laborers dig a ditch at the Cucaracha Slide, October 11, 1913.* Washington, D.C., National Archives.

**134**
"Official Photographer of the Isthmian Canal Commission," (Ernest Hallen or unknown predecessor), *Mudslide engulfing U.S. steam shovel 201, February 7, 1913.* Washington, D.C., National Archives.

**135**
*Map of the Panama Canal Zone, showing the levels of the canal.* From J. and M. Biesanz, *The People of Panama* (New York: Columbia University Press, 1955). Photo: Julie Wolf.

**136**
"Gatun Upper Locks, East Chamber," in Logan Marshall, *The Story of the Panama Canal. The Wonderful Account of the Gigantic Undertaking commenced by the French, and brought to triumphant completion by the United States*, Boston and Chicago, 1913, p. 173. Photo: Julie Wolf.

**137**
L. Hardy, *Le Pavillon de la Compagnie de Suez, Élévation,* 1889. Paris, Archives National.

**Currency, the terrible precision instrument, clean to the conscience, loses even its meaning.**
**Stéphane Mallarmé, "Or," 1897**

Panama's mud, its sacrificed workers, its duped subscribers, Lesseps' desperation:—Eiffel had profited from them all. He had been paid no less than sixty-three million francs, ten times the price of the tower, to save the Panama Canal, at a time when thousands of subscribers faced bankruptcy. Headlines screamed "THIRTY-THREE MILLION NET?" One paper caustically referred to the "pyramidal farce."[108]

In an article on the Panama scandal, published in a British paper in 1893, the poet Stéphane Mallarmé explains why "the simple man" had trouble comprehending the enormous sums of money that had been lost. Writing in the first person as a witness to the disaster, he begins with the meltdown of capital that

> flows, spreads, gleams on the horizon. I thereby gain an impression of what such sums might be, millions by the hundreds and beyond.... And yet, it is the inability of figures, however grandiloquent, to translate it, [that] truly springs out of this case. Nothing in me can explain it; though one gets a hint from the fact that the more a sum increases or backs up, as far as the simple man in the street is concerned, toward the improbable, it includes as it inscribes itself, more and more zeros; signifying that its total is equal to nothing, almost.[109]

Endless zeros do not enlarge the sums but reduce them almost to nothing. The numbers upon which accounts of the colossal had relied are pronounced all but incomprehensible. Mallarmé further meditated on money in the poem "Or" (Gold) he developed from his article. In this poem, Barbara Johnson points out, Mallarmé chose to erase the specificity of the poem's origins in the Panama scandal. In "Or," the word "Panama" is never mentioned. But article and poem do share the image of liquid money: "a treasure liquefaction crawls, gleams on the horizon."[110] The identity of the "horizon" is irrelevant. What matters is the capitalist dream that underwrote the desire to cut canals across continents; the dream of the endless flow of capital, spreading, gleaming, unhindered. Canals were meant to ensure the flow of commerce.[111]

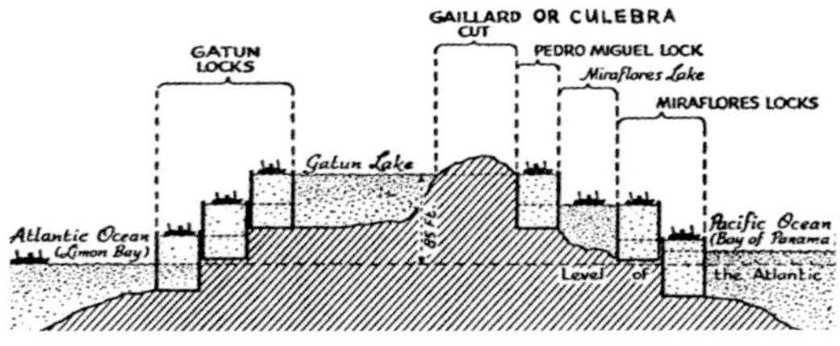

The Panama scandal of 1892—it occurred while Freycinet was prime minister—permanently stained Eiffel. There was no stopping the sensationalist indictment of the colossal financing of colossal engineering: the behind-the-scenes traffic in money and profit, the millions of francs used to bribe government officials, the ruthless sacrifice of subscribers' investments.[112] Camille Pissarro and other critics, many of them anarchists, seized the opportunity to brand the Eiffel Tower as the sign of capital. The funicular structure optimizes the use of materials, which means that it minimizes cost and increases profit (fig. 138).[113] And profits had been huge. Workers had been sacrificed to profit. Two men had died building the Eiffel Tower, but twenty-two thousand West Indians and Frenchmen died, many from disease, while digging the Panama Canal during the French phase of work.[114]

Belated and unsuccessful, the attempt to move the mud of Panama ruined Eiffel. In newspaper after newspaper, illustrations lampooned him (figs. 139-140). He might have been only one among many guilty men, but he could not hide in the crowd. Always the Eiffel Tower gave him away. The scandal had diminished his giant tower to the human scale of a commodity. The structure that had once loomed over ancient Egyptian pyramids shrank pitilessly into an object, or perhaps worse, into a model. In the press of the early 1890s, the tower was borne on Eiffel's back, pushed in a cart, or displayed on a mantel. Once upon a time, the tower's colossal scale had seemed all but unimaginable, but compared to the sums of money that had vanished into the pockets of a few, its physical size became paltry. What were one thousand feet of structure compared to the unfathomable number of millions lost—"more and more zeros"?

Eiffel was sentenced to two years in prison. Although he was spared jail, he never built another monument. He spent the rest of his life conducting scientific experiments at the top of the tower once heralded as evidence that engineering could lift you high above the mud and corruption that swallowed French machinery and French fortunes in Panama. Still Eiffel persisted. The next steps up from the tower into the air were the focus of his last experiments. He probed into telegraphy, meteorology, and aerodynamics, all free of the problems of earthbound structures. Giving mass flight, that became Eiffel's final goal for reasons the Socialist Jean Juarès wove into a parable published as an editorial in 1901. The parable centers on the flight of a balloonist:

But he does steer: he makes the balloon turn in every direction and then go like an arrow to the point he has fixed upon. For the first time the line of a human will has been marked in space, the plan of a human thought developed. Until now balloons could only be steered in a vertical direction, and that very clumsily.... Now at last man with his imperious will and his definite and vigorous thought is asserting himself in the upper spaces...

In that frail balloon moving deliberately toward its goal I see a part of the immense human problem. I might express it in this way: to make life, social life as well as natural life, a thing that can be steered.... While I was rejoicing in a free and impersonal pride, the pride of the human race and of Socialism, and was looking with emotion on the spectacle presented by victorious man, master of nature and of himself...I recognized one of my friends whose conclusions often distress me, on the outskirts of the group.... "How strange!" he murmured; "here is a justification of all our suspicions. He could turn from right to left and he turns from left to right, the direction of every treachery.... Don't you see that this man has agreed to go around the Eiffel Tower that was built with the stolen Panama money? Don't you see that in bringing the Eiffel Tower into an experiment that is, anyway, of very doubtful value but that has excited all the faddists of progress and science, they wished to rehabilitate the Panama Company and Eiffel...? I say to you, I who have not been bought by either cheats or fools, what you see up there is a trick of the Ministry and the Panama Company. That man has stolen right and left: he has stolen from public secret funds and I, I alone will denounce him."

And as the balloon disappeared behind the glowing tops of the autumn trees, he cried in a voice that was rather sharp and shrill: *"Panamiste! Panamiste!"* [115]

**138**
*Eiffel Pavilion.* From L. Farge, *Constructions francaise et étrangères.* Paris, Bibliothèque Historique de la Ville de Paris.

The suspicious onlooker mocked in Juarès's story recounts a truth: it was the failure of Lesseps' canal in Panama that had provided the funds for the Eiffel Tower. At the Universal Exhibition of 1889 visitors at the top of the tower saw Paris recede into a panorama that stunned them in its silence, maplike stasis, and leveling of difference. From the Eiffel Tower, one commentator remarked, "nothing appeared to dominate anything." The ironies are multiple, tragic. The fiasco in Panama had bankrupted thousands of subscribers, squandered labor and money, and yet helped to build a tower that gave visitors a panorama in which everything seemed equal.

Juarès's tale of ballooning can be applied to Eiffel and Lesseps in more ways than one. In his parable, geometry is what demonstrates and makes visible man's will and his power. Only the pilot's capacity to steer the tossing balloon to an intended point, to trace a line, indicates his control over chaos, and the straighter the path, the greater the achievement. Mastery's sign is geometry, even drawing, in the midst of a turbulent and beautiful nature, but not engineering, not mechanics, not prosthetics, not locks. Lines in space. I understand the seduction.

The extraction of mass to make simple volumes is, Freycinet argued, one of our most enduring—and reckless—habits. And colossal mass proves surprisingly difficult to keep in mind. Millions of cubic yards of earth are hard to fathom. And while mathematics homogenizes its quantities—we do not subtract three apples from five oranges—a cubic yard of matter is an exceedingly diverse thing. Egypt's sand and Panama's mud are not the same; flesh and rock are not either. Nor in modern manufacture are colossi and human lives. They cost more in Paris than in Panama. Eiffel had computed the equilibrium of forces on paper and had successfully translated that drawing into colossal structure. But visualizations on paper could not predict the disequilibrium of forces in Panama. Eiffel the engineer had misled Eiffel the egotist; drawing cannot prophesy the complex variables of geography as it can those of engineered structures.

Volumes do not indicate mass. Cubic yards can be light as a feather or weigh five tons. Nevertheless, in 1913, the year of the Panama Canal's opening, when Americans were eager to boast about accomplishing a colossal removal of earth where the French had failed, *Scientific American* published an image in which sixty-three pyramids are set among the tall buildings of New York City (fig. 141). To clarify the point of the illustration, a caption was added: "A graphic comparison. The 'spoil' taken from the canal would build 63 pyramids the size of Cheops in Broadway from the Battery to Harlem."

Modern channels, even Panama's, could not be conceived without ancient Egypt or the simple geometric shapes Egypt's solid stone monuments had left to haunt posterity. From these emptied shapes and New York City's buildings, Americans were being asked to imagine the mass such pyramids represent. Their job, now our job? Putting mass back after geometers and so many valiant, sometimes desperate, workers had taken it away.

22e ANNÉE — No 1.129 FRANCE : 15 CENTIMES 27 Novembre 1892

LE GRELOT

BUREAUX
5, Cité Bergère, 5
PARIS

ABONNEMENTS
FRANCE
Un an ........ 8 fr.
Six mois ...... 4
Trois mois .... 2
15 c. le numéro

PARAIT LE DIMANCHE

ADRESSER
Lettres et Mandats à M. J. MADRE
Administrateur.

BUREAUX
5, cité Bergère, 5
PARIS

ABONNEMENTS
ÉTRANGER
Un an ........ 10 fr.
Six mois ...... 5
Trois mois .... 2 50
20 c. le numéro

PARAIT LE DIMANCHE

PUBLICITÉ
Les Annonces sont reçues aux bureaux du Journal.

Voir en tête de la deuxième page les conditions auxquelles on peut recevoir gratuitement le GRELOT

LES MARTYRS DU PANAMA



**139**
Camille Pissarro, *Capital*, 1891. Pen and ink drawing from *Les Turpitudes Sociales.* Oxford, Ashmolean Museum.

**140**
"The Martyrs of Panama," *Le Grelot*, 27 November 1892. Photo: Julie Wolf.

**141**
*Scientific American* illustration, reproduced in Willis J. Abbot, *Panama and the Canal in Pictures and Prose* (London and N.Y., 1913), p. 134.

Courtesy Scientific American

A GRAPHIC COMPARISON

The "spoil" taken from the canal would build 63 pyramids the size of Cheops in Broadway from the Battery to Harlem

# Panama's Cut

## Stereoview / Painting

**Matter in large masses must always be fixed and dear; form is cheap and transportable.**
**Oliver Wendell Holmes, "The Stereoscope and the Stereograph," 1859**

The job seemed easy. The isthmus is only fifty miles wide. In one postcard, Uncle Sam chops it with an axe while Teddy Roosevelt looks on (fig. 142). In another Panama is so narrow that the canal appears to be little more than the kissing lips of two oceans (fig. 143).

Early modern mapmakers had been unable to find the correct category for Panama. Isthmus or strait? Finger of land or finger of water?[1] Connection or opening? Conjunction or gap? But these questions faded when Panama began to be seen as a bridge between two vast masses of land. Then it shrank into the most slight of land forms.

To cut through tiny Panama seemed to require little more than cognitive control: make some plans, obtain agreement fom concerned parties, proceed. The case had the ring of the inevitable in this era of colonialism; no one bothered to take a closer look. The hubris of Théophile Gautier, writing in 1869 when the Suez Canal was opened, is typical. "The isthmus of Suez forms a sort of depression between Africa and Asia.... [T]his weak obstacle, this thin tongue of earth [is] hardly visible on the map... An analogous operation on the isthmus of Panama, that point of suture connecting South and North America and preventing the Atlantic Ocean from opening onto the Pacific, will permit man freely to circle his globe and to eliminate enormous useless detours."[2]

In expressing the imperialist delusions of his time, Gautier shows how automatic and pervasive was the connection of Suez and Panama, "thin tongues" both. In poems and prose Panama inevitably followed Suez. But if an isthmus sutures continents, canals were meant to disconnect them—Africa from Asia, North from South America—in order to link the oceans and facilitate the circulation of goods. The vision of severing continents to connect oceans assumes that, even in this age of railways, water continued to be the best means of long-distance transport.

Maps permit men to peer at paper and mistake representation for its referent (see fig. 131). But they are likely to overlook the irreducibility of physical matter. Representation simplifies, and it typically miniaturizes. Maps, paintings, photographs, stereoviews, medals: all shrink the world. How can these things convey immensity? The question of scale is pertinent because the Panama Canal was considered a colossal achievement, indeed "the greatest engineering feat in the world."[3]

Lesseps' plans for "his" second canal repeated the straight line that had so effectively secured the achievement of Suez. The thousands of hapless French subscribers who underwrote the mounting costs received certificates with female personifications of North and South America holding hands above a straight arrow of water receding to the horizon (fig. 144). That idealized straight passageway is all the more remarkable given the impenetrable jungle in illustrations to books such as Napoleon Bonaparte Wyse's *Le canal de Panama, l'isthme américain* of 1886 (figs. 145–146).[4] In these pictures, French surveyors, some with imperialist swagger, attempt to survey a land encroached upon by vegetation. The surveying equipment seen in these images was meant to provide cartographic knowledge that would assist French engineers in the ordering and leveling of the land. The same illustrations show the difficulties newcomers faced when traveling on foot. There were no long views or horizons for guidance; the ground level could not be seen and was uneven.[5] The black vegetation, black shadows, and black bodies inscribed with black ink occluding the white paper stop our view as they did the view of the nineteenth-century explorers. Up close Panama was confusing.

It is no less daunting when viewed from a great distance as in a map of the Western Hemisphere. With the Pacific at its west, the Atlantic at its east, North America above it, South America below, the isthmus gives the impression that it can be charted with a compass. But curving, twisting, the isthmus and its canal confound simple north-south and east-west axes. Direction in Panama is perplexing. The canal runs from Pacific to Atlantic; but not from west to east so much as from north to south. Even more bewildering is the fact that the Atlantic side of the canal is farther west than the Pacific side. The sun rises over the canal, not in the east on the side of the Atlantic, but in the west on the side of the Pacific. And, against all common sense, the sun sets on the Atlantic which in Panama is farther west.

A map of the canal made after its completion in 1914 indicates how Panama's curves undermine certainty about direction, predicated as it is on a perpendicular axis (fig. 147). Engineers designing the canal had to survey Panama's daunting terrain and calculate how the canal could cross mountains, lakes, and the torrential Chagres River, then capable of rising forty-six feet in

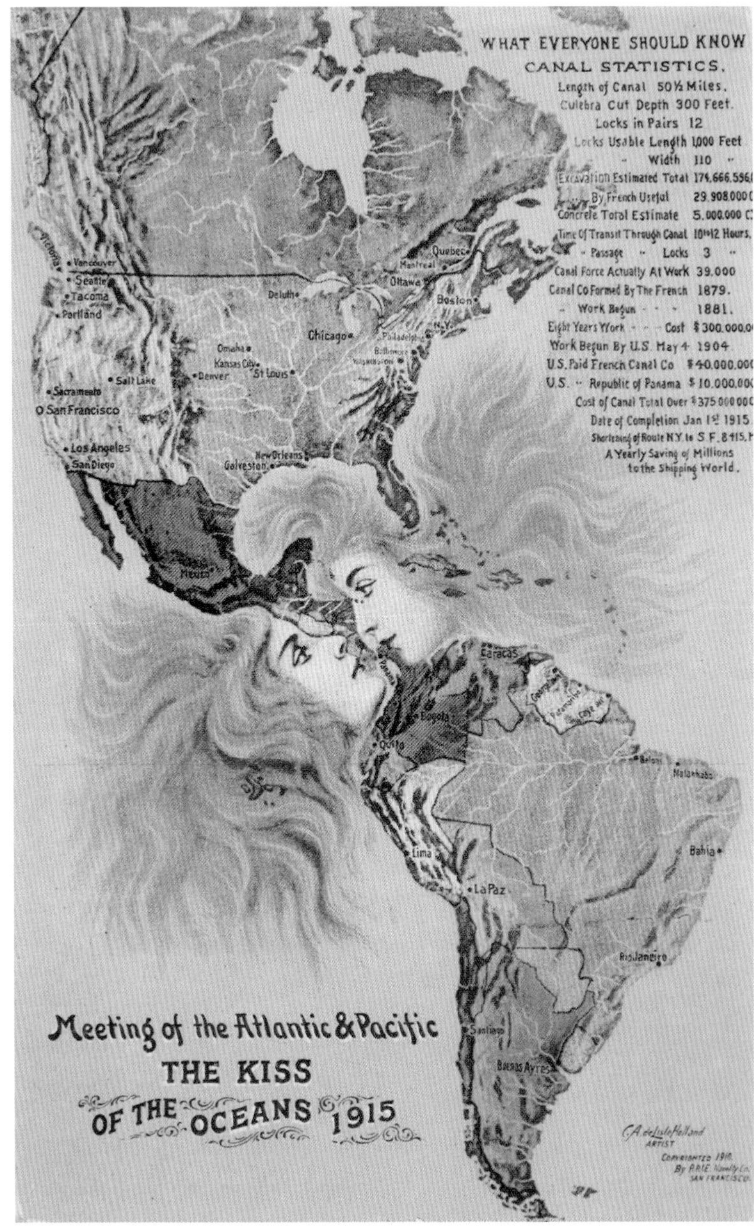

**142**
Postcard, "Ground Broken Oct. 14, 1911, Panama-Pacific International Exposition San Francisco 1915." Copyright Richard Behrendt, 1911. Author's Collection. Photo: Julie Wolf.

**143**
Postcard, C.A. de Lisle Holland, *Meeting of the Atlantic & Pacific*, 1910. Copyright P.P.I.E. Novelty Co., San Francisco. Author's Collection. Photo: Julie Wolf.

**144**
Detail of French subscription. "Compagnie Universelle du Canal Interocéanique de Panama. Action de Cinq Cents France au Porteur," 1886. Author's Collection. Photo: Julie Wolf.

**145**
"M. Lacharme having a trail cut in the forest."
From Lucien N.B. Wyse, *Le Canal de Panama, L'Isthme américain; explorations; comparaison des traces étudiés; négociations; état des travaux*, Paris, 1886. Photo: Julie Wolf.

**146**
"Tidal pools, Caquirri, upstream from the hill of Cristal."
From Lucien N.B. Wyse, *Le canal de Panama, L'Isthme américain; explorations; comparaison des traces étudiés; négociations; état des travaux*, Paris, 1886. Photo: Julie Wolf.

**147**
*Souvenir of the Panama Canal*. Author's Collection. Photo: Julie Wolf.

**148**
Thomas Nast, "The European plan," *Harper's Weekly*, 13 March 1880. Washington, D.C., Library of Congress

**149**
Udo J. Kepple, "Waiting," *Puck*, 21 June 1904. Washington, D.C., Library of Congress.

**150**
"A Crown he is entitled to wear," *Judge*, 4 June 1904. On the crown: "The Greatest Achievement for Trade in Modern Times." Washington, D.C., Library of Congress.

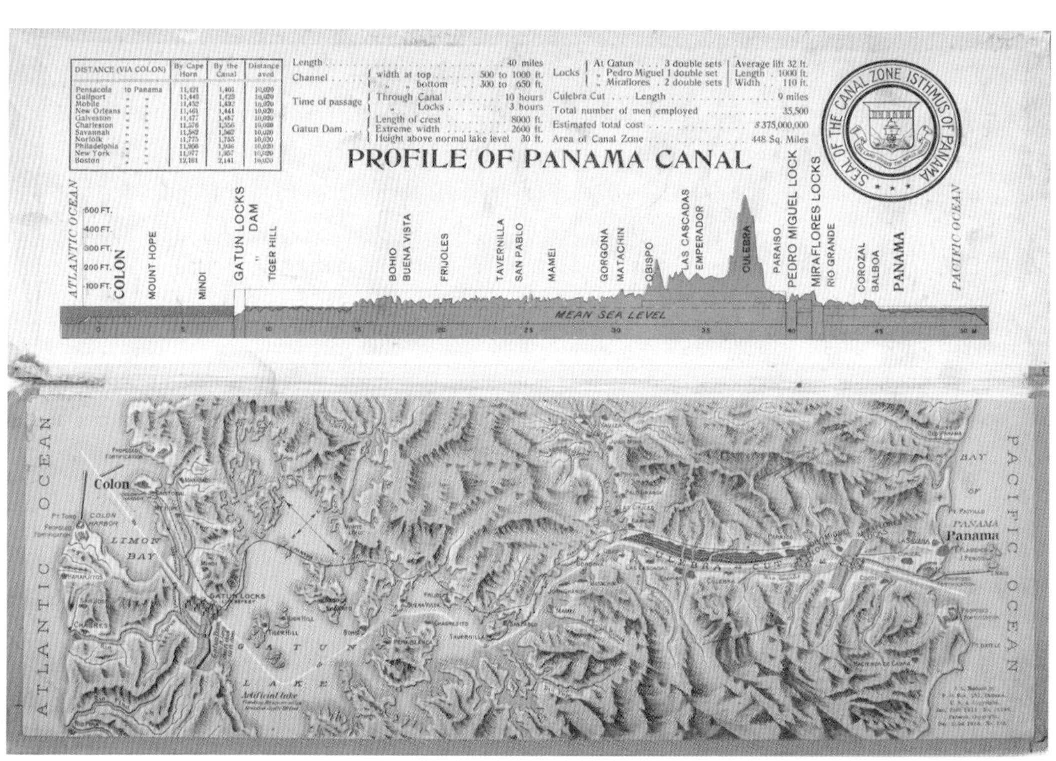

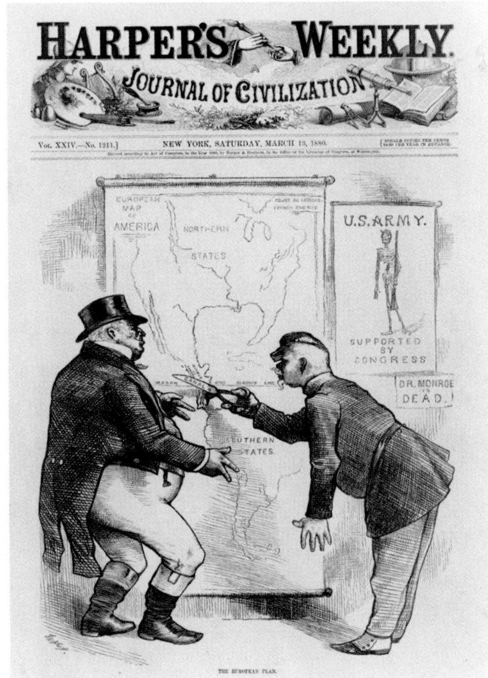

three days, releasing 1,000 cubic feet per second during the dry season, and discharging eighty times that amount during the floods of the rainy season. Lesseps nonetheless intended to carve a canyon through a 330-foot mountain pass at Culebra. Neither an engineer,[6] nor a geographer, he failed. Endless mudslides refilled the cut, which had to be made wider and wider. Most eerily, the bottom of the Culebra Cut would rise in perceptible ways underneath workers' feet; sometimes the land would push upward as much as six feet in minutes.[7] The earth was not giving way to water. Panama's mass would not be emptied.

---

**Beware also of those who, seeing two rivers separated on the map of France by a little scrap of white paper, propose to join these rivers and call that a project.** **Condorcet warning Turgot, 1774**

There was no avoiding a paradox. The isthmus of Panama was imagined as ever so slender and finite (just 50 miles), but excavating a canal across this slender isthmus was a monstrous, never-ending task. After six years the French admitted defeat; the failed canal had cost tens of thousands of lives, at least five hundred men per mile. Americans would require an additional eleven years and three million dollars to finish the job. But in 1889, nine months after the bankruptcy of the Panama Canal Company, Edison was already mocking France's dandified engineers. His sense of superiority reflected his countrymen's belief that they could finish the job.[8] The United States had never liked French intervention in the Americas. As early as 1880 the cover of *Harper's Weekly* featured "The European Plan": Maréchal MacMahon of France uses scissors labeled "Canal" to cut the continents; British John Bull looks on approvingly; a sign declares that the Monroe Doctrine is dead (fig. 148).

Nineteen years later, in 1899, Uncle Sam would be depicted encouraging President McKinley to "Finish the Canal...and make our national expansion complete in your first administration." U.S. flags flying over the Philippines, Hawaii, Alaska, Cuba, and Puerto Rico marked that expansion.[9] In the end, after McKinley's assassination in 1901, Teddy Roosevelt would seek to complete America's "national expansion" in Panama. Although critics claimed Panama was no more than a mass grave (fig. 149), Roosevelt was eager to wield his "big stick" in Latin America. The same year that death loomed over Panama on the cover of *Puck*, the president appeared on the front of *Judge*, sporting a crown inscribed "The Greatest Achievement for Trade in Modern Times" (fig. 150).

The year was 1904. Months before, in November 1903, the United States had declared Panama an independent republic. When Colombia failed to ratify a treaty transferring the French New Canal Company's concession to the United States, along with a ten-mile-wide strip of the isthmus, Roosevelt resorted to gunboat diplomacy. He had U.S. ships stationed off shore; a popular uprising against Colombia ensued. Three days afterwards, on 6 November 1903, the

United States recognized the new republic and a few weeks later paid it ten million dollars for rights to the canal; the New Canal Company was paid forty million.[10] A cartoon of 1903 represents the president dropping a shovel of Panama soil on top of Bogotá (fig. 151). The 1904 covers of *Puck* and *Judge* would pose the question: was the Panama Canal modernity's greatest boost to trade or its cavernous graveyard?

Teddy Roosevelt was not the kind of man who hesitated. Lesseps' equal in arrogance and ambition, he was similarly prone to imagine the successful completion of the canal as a matter of his own personal volition and prowess. During his 1906 visit to Panama, he posed for photographs. In the most famous of them, Roosevelt sits in a huge steam shovel as if he presided over the digging himself (fig. 152). Later, in 1911, he crowed: "I took the Isthmus [and] started the canal," as if he, not Lesseps, had begun the canal.[11] These two were quite the pair.

In some ways the Americans were better suited to meet the difficulties of Panama's terrain, but not because they worked harder than the "dandified" French, as Edison would have it. The United States succeeded where the French had failed for more systemic reasons. Whereas the French government had had no overt role in the canal enterprise, the American government oversaw and controlled the canal's construction; the army was mobilized, and the government subcontracted supply companies. The historian of engineering Tom F. Peters has argued, "George Washington Goethals treated the problem like a military problem: he orchestrated and controlled the hierarchy and interaction of all the parts," including the management of disease.[12] But most decisively, the United States adopted Eiffel's plan for a lock-based rather than a sea-level canal. The mountains were to be climbed by ships, not leveled.

Lesseps' infatuation with the straight line was characteristic of the French. In these same years, at Napoleon III's behest, Baron Haussmann was replacing the narrow, crooked medieval streets of Paris with new "cannonshot" boulevards. His modernization of the city earned him the name "Attila of the Straight Line."[13] Americans were different; they were responsive to the character of a territory—its mountains, rivers, and canyons."All European observers noted how American railroad lines proceeded by curves rather than straight lines."[14] The aesthetic differences were pragmatic in origin. The German cultural historian Wolfgang Schivelbusch has observed:

> In England [for example, the railway] line was to be built as straight as possible, partly because railroad technology favored this, partly for economic reasons. Labor was cheap and land expensive. Thus it paid to construct tunnels, embankments and cuttings in order to make rails proceed in a straight line, at a minimum of land cost. The diametrically opposed American conditions produced opposite results. Labor was expensive, land practically worthless.... The American railroad did not proceed in a straight line through natural obstacles, but ran around them like a river not so much out of respect for nature as for cheapness. Von Gerstner, one of the first European Railway experts to visit the United States in the 1830s noted: "A great deal of earthwork is avoided."[15]

The cost per mile of railway in the United Sates became a fraction of that of England. In 1876 Bartholdi had maintained that American engineers were predisposed to straight lines because of their "hard" pragmatism and indifference to the arts. But Bartholdi was wrong. American engineers utilized curves for practical and financial reasons. Bartholdi had been speaking as a sculptor who assumed that Americans would never learn to appreciate the fine arts even if for the engineering of territory Americans were more than happy to rely on curves to save money. What Bartholdi thought was their penchant for engineered lines, rather than the gracious undulations of fine art, derived from a skewed view of American pragmatism. The French were superior. Even their engineers were more likely to be committed to ideas, to abstractions; and they could afford to engineer that way because their projects were generally government funded.

Given the American willingness to circumnavigate natural landforms, it is puzzling that they chose to continue the most impossible job the French had ever undertaken. Naive, they thought the French had made too much of the landslides at the Culebra Cut; they were sure that they could control the mud in this slippery terrain. Optimistic, they chose to focus first on the locks and dam. A *Scientific American* headline of 1910, four years before the canal's completion, boasted: "Rapid construction gives promise of an early opening."[16] Building did go smoothly, but once they returned to the cut, they came to realize that they had been far too confident. Excavating earth proved far more difficult than building structures. And now those finished structures—the

**151**
W. A. Rogers "The News Reaches Bogotá," *New York Herald*, December 1903. New York, New York, The Granger Collection.

**152**
"President Theodore Roosevelt sitting on a steam shovel at the Panama Canal," *New York TImes*, 15 November 1906. Washington D.C., Library of Congress. Photo: Corbis.

**153**
"Average Shape and Dimensions of the Culebra Cut," illustration in Frederick J. Haskin, *The Panama Canal*, Garden City, N.Y., 1914, p. 75. Photo: Julie Wolf.

locks and the dam—left the Americans with no alternative but to finish the Culebra Cut. With concrete and steel, they had locked the design into place. The cut, the United States belatedly came to realize, would decide the canal's success or failure. They continued to dig at the Culebra Cut—the mud continued to fill in their excavations.

How could the Americans possibly succeed? Dynamite, Alfred Nobel's contribution to the modern era. The United States would eventually use sixty-one million pounds of dynamite to explode holes in the mountainside.[17] For seven years the Culebra Cut was seldom silent; 6,000 men worked there daily, half of them doing the dangerous work of dynamiting. Despite the incessant accidents that hurled rocks onto railways; despite constant mudslides; despite continual overturning of railway tracks, the workers managed to excavate 232 million cubic yards, more than seven times as much as the French had dug in Panama, and three times the excavation at Suez (fig. 153). The job was never-ending and treacherous. To cite workers, primarily West Indians, whose firsthand accounts were solicited by the Isthmian Historical Society in 1963: "Work in water and mud. Rain and sun day and night." "Condition in the Cut was very bad, rain all day and then mud-mud-mud- and more mud." "The amount of West Indians that lose their lives on the job was mournful to talk about."[18] One worker from St. Lucia deserves to be quoted at length.

Man die, get blow up, get kill or get drown. During the time someone would ask where is Brown he diede last night and burry where is Jerry he dead a little before dinner and buried so on and so all the time Malaria was raging yellow fever was raging another fever was called tyfod fever rageing in matachin section United States Citensin and West Indian lives and blood was taken to put through this Canal Uncle Sam had to run through the door left it open and get foreneners to do his wark we had Colored Americans working good men skillful men but they can't pull with the White Americans always a fight and trouble if not West Indians could never be hear because Uncle Sam have plenty Colored Americans to do his work also they don't like down hear to get away they make plenty of trouble at that rate West Indians get a break if not so when we had arrived from our native land to Cristobal Dock no. 2 we would have to take the next boat back home it would be too many dogs for the pice of bone.... Culebra Cut that is call Gaillard cut that was where the Goverment had the stiffest job which I and others never believe will ever put through because today you dig and it grow tomorrow beside it slides every day the Government wash down the hill give it a bath night and day until the hill catch cramp then blass it up with dannimite that was done year after year.[19]

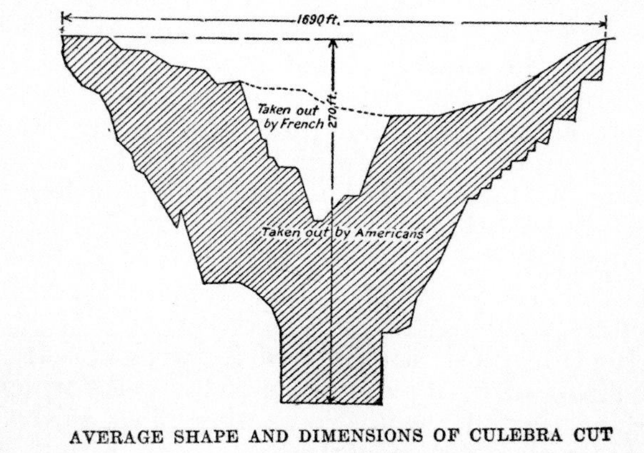

AVERAGE SHAPE AND DIMENSIONS OF CULEBRA CUT

Digging, dynamiting, more digging, disease and death, ongoing racial tension, and boatloads of new workers from the Caribbean—the man from Santa Lucia knew that the canal was a quagmire even for Uncle Sam. But the jobs, dangerous and grueling, had to be taken. West Indians and "Colored Americans" were pitched against one another in a dog-eat-dog world. The man from Santa Lucia knew that too. No wonder. African Americans—"working good men skillful men"—were treated badly, paid less well, did not like the work, and found ways of returning home, "always a fight and trouble." And the cut as always is characterized as the toughest job: "today you dig and it grow tomorrow beside it slides."

In 1915, two years after the Panama Canal's opening, yet another slide at Culebra would close it for seven months. Even today slides continue to occur.[20] The persistent failure to secure the excavation at Culebra ultimately made the cut an almost mythical labor. Hercules, gigantic and more muscular than ever, forces the Cut into being in the poster for the Panama-Pacific Exhibition of 1915 (fig. 154). In his five-volume 1921 publication, Frank Morton Todd, the exhibition's official historian, criticized the poster because Hercules was "a sheer misrepresentation" of "the real wonders of the work."[21] Recently, Bill Brown has added that "this classical body subsumes the work of 30–40,000 'white and negro workmen,' primarily West Indians, employed to construct the canal. It aestheticizes labor into the abstraction of 'the thirteenth labor.'"[22] The tactic was not new. Lesseps had been represented as Hercules parting the land of Egypt to make the Suez Canal (fig. 155).

The Culebra Cut seemed to condense and simplify the fundamental question that the desire to build canals posed: Could the land be parted? The "weak obstacle" of the slender isthmus proved to be no such thing (fig. 156). The cut grew wider and wider and still the sides would collapse. The digging, the dynamiting, the widening, the slides, the refilling, and the land rising beneath workers' feet: Culebra was a morass, at once grueling and entangling.

**154**
*The Thirteenth Labor of Hercules*, Cover of *Panama Pacific International Exposition. San Francisco, 1915*, San Francisco, 1915. Author's Collection. Photo: Julie Wolf.

**155**
Étienne Carjat. "Ferdinand de Lesseps separating the two continents," lithograph published in the journal *Le Boulevard*, 29 June 1862. Collection de l'Association du Souvenir de Ferdinand de Lesseps et du Canal de Suez.

**156**
Photograph. *Culebra Cut, Culebra. Deepest excavated portion of the Panama Canal, showing Gold Hill on right and Contractor's Hill on left. June 1913.* Author's Collection. Photo: Julie Wolf.

**Yet if some survivor of the ancient Egyptian work could have seen Culebra, he might have been pardoned for wondering whether these were men or devils, so strikingly were ingenuity and audacity on display.** Frank Morton Todd, *The Story of the Exposition*, 1921

Whatever the canal workers displayed in the way of "ingenuity and audacity," Panama would confront the American artist William Brantley Van Ingen with the most difficult—and most enthralling—challenge of his career. Although almost forgotten today, in 1914 when Colonel George Goethals awarded him the commission for painting murals in the rotonda of the new Panama Canal Administration Building, Van Ingen had attained a national reputation as a muralist (fig. 157). A Philadelphian, Van Ingen had studied at the Academy of Fine Arts and then moved to New York City to apprentice with the respected decorative and stained glass artists Louis C. Tiffany and John La Farge, the latter having been president of the National Society of Mural Painters from 1899 through 1904.[23] By 1914 Van Ingen had completed numerous public murals and stained glass windows for the Library of Congress, the Philadelphia Mint, and the Union Club and Edison Electric Building, both in New York City. His work for the Electric Building celebrated technology and portrayed Edison experimenting in his laboratory.[24] He also decorated private residences, even traveling to Japan in preparation for a Japanese-style room.

But he preferred public commissions, primarily because of their large scale.[25] In a 1917 essay Van Ingen treats size as a gauge to the "majesty" of a subject."

> Size, we know, is an element of grandeur. The canvas that is small carries with it an unescapable implication that the scene it represents is small whereas the wall space that is noble, like the sonority of the voice of the orator or the rhythmic roll of verse, prepares our minds to receive the profound teachings of Nature's handiwork.... Where can these great spaces be found save in our public buildings? Where else can we avail ourselves of size?[26]

Experienced, disciplined, and committed to large-scale public painting, the fifty-six-year-old artist was well suited to the task Goethals had given him. His contract with the Isthmian Canal Commission is dated 3 March 1914. Van Ingen took the commission seriously and traveled twice to Panama, where he made studies.[27] In his studio in New York City, with two assistants, he painted some 953 square feet of canvas for which he was paid almost $24,000, twenty-five dollars a square foot, plus expenses.[28] In 1915 he returned to Panama to supervise the installation of his paintings in the new beaux-arts building.

In an essay about the cycle published in an art journal in 1917, Van Ingen emphasized that his commission was "simply to show, as far as possible, the making of the canal," and his primary difficulty conveying immensity of the undertaking.[29] "How to express magnitude was in reality the problem imposed on me by the conditions; my constant occupation a study of the expedients of composition by which length and width, height and depth might be displayed."[30] The canal, he pointed out, had been characterized as "the Wonder of Work [but] it might also be addressed as His Majesty Magnitude." Work and colossal scale: Van Ingen interprets magnitude as labor's sign. For this American painter, the work required to make the Panama Canal could not be conveyed without expressing its gigantic size and vice versa. For Van Ingen, much as for Volney

**157**
The Panama Canal Administration Building, Balboa Heights, Canal Zone, photograph, 1937. Washington, D.C., Library of Congress.

and the French draftsmen who contemplated the pyramids in Egypt more than a century earlier, colossal size meant colossal exertion. If your job was to represent one, you needed to find some way to suggest the other: "How to express magnitude was in reality the problem."

Van Ingen understood the ways immensity confounded understanding. He opens his essay by addressing the difficulty of comprehending the scale of the great Culebra Cut.

> The Panama Canal appeared to contradict logic: in that its parts were larger than the whole. From the narrow bridge spanning the Great Cut it was evident to me that the whole canal, from ocean to ocean, could be put into that part of it which was being excavated there. This illusion was not entirely a revelation. I recalled looking into the empty hold of the steamship *Gaelic*, years ago, in the harbor of Honolulu, and, were my eyes to be trusted, the entire vessel could have been readily transported in her own hold.[31]

Van Ingen was right. The Culebra Cut seemed to exceed the size of the canal itself. This part threatened to swallow the whole. Knowingly or not, he was reiterating Kant: apprehension of the part makes the whole difficult to keep in mind; colossal scale confounds comprehension.[32] Yet for Van Ingen the colossal correlates not merely with the sublime—that which overwhelms rational assessment—but with the amount of work required to fashion disorienting enormity. The isthmus is narrow, but the cut is gigantic and the labor unceasing.

---

**I remember well the first time I saw a stereoscope and stereographs....I seemed let out to the ends of the earth.** Albert E. Osborne, *The Stereograph and the Stereoscope*, 1909

The proliferation of American images representing the construction of the Panama Canal makes it clear that the canal was an instant icon of the Roosevelt Era and Big Stick Diplomacy. In postcards, medals, photographs, and stereoviews, Americans had tokens of their success where the French had failed (figs. 158–164). "The American cut" was repeatedly contrasted to "the French cut" even when the comparison inadvertently turned both into unimpressive streams (see fig.158). In other images, French machines were shown rusting, overturned, or overwhelmed by the jungle's growth—totems of impotence and failure (fig.165).

Many mementoes were produced to coincide with the canal's completion, but it is important to underscore that the production of representations spanned the entire eleven-year period of American excavation. During much of that time success was far from certain, although Americans, with typical bravado, did not always acknowledge the uncertainty. The tremendous number of American representations reflects a characteristic overconfidence, but it suggests as well a desire to delimit the limitless, to give the Culebra Cut some kind of form. Once again the goal was contradictory: to turn matter into form; to register the colossal scale of the task. On the one hand, the photographs, postcards, and stereoviews of the Culebra Cut compensated for the narrowness of the isthmus in their celebration of the heroic achievement of the Cut. On the other, Americans working on the Panama Canal probably sought to convey the project's difficulty as much as its ultimate success.

In this era of innovation in photography and expansion in mass culture, pictures were called upon, as never before, to convey the colossal to far distant audiences. The American physician and writer Oliver Wendell Holmes famously claimed: "Matter in large masses must always be fixed and dear; form is cheap and transportable."[33] Holmes was writing in 1859 about the stereoscope and the photographic stereoview, an invention he deemed so marvelous no overstatement seemed unwarranted."*Form is henceforth divorced from matter.* In fact, matter as a visible object is of no great use any longer, except as the mould on which form is shaped. Give us a few negatives of a thing worth seeing, taken from different points of view, and that is all we want of it. Pull it down or burn it up, if you will."[34]

Holmes is imagining an archive of images that renders the material referent redundant. Form will be divorced from matter; form is cheap and transportable, whereas matter in large masses must always be fixed and expensive. Both Alan Trachtenberg and Allan Sekula have pointed out that Holmes's hypothesis depends upon an economic model in which paper currency replaces gold.[35] Holmes was eventually disappointed with public response to the stereoscope. The anticipated revolution whereby paper archives summarized and replaced the world of things did not come to pass, but the second renaissance in the commercial manufacture of stereoviews at the end of the nineteenth century and the beginning of the twentieth would have delighted him.[36]

**158**
"The French Cut, the American Cut" *A Trip. Panama Canal, Panama City and New Orleans*, 1911, p. 60. Photo: Julie Wolf.

**159**
Postcard, *The Canal Which Cuts a Continent.* Copyright Underwood & Underwood, N.Y. Author's Collection. Photo: Julie Wolf.

**160**
Postcard, *Landslide Culebra Cut.* Author's Collection. Photo: Julie Wolf.

**161**
Postcard, A. Pienkowski, *Trains hauling the excavations from Culebra Cut—Panama.* Author's Collection. Photo: Julie Wolf.

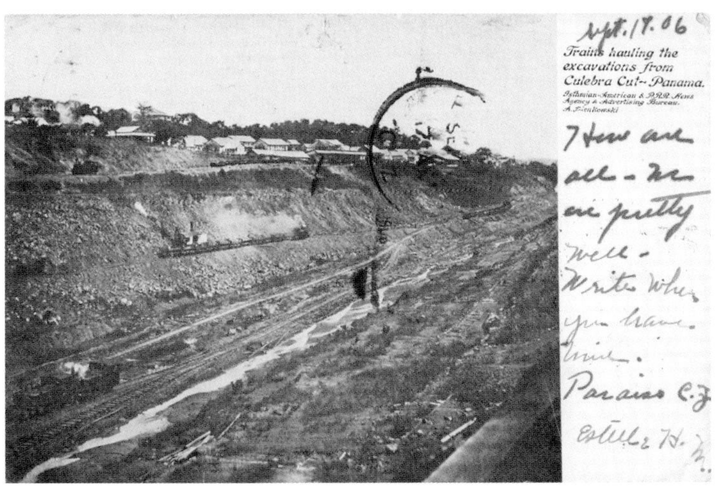

**162**
Medal, *The Land Divided—The World United.* Reverse: *Culebra Cut.* Author's Collection. Photo: Julie Wolf.

**163**
Stereoview, *Culebra Cut, Looking North—The Deepest Excavation Along the Panama Canal.* Keystone View Company. Author's Collection. Photo: Julie Wolf.

**164**
Fold-Out Double Postcard, *Culebra Cut, looking towards village.* Copyright L. L. Maduro Jr., Author's Collection. Photo: Julie Wolf.

**165**
Postcard. Untitled. Caption states that this deserted French car was enveloped by a tree. Underwood and Underwood, n.d. Author's Collection. Photo: Julie Wolf.

In 1898 Holmes's essay was reprinted as a book by a prominent stereoview publishing company.[37] In the early 1900s, hundreds of stereoviews were devoted to the construction of the Panama Canal.[38] Industrially produced cards were sold individually; in addition, there were "highly organized merchandising schemes" involving door-to-door salesmen, advertising campaigns, and the sale of boxed sets to school libraries.[39]

Stereographs, photographs, and photographic postcards served many of the same purposes: "dream traveling," to repeat the felicitous wording of a 1904 journalist, and the ever more voracious consumption of the foreign in Europe and the United States.[40] What one historian attributes to stereography can just as aptly be applied to photographs and photographic postcards: "A parallel between the expansion of the stereograph industry and this nervous period of imperialistic expansion was certainly more than coincidental. As a medium, stereography allowed the viewer to participate in the visible effects of the age's political and economic conquests. It also confirmed the growing social prejudices of a nation of immigrants bent on playing 'king of the mountain.'"[41]

Only industrial production made possible mass consumption at this scale.[42] The official photographer of the Panama Canal during the American phase, Ernest Hallen, took some 16,000 photos of the American phase of the building of the canal.[43] He was only one among many photographers to record its realization. Photographs were published as postcards and appeared in the press. *National Geographic Magazine* alone published twenty-five articles between 1889 and 1909 on the progress of the canal.[44] *Scientific American* also devoted amply illustrated articles that offered double-page spreads of panoramic shots of the canal.[45] The explosion of images accompanied the development of geography as a discipline. Economists who worked for the Isthmian Canal Commission founded a geography department at the University of Pennsylvania.[46] The canal project had proven that "a grasp of geography was necessary for the future growth of American trade."[47] No wonder Panama's canal was so prominently featured in the media.

"Matter in large masses must always be fixed and dear; form is cheap and transportable." Holmes' axiom has a bearing on the history of the Panama Canal. Mass needed to be excavated in order to increase the speed and lower the price of circulating goods. Boosting international trade, this was the canal's purpose. And the canal itself became mobile through its representation, its form. And when the canal was being built, the most popular medium to turn matter into cheap, transportable form was the stereoview, which combines "the detail and intimacy of the daguerreotype with the range of subject matter of the illustrated magazine."[48]

A photograph moves viewers from cartographic space, Panama as slender isthmus, to an indexical image of matter, Panama as rubble (fig. 166). (And I confess to believing there is no better subject for photography than broken rock.) But the stereoview seems to take viewers even closer (fig. 167). Exploiting the fact that our two eyes see the world differently because they are some two and a half inches apart, the stereoview provides two unlike images which we optically conjoin; it reproduces our binocular parallax and in so doing reproduces our sense of depth.[49] Stereoscope, a word coined by Charles Wheatstone who invented the medium, means to see solids, but the term solid is misleading because of its implication of material density.[50] Stereoviews offer not so much a sense of solidity as a sense of dimensionality or volume, but even here we need to be cautious.

In a stereoview the illusion of depth depends on the overlapping of clear-cut, flat shapes (fig. 168). Like theater wings, these flat shapes create a sense of layered space even as they tend to flatten volumes. Human figures can be especially frightening in stereoviews (figs. 169–170). Though at first glance the figures appear to have three-dimensions, considered again, their far side disappears. Bodies become eerie phantoms: they have three dimensions, then again they don't.

Stereoviews dramatize the incommensurability between one lateral plane and another. Their most powerful effects derive from staggered hard-edged shapes like rocks, cliffs, or branches in the foreground or middle ground. Looking at *Excavations Measuring 500 Ft. Deep in Gaillard [Culebra] Cut, Panama Canal* (see fig. 168), for example, our heightened sense of depth results less from an illusion of the three-dimensionality of solids or volumes and more from acute apprehension of the abrupt gaps between things. The stereoview is a mechanism through which emptiness is conjured. Materiality only appears to erupt in a sequence of flat edges that accentuate the intervening spaces. And scale? Seen with the naked eye the stereoview consists of two slightly unlike photographs, each of which suggests a deep recession into the distance

**166**
Untitled Photograph. Author's Collection. Photo: Julie Wolf.

**167**
Stereoview, *Site of the Gatun Lock. Looking South from the Lowest Lock towards Lake Gatun. Panama Canal Route*, 1907. Keystone View Company. Author's Collection. Photo: Julie Wolf.

**168**
Stereoview, *Excavations Measuring 500 Ft. Deep in Gaillard Cut, Panama Canal*, 1907. Keystone View Company. Author's Collection. Photo: Julie Wolf.

**169**
Stereoview, *Culebra Cut at its Most Interesting Point*, 1913. Copyright Keystone View Company. Author's Collection. Photo: Julie Wolf.

**170**
Stereoview, *Culebra Cut looking North showing Land Slides on Both Sides*, 1913. Keystone View Company. Author's Collection. Photo: Julie Wolf.

because of the precipitous shrinking of the size of the train as it recedes in space. Our eyes rush down the angled tracks until they reach the haze at the horizon and the space becomes indeterminate. The right ledge that fills more than half of the foreground remains the uninteresting ground from which the drama of perspectival illusion is launched.

But with the help of a stereoscope the stereoview seems to change; the illusion becomes riveting. Now all the contrasts take on bold drama; each piece of grass, each rock, each section of cliff is distinct and separate, and the closest train car, below the cliff face, appears three-dimensional. But the force of the illusion resides not in the discrete things but in the apprehension of the space between them; *the empty gaps between things rivet our attention.* Yet the illusion of depth suffers. The most distant train cars appear larger and closer than they do when viewed without the help of a stereoscope. Unaided our eyes see the farthest train cars as lilliputian, and the train seems to diminish abruptly into what we presumed to be a great distance.

The differences between the effects of photographs and stereoviews are the result of what scientists call size constancy.[51] When we look at the world, we tend to "restore the 'real' characteristics of an object despite adverse stimulus-conditions."[52] This, according to one scientist, is a "phenomenal regression to the 'real' object" (fig.171).[53] We magnify the size of distant persons because of our familiarity with their "real" size. Representations tend to mitigate this effect but not entirely. In figure 171 it is size constancy that leads us to see the distant woman as much larger than her actual size on the surface of the picture. That illusion is harder to sustain in a photograph reproduced as a photogravure or a photocopy, because the more we are aware of the representation's surface, the more we acknowledge the discrepancy in the size of near and far objects.

Using a stereoscope to look at a stereoview yields an approximation of "normal" binocular vision impossible in the perception of a photograph. This illusion of binocular vision means that size constancy operates when we see a stereoview through a stereoscope, as it does not when viewing ordinary photographs. Our awareness of the surface of the photograph inclines us to "falsify" the diminution of distant shapes; in a photograph the distant train car appears far smaller than the near one, and we therefore see the whole train as receding into a much greater distance in the photograph than in the stereoview. Looking at a stereoview we are less aware of the surface and approach binocular vision, and our awareness of size discrepancies diminishes. Objects in the distance appear larger, the distance itself more shallow.

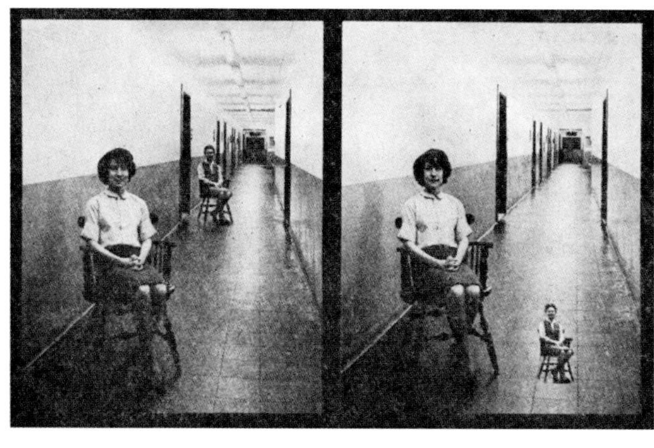

**171**
Illustration in Edwin G. Boring, "Size-Constancy in a Picture," *The American Journal of Psychology* 77, no. 3 (September 1964), p. 497. Photo: Julie Wolf.

Photographs indicate certain kinds of immensity far more effectively than stereoviews; they better evoke extension back into space. Nonetheless the stereoview does do one thing the photograph cannot: show *downward* extension—distance down, depth into the earth not across it. When we look through a stereoscope at *Excavations Measuring 500 Ft. Deep in Gaillard [Culebra] Cut, Panama Canal* (see fig. 168) the staggered levels of ground in the foreground are nothing short of startling, abruptly dropping below our feet into darkness. In a stereoview like this, ten feet down commands more interest than would three miles back. Stereoviews were therefore the ideal medium to represent the Culebra Cut in Panama as depth rather than as distance. Figure 166 shows a carving out of the earth; the staggered levels and deep black spaces heighten the drama of excavation. Is it possible to doubt that Edmund Burke, author of *A Philosophical Enquiry into the Origin of Our Ideas of the Sublime and Beautiful* (1756), would have approved the stereoview? To Burke, vastness is sublime, and great depth, more than either great height or length, is likely to awakens that feeling of awe, fear, and attraction.[54]

The stereoviews taken to document the excavation still survive (see figs. 167–170). In one a man (probably a West Indian following the directions of the photographer) stands on a mountaintop and looks down upon an immense and desolate canyon (see fig. 170). Seen without the benefit of a stereoscope, the scene is dramatic but apprehended in terms of landscape as an extension towards the horizon. Looking at the single photograph, we see the cut through the conventions of landscape. When we look at the stereoview through the stereoscope, the entire scene rises up; and the foreground once again seizes our attention. As before, we are preoccupied by the scene's depths below our feet, but now there are fewer levels by which space is suggested as it is traversed; there are hardly any steps down. Instead the wire plunges from the sky down into the deep darkness at right. The man hovers oddly in the foreground; we are unsure where he stands. At right, his shirt puffs out—was there a breeze that day?—with all the material specificity so effectively presented by photography (the indexicality that Holmes called the marks on the head of a drum).[55] But the photograph was too underexposed to indicate the volume of the man's dark head; instead it flattens out and we feel unease when details like his collar turn him into an inanimate and uncanny cutout. Between the figure of the man and the ground below there is a free fall of space. Only the tensed cables offer something to hold on to. But these vibrant lines also enhance our sense of emptiness by marking the void.

The deeper the Culebra Cut became, the less graduated became its depths. Once it began to resemble a wide valley, not a precipitous canyon, stereoscopic photographers needed to put men at its top in order to evoke the gaps between here and there. Without such foreground figures, the stereoview became more and more like a photograph; that is, it relied on landscape conventions to convey enormity rather than suggesting how vertiginous is a drop of any size into space.[56]

Sixty years after Bartholdi's *Colossi of Memnon* (see fig. 52), photographers were still trying to evoke faraway colossi. But there is a difference. Whereas the Egyptians and Nubians had been posed in the distance next to monuments in order to provide a measure for ancient Egyptian colossi, in Panama photographers of stereoviews had dark-skinned men stand in the foreground, usually with their backs turned to the camera. It seems probable that stereographic photographers relied on the same assistant; one man may have posed in the foreground of many of the Keystone stereoviews. He serves as the first in the series of flat shapes that with the help of a stereoscope produce the illusion of gaps in space. In these double images the foreign man functions as our surrogate, another viewer, but also as the first plane, the launch pad, that enables us to perceive space. His back to us, he is meant to remain anonymous. He is not one of those "co-operators," Ishmael-Hadj, for instance, who faced the "operators" Bartholdi and Du Camp. He serves instead as an interface, a mediating means of entry and a sign of the smallness of the human body before looming and precipitous depths.

---

**Van Ingen had the practically impossible task of [painting] the impression produced on his mind of vastness.**

***New York Times*, 6 November 1914**

And painting? In his cycle for the Panama Canal Administration Building, Van Ingen needed to depict "His Majesty Magnitude." Although the painter had traveled twice to Panama to witness the building of the canal, he was also undoubtedly familiar with the vast array of images and texts circulating in the United States in advance of the canal's completion, including the numerous photographs. Another American artist, the gifted lithographer Joseph Pennell, kept track of the progress of the building of the canal through photographs. In 1912 Pennell worried that it was "too late" to travel to Panama; he was "afraid the work was finished and that there would be nothing to see, for photographs taken a year or eighteen months before, showed some of the locks built and their gates partly in place."[57] Illustrators and painters were now accustomed to comparing their representations to machine-made photographic images.[58]

Pennell is most famous for his hostility to photography, which threatened his livelihood as a lithographer and illustrator. Fifteen years before he published his series on the Panama Canal, he had attacked the photographer, who had

> discovered a machine to make a masterpiece for him. No wonder he laughs at the poor artist who must humbly toil to create beauty, which a camera manufactures for him at once. What a farce it is to think of Titian and Velasquez and Rembrandt actually studying and working, puzzling their brains over subtleties of drawing and modeling, or light and atmosphere and colour, when the modern master has but to step into a shop, buy a camera, play a few tricks with gum chromate—I believe it is called—to turn you out a finished masterpiece which is far more like the real thing, he says, than any mere handmade picture ever could be. Is he not doing for art what Watt and Stephenson have done for labour? There are to be machine-made pictures, as there are machine-made shirts and carpets.[59]

For Pennell the camera leads inexorably to the steam engine and locomotive; photographs lead to machine-made shirts and carpets. But what does this imply about the impact on labor of James Watt's steam engine and George Stephenson's railway locomotive? Though the camera's impact on art is unambiguously condemned in Pennell's text, it is less clear whether he also means to imply that labor-saving machines are equally pernicious. Pennell devoted his art to the building of skyscrapers, urban transport, trains, and the Panama Canal, even as he distinguished the manual labor essential to art from the modern machine-made city. He was therefore in a hopelessly compromised position, asserting that photographs were counterfeit but skyscrapers were not. Only the photographer "sold margarine for butter, and chalk and water for milk."[60]

There is no evidence that Van Ingen shared Pennell's hostility to the camera. At least one of the artists with whom he studied, La Farge, regularly used photographs as the bases for his pictures, including landscapes of both domestic and foreign sites. Indeed La Farge is known to have based one watercolor on a stereoview he owned.[61] I believe that Van Ingen learned from the many photographs of the Panama Canal but still endeavored to take advantage of the opportunities and resources painting afforded him. He was keen to exploit effects no photographer could produce. How, as a painter, could he represent the strange, disorienting character of the Panama Canal, above all the Culebra Cut? He could not rely on presenting a series as did the publishers of stereoviews or photographers such as Hallen, who made those 16,000 images for the United States government (Pennell's despised instant masterpieces).[62] Van Ingen's choice was a cycle of only four large scenes, each measuring about eighteen feet by eleven feet; and a narrow frieze, about two and a half feet high and ninety feet long, circling the entire circumference of the rotunda. He devoted one large scene above and the whole frieze below to the Culebra Cut (fig. 172). The circling frieze was to encompass, in the words of Van Ingen, "the processes of making [this] cut nine miles long through the mountains."

The three other major paintings portray another canal, the American Canal and portray not excavation but elevation, not the digging out of earth but the building up of structure, not the emptying of mass to create a volume, a channel, but the accumulation of mass upward (figs. 173–175). Rather than celebrations of straight channels cut through flat land, the scenes commenmorate colossal monuments—immense locks and dams and cranes. The pictures owe a debt to the building of sublime skyscrapers, not to sublime landscapes.[63] Van Ingen was explicit about the association: "The construction of the lock gates reminded me of the steel gage construction such as may be seen in our 'skyscrapers'; and it might be added that if all the gates in use in the locks were laid flat, piled one on the other there would be made a tower higher than that of the Singer Building."[64] Van Ingen was by no means unique in assimilating locks to skyscrapers. In his 1912 publication Pennell had deployed looming structures filling a vertical format to depict the Panama Canal's locks, much as he had depicted New York City's skyscrapers some eight years before (figs. 176–177).[65] (Both Van Ingen and Pennell also depicted the towering structures—skyscraper, locks, and dams—from above.) Yet the Americans had raised structures reminiscent as well of ancient Egypt's pyramids. Van Ingen explained how composition enhances the viewer's sense of the magnitude of the scene in his picture of the construction of the Miraflores Locks. By eliminating a lock wall at the far right he could show:

> the depth to the bottom of the lock. Then, the placing of the enormous boom close to the eye helped to convey the feeling of a person standing, as it were, upon the actual lock wall—though as a matter of fact this section of lock wall was removed from the picture. Then the selection of the point of view from which might be seen the great six-foot steps that formed the side walls of the locks seemed to bring to mind thoughts of the Egyptian pyramids, which we so generally associate in our minds with magnitude. And the peopling of those steps with workmen (this I did not do in the original sketch) gave a standard of measurement which reinforced the suggestion of the pyramids, because there exist similar steps in the Egyptian Wonder of Work.[66]

To see the canal in relation to the Egyptian pyramids was not idiosyncratic. Half a century earlier the construction of the Suez Canal had been contrasted to the expense and labor required to build the pyramids. Now the same point was being made about Panama's canal; the following account was written the year the canal opened:

> On the canal the illusion of being in Egypt was very strong. We are told that it required a hundred thousand men 10 years to make ready for the building of that great structure [the Pyramid of Cheops], and 20 years more to build it. There were times at Panama when, in 26 working days, more material was removed from the canal than was required to build Cheops.... Were it all placed in one such structure, with a base as large as that of Cheops, the apex would tower higher in the sky than the loftiest mountain on the face of the earth.[67]

**172**
William Bradley Van Ingen, *Culebra Cut* and frieze [of the Culebra Cut]. Oil on canvas, 1915. Panama Canal Administration Building, Balboa Heights, Panama Canal Zone, Panama. Photo: Panama Canal Authority.

**173**
William Bradley Van Ingen, *Constructing a Miter Gate at a Lock* and frieze. Oil on canvas, 1915. Panama Canal Administration Building, Balboa Heights, Panama Canal Zone, Panama. Photo: Panama Canal Authority.

**174**
William Bradley Van Ingen, *Miraflores Locks Side Wall Culvert Construction* and frieze. Oil on canvas, 1915. Panama Canal Administration Building, Balboa Heights, Panama Canal Zone, Panama. Photo: Panama Canal Authority.

**175**
William Bradley Van Ingen, *The Construction of the Gatun Dam Spillway.* Oil on canvas, 1915. Panama Canal Administration Building, Balboa Heights, Panama Canal Zone, Panama. Photo: Panama Canal Authority.

**176**
Joseph Pennell, "At the Bottom of Gatun Lock," lithograph illustration in *Joseph Pennell's Pictures of the Panama Canal. Reproductions made by him on the Isthmus of Panama, January-March 1912, together with Impressions and Notes by the Artist.* London, 1912, Plate IV. Photo: Julie Wolf.

**177**
Joseph Pennell, "The Avenue," *The Great New York,* Boston, 1912, Plate 22. Photo: Julie Wolf.

**178**
"The 'Spoil' from Culebra Cut Would do This," *Scientific American*, reproduced in Willis J. Abbot, *Panama and the Canal in Pictures and Prose*, London and New York 1913, p 135. Photo: Julie Wolf.

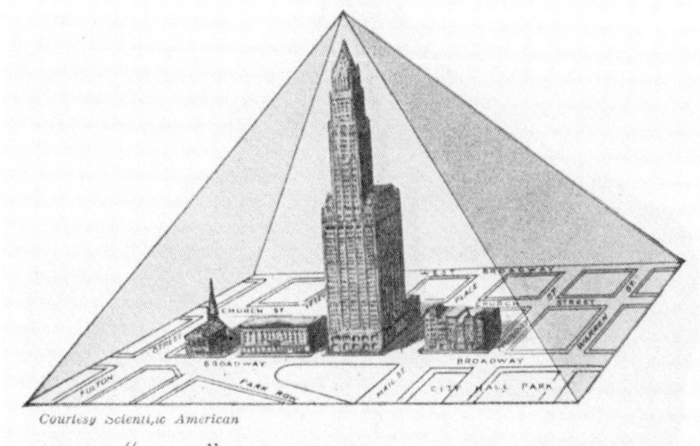

Courtesy Scientific American
THE "SPOIL" FROM CULEBRA CUT WOULD DO THIS

In a 1913 illustration the outlines of the Pyramid of Cheops are laid over a cityscape of Manhattan in order to indicate how much earth had been excavated in Panama (see fig. 140). Another illustration places a transparent pyramid over a skyscraper and seventeen city blocks to gauge the amount of earth removed from the Culebra Cut alone (fig. 178). In chapter 4 I discussed the fact that engineers understood both excavation and construction to be the job of the engineer. Nonetheless I want to stress how strange is the continual comparison of the Culebra Cut with the Egyptian pyramids. When an excavation is likened to a geometric mass, it is given a shape and thereby made to seem discrete—a thing, rather than formless, ever-shifting earth.

Although the official historian of the Panama Pacific Exhibition in 1915 linked the making of the cut to the pyramids, he went on to use the ancient Egyptian monuments to make a very different point: "The dynamite used in the [Culebra] Cut alone averaged 6,000,000 pounds a year for several years.... The heaviest blast was a charge of 26 tons of dynamite and black powder in the solid rock of Contractor's Hill in November 1906—enough to have blown the roof off the pyramid of Cheops."[68] The pyramids, this statement makes vivid, were subject to continual imaginative manipulation—sometimes constructed, sometimes exploded—but they remained the preferred term of comparison.

Van Ingen was intent on revealing "the depth to the bottom of the lock." The height of the locks made that effect imperative. When Van Ingen and Pennell painted steep heights and the construction of vertical monuments, they were forcing the Americans' lock-based canal to rise to the triumphant heights of Eiffel's tower. The American competition with the French was lateral, horizontal, geographic, a matter of managing and excising land to form a channel; and also vertical, architectural, engineered, a matter of building structure and consolidating concrete mass. Yet Van Ingen consistently places the viewer at the top of the skyscrapers, not at their base looking up. As in stereoviews, space seems to drop away in immeasurable ways. Where is ground level in representations such as these? Where is sea level? We are entirely unsure. The Americans had erected structures as enormous as ancient Egypt's pyramids, but these structures no longer adhere to the land. In these paintings the prospect has been divorced from the perch that had enabled it to come into being. Van Ingen after all had wished "to convey the feeling of a person standing, as it were, upon the actual lock wall—though as a matter of fact this section of lock wall was removed from the picture." The painter relies on a structural elevation to construct a view but then drops the ground out from under our feet to suggest indeterminate depths.

Van Ingen's paintings propose that the Americans manipulated all coordinates at the canal—height, width, depth. According to these pictures commemorating their achievement, the Americans managed to complete the canal because they were capable of thinking multi-dimensionally. The space of the rotunda allowed Van Ingen to make paintings representing the simultaneity of different operations.

**The very largeness of the American problems has helped to make a people able to solve them.** Albert Perry Brigham, *Geographic Influences in American History*, 1903

Van Ingen's paintings of the Culebra Cut transform into a radiant mountainous landscape the bleak, dark canyons of rubble and train tracks in black-and-white photographs and stereoviews (fig. 179). This large picture of the cut is already familiar; it resembles the numerous colored postcards which preceded its making. That said, Van Ingen's picture is far more beautiful. The distant view, the clouds against a blue sky; the rusty red hillside, and lovely green promontories distract us from the laborers in the shaded foreground and the distant trains and rows of train tracks at the lower right. In this painting the Culebra Cut is naturalized and made to seem lovely and therefore manageable, perhaps inevitable, a channel nestled in the crevice of a valley. Such a painting, its duplicities included, is of little surprise, but familiarity is one of its achievements. Van Ingen's Culebra Cut looks like an American landscape because it is made to look like a nineteenth-century American painting. The canal is American in scale, not French, the picture asserts: we who are Americans know this scale well.

Lesseps had envisaged a straight canal even in Panama, whereas Van Ingen's American canal is responsive to nature and therefore capable of managing it. The excavation seems to wind its way along a canyon rather than to blast its way through the mountains. In fact the large picture prominently features a landslide; the large patch of red pigment in the middle foreground is earth covering railway tracks. In this way pigment represents matter's capacity to obscure form. Red pigment is made of earth; it is matter. And yet it is also a color that produces an immaterial optical effect, and as optical effect it hovers free of the material constraints it describes. Red as color dematerializes the heavy, stubborn dirt and mud, its mass and also its volume. It offers a gorgeous screen, neither thing nor painted surface but pigment transmuted into light. This red is seductive and difficult to condemn although it is used to represent a landslide. Both as pigment and as light, this color underscores the fragility of form and structure and implies the earth's resistance to human organization. Still the painting as a whole shows another possibility: beautification, even naturalization, of the landslide veils the threat posed by Panama's geology.

Below the landscape of the Culebra Cut, the panoramic frieze provides a circling scene, the first Van Ingen had ever painted (fig. 180). The frieze is an amplification of the landscape above and relies just as heavily on the conventions of landscape. But the Panama Canal did not lend itself to the panoramic view predicated on stasis, spatial logic, and the viewer's distant and privileged view of "all." Numerous nineteenth-century panoramas eliminated barriers that could block so commanding a sight. While *stereoscope* means "seeing solids," panorama means "all seeing;" it promised a total view.[69] Yet the winding mountainous terrain of Panama afforded few opportunities to attain a magisterial gaze. Although people tried, it was never possible to find a prospect that made visible the complexity of the canal from beginning to end. A photograph of the Suez Canal relies on synecdoche: a part of the straight channel is presumed to represent the canal as a whole (see fig. 112). Because engineering has created simple mathematical form, it is presumed to be predictable and consistent. Not so with Panama. Both locks and mountains block the view (see fig. 135). Of course Van Ingen could have made a panoramic view of the entire canal, perhaps from above, something like the bird's-eye view carved on a commemorative medal (see fig. 162). Still the rotunda presented him with a formidable problem: the 360-degree format ill-suits the depiction of a canal cut across an isthmus. The point of the canal, after all, is not to return you to where you started.

Van Ingen nonetheless found ways to exploit the circular format to great effect in representing the canal. Rather than using the 360 degrees of wall surface to provide an all-encompassing view, he decided to represent, in his words, "the processes of making a cut nine miles long through the mountains." The frieze weaves the canal's cut in and out of a lush, gently rolling, tropical landscape. We are above the cut, at its crumbling banks, and the cut itself is glimpsed, obscured, and revealed again. Yet more important is Van Ingen's adaptation of the particularly American technology of the moving panorama; he uses the circular frieze to portray seemingly continuous labor and thereby introduces narrative into the panorama.[70] As we circle around the frieze, we see labor enacted again and again. And throughout we become aware of men working, many of them dark-skinned as are their counterparts in the four tableaux above.

**179**
William Bradley Van Ingen, *The Culebra Cut*, Oil on canvas, 1915. Panama Canal Administration Building, Balboa Heights, Panama Canal Zone, Panama. Photo: Panama Canal Authority.

Given his commission to memorialize the building of the Panama Canal, it is not surprising that Van Ingen's paintings focus attention on workers. But in the context of racial prejudices of the early twentieth century, the prominence he accords the West Indians, who had constituted a large portion of the work force, is noteworthy. Though one of the upper tableaux, *The Gatun Dam*, presents two men carrying a chain and hence stirs up memories of enslavement, most of the other figures appear fully autonomous, even heroic (see fig. 175). At the Philadelphia Mint the painter had shown the processes of making coins with sprightly young girls serving as cloying substitutes for laborers.[71] But in Panama Van Ingen rose to the challenge of a commission to memorialize the making of the canal. Work and workers became his subject.

The circularity of the wall of the rotunda of the Panama Canal Administration Building offered Van Ingen certain opportunities even as it also limited his choices. It evokes movement but also repetition, developments realized later, winding climbs and descents, a process without climax. Most simply a circular format disallows linear trajectories beginning at point A and ending at point B. Any pathway leads back to its beginning and leads to yet another route. It is impossible to keep the whole scene in mind; one portion after another dominates the experience of the beholder. She or he circles without ever finishing the narrative. Though this contradicts the purpose of a canal, it suits the representation of the endless excavation at the Culebra Cut. If Van Ingen makes the canal deceptively lovely, the circular format reminds us of the endlessness of its making. And he shows both the relative successes and the relative failures of the cut. In one view of the deepest part of the excavation, trains and machines send up clouds of steam; in another a landslide overturns railway track (figs. 181–182). Nowhere is the cut over and done with. Colossal scale is made manifest less by size than by unflagging industry—less by space, more by that other dimension, time.

**180**
William Bradley Van Ingen, Frieze of the Culebra Cut, oil on canvas, 1915. Panama Canal Administration Building, Balboa Heights, Panama Canal Zone, Panama. Photo: Panama Canal Authority.

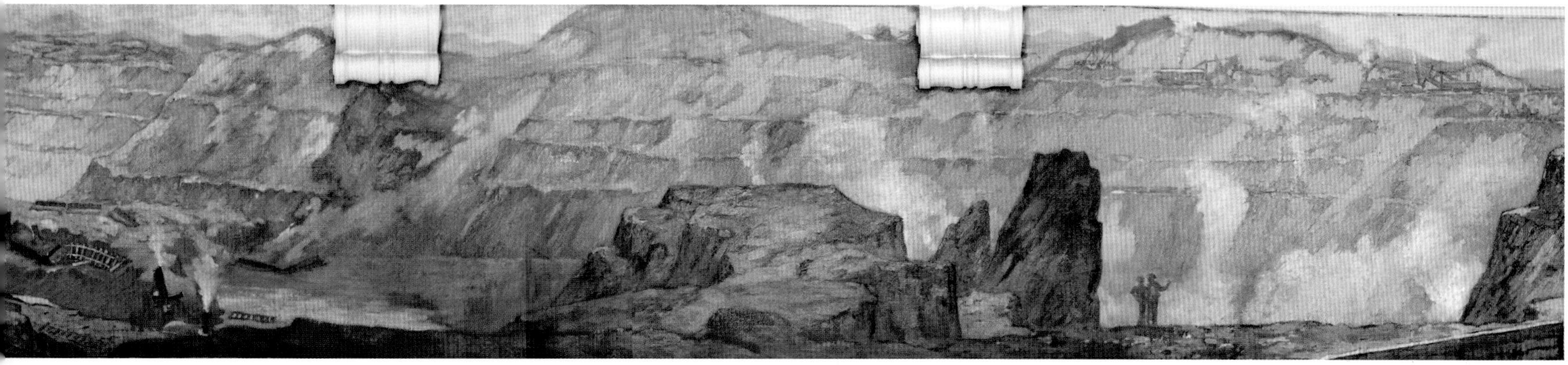

**181**
William Bradley Van Ingen, (Relatively Successful Culebra Cut). Detail of the frieze of the Culebra Cut, Oil on canvas, 1915. Panama Canal Administration Building, Balboa Heights, Panama Canal Zone, Panama. Photo: Panama Canal Authority.

**182**
William Bradley Van Ingen, (Relatively Unsuccessful Culebra Cut) Detail of the frieze of the Culebra Cut, Oil on canvas, 1915. Panama Canal Administration Building, Balboa Heights, Panama Canal Zone, Panama. Photo: Panama Canal Authority.

**183**
Panoramic Photograph. *Construction of Panama Canal*, stamped on front: "Isthmian Historical Society" photographic print, gelatin silver, 10 x 58.5 in., c. 1913. Author's Collection. Photo: Julie Wolf.

**184**
Panoramic Photograph. *Spillway, Gatun Dam. Panama Canal*, 15 x 74 in., c. 1914. Gordon Panoramic Company. Washington, D.C., Library of Congress.

**185**
Photograph. "Culebra Cut, looking south, Panama Canal," n.d. Detroit Publishing Company. Author's Collection. Photo: Julie Wolf.

A cut winding its way through the mountains of Panama was of special concern to Van Ingen. While most painted panoramas provided at least the illusion of a magisterial, complete view, that illusion was beyond the means of panorama photographs of the early twentieth century. These bend the space of their views in ways that leave the viewer uncertain of the land's form and disposition (fig. 183). Straight streets bend; bridges curve and seem to connect to the same side of the river; dams fold (fig. 184). Rather than providing more information, as they promise, early panorama photographs render spatial relations all the more confusing.

Van Ingen realized that the shape of the wall at his disposal could be fortuitous. The circular format of his frieze turns the straight line into a curve. And though the painter could have minimized, if not excised, impediments to the view, Van Ingen avoided this option. His frieze bends the cut in and out of the horizontal format and fully exploits the intrusion of the objects so typical of photographic foregrounds. Obstructions were maddening to photographers in search of a commanding view. The British photographer Frances Frith aired their frustrations:

> A photographer only knows—only he can appreciate the difficulty of getting a view satisfactorily into the camera: foregrounds are especially perverse; distance too near or too far; the falling away of the ground; *the intervention of some brick wall or other commonplace object which an artist would simply omit;* some or all of these (with plenty others of a similar character) are the rule, not the exception. I have often thought, when maneuvering about for a position for my camera, of the exclamation of the great mechanist of antiquity—"Give me a fulcrum for my lever, and I will move the world." Oh what pictures we would make, if we could command our points of view![72]

The inevitable foreground obstructions that exasperated panorama photographers were nonetheless essential to the stereoview's illusion of relief. Stereoview photographers needed to find objects and planes to fill their foregrounds and middle grounds in order to articulate the extension of space back as well as down. Van Ingen also knew how helpful obstructions could be. They frame vignettes even as they enhance the sense of continuous unfolding as in panoramas; and they imply extension beyond what we can see, both across and below, as in stereoviews. Understood in this way, foreground objects are an economical means to imply the existence of a larger world. Van Ingen had already deployed views glimpsed from hilltops in a rectangular landscape frieze, but his adaptation of the strategy to a 360-degree format was unique and indebted to the panorama photographs' curving of space, the ways they turned straight lines into a circle.[73]

In Van Ingen's circular frieze, it is often difficult to establish whether the curving landscape presents Panama's geography or the workers' intervention. As in the tableau of the cut above, in the frieze the distinction between the natural landscape and human artifice is not certain. This is both an achievement and a loss. The canal is made to seem natural and inevitable rather than the outcome of violence. But it is also made to seem natural, not man-made. This was not what Goethals had hoped for. He had wanted everyone to know that the canal exacted years of backbreaking and dangerous labor; he wanted people to appreciate that the canal is an achievement against all odds. While structures with straight lines are obviously man-made, those with undulating, irregular curves can appear to be nature's handiwork, particularly if they are, like a river, filled with water. Water covered the Culebra Cut as soon as it was completed. Its success guaranteed that all the work and skill and lives consumed in its making were hidden under water. Van Ingen could not avoid painting colossal exertion as if it were a wonder of nature. The straight line is obviously man-made, the undulating, irregular curve is often a sign of nature, especially when filled with water. Although the Culebra Cut had come to stand for the achievement of the Panama Canal, its successful completion guaranteed the ultimate erasure of its inordinate labor. Van Ingen was painting a colossal exertion hidden under water.

When filled the Culebra Cut resembled a complacent river, not the Chagres so much as the Mississippi (fig. 185). Engineers and workers knew this would be so. The image makers knew this as well. So too did Goethals who had ordered Hallen to make 16,000 photographs and who had commissioned Van Ingen's paintings just as the Gatun Lake was rising to fill the locks. A 1914 article in the *New York Times* explained why. Rather than a "synthesis," Van Ingen was expected to provide a "record of conditions necessarily of short duration. The water has covered all this scaffolding erected in opposition to the angry defiance of nature."[74] It is noteworthy that with the

**186**
"A giant blast in the Culebra Cut," in Ralph Emmett Avery, *Greatest Engineering Feat in the World. Panama*, New York, 1915, p.182. Photo: Julie Wolf.

**187**
"Drilling for the blasts in Culebra Cut," in Walter B. Stevens, *A Trip to Panama*, Saint-Louis, Missouri, 1907, p. 160. Photo: Julie Wolf.

**188**
William Bradley Van Ingen, (carrying boxes of dynamite and smoke from dynamiting). Detail of the frieze of the *Culebra Cut.* Oil on canvas, 1915. Panama Canal Administration Building, Balboa Heights, Panama Canal Zone, Panama. Photo: Panama Canal Authority.

**189**
Stereoview, *Loading Holes with Dynamite, Point 2. June 6, 1909,* J. A. Bruce, *Panama Canal Scenes.* Washington, D.C., Library of Congress.

**190**
"The Great Fill at Balboa where the Culebra Cut is Dumped," in Willis J. Abbot, *Panama and the Canal in Pictures and Prose*, London and NY, Syndicate, 1913, p. 223. Photo: Julie Wolf.

**191**
"Bottom of the Canal," in *A Trip to Panama, Panama City*, Avery & Garrison, 1911, p. 48. Photo: Julie Wolf.

use of the word "scaffolding" this writer categorizes the making of the canal as the building of a structure. But the Culebra Cut was fundamentally made through the removal of earth to create a void. The Americans were digging a hole.

Emptiness is a strange achievement. Where did everything go? The Americans' reliance on dynamite made it seem that all the soil disappeared into thin air. The roof of the pyramid could be "blown off." Without exception, photographs, stereoviews, and Van Ingen's murals feature the great bursts of smoke that followed detonation. In these images rock seems to have disappeared into the sky (figs. 186–189). In illustrated books and stereoviews, captions were often added to indicate which distant billows were exploded matter and which the steam produced by machinery (and also which explosions were intentional or accidental). In his painting cycle most strikingly in the frieze, Van Ingen exploits the resemblance between the steam produced by modern industry and the smoke from dynamite explosions. Everywhere in the frieze, plumes of white smoke rise from the unseen depths of the cut; they rise too from train engines. Whether produced by steam or dynamite, these white clouds are signs of men and machines at work.

To specify that the rising plumes sometimes come from explosions, Van Ingen painted a line of men carrying wooden boxes on their heads (see fig. 186). Boxes of dynamite can also be seen in numerous photographs of the canal (see fig. 187). Compact and geometric, these shapes portend the shattering and disappearance of the landscape. Another irony emerges. The small boxes contain the dynamite that will destroy land while giving the artist the opportunity to spread paint into the semblance of a colored haze. Explosions caused dust to rain down upon the site and clouds to rise high into the sky. Van Ingen was a happy painter.

In many ways the Panama Canal is the product of a fantasy of disappearance. Man can make the land go away; we don't need it anymore. Conspicuously absent was any thought of redistributing the land for other uses. The copious visual and textual documentation of the digging and building of the Panama Canal records the dynamiting and loading of earth onto trains. It registers the number of trains that were filled each day, the tonnage of the rubble that was removed. But there is little if any mention of where all the earth was taken. The excavated mountain had to have been moved somewhere. The existence of that dump was repressed. The trains left, came back empty; the unwanted substance had disappeared.[75] Barely acknowledged in the proliferating representations of the Panama Canal was the continual dumping of earth into the Pacific Ocean at Balboa, only miles from the administration building where Van Ingen's paintings hung (fig. 190).

The repression has one plausible explanation. There is nothing monumental about the spit of earth that extends into the sea. It is not an impressive form and does not demonstrate the extraordinary amount of earth removed. How could such a narrow strip of land be the equivalent of the cavernous gap cut out of a 330-foot mountain? The digging up of matter at the cut was a manifestation of virile empire's insatiable appetite, while disposal connoted elimination, the wrong end of the digestive process. So much waste.

A small portion of the excavated earth is visible in the spit at Balboa; the rest is below water. The extension appears meager because we cannot see its size. The excavated mass disappeared under water at Balboa; at Culebra the size of the emptied volume was hidden in the same way. After the seas rushed into the canal, nothing save its depth attested to over thirty years of digging and 25,000 lost lives. But the water's depth is difficult to judge; only its reflective surface can be seen. No wonder an American would label an uneventful photograph "bottom of the canal" (fig. 191).

Water is notable for its absence in Van Ingen's painting cycle. The canal's future as a waterway is nowhere visible. Just the architectural frame with its pattern of waves refers to the canal's ultimate purpose (see fig. 172). The stylized waves circle the rotunda, dividing the frieze from the scenes above it, playfully (or is it menacingly?) conjuring the waters that had already risen outside. Van Ingen was portraying the past of a specific place, and his panoramic frieze has been seen in its entirety no place but there. Reproducing this 90-foot circling picture is exceptionally problematic. Photography can entail turning Panama's curves into straight lines; perhaps, this difficulty explains why the frieze has never before been reproduced. More puzzling is the fact that it was made in New York City but never exhibited there. And although, like the Statue of Liberty, like Villiers' fictive Eve, the frieze was once transported on board a ship, after arriving in Panama it has never traveled again.

At the Panama-Pacific Exposition held in 1915 to celebrate the opening of the Panama Canal, a speaker asked the audience "'Who built the Panama Canal?' "Teddy! yelled the crowd."[76] The Honorary President of the Engineering Congress, convened at the same Exposition, disagreed. In his opening remarks, President Goethals, head of the Corps of Engineers during the construction of the Panama Canal, offered a panegyric not to Teddy Roosevelt but to engineers:

> The Canal is another illustration of the functions of the engineer, his uses of the forces and materials of nature for the benefit of man. It is another instance of the fact that engineers are fitted for great executive and administrative functions, and also that they can accomplish and manage a government to the satisfaction of those governed.[77]

Now a Major General, Goethals sustains the oft-repeated nineteenth-century tribute to the engineer as master of "the forces and materials of nature," but he also expands the engineer's expertise to the governance of peoples. Goethals made a point, however, of keeping governance separate from politics: "Believing in straightforward, practical administration, as the engineer does, such a government to be successful must not be political but autocratic, for with politics involved there would enter an unfamiliar factor opposed to the engineer's training and ideals, and he would fail."[78] The Major General argues that the engineer is far too practical to waste time and energy on politics. His success depends on imposing an "autocratic" administration as had been done in Panama. Goethals' speech demonstrates how seamlessly engineering merged with colonial rule; in the name of efficiency (and "satisfaction"), a military corps could make occupation of a foreign country appear benevolent. Goethals knew what he was speaking about. He had been Chief Engineer in Panama from 1907 and governor the Panama Canal Zone from 1914 to 1916. "I believe in a strong executive, I believe in power," remarked this "Czar of the Zone."[79]

Since 13 December 1999, when the United States relinquished control, the paintings Goethals had commissioned from Van Ingen have been located in a canal zone under the control of Panamanians. Few tourists visit the Administration Building in Balboa. If the workers who come in and out of the building notice the paintings, they see a celebration of the canal's manual laborers. "Who made the Panama Canal?" Workers, not Teddy Roosevelt, not engineers, Van Ingen answered.

His allegiance with "the man in the ditch" started during his trip to Panama:

> never did an artist have more sympathetic help than I had from everyone high and low that I met on the canal. I forgot I was an artist and had genuine regret at not being entitled to a number and a brass check, while any success the paintings may have had came, I believe, from an endeavor to see with the eyes of the man in the ditch. I was a translator, not an originator.[80]

"A number and a brass check" are the identification tags assigned to every worker on the Panama Canal. Van Ingen does not mention that whites were paid in gold and were called "gold workers," whereas blacks were paid in Barbados silver coins and were "silver workers." To him there was simply "the man in a ditch" with his "number and brass check." In his paintings the workers are often dark skinned; they stand below the colossal structures planned but not built by American engineers. This is a profound achievement in an age when engineering was regarded as a white enterprise. The box of the 1914 version of the Meccano "erector" set features a white boy in a landscape that he rules with evident pleasure (fig. 192). The set's instruction book teaches boys to build bridges, towers, windmills, dredges, and even stools, wheelchairs, and other domestic objects.

The future, Meccano promises consumers, will be engineered by men who had been learning engineering skills since childhood. In 1914 children would have confronted only one structure with a human figure, "Drop the nigger!" According to the diagram (fig. 193), this device allowed children to move a black doll along its uppermost track, then suddenly drop the doll as if in execution. The matter-of-fact attitude towards racial violence—its explicit encouragement—are shocking. The device goes a long way towards explaining why African Americans resented work in Panama and never romanticized American achievement there as did some West Indians. And Van Ingen's celebration of black men's building of the canal acquires yet greater power when considered alongside this ghastly reminder of U.S. racism. His murals show that black and brown men struggled to fulfill the plans of engineers.

Panamanian visitors to the Administration Building and the many employees who work there are likely to be alert to the prominence of the brown and black men in Van Ingen's murals. Panama's population is exceedingly diverse. Some citizens may be pleased to see an homage to the canal that also pays tribute to Panama's tropical habitat, a habitat at once lovely and omnivorous and capable of swallowing settled land and abandoned machines. These portions of the paintings are probably most significant to the gardeners who maintain the manicured lawns that are another vestige of U.S. engineers' plans for "the Zone."

Stereoviews of the building of the Panama Canal still circulate around the world giving far distant viewers virtual experiences of this "wonder" of engineering. But Van Ingen's murals, no matter their alternative interpretation of the canal, receive no mention even in comprehensive histories of art and are now all but forgotten, except in Panama. Van Ingen ensured that the old-fashioned cycle of paintings would commemorate canal labor at the canal itself. This means that Van Ingen's murals belong to the Panamanians who are their primary viewers. Histories of colonialism are always ironic; there are at least two points of view, each of which subverts the other, and they change over time. The "Czar of the Zone" commissioned site-specific paintings to celebrate the accomplishment of American engineering. Today the same pictures provide Panamanians with a fictional and appealing representation of their collective achievement by erasing the violence of their exploitation.

**192**
Meccano Construction Toy, 1913. Author's Collection. Photo: Julie Wolf.

**193**
Diagram. Meccano Construction Toy, 1913. Author's Collection. Photo: Julie Wolf.

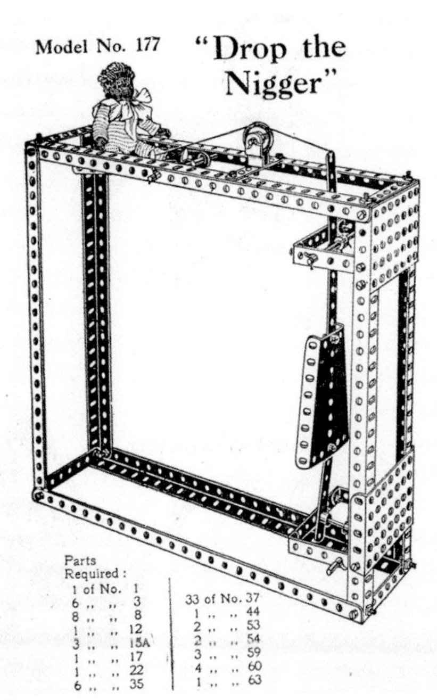

# Toyland

## Model / Miniature

**Paris is no longer in Paris: one would swear that it fits entirely into the phenomenal, attractive, troubling work of the great engineer to whom all these street vendors, in their way, pay homage.**
**Paul Bluysen, *Paris en 1889: Souvenirs et croquis de l'Exposition,* 1890**

In chapter 15 of *Capital* Karl Marx remarks upon the machines invented to build other yet larger machines:

> The mechanical lathe is only a cyclopean reproduction of the ordinary foot-lathe; the planing machine, an iron carpenter, that works on iron with the same tools that the human carpenter employs on wood; the instrument that, on the London wharves, cuts the veneers, is a gigantic razor; the tool of the shearing machine, which shears iron as easily as a tailor's scissors cut cloth, is a monster pair of scissors; and the steam-hammer works with an ordinary hammer head, but of such a weight that not Thor himself could wield it.[1]

Though each object has the massive size of a factory machine, each replicates the shape of an artisan's tool and performs his work. The machine-tools cut, plane, and hammer; just what the worker wielding his handheld tools accomplished albeit more slowly. No mystery about the change in scale or the displacement of the worker—call it industrialization. But for the moment in this passage from a section in "The Development of Machinery" in chapter 15 of *Capital*, Marx fixes his gaze upon a spectacle that boggles the senses. "Cyclopean," "gigantic," and "monster" planers, razors, scissors, and hammers—magic tools for a giant or ogre in a fairy tale, perhaps, but Marx chooses the other plot, the one with weapons or instruments that defy the mastery of even the mythical beings summoned to the pages of *Capital*. "Not Thor himself," the Nordic god of thunder, claims Marx, could wield the "steam-hammer."

Machines belong to a new order of things in Marx's account of the technology of industrialism. Tools once commensurate with the human body and human control have acquired the power of generation; they beget ever larger versions of themselves, eventually morphing into something that belongs to a new regime of work and production. Isolated from narratives of invention or progress that would explain the burst in size, the machines take on a life of their own. Nowhere does Marx connect them with an energy source or a human worker. Machines appear autonomous, an illusion at the Universal Exposition of 1855 that the artist Eugène Delacroix lamented.[2]

Delacroix's lament, Marx's testimonial—both mark the advent of the age of machines in which the Statue of Liberty, the Eiffel Tower, and the Suez and Panama Canals were to be hailed as triumphant achievements. To trace their history is to witness the increasing size and importance—the increasing autonomy—of machines. When the French yielded to British criticism about slave labor at the Suez Canal, they replaced Egyptian fellaheen with dredging machines. Even earlier Conté invented a machine to engrave straight lines in the plates of the *Description de l'Égypte*, a substitution that the unprecedented immensity of its pages called forth. In the text on "cyclopean" tools Marx marvels at the colossal hammer that James Nasmyth had invented to forge gigantic paddle shifts for steamships. Numerous other machines were developed in response to enlargements of scale.

The shift from manual to machine labor notwithstanding, workers were still hammering on the folds of copper for the Statue of Liberty and on the rivets of the Eiffel Tower and the locks of the Panama Canal. The Eiffel Tower may have appeared to rise autonomously because its workers disappeared from view, but it did not appear to be made by another machine. Indeed Eiffel had hidden the making of the huge iron beams from view. Men were still working, but discerning how the Statue of Liberty and the Eiffel Tower were fabricated—this was not easy once the projects had been completed. For all the hyperbole about the logic of engineering and the precision of mathematics, these colossi could appear opaque: a material fact with veiled origins. That they were called wonders of the world is as it should be. But their makers did not wish viewers simply to "wonder" before these outsize things.

Many representations were attempts to make visible the immensity of the intelligence, engineering, and labor required for constructing them. To convey the accomplishments was never easy. The key to Marx's success in the endeavor is the surreal coupling of near opposites. Ordinary tools held in the hand yield gigantic razors or monster scissors. Unexpected transformations in size, when combined with movement, give the human observer a good indicator of humongous structures.

The process is volatile; it can easily be reversed and used to shrink things. The gigantic machine is a pair of scissors or a hammer (fig. 194). Marx teaches a lesson that extends beyond the growth in the size of machines and the displacement of labor to the curious interdependence of model and colossus. Models are diminutive, humble, and relatively simple three-dimensional

**194**

Miniature Eiffel Tower as scissors inscribed "Exposition Universelle," 5 3/8 inches tall, 1889. Courtesy of Ace Architects, Oakland, CA. Photo: Julie Wolf.

**195**

Miniatures of the Statue of Liberty and Eiffel Tower. American Views Stereoview of Statue of Liberty. Brochure, Panama-Pacific International Exposition Company, *The Panama Canal at San Francisco*, 1915. Medal, *The Land Divided—The World United*. Reverse: *Culebra Cut*. Medal of Eiffel Tower. *(Souvenir de mon ascension au 1er étage de la Tour Eiffel 1889* venir of my ascent to the first floor of the Eiffel Tower, 1889). Reverse: *Les travaux ont commencé le 27 janvier 1887. Le monument a été inauguré le 6 mai 1889* (Work was begun 27 January 1887. The monument was inaugurated 6 May 1889). Author's Collection.

constructions that assist in the design and construction of full-scale buildings, structures, and sculptures.[3] Such models are assumed to be preliminary and subject to revision. They are meant to offer designers a quick means to experiment: "Models in practice are quicker than drawings, they don't need to be perfectly crafted, or perfectly scaled, to represent a project clearly."[4]

Models articulate the distribution of large volumes; they are used to organize and distribute parts as if seen from outside the structure. Specialists assume that the small-scale object permits an overall view of the eventual full-size structure itself; they assume that apprehension of the model is comparable to that of the finished project. Further, engineers understand that models afford some viewpoints unavailable in full-scale structures: for instance, how the distribution of masses appears when seen from above. But designers are aware that models have limitations; they can convey only certain characteristics to the exclusion of others, such as detail, color, interiors, and, most significantly, the impact of scale.[5] From the outset of industrial engineering, the model's limited ability to predict effects of changes in size was a key issue in the designing of colossi. J. E. Gordon is worth quoting on this crucial point: "models" are all very well if one just wants to see what the thing will look like, but they can be dangerously misleading if they are used to predict strength." They simply show a form in space, a form which may or may not be feasible at a particular scale.

Bartholdi used three-dimensional models to design his statue and left it to Eiffel to devise an armature capable of supporting its weight in an outdoor setting. There are models of the Eiffel Tower, and the Suez and Panama Canals, but they were fashioned at a late stage in work, after the design had been established, and were intended not for engineers but for the public. Bartholdi would turn out many models for publicity as well. Rather than anticipating a future, models of this type replicated an achievement.

The Statue of Liberty, the Eiffel Tower, the Suez and Panama Canals were all converted into small-scale, two-and three-dimensional reproductions (fig. 195). One reason for this is obvious. Immense monuments are site-specific and defy relocation (the Statue of Liberty is the exception, and it was moved just once for installation). Wasn't this a source of the pyramids' fascination for Europeans? The pyramids strained the cognitive powers of the few who saw them in person; visitors attempting to represent the sublime scale of the monuments to those back home faced yet greater difficulties. Even French engineers never imagined rebuilding Egypt's colossi and pyramids in France. Instead they turned them into reduced representations, whether texts, two-dimensional drawings and prints in the *Description de l'Égypte*, or three-dimensional porcelain dessert services (see fig. 16).

The colossal monument is made small so that more people can see and revere it. It is also reduced in size in order to raise money either to fund the monument in advance or to profit from it after the fact. Most conspicuously the colossal is shrunk so that it can be possessed. Miniaturization turns the public monument into a mere thing, yet a thing that is mobile and a commodity. Marx famously had this to say on commodity fetishism: "the whole mystery of commodities, all the magic and necromancy that surrounds the products of labour" when "the social character of men's labour appears to them an objective character stamped upon the product of that labour."[6] But his tale of enlargement and reduction intimates that shifts in scale also produce effects strange, at times fantastic. Things not conforming to our expectations of dimension, whether they are too large or too small, can elicit both pleasure and disorientation.

---

**I am assured that my legal right exists, because the model has been deposited with the commercial court since 1885 and, well before my treaty with the State and the City, I made sure of this ownership.** Gustave Eiffel, Letter to the Conseil d'État, 26 February 1889

Visitors to the Universal Exhibition of 1867 in Paris could inspect models of the Suez Canal, although it was not yet finished (see fig. 47). In the Suez Canal Company Pavilion, they walked around two reliefs of almost the same size but representing the canal at two different scales: one at a smaller scale so as to provide topographical information about the isthmus of Suez, the other at a larger scale that zoomed in on a small portion of the canal to highlight the newly invented dredging machines. Many earlier representations, among them the *Description de l'Égypte*, would have prepared viewers to move effortlessly from distant to proximate views. The map of the isthmus of Suez afforded the viewer an opportunity to see land from a bird's-eye view—a position higher than most had ever before experienced. The second model representing a portion of the straight-edge canal brought viewers closer to the earth but nonetheless sustained an elevated view. Between one model and the other, viewers not only had to shift their apprehension of scale but also somehow to reconcile the curving paths of water with the undulations of earth in the topographical map and the hard-edge, straight channel in the display of machines. Reconciliation may be too much to ask. The two models, side by side, offered discrepant views of what a canal crossing an isthmus had to do: in one, geography needed to be accommodated, in the other it did not. Visitors had to interpret the discrepant ways information was conveyed. The aisle between models served, much like the blank page framing the repre-sentations in the *Description de l'Égypte*, to signal the gap, the need to start over required by a different mode of representation.

Lesseps had been remarkably successful at drawing the French people into his fantasy: they trusted that cutting two isthmuses would yield fortunes. Yet, except for the displays at the Universal Exhibitions, Lesseps offered merely a few images of the Suez and Panama Canals to subscribers, whereas a veritable avalanche of representations was on offer during the American phase of work in Panama. For the French an investment in engineering a canal—a link in a system of transportation—did not proffer ownership of a thing that could be pictured; it meant quite simply a portion of future profits and, perhaps, for a few patriots, national glory. Instead of replicas French investors received ornate certificates with stamps and signatures galore, pieces of paper that promised future wealth (fig. 196).

Tokens of the statue and tower were far more literal and, for the most part, these monuments stood outside the capitalist system of stocks and profits. The public regarded them as achievements, marvelous things, even as works of art. Bartholdi took this perception for granted. Time and again the sculptor attempted to attract subscribers through the offer of a representation. Though much of the publicity depended on easily reproduced images, subscribers received sculpted miniatures of sizes calibrated to the size of their donation.[7]

Bartholdi clearly understood the value of his design for the Statue of Liberty and went to great lengths to secure exclusive rights to its reproduction. He filed a patent in the United States and often appended copyright dates and patent numbers to souvenirs of the statue (fig. 197). In another effort to assert (and exploit) his rights, he issued souvenirs made out of the material left over from building the monument. These small pieces of copper were inscribed "Fragment of the Colossal Statue of Liberty executed by A. Bartholdi, 1878–1883. Souvenir of a visit to the worksite."[8] Anyone lucky enough to possess one of the pieces of copper had more than a mere souvenir, she or he had a relic that confirmed belief in the exalted status of the statue.[9]

Bartholdi's patents performed a different function; they concerned the image or what he called the "Design." "Be it known that I, AUGUSTE BARTHOLDI, of Paris, in the Republic of France, have originated and produced a Design of a Monumental Statue, representing 'Liberty enlightening the world,' being intended as a commemorative monument of the independence of the United States."[10] Except for the words "monumental" and "monument," Bartholdi did not emphasize the colossal dimensions of his proposed statue. He preferred to file a patent for a design which could be copied in two or three dimensions in any medium at any size. "This design may be carried out in any manner known to the glyptic art in the form of a statue or statuette, or in alto-relievo or bas-relief, in metal, stone, terra cotta, plaster-of-paris, or other plastic composition. It may also be carried out pictorially in print from engravings on metal, wood, or stone, or by photographing or otherwise."[11]

Bartholdi was nothing if not audacious. He was seeking to patent a venerable personification of Liberty as his own creation. To give him his due, his claim was based on the supposed originality of having his statue hold aloft a light. Still his own verbal description was of little more than a female figure draped in the classical way. Bartholdi tried as well to patent the sculpture's two-dimensional image. The only pictorial evidence accompanying the patent was a drawing of the statue seen frontally. A drawing of so generic a character could hardly serve to specify the details of the sculpture in the round. The drawing functioned as a placeholder for the projected monument, whose reproductions in all media Bartholdi claimed as his own. Bartholdi was dangerously close to claiming sole rights to the image of Liberty tout court.

The numerous letters Bartholdi sent to contacts in the U.S. make it clear he was a persistent man who left no stone unturned in his pursuit of patents and rights of reproductions.[12] (And indeed they were of special importance to sculpture as Jacques de Caso has demonstrated.)[13] Bartholdi was repeatedly challenged because he was trying to control the rights of reproduction in France as well as the United States. Sometimes his contracts with parties in one country were at odds with contracts in the other. Avoiron and Company, to whom he had assigned the rights to reproductions in zinc (called imitation bronze), contested, for example, Bartholdi's right to permit an American manufacturer to produce similar replicas. The miniatures produced by Avoiron were inscribed with Bartholdi's first U.S. patent number, issued in 1876.[14] Bartholdi had reserved for himself the rights of reproductions in bronze. These finer, more expensive reproductions he had ordered from Thiébaut Frères, a respected Parisian foundry.[15]

Bartholdi's all-inclusive claim in his filed patent was too general to be defensible. In 1885 Eiffel had also tried to protect his rights to his design by depositing a model of his tower at the Tribunal of Commerce in Paris. Aware of Bartholdi's success six years earlier, Eiffel believed that deposit of the model legally defined the tower and its design as his property. With no reason to doubt his rights, in 1887 Eiffel went ahead and formulated a contract with Jules Jaluzot, the founder of the department store Printemps. Eiffel agreed to sell metal scraps from the construction of the tower "to be used to make all sorts of objects of fantasy, whether reproducing or not, the silhouettes and models of the actual tower, but systematically mentioning that they were made of the same metal."[16] Eiffel would receive 25 percent of the profits. The contract stressed material continuity over the reproduction of the tower's form; "all sorts of things" would be devised from metal scraps. In addition Jaluzot appears to have presumed he had the sole right to sell three-dimensional reproductions of the tower.

In March 1889 Eiffel's rights to execute a contract for the manufacture and sale of derivatives from the tower were overturned. The Conseil d'État ruled that Eiffel had never been the owner of the tower; he was merely the contractor (*concessionaire*).[17] Moreover, because "Eiffel had only deposited a model of the Eiffel Tower itself in 1885, without protecting its image in any way, the tower according to the convention of 1888 must remain part of the public domain of the State during the Exhibition, then become the property of the Ville de Paris."[18]

The case could not be resolved within legal protocols of the time. On the one hand, the "model" of the tower did not protect "its image in any way." On the other, the "model" did not protect the monument itself. The tower therefore was consigned to the public domain. Would Eiffel have maintained possession of the tower if he had protected its "image"? Is a difference between the two-dimensional and three-dimensional, between image and model, implied here? Or is the intended contrast between the abstract concept of the tower and the specific material thing that the model anticipated? The distinction between a model of the tower (which refers solely to the edifice it projects) and the subsequent reproduction of its image seems to have been crucial.

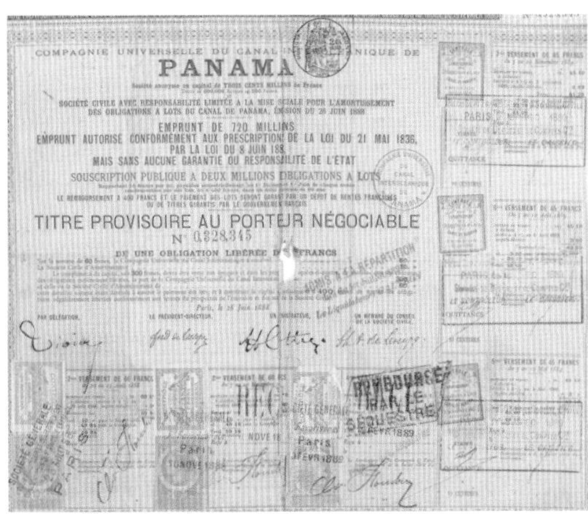
COMPAGNIE UNIVERSELLE DU CANAL [illegible] NIQUE DE

PANAMA

EMPRUNT DE 720 MILLIONS

EMPRUNT AUTORISÉ CONFORMÉMENT AUX PRESCRIPTIONS DE LA LOI DU 21 MAI 1836, PAR LA LOI DU 8 JUIN 188[illegible]

MAIS SANS AUCUNE GARANTIE DU RESPONSABILITÉ DE L'ÉTAT

SOUSCRIPTION PUBLIQUE A DEUX MILLIONS D'OBLIGATIONS A LOTS

TITRE PROVISOIRE AU PORTEUR NÉGOCIABLE

**196**
Compagnie Universelle du Canal Interocéanique de Panama Titre Provisoire, 1888. Author's Collection. Photo: Julie Wolf

**197**
Miniature head of the Statue of Liberty. Inscribed "Souvenir de l'Exposition 1878. Statue de la Liberté. Bartholdi Copyright August 1878" 1878. Courtesy of Ace Architects, Oakland, CA. Photo: Julie Wolf.

The model apparently wielded no control over what people could choose to do in response to the finished structure. A model by this definition comprises a stage in the building of the tower and bears no relation to the similar small objects produced after the tower was finished.

A week before the Conseil d'État's adverse ruling, Eiffel realized that selling Jaluzot full rights to the tower's reproduction had been a mistake. Too many parties were angry. In a letter to the Conseil he indicated his willingness to revoke the contract with Jaluzot and to permit "complete liberty" of reproduction. "I had already specially reserved for myself the rights of reproduction by engraving, photography, and the print trade, etc., in order to be able to allow, without any levy, complete liberty for these kinds of reproductions.... I would like today, owing to the considerations that I have just put forward, to do the same for all other reproductions of the tower."[19]

Eiffel was sure that the model he had filed with the tribunal gave him comprehensive rights to all reproductions of the tower. He believed as well that he had granted Jaluzot only the right to sell objects made from metal scraps. He had, he argued, retained the rights to all two-dimensional reproductions of the tower in order that anyone could freely fabricate them. The engineer had finally realized the importance of unrestricted production and circulation of images of the tower, though evidently he retained a more limited view of three-dimensional miniatures; these were commodities from which he expected to profit. It is conceivable that he regarded the miniature objects as easier to control and more valuable than photographs and postcards. If he did he had erred. Jaluzot had already built a factory to manufacture various bibelots from tower detritus. He had also subcontracted thirty-one industrialists, including a French jeweler who had hired 150 workers solely for the production of expensive miniature versions of the tower. Eiffel's formidable skills were of little use in controling commercial reproduction of what had previously been "his" tower.

---

**The knickknack of the year, the king of knickknacks taken away by all foreigners and provincials, is the Eiffel Tower, the famous tower that illuminates all of Paris, immense or miniscule.**

**Paul Bluysen, *Paris en 1889: Souvenirs et croquis de l'Exposition*, 1890**

It is often assumed that a miniature entails more refined craftsmanship than the larger original.[20] From Edmund Burke to Robert Morris, smallness has been aligned with decorative beauty, femininity, and detail—and the huge with power, masculinity, the sublime, and the potential for transcendence.[21] The jeweler commissioned to craft expensive jewelry based on the Eiffel Tower for the department store Printemps probably thought along those lines. But the jeweler would have been mistaken; the number of proponents notwithstanding, an aesthetics in which the small-female-exquisite opposes the large-masculine-sublime suffers from serious flaws. Miniatures can never be more "finely crafted" than the colossal originals (figs. 198–199). The relative proportions of the small-scale reproductions vary greatly, as anyone who has been inside a New York City or Paris souvenir shop knows: shelves are lined with skinny, fat, big-headed, squat, blocky, and elegant miniature Statues of Liberty; and the same is true of rows of souvenir Eiffel Towers. Their interpretation varies as does their cost. The vast differences between the miniatures of the Statue of Liberty and the colossal sculpture itself are immediately evident because the reproductions range in "body type" and everyone is accustomed to discriminating among bodies. Then too few miniatures of the Statue of Liberty capture the elegant simplicity of the original, despite Bartholdi's concerted attempts to regulate the quality of replicas. He even provided models of varied sizes to manufacturers during the statue's construction, but the crude miniatures are proof that his efforts failed.

Although it has a strong and symmetrical shape, the Eiffel Tower posed its own problems for the souvenir business of the late nineteenth century. The tower presented manufacturers of miniatures with a paradox: nothing could be easier to reproduce than the tower's silhouette—the simple shape, pyramid and/or two identically curving lines—that made possible its unprecedented height (see fig. 194). But the tower's open structure is quite another matter. Thousands of its constituent parts are fully visible, and even if they are largely brute, prefabricated pieces of iron, the colossal size of the tower makes them appear to be delicate members of a delicate web. Albeit an industrial structure, the tower is infinitely more intricate than any small-scale reproduction could ever be.

To diminish in size is necessarily to diminish in detail, not because any given detail cannot be included, but because all of them cannot. The manufacturer has to decide which parts or details to reproduce, and those decisions are evident in the final products. The decision in

**198**
From left to right: Miniature Statue of Liberty, committee model on correct pedestal, 11 5/8 inches tall, base inscribed "Pat. Nov. 5, 1878 and Feb. 18, 1879;" Miniature Statue of Liberty inscribed "Liberty Enlightening the World," and "Pat. Feb. 18 1879, July 16, 1885," 5 7/16 inches tall; Miniature Statue of Liberty on Globe captioned "Liberty always right side up," 6 3/8 inches tall, 1885; Miniature Statue of Liberty model with incorrect base, 12 9/16 inches tall; Miniature Statue of Liberty perfume container, inscribed "Patent applied for," "From the Wenck Perfumes Mfg. Co." 5 3/4 inches high. Courtesy of Ace Architects, Oakland, CA. Photo: Julie Wolf.

**199**
From left to right: Miniature Eiffel Tower to wear at one's wrist with a dance card, 4 11/16 inches tall, 1889; Miniature Eiffel Tower with peep hole through which one sees a black and white image of the Universal Exhibition of 1889, 5 inches tall, 1889; miniature Eiffel Tower with thermometer, 5 3/8 inches tall 1889. (All measurements include pedestals). Courtesy of Ace Architects, Oakland, CA. Photo: Julie Wolf.

one diminutive Eiffel Tower to include an open trellis at each landing is striking because that openness is not sustained elsewhere and because other miniatures seldom include it. Most Eiffel Tower miniatures are solid. They represent the tower's silhouette and sometimes the spaces between its four piers, they do not reproduce the open trelliswork or the structure's voids, and like all miniatures, they fail to reproduce its complexity. But they do fulfill their function as souvenirs: miniatures, they give anyone who holds them or looks at them a sense of mastery. Miniatures are about exteriors and possession.

George Seurat's painting of 1889—measuring a mere 9.5 x 6 inches—is the one "miniature" to identify the tower with its open spaces, which is also to say the painting treats the modernity of the tower as its subject (fig. 200). Seurat's understanding of Eiffel's work and Seurat's achievement as a painter stem from the same source: belief that things become visible in and through the flux of light and color. Hence there are no clear lines in Seurat's painting, no definition of structure, no evenly lit, continuous surfaces. It replaces all those with hundreds of tiny dots of oil paint applied in the pointillist technique Seurat invented. When viewed from a distance the skein of dots configures the tower—it is instantly recognizable in the oranges, browns and lavender suggestive of matter alternating with the pale greys, peaches, and blues suggestive of sky.

The tower had not yet been completed when Seurat made his painting. But this is not clear to the viewer. Eiffel's tower appears so delicate at its pinnacle as to disappear into the bright light. Seurat calls attention to the openness of the entire structure. Differentiated in hue and value, the dots of paint evoke sky yet do not create a background. Quite the reverse happens: the sky overlaps the tower; some dabs of pale blue can be detected on top of orange dots constative of the tower. Sky invading a triumph of nineteenth-century engineering?

According to Claude Lévi-Strauss, objects of enlarged dimension are comprehended through their parts; we learn about them beam by beam, stone by stone, but miniatures offer immediate knowledge of the whole; they offer a mental as well as physical possession.

To understand a real object in its totality we always tend to work from its parts. The resistance it offers us is overcome by dividing it. Reduction in scale reverses this situation. Being smaller, the object as a whole seems less formidable. By being quantitatively diminished, it seems to us

qualitatively simplified... In the case of miniatures, in contrast to what happens when we try to understand an object or a living creature of real dimensions, knowledge of the whole precedes knowledge of the parts.[22]

Lévi-Strauss' argument finds support in the diminutive representations of buildings installed on the walls of some early skyscrapers.[23] Since the totality of a colossal structure cannot be apprehended, it requires compensatory reminders of its whole form for visitors making their way through its parts. Lévi-Strauss' absolute statement can be contested, yet it bears comparison with Kant's discussion of apprehension and comprehension before the Great Pyramid. Against Kant, this modern intellectual believed that looking at a pyramid up close with a small-scale model in hand permits the simultaneous apprehension and comprehension of its form.

Lévi-Strauss adds an important qualification to his point: "And if this [knowledge of the whole] is an illusion, the point of the procedure [of miniaturization] is to create or sustain this illusion, which gratifies the intelligence and gives rise to a sense of pleasure which can already be called aesthetic on these grounds alone."[24] Miniatures offer the illusion of heightened knowledge. Quantitative diminution leads to a sense of qualitative simplification: all can be known. Therein lies the aesthetic pleasure miniatures afford. Moreover, to hold one's own colossus in one's palm is to enjoy a sense of command over it. The tremendous number of small-scale replicas of the Eiffel Tower attests to people's desire to own it in a diminutive form.[25]

There is a special pleasure in the experience of dramatic shifts in scale. In 1889 one Parisian wrote: "Is it necessary to enumerate the models of the tower in leather, gold, silver, lead, nickel, rolled gold, zinc, crystal, which have no practical usefulness and which one puts in one's pocket simply to possess as a good luck charm the colossus of the Champ-de-Mars?"[26] As in so many other contemporary accounts, the author is compelled to list the many different materials out of which replicas were made. Jaluzot had been granted rights to make anything he wished out of the iron scraps Eiffel provided. But the appeal of these miniatures did not depend on their material substance nor could these reproductions proffer fine craftsmanship with unexpected detail. The game they played was that of scale itself. If Eiffel's tower had been accused of uselessness, here were things that were doubly useless, unless one believes in the power of charms. In that case they were invaluable. A colossus in your pocket? Magic, not knowledge, is the prize.

**200**
Georges Seurat, *The Eiffel Tower*, 1889.
Oil on canvas, 9.5 x 6 inches. San Francisco, Legion of Honor. The Fine Arts Museums of San Francisco.

In her classic book *On Longing*, Susan Stewart writes that "the observer is offered a transcendent and simultaneous view of the miniature, yet is trapped outside the possibility of a lived reality of the miniature."[27] Stewart is correct but only in part. She fails to recognize the ways in which miniatures invite fantasy, what one art historian has called the "symbolic—relatively magic — implications of the reducing process."[28] It is also worth remembering that Gaston Bachelard maintained the non-sense of miniatures liberates people from "the obligation of dimension."

We are inclined to think the narrator [of a *Dictionary of Christian Botany*] would have been more cautious had he had to describe an object of ordinary dimensions. But he entered into a miniature world and right away images began to abound, then grow, then escape. Large issues from small, not through the logical law of a dialectics of contraries, but thanks to liberation from all obligations of dimensions, a liberation that is a special characteristic of the activity of the imagination.[29]

This awareness of the playfulness of the miniature modifies received notions about the tourist souvenir— that mass-produced commodity art historians regard as at best kitsch.[30] But to me extreme shifts in scale are wondrous. And nineteenth-century consumers are known to have been astonished at the sight of a structure of three-hundred meters in height somehow shrunk down to a bauble a few centimeters high. A tiny colossus lends itself to use as a personal fetish, held close to the body, in a pocket or on a chain around the neck or the wrist. This is a relationship that challenges Lévi-Strauss' notion that possession is primarily a visual experience. These uses turn the miniature colossus into something felt rather than regarded, something pressed against warm skin.

**One had, at the first sight of the giant, been surprised that three hundred meters were not more, but now became surprised that it stood there so immovably firm in spite of its airy lightness which made it look like a toy.** Henri Girard, *La Tour Eiffel*, 1891

There are two constants in this story: an impulse to make colossal things and an impulse to devise means to shrink the colossus into something hand-held and portable. The plates in the *Description de l'Égypte* and the dessert service with replicas of the Colossi of Memnon are products of the second impulse, as was photography. Early on in its history, 1849, the theorist of vision David Brewster salutes the sculptor who could now "virtually carry in his portfolio... the gigantic sphinxes of Egypt."[31] And herein lay the power of stereoviews of faraway people and places.

But stereoviews have an oddness about them. They convert things into images in which huge things appear to be mere miniatures. To some commentators in the nineteenth century the stereoview made the world look like a model. A writer reviewing the Crystal Palace Exhibition for a London newspaper recorded this experience and offered a physiological explanation for it.

...a view as if the pictures were taken from a small model of the building brought sufficiently near for the whole to be within the distance influenced by the angle of the eyes. In fact, instead of seeing the object itself, you see a miniature model of it brought close to the eyes; so that, in this instance, the stereoscopic Daguerreotypes actually surpass the reality. No one has ever seen the interior of the Exhibition from end to end with such clearness as it is seen in M. Claudet's [stereoview] pictures.

The stereoscope was celebrated for producing images that the eye alone could never have achieved. David Brewster believed that the lenses of stereoscopic cameras should not be farther apart than human eyes, which he calculated as a distance of two and a half inches. He allowed only one exception, and it was for "colossal statues" and buildings, which needed to be viewed at a great distance to be seen in their entirety. The problem is that distance diminishes the appearance of three-dimensional relief. Human eyes are too close together to allow for the binocular parallax required to create a sense of relief in very distant objects. Brewster posed the question: "As we cannot increase the distance between our eyes, and thus obtain a higher degree of relief for bodies of large dimensions, how are we to proceed in order to obtain drawings of such bodies of the requisite relief?" Brewster's answer was to propose increasing the distance between the stereoscopic camera's two lenses:

If the lenses are placed at this distance [25 inches apart], and pictures of the [ten-foot-wide] colossal statue taken, they will reproduce by their union a statue of one foot high, which will have exactly the same appearance and relief as if we had viewed the colossal statue with eyes 25 inches distant. But the reproduced statue will have also the same appearance and relief as a statue a foot high, reduced from the colossal one with mathematical precision, and therefore it will be a better and a more relieved representation of the work than if we had viewed the colossal original with our own eyes, either under a greater, an equal, or a lesser angle of apparent magnitude.[32]

The stereoview produces, to cite Robert Silverman, "the impression of viewing a reduced copy of the oversized structure."[33] A giant would be able to see a very distant colossal building in relief, but an ordinary human being cannot. The stereoview compensates for this human limitation by offering the viewpoint of a giant with eyes twenty-five inches apart. This view is strange: whatever is seen appears like a model, particularly to those unaccustomed to seeing the totality of immense things or vistas in bold relief. There is a perceptual bind here: knowledge of the entire real colossus is gained at the cost of making it small and unreal. Is this yet another way that miniatures produce a sense of magic? Looking at stereoviews, people perceive the world as a kind of theater set. Everything is compressed and flattened into disparate planes; gaps between the planes acquire heightened clarity. The world becomes like a toy in which looming spaces separate miniature things.

Do I exaggerate the difference between seeing the monumental in a stereoview and seeing it in life? Even in 1889 the Eiffel Tower, its unprecedented height of 1000 feet notwithstanding, disappointed some visitors and angered others. The author of *Against Nature [À rebours]* Joris-Karl Huysmans denounced the tower in "Iron," a vitriolic essay of 1889. And even he was two years late in launching an assault. A group of French writers and artists had attacked the "tower, dominating Paris...the barbaric mass of a gigantic black factory smokestack crushing Notre-Dame, the Saint-Chapelle, the Tour Saint-Jacques, the Louvre, the dome of Les Invalides, and the Arc de Triomphe. One need only imagine, all our buildings shrunken, disappearing in this stupefying dream."[34]

"Not even enormous," asserted Huysmans in a riposte to earlier critics. The tower was indeed a blight on Paris not because it was gigantic but because it was "paltry." Lacking in "art's forms," it should have been enormous, he wrote, opening a new line of attack on the great symbol of modern progress.

The Eiffel Tower is truly of an ugliness that disconcerts, and it is not even enormous!—Seen from below, it does not seem to attain the height of which we have been told. It is necessary to consider points of comparison, but imagine, stacked, one on top of the other, the Pantheon and the Invalides, the Vendôme Column and Notre-Dame and you cannot persuade yourself that the belvedere of the tower scales the summit attained by this unlikely pile.

Seen from a distance, it is even worse. This shaft barely overtakes those monuments. From the Esplanade of the Invalides, for example, it barely doubles [in height] a five-story house.... From close range, from a distance, from the center of Paris, from the depths of the suburbs, the effect is identical.... Finally, drawn or engraved it is paltry....

Wherever you turn, this work deceives. It is 300 meters high and seems 100; it is finished and it seems barely begun. For lack of art's form, difficult to achieve with these trellises that are only piers built up of decks, the tower should at least have been made gigantic to suggest to us the sensation of the enormous; it was necessary that this Tower be immense.[35]

Eiffel had every right to be outraged. First he had been attacked for creating an ugly "factory smokestack" that "crushed" the revered monuments of Paris; then Huysmans accused him of making the smokestack too small to compensate for its ugliness. Did Eiffel realize that Huysmans was playing faux-naïf? The view from up close leads him to measurement: in this case, the conventional piling of monuments one upon another to comprehend the tower's height, a height he does not believe to be true. For Huysmans the tower just does not appear that tall. From up close it appears, he claimed, 100 meters tall rather than 300. From afar, it shrinks. appearing barely twice as high as an apartment building of five floors. Huysmans, naive or jeering, blames Eiffel for the effects of distance: objects of any size look smaller the farther they are away from the beholder. Distance miniaturizes no matter the size of the edifice. Huysmans knew no shame in mocking Eiffel for failing to design a tower of absolute scale. His argument is outrageous or silly or both, but it points to one of the problems in building something to attain great height. The experience of size is determined through comparison, whether to a yardstick or to a person.

Relative size is the subject—occasionally the source of humor—in Henri Rivière's series of lithographs, *Thirty-Six Views of the Eiffel Tower*.[36] Several of the prints reinterpret photographs Rivière had taken during his ascent of the tower while it was under construction (see fig. 4). In these prints emulating Japanese woodcuts, he flattened and simplified the silhouette of worker and beams against the sky. (Rivière's model was Hokusai's *Thirty-Six Views of Mount Fuji*.) But the great majority of his images depict the tower as seen from locations throughout Paris and its outskirts: from the Seine where the barges load and unload, from rooftops, from faraway pathways and roads (figs. 201–204). In several of Rivière's prints the tower is an extraordinary modern colossus looming over the uneven heights of old stone buildings from which laundry hangs. But in most Rivière jokes about the difficulty of seeing the Eiffel Tower, resembling as it does smokestacks or trees or lampposts or muted as it is by its great distance, a mere slip of pale grey. Still in all thirty-six views, from various points in the city, the Eiffel Tower is there, even when it seems to have vanished. A scene at the Bois-de-Boulogne featuring ducks is sweet, insipid, and surely tongue-in-cheek (fig. 205). Adorable Paris sans the offensive tower, yet it is still there at top right, a pale streak caught between the trees. What Rivière gets right in his series is that the colossal monument will not always appear colossal but appear it will. And it will always appear the same because the tower itself (unlike the Statue of Liberty) is identical on all four sides. From afar, whether from north, south, east, or west, the tower appears the same. The celebrated writer Guy de Maupassant had signed the 1887 petition protesting its construction; he is said, later, still indignant, to have eaten lunch at the tower everyday in order not to have to see it.[37] The colossal, especially if symmetrical, produces omnipresence. This is one reason the anecdote about Maupassant is often repeated.

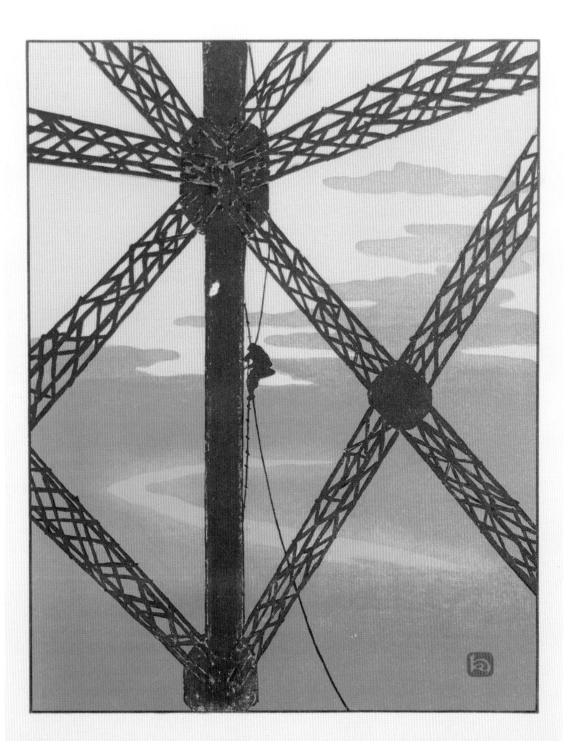

**201**
Henri Rivière, *Thirty-Six Views of the Eiffel Tower: Le Peintre dans la Tour*, 1902. Color Lithograph. Cleveland, The Cleveland Museum of Art.

**202**
Henri Rivière, *Thirty-Six Views of the Eiffel Tower: Rue Beethoven*, 1902. Color Lithograph. Cleveland, The Cleveland Museum of Art.

**203**
Henri Rivière, *Thirty-Six Views of the Eiffel Tower: De l'Estacade*, 1902. Color Lithograph. Cleveland, The Cleveland Museum of Art.

**204**
Henri Rivière, *Thirty-Six Views of the Eiffel Tower: De la Rue Rochechouart*, 1902. Color Lithograph. Cleveland, The Cleveland Museum of Art.

**205**
Henri Rivière, *Thirty-Six Views of the Eiffel Tower: Du Bois de Boulogne*, 1902. Color Lithograph. Cleveland, The Cleveland Museum of Art.

**Seen thus from above, the entire landscape looked inert, like a painting.** Gustave Flaubert, *Madame Bovary*, 1857

If the Eiffel Tower was repeatedly miniaturized and turned into mere representation—an icon of Paris—the tower itself afforded visitors the opportunity to see the city as a diminutive model (fig. 206). The tower is after all a viewing platform from which to behold Paris and its environs as a panorama. And it was erected when panoramas were enjoying great popularity in Paris; the Universal Exhibition of 1889 displayed no fewer than seven.[38]

Architects are taught that it is extremely difficult to design a structure intended to serve as a viewing platform. One student of architecture has summarized it this way: "Firstly, one is always observing, and thus the space of observation is not easily distinguished from any other. Secondly, designing a space for observation is to make the visitor focus on another space even as they are within yours; the space is designed, that is, to dissolve its own presence in favor of what is being observed."[39] The Eiffel Tower is a brilliant solution to this problem; it initially forces awareness of its particularity as a structure, and then, as the visitor ascends, it drops away from sight so that the city of Paris dominates the view.

The experience of that view from the top enthralled nineteenth-century visitors, many of whom recorded their experiences:

> The panorama develops the higher you climb. What you see at first are the hills that surround Paris, then the view drops back to a distance.... Paris and the surrounding area look detached as on a map.[40]

> The crowd there takes...stairs, elevators, Jacob's ladder, to the sublime heights from which it will admire in absolute silence the panorama of an immense magical radius—but it will have under its surprised gazes no more than a geometric plan— in place of Paris, nothing there dominates any-thing any longer—three hundred meters below, those who seemed our masters are dwarves like us.[41]

> From this height, Paris looks like an enormous game of Biribi played by a giant on a green carpet.[42]

> At this point the city already had the immobility of a panorama. Life and movement were not apparent. The silhouettes of the pedestrians and the fiacres were small ink stains, very black and very clearly outlined. They had the look of hurrying throngs frozen to the ground, the look of horses in drawings, halted around the department stores. Only the Seine was still alive, because of the watery effects on its muddy surface. The scene was like a canvas puffed out by a gust of wind.[43]

From the top of the Eiffel Tower these visitors saw a city stilled, inert. Paris became a map, a geometric plan, a game board, a panorama, a drawing, a painting. To climb the tower was to enter a machine that turned Paris into a miniature. And in the throes of that experience of transformation, visitors gained a visceral sense of the tower's height. When Eiffel erected a 1000-foot tower in Paris, he inserted a device that increased everyone's awareness of scale, its deceptions as well as its playfulness."Paris is no longer in Paris: one would swear that it fits entirely within the phenomenal, attractive, troubling work of the great engineer to whom all these street vendors, in their way, pay homage."[44] Paris fits inside the tower and, thanks to the vendors, the tower fits inside your pocket. Child's play.

---

**In the preparation of these plans and all during its construction this work was treated as an engineering problem and not as a theatrical venture, and it is due to this that such perfect results have been attained. All the mechanical and electrical features here developed are fully covered by patents.** *The Panama Canal at San Francisco*, 1915

At the close of his essay on the murals of the Panama Canal, Van Ingen remarks: "When the pictures had been placed [in 1915], I took a trip, one fine morning, through the Great Cut. Returning to the Administration Building I hurried to the rotunda to test the effect of the paintings, and received the impression that as *miniatures* they were not bad!"[45] Van Ingen italicizes "miniatures" to reflect his experience of seeing his paintings with the reality of the canal fresh in his mind. The discrepancy in size could not have come as a surprise to him. Throughout the essay he acknowledges that the primary challenge of the Panama commission had been "to express magnitude."

Few Americans saw Van Ingen's painting cycle after he finished it in 1915. But that same year thousands of visitors at the Panama-Pacific Exposition paid to see a three-dimensional model of the recently completed canal. An official brochure extolled it as "a complete, correct and faithful working reproduction of the Panama Canal and Canal Zone." Though the models

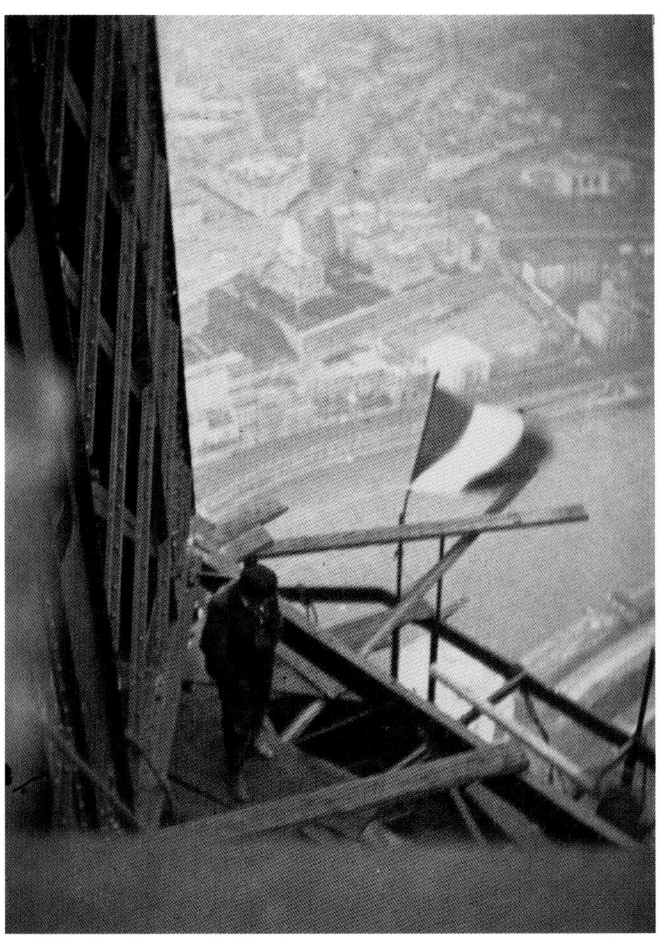

**206**
Henri Rivière, *The Eiffel Tower. Visitor on the Scaffolding on the North Pier; in the background a flag, the Seine, and the Right Bank*, 1889. Photograph. Paris, Musée d'Orsay, fonds Eiffel.

of the Suez Canal had been exhibited at government pavilions, the U.S. model was located in a strip of private concessions called the Zone. The location of Van Ingen's murals was similar: a five-mile-wide strip of land, known as the Zone, on either side of the full length of the canal.

The Zone was where Americans lived in the early twentieth century after expelling native inhabitants. In the Zone sidewalks were straight, houses looked American, lawns flourished, and the feared jungle was kept at bay. Cheap labor for the maintenance work was at hand in the native and West Indian population.[46] With their help American women kept manicured gardens which reproduced the botanical richness of the jungle at a small scale but, according to a government report, avoided "the close confusion of the jungle into which native vegetation lapses when left alone or indiscriminately cultivated."[47] Photographs continually underscored the contrast between the chaos of the jungle and the paved streets of the Zone (figs. 207–208). A photograph of me, aged two, in a traditional Panamanian dress, standing on a Zone sidewalk, inadvertently reproduces the hard-edge order celebrated in engineering as well as in the "taming" of the Isthmus.

In San Francisco at the Panama-Pacific Exposition, the Zone was where visitors paid for food, entertainment, and thrills. It cast the rest of the exhibition as official and pedagogical. Every exposition in Europe as well as in the United States made similar distinctions, and the public was ready to be educated. Only fifteen of the 455 concessions on the Zone made over $100,000, whereas the Panama Canal exhibition earned almost $340,000, according to the exposition's official historian.[48] The model was a resounding success, except for the fact that it failed to realize a profit; it had cost $500,000 to fabricate.[49]

The model, itself a feat of engineering, was the brainchild of "L. E. Meyers, head of a Chicago corporation engaged in the manufacture of equipment for public utilities."[50] He had gotten the idea for the model during a visit to the Panama Canal in 1911, a year before Joseph Pennell's trip and three years before Van Ingen's two visits. Engineer, lithographer, and painter visited Panama, one after the other, each in search of a way to represent the immensity of the canal, each in competition with photographers whose pictures were already circulating and defining public perception. The lithographer Pennell was the first to present his work to the public; a book of his lithographs appeared in 1912. The painter and engineer completed their work in 1915. But the engineer's model took the longest to prepare: "More than two years were devoted to designing and planning ways, means and methods for operating the locks, ships, trains and other moving objects, also to provide some method by which it would be possible to satisfactorily explain to each individual spectator the construction and purpose of the Canal, and this, too, in a way that would be easily understood."[51]

But Meyers had begun the extensive work of solving what he considered a problem in engineering long before the government had shifted its attention from the canal to the exposition in its honor.[52] After prolonged negotiations in San Francisco and Washington, D.C., the government finally allowed work to proceed, partly because it came to admire the engineer's plans and partly because it had no better way to show "all that [visitors] should know with respect to the Panama Canal."[53] The government conceded rights of reproduction to a private entrepreneur because his model had been designed to impart information to the masses. In the official brochure Meyer's company reproduced a letter of congratulations and open admiration from "F. C. Boggs, Chief of the Washington Office, Panama Canal." The model would win Grand Prize as a Liberal Arts exhibit because of its "educational value."[54]

The model covered five acres and attempted to replicate "more than one thousand square miles, with every minute detail worked out with engineering accuracy from plans and drawings furnished by the United States Government."[55] No fewer than 1,200 people eventually sat in "trains" on an elevated platform that electric motors propelled to circle the display. The organizers supplemented the model with lectures:

As the spectators sat in comfortable chairs and passed the various points of interest, they held telephone receivers to their ears, and heard lectures from phonograph records which were switched on and off to correspond with the various sections of the journey. The system by which the lecture was delivered was invented for this Exposition and was perhaps something entirely new. It required 45 phonographs, with 15 "spares," in a nearby room, to deliver the message into telephone transmitters, which in turn delivered it to the receivers at the seats. A lecture record lasted about six weeks. The details of the invention were worked out in the laboratory of Thomas A. Edison.[56]

The lectures were paced to correspond to what visitors were seeing. Thanks to engineers, thanks to Edison's invention, and thanks to the United States government, the private entrepre-neurs had made a model that in less than half an hour purportedly"impart[ed] to anyone a more complete knowledge of the Canal than a visit of several days to the waterway itself."[57]

If the Panama Canal was touted as the greatest and largest engineering achievement of its kind, its model was advertised as "the largest reproduction of any subject ever created."[58] Leave it to early twentieth-century Americans to boast that they had made the largest miniature of the colossal. Models by definition are meant to be small, small enough for makers to manipulate them; small enough for makers and viewers to apprehend the whole rather than its parts. The models of the Suez Canal had conformed to this expectation. But the location of the Panama Canal model points to a key difference. In the Zone entrepreneurs were competing to sell food and entertainment. The model of the Panama Canal vied with those many quintessentially nineteenth century spectacles with names ending with -orama (panoramas, cosmoramas, and so forth), even as it sustained its commitment to accuracy.

---

**Up, up, up. Faster and faster and faster and faster the little engine climbed.**
**Watty Piper, *The Little Engine That Could*, 1930**

Visitors to the Suez Canal Pavilion at the Exposition of 1867 were depicted as relaxed yet involved; they stroll around the Pavilion and appear to discuss the models and their different modes of presenting information (see fig. 47). They could scrutinize a rock from a particular site and then turn to a map to locate that site. A scant half century later, at the Panama-Pacific International Exposition, the public was subjected to a program of instruction. If attracted to the centerpiece of the Exposition, the Panama Canal model, visitors of all ages faced a "tour" with few choices. They sat in an ever-moving, mechanized assembly line, listening to phonographs. As in trains they became static objects inside the machines that moved. From above they saw a miniature canal around which "boats, trains, 'electric mules,' and lighthouses [were] in operation, and the ships were timed to pass through the miniature Canal and locks at the same pace relatively at which the originals would have passed through the real Canal"[59] (figs. 209–214).

Lévi-Strauss claims that miniature versions of things function much like toys. They endow their owners or observers with a sense of mastery. Canals are an exception to his rule. How can someone hold a canal in their mind or their hands? It is very difficult to visualize work that encompasses large stretches of terrain. Its forms are tied to the peculiarities of a site that are best learned through repeated direct experience. Lesseps had made the Suez Canal easy to apprehend by smoothing the irregularities of surrounding land and accentuating its straight edges. The Panama Canal could not be simplified in this way. Even the exposition's model of the Panama Canal was so large that it could not be seen all at once, so large that the trip around it took twenty-three minutes.

**207**
Tropical Vegetation in the Heart of the Panama Canal Zone. Half of Keystone Stereoview. 1907. Author's Collection. Photo: Julie Wolf.

**208**
Photograph of Author, age two, in traditional Panamanian Carnival Dress, Panama Canal Zone. Author's Collection. Photo: Julie Wolf.

Yet compared to the Panama Canal itself, the model was a miniature. A trip that required a day in Panama took twenty-three minutes in San Francisco. Because of the brevity of the trip Meyers was confident the audience would listen to an accompanying lecture. The entire experience was planned to give visitors a grasp of the canal as a whole. The illusion of comprehensive knowledge was reinforced by the visitor's elevated point-of-view, twenty feet above the model: "The effect being that of a general bird's-eye view, not only of the Canal, but the territory lying within and adjacent to the Canal Zone."[60] In a huge, sheltered amphitheater the visitors looked down upon the full Panama Canal much as had the visitors to the Suez exhibition. But here the point of view was even higher and sustained as far as the eye could see. A panorama furnished the model with 10,000 miles more illusory space. Carefully controlled lighting helped to unify the ensemble which looked very much like an aerial photograph of the isthmus.[61]

The model of the Panama Canal conjoined the two separate models that had been exhibited at the Suez Canal Company Pavilion. There was a view from above of the canal cutting between mountains, incorporating a lake and gradually winding its way from the Pacific to the Atlantic. Once again there were machines, though not the dredging machines seen at the Suez

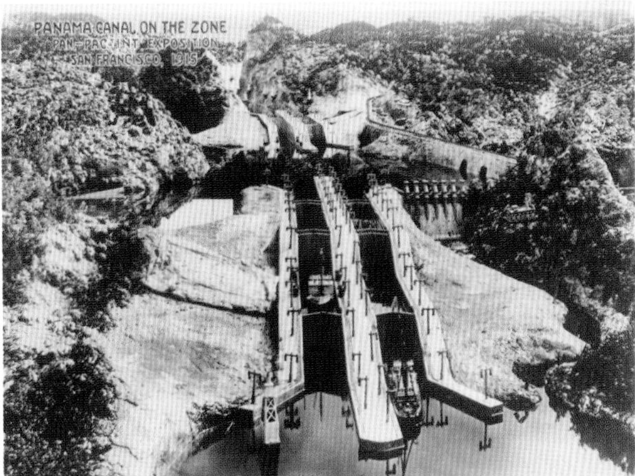

**209**
Panama Canal Building. Illustration in Panama-Pacific International Exposition Company, *The Panama Canal at San Francisco*, 1915. Author's Collection. Photo: Julie Wolf.

**210**
Postcard. "Panama Canal on the Zone. Panama-Pacific International Exposition, San Francisco, 1915," 1915. Author's Collection. Photo: Julie Wolf.

**211**
"Panama Railroad Train Crossing Gatun River Bridge," Model of the Panama Canal. Illustration in Panama-Pacific International Exposition Company, *The Panama Canal at San Francisco*, 1915. Author's Collection. Photo: Julie Wolf.

**212**
"Gatun Locks," Model of the Panama Canal. Illustration in Panama-Pacific International Exposition Company, *The Panama Canal at San Francisco*, 1915. Author's Collection. Photo: Julie Wolf.

**213**
"City of Colón with Gatun Lock in the Distance," Model of the Panama Canal. Illustration in Panama-Pacific International Exposition Company, *The Panama Canal at San Francisco*, 1915. Author's Collection. Photo: Julie Wolf.

**214**
"Darien Wireless Station," Model of the Panama Canal. Illustration in Panama-Pacific International Exposition Company, *The Panama Canal at San Francisco*, 1915. Author's Collection. Photo: Julie Wolf.

Canal Company pavilion. On display in San Francisco were the machines needed for the working of a lock-based canal, most notably the electric "mules" along the canal's edge as well as trains and lighthouses.

These diminutive working and moving machines were considered one of the exhibition's marvels: "By far the most interesting feature of the model is the mechanical operation of the boats, trains, lighthouses, buoys, etc., all of these features being shown in full operation, exactly as they are on the Isthmus. The boats that pass back and forth thru the Canal are controlled by magnets operated on tracks placed beneath the floor of the model, the magnetic influence being exerted thru a 3-inch gap of air, wood, tar, felt, cement and water."[62] Hidden machines thus made possible the illusion of autonomous movement.

While Van Ingen's "miniature" was devoted to the labor that had built the Panama Canal, the San Francisco model promoted the efficacy and efficiency of its engineering. The canal system is autonomous in its workings, or so the model with its rotating platform and synchronized lectures piped into visitors' ears would have the public believe. The fit between the actual canal and the display in San Francisco was perfect, except to the serious-minded alert to a major shortcoming. The model—ingenious, educational—changed the Panama Canal into a toy. Choo choo went the train, ding ding went the boat, flash flash went the lighthouses.

Heroic toy machines were becoming popular in American children's literature of the early twentieth century. *Katy and the Big Snow, Choo Choo—The Story of a Little Engine Who Ran Away, Scuffy the Tugboat* are among the books that continue to be favorites of teachers, parents, and children. Although some of them appeared after the 1930s, versions of *The Little Engine That Could* first appeared while the Panama Canal was being dredged.[63] "I think I can, I think I can," says the little Blue Engine determined to deliver carloads of good things to the boys and girls on the other side of the mountain. Turned into a toy to "ride," seen from above in aerial perspective, the Panama Canal was the little system-that-could.

**215**
"Toyland Grown Up," 1914. Illustration by Cardinell-Vincent, the official photographer of the Panama Pacific Exposition, Donald G. Larson Collection on International Expositions and Fairs, Henry Madden Library, California State University, Fresno.

Of course it could. Engineers had changed the scale of Panama; it was now small, manageable, and an outpost of American power that ushered in a new era in international commerce. They had also erased the workers and their excruciating toil. It is conceivable that laborers were mentioned in the lectures piped through phonograph tubes to visitors to the model in San Francisco, but they were nowhere to be seen in the grand mechanized system-that-could. The workers stayed in Panama. In San Francisco Americans enjoyed the ride.

After visiting the five-acre model of the Panama Canal, people could try an attraction that occupied almost three times as much area as the Panama model and is estimated to have cost twice as much to build. All these resources were used to present a big, really big version of the world of children (fig. 215). "'Toyland Grown Up' is the million dollar concession of Frederick Thompson and covers fourteen acres.... In this new enterprise Thompson has reversed the fairy tales of childhood and the giant's stove, his skillet, the blocks of the children, Noah's Ark, and every hero, heroine and villain of nursery rhyme will be so large as to make the humans who visit the toyland appear very small and insignificant."[64]

Never mind the silliness of enlarging a giant's possessions (and calling this a "reversal"), Toyland Grown Up made real people appear "small and insignificant," much as the ancient Egyptian pyramids, the Statue of Liberty, Eiffel Tower, and the Culebra Cut had done. What had been sublime, sometimes tragic, about these engineering feats had devolved into an amusement park.

Small, solid blocks of wood teach children about weight, gravity, and balance, about what is or is not possible in the physical world. You made the tower as tall as you could; if you did not build it well, placing the large blocks at the base, slender ones at the top, it fell down. And even if you built it well, the higher you went, the more likely a fall. You learned not all heights are possible. And you were delighted with both the building up and the tumbling down.

There were blocks at Toyland Grown Up, colossal blocks that seemed to be accurate facsimiles of children's blocks so long as a certain distance, a certain decorum was maintained. Seen up close, pushed or pulled, the blocks proved to be hollow and locked in place. The same method was used to manufacture the other giant toys. They were hollow, their defiance of gravity an illusion, and so too their invitation to play. They were all static models. Yet visitors to Toyland may have felt pleasure, even wonder. Colossal things are always wondrous. Often they mask the fact that unless correctly engineered they, like towers of blocks, will fall down.

TOYLAND GROWN-UP.
PEARL TOP
ALLADIN
WISHING WELL
T.A.

# Coda, Tallest?

The past is never dead. It's not even past.
William Faulkner, 1951

The joke is an old one by now: show someone talking on a cell phone the size of a shoe, get a laugh. Technology of a few years ago is just so gauche. Hollywood uses the gag all the time: oversized cell phones, oversized video cameras, secret agents of normal size brandishing XL spook devices. Ridiculous.

In the 2002 movie "I Spy," Owen Wilson knows he is considered second-rate when he is assigned clunky equipment that looks as if it came "from Radio Shack in 1972." He whines: "Look at the size of this thing! Size matters! But in the spy world it's the reverse; you want people to say, 'look how small and sexy and sleek this is!' "Technology has shrunk devices. One hears these days of the imminent insertion of computers into our bodies as skin keyboards or screens on our retinas. The future looms very, very small. Or does it?

The twentieth century was the age of the skyscraper, the hydroelectric dam, and Mount Rushmore, all indebted to technological innovations of the nineteenth century. The systems of construction introduced at the Statue of Liberty and the Eiffel Tower won international acclaim and were soon copied and developed. The skyscraper would never have been possible without the innovations achieved in those nineteenth-century monuments. In the 1930s U.S. engineers used the locks and Gatun Dam of the Panama Canal system to design Hoover Dam, still the largest dam in the world. The Statue of Liberty inspired the Mount Rushmore Memorial (1927–41), but engineers at the Panama Canal had perfected the techniques the sculptor Gutzon Borglum would later adapt. To create the portraits, he and his four hundred assistants exploded dynamite along the face of the "stone mountain," much as workers had blasted the mountains of Panama. It is fitting that Teddy Roosevelt is one of the four presidents portrayed at this beloved yet bizarre monument.

A decade into the twenty-first century, the colossal lives on, ever bigger if not better. Nations are still investing in structures of immense size, often to claim power (real or illusory), sometimes out of financial necessity. The Republic of Panama has decided its economy requires a return to grandiose ambition. Because ships, especially oil tankers, have steadily become larger since World War II, the Panama Canal has turned into an anachronism. It is too small—although modified time and again—for today's "post-Panamax" ships. A strange maritime term, "post-Panamax" refers both to time and size; to ships that exceed the size limitations (depth as well as length and width) of the now outdated Panama Canal. In order to fit within the current system of locks, a container ship must measure less than 105 feet in width, 956 feet in length, and 39 feet in draft—the portion of the vessel submerged below the water line.[1]

It is difficult to appreciate the sheer immensity of today's ships. Allan Sekula's film, *The Lottery of the Sea* (2000), helps in imagining their size; so too does a chart of 1979 comparing the Empire State Building and other colossi to the world's largest supertanker (fig. 216).[2] Initially named the *Seawise Giant* (a name likely to have pleased Jules Verne), and now awaiting the scrap yard after many changes of ownership, the tanker measures some 1,504 feet in length; turned on its bow, it would be taller than the Eiffel Tower and Empire State Building. *Seawise Giant* was too wide to pass through the English Channel, let alone the Panama Canal.[3] In the 1980s, about 92 percent of the world's cargo ships could use the Panama Canal; by 2000 the percentage was down 10 points. Post-Panamax ships transporting cargo from Asia to the east coast of the United States are now unloading goods on the west coast and shipping them across the continent via railway. Although more costly and less dependable, transcontinental shipping has over 60 percent of the market share today, the Panama Canal only 38.[4]

Panama, staking its future on the canal that brought it into being, has decided to construct a third set of locks. A report from the Panama Canal Authority describes at length the need for expansion, all the more pressing because the Suez Canal already accommodates post-Panamax ships.[5] A third set of locks can easily be installed beside the existing locks, and the Gatun Lake offers various outlets to the Atlantic, but the Canal's passage through the Culebra (Gaillard) cut is fixed in place just as it was when the Americans inherited it from the French over a century ago. Yet again the only option is to widen the Cut, something already done several times: from 300 to 500 feet (1957–71); to 630 feet (since the 1980s). Now the Panamanians will expand to 715 feet the very excavation that defeated the French, delayed the Americans, and still remains subject to landslides.[6] If Panama succeeds, it will be adding a chapter to a late nineteenth-century story of achievement and incalculable human suffering. In the twenty-first century, Panama is gambling that a nineteenth-century project can continue to yield wealth and power. And as before Panama is competing with its predecessor in Egypt's desert.

9/11 was widely expected to bring an end to the building of "the world's tallest" structures, each taller than the last, each a possible provocation to terrorists. The towering skyscraper carries so much symbolic baggage, starting with the Old Testament Babel, it is indeed a perfect target for those who wish their violent acts to be perceived as an attack on power, capitalism, and modernity itself. Be that as it may, nations in Asia, the Middle East and Eastern Europe are eagerly competing to construct emblems of modern technological know-how. The risk of inciting vengeance has no more weight than the fleeting nature of the prize.

To boast of having the world's tallest skyscraper is futile sooner not later. "Five years, it turns out, is an eternity in the record-breaking skyscraper business" concludes *New York Times* journalist Howard F. French. When the game began in the nineteenth and early twentieth centuries, upstaging by height was novel, linked to the development of iron and steel construction, and proceeded more slowly.[7] Today buildings are surpassed even before they are completed. In 2004 the unfinished Shanghai World Financial Center (fig. 217) had to cede first place to the just completed Taipei 101 (fig. 218) in Taipei, Taiwan. Given that nationalist rivalry is predicated on the equating of power with height, Taiwan's achievement was a humiliation for China. Over a hundred feet were "quietly" added to the Shanghai building; a lavish multimedia "event" on its ground floor declared it to be the higher of the competing towers.[8] But the Shanghai claim is moot. If antennae are allowed into the calculations—and not everyone agrees that they should—Taipei 101 wins the title.

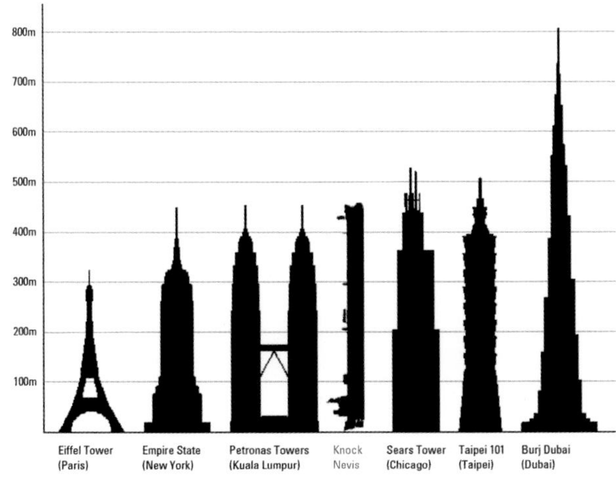


**216**
Comparison Knock Nevis (Seawise Giant) with Large Buildings," 2008
Photo: Wikimedia Commons

Be that as it may, in a few short years the China-Taiwan competition of 2004 would be at best a backstory. No matter an horrendous financial crisis, in 2010 Dubai opened "the world's tallest building," the Burj Khalifa (fig. 219), over 2700 feet in height, more than a thousand feet higher than either building in Asia. The rivalry between the Shanghai and Taiwan buildings was so dramatically eclipsed, it came to seem minor league and not a little pitiable. Disputing the significance of an antenna or the addition of a hundred feet lost all significance after the inauguration of a structure indubitably a staggering thousand feet taller than its closest competitors. Opulent, ostentatious, in my view repellant, the Dubai skyscraper has 160 floors, all accessible via 54 elevators moving at 40 miles per hour; it also features the world's highest swimming pool (76th floor) and the world's highest mosque (158th floor). Visitors who venture to the top are promised a territorial panorama of sixty miles in all directions. Twelve thousand people will eventually live and work in the air-conditioned Burj Khalifa, which cost investors some $1.5 billion to build.

Geraldine Bedell was one of the first journalists to recognize the political impact of the new building:

> Not since 1311, when the spire of Lincoln Cathedral first topped the Great Pyramid of Giza, has the tallest structure in the world been located in the Arab world. Some Arabs, not unreasonably, interpret criticism of the building as resentment at Dubai's presumption in setting itself up as a world city.[9]

Seven hundred years after a cathedral outstripped the height of the Great Pyramid, a prestigious skyscraper reminded the world of the oil emirates' capabilities. Yet in design and aspiration the Burj Khalifa is Western. Skidmore, Owings, and Merrill of Chicago, renowned for building such icons of modernism as Lever House, designed the tower and its complex engineering; planning for a hotel and a small group of "residences" in the tower was turned over to Giorgio Armani, the "world's most successful" fashion designer.

Descriptions of the Burj Khalifa dwell on the abstract forms that brand it as a modernist skyscraper belonging to an international elite of buildings. It looks, said one critic, "like a cluster of variously sized metal rods, the tallest at the center."[10] Paul Goldberger of *The New Yorker* defended the building's design, largely on the basis of its dialogue with modernist precursors. He compares the tower—"a shimmering silver needle"[11] to the Eiffel Tower and earlier skyscrapers that sacrificed floor space in order to possess a "lyrical profile." (In recent years, the reverse choice—"lots of horizontal space"—has prevailed in the U.S.) The morphing of the tower into a heroic figure, Ayn Rand's notorious trope, enters Goldberger's assessment by way of praise for its level-by-level setbacks that serve to prevent wind damage yet also enhance its ability to afford "visual pleasure."[12]

In the end irony more than nostalgia colors Goldberger's assessment of the Burj Khalifa. He sees it as a building, haunted by what I too regard as the fundamental contradictions of record-breaking monuments. They are symbols allowed exorbitant budgets and asked to express superhuman dreams; yet, at some point, calculations of cost-effectiveness and function are brought into play and the fissures in the enterprise emerge. The Burj Khalifa is no exception. It has less office space than the Shanghai World Financial Center—four hundred thousand square feet less. It consumes energy at a staggering rate in a city with the world's highest per capita carbon footprint.[13] The 40 miles per hour elevators are already causing problems; on one occasion visitors were trapped in an elevator on the 124th floor for forty-five minutes, an experience that left at least one person in tears;[14] the building was closed a month after its gala opening. All these failings point up the absurd extravagance of the Burj Khalifa's planners; they erected the world's tallest building. It is close to being pure spectacle.

Of course Dubai was prosperous when the tower was first conceived as the Burj Dubai, a symbol of the country's importance in the world of finance capital. Its new name Burj Khalifa honors Sheik Khalifa bin-Zayed al-Nahyan, the president of the United Arab Emirates, who provided $10 billion to bail out a country, suddenly, in 2009-10, on the brink of bankruptcy. When office space was sacrificed to vertical surge in the tower's profile, it was assumed that investors would snap up the residential spaces as investment properties, not homes, at prices that would compensate for lost revenue from potential business clients. The recent financial crisis has stymied the plan. Empty, the Burj Khalifa is surrounded by numerous other empty skyscrapers, now "monuments to architectural vacancy," though once ostentatious celebrations of capitalism. There are yet more contradictions. A symbol of megalomania, the Burj Khalifa is also a symbol of dependency; of outsize gains and outsize losses; of success and failure; of exploitation of the impoverished workers who have been called "slave laborers" in the press, foreigners primarily from Asia, who continually protested their conditions and the high injury and death rates.[15] It is also a symbol of humiliation. The Burj Khalifa is, after all, an ostentatious emblem of wealth that disappeared before all the bills were paid. Rather than drawing the world's attention to Dubai's wealth, it has dramatized its debt. As "a monument to the excesses of the emirate's bygone boom,"[16] it is perfection. The rounded towers—horizontally striated in silver and gold—resemble stacks of coins.

Mere measurement has never been the source of the drawing power of the colossal. Immensity represents power, the power to build enormous things and the power to finance them. The "Panama Canal Expansion is '2009 Project Finance Deal of the Year,'" crows the headline of a press release from the Panama Canal Authority.[17] *City of Gold: Dubai and the Dream of Capitalism* is the title of a 2009 book by Jim Krane, a reputable Middle East correspondent; the book's jacket features a host of skyscrapers.[18] Immense building and immense engineering are possible only because of immense financing and its attendant corruption.

Mallarmé's article on the Panama scandal of 1892 comes to mind every time I read about the financial crisis begun in 2008. "Currency," observed Mallarmé, loses meaning, especially for "the simple man in the street" as its numbers include "more and more zeros." Such numbers, strings of zeros, seem "equal to nothing."[19] And they are characteristic of the twentieth-century economy wherein colossal finances, whether gains or losses, elude control. In the United States, the government bailout of the banks was in the billions or was it the trillions? And whose money was it anyway?

No twentieth-century statue has acquired the fame of the Statue of Liberty, at least not in the United States. But it has clones and competitors. Before the government of the Soviet Union began to collapse in 1985, it placed immense statues of Vladimir Lenin and "the Motherland"—an almost mystical evocation of Russian identity—in major cities thoughout its farflung territories. When completed in 1967, Motherland Calls (fig. 220) in Volgograd (the former Stalingrad) was pronounced the tallest sculpture in the world. Although the concrete figure measures only 170 feet, she holds aloft a stainless steel sword that adds another 108 feet to her height.[20] The statue was erected as a memorial to the million or more people, many of them civilians, who died in the Battle of Stalingrad (1942–43), one of the largest battles ever fought and a turning point in World War II. Again the colossal is meant to stand for huge numbers, in this case the number of dead as if immense size can represent the horrific slaughter—as if it can ensure lasting memory and public meaning for the human sacrifice.

Fourteen years later, in 1981, a statue of the Motherland (fig. 221) was placed at the summit of the World War II museum in Kiev; with the pedestal, this titanium statue rises 335 feet, thirty feet taller than its rival in New York Harbor. After the fall of the Soviet Union, many sculptures of Lenin were destroyed in acts of iconoclasm laced with regicide that have a long history and are still common. In 2003 in Baghdad, the United States choreographed the toppling of a colossal statue of Saddam Hussein. No similar violence has ever been meted out to the statues of the Motherland in part because of their association with World War II. Female personification of national ideals has this advantage: it can withstand regime change. Still the future of one of the Motherland statues is in jeopardy. Bad Soviet engineering is slowly leading to the demise of the Volgograd statue. The 7900-ton statue has begun to lean because nothing except its weight holds it in place on its foundation, and the groundwater level is changing. No Eiffel advised the Soviet sculptor.

Four hundred twenty feet in height from the base of its lotus throne, finished in 2002, the Spring Temple Buddha in Henan, China (fig. 222) is currently the tallest statue in the world. Though not a replica, the sculpture was planned in response to the Taliban's destruction in 2001 of the Bamiyan Buddhas in Afghanistan, invaluable monuments from the sixth century, which at 165 and 114 feet high had been the largest standing figures of Buddha.

The Chinese project is not without ironies. The timing of the Spring Temple Buddha is a clear signal that hostility towards Tibetan Buddhism had a part in determining China's decision to erect the colossus. China launched the project soon after a Tibetan exile organization—the Foundation for the Preservation of the Mahayana Tradition—announced its plan to build a 500-foot statue of the Maitreya Buddha in a temple complex in Northern India. The Chinese and Tibetan statues are hollow metallic structures designed much like the Statue of Liberty. The Chinese sculpture consists of approximately 1,100 pieces of copper with a total weight of 1,000 tons. The Maitreya Buddha will have an internal structure of steel trusses that is to be covered by thin bronze sheets, cast from resin-bonded sand molds.[21] As if alarmed by the instability of the Vologograd Motherland, the Foundation had the contract for the Maitreya Buddha stipulate that it must last for at least 1,000 years.

Again and again political struggles are enacted through colossi: Soviet statues appropriating Russian patriotism, competing Chinese and Taiwanese skyscrapers, Chinese Buddhism pitted against Tibetan Buddhism; and on a hilltop overlooking the Atlantic Ocean and Dakar, the capital of Senegal, a tremendous copper statue pointing to the horizon of a continent. African Renaissance (fig. 223) was inaugurated on 3 April 2010 and immediately logged into the catalogue of colossi. Abdoulaye Wade, president of Senegal and the statue's main promoter, told the crowds that the 164-foot bronze structure topped the Statue of Liberty by a foot and was now the world's tallest sculpture. He did not mention Asia's taller *Buddhas*. The press followed Wade's lead; the story of the Senegalese statue was linked to the story of its precursor and presumed rival. The assumption seems to be that if a twenty-first century colossus does not surpass contemporary competitors, its gain on the most famous colossus of the nineteenth century has great historical significance. Neither financial crises nor charges of extravagance were allowed to block the raising of this monument, President Wade's brainchild. To finance it, he made a deal, pledging Senegalese land to have a North Korean conglomerate carry out construction.

The colossus, designed by President Wade in collaboration with the architect Pierre Goudiaby, is unlike all its kin, not least the majestic, ancient Egyptian statuary that had enthralled Bartholdi back in 1855. The figures in the *African Renaissance* appear to be struggling free from a mountain; the theme is liberation and rebirth; the dynamism of their twisting bodies had never before been attempted in sculpture at so grand a scale. African Renaissance is also the first colossal statue to represent a knot of figures—a family—rather than a single figure like a Buddha, a Liberty, or the Motherland. A muscular male dominates the group; the African woman is represented as young and slight; she looks towards the baby perched on the man's shoulder but seems haplessly separated from both. Claims about the expressive richness of the statue—Wade speaks of it as showing "Africa standing tall and more ready than ever to take its destiny into its hands"—have failed to quell the controversy attending its unveiling. The statue has been attacked as extravagant, idolatrous, and misogynistic, and President Wade's angry opponents have agitated for its removal.

But colossi do not necessarily have to exist to enter the fray. After all, the Maitreya *Buddha* has not yet been constructed, and it has already sparked the building of a competitor. Like many architectural projects, the colossus begins as an announcement that is apt to sound megalomaniacal. In the next step, the proposals in and of themselves function as competitive tokens: Bartholdi and Eiffel both knew that big ideas could be sold at high prices. Dematerialized spectacles on glossy paper, newsprint, or the internet can trump any structure that has already

**217**
Kohn Pedersen Fox Associates
Shanghai World Financial Center, 2008
1614 feet, steel, concrete
Shanghai, China
Photo: Keren Su/Corbis

**218**
C. Y. Lee & Partners
Taipei 101 (Taipei World Financial Center), 2004
1667 feet, steel, concrete, aluminum
Taipei, Taiwan (China)
Photo: Jose Fuste Raga/Corbis

**219**
Skidmore, Owings, & Merrill, Adrian Smith
Burj Khalifa, 2010
2700 feet, steel, concrete, aluminum
Dubai, United Arab Emirates
Photo: AFP/Getty Images

**220**
Yevgeny Vuchetich, Nikolai Nikitin
Motherland Calls, 1967
170 feet to top of head, 278 feet to top of sword
concrete, wire ropes, steel
Volgograd, Russia
Photo: Getty Images

**221**
Yevgeny Vuchetich, Vasily Boroday
Mother Motherland, 1981
335 feet with pedestal
stainless steel
Kiev, Ukraine
Photo: Corbis

**222**
Spring Temple Buddha, 2002
420 feet inclusive of the 66-foot lotus throne, copper
Henan, China
Photo: Wikimedia Commons

been constructed and is subject to the constraints of reality. The *Spirit of Houston,* (fig. 224) a "chrome sky goddess," can be summoned onto any computer screen. Announcement and dream-sell merge in the text accompanying the pictures of the goddess-to-be. "At 555 feet," she will be "the World's Tallest Woman," designed and constructed by Michels Bollinger, Inc; "eye-to-eye with erect downtown skyscrapers"; a "visionary silver icon for new century Houston"; and "a proud TEXAS ICON."[22] Architect, industrial designer and sculptor are purported to have collaborated in the design of this plan for a glitzy statue of a woman with hands lifted to the sky, clinging drapery rippling across her body and gathering between her legs—a sculpture resembling Cordier's small sculpture of a fellah woman more than Bartholdi's chaste giant.

And why not? The statue will not be built and does not need to conform to limitations of time, material, money, or structural necessity. Bartholdi's statue looks the way it does in part because he knew it needed to be stable in design if it were to be built; once construction is no longer the goal, the colossus is free to imitate Cordier's serpentine lines. 555 feet tall (the specificity is witty), but the designers might as well have said 8,555.

The rhetoric of the colossus has changed little over the centuries. The colossus is pitched as a symbol and a trademark of progress, profit, and local pride, no one of which can be separated from the other. And when it comes to monuments for touristic city-branding, the twenty-first century repeats the refrains of the nineteenth. Writing about the sculpture to be raised in London to mark its hosting of the 2012 Olympic Games, Mark Brown treated readers of *The Guardian* of 31 March 2010 to a round of the usual. The sculpture by Anish Kapoor (fig. 225)

> ...will be slightly taller than Big Ben and the Statue of Liberty, just short of the Great Pyramid of Giza and considerably shorter than the structure to which it is being compared—the Eiffel Tower. And even though it is still just a computer-generated model, it is already gathering nicknames...[23]

The previous fall, a headline in the *Telegraph* ran: "London 2012: new Olympics structure would rival Eiffel Tower."[24] 377 feet tall, the Olympic sculpture will be "twenty-two meters higher than New York's Statue of Liberty," but 600 feet shorter than the Eiffel Tower.

By setting the proposed statue in the canon of the world's great monuments and tourist attractions, journalists justify its price tag of 19.1 million pounds. In an attempt to deflect charges that their colossal monuments were useless, Bartholdi and Eiffel compared them to the pyramids of ancient Egypt. Kapoor has been commissioned to repeat the gesture and that gesture, the journalists and promoters all but admit, cannot be understood without the lineage of the nineteenth century.

The pyramids were the measure of all large things throughout the nineteenth century, even the amount of earth moved in the Culebra Cut at Panama. Now the Statue of Liberty and Eiffel Tower are units of measure and exemplars of extravagant spectacle, proof of how emblems of nation, capital, and modern tourism can be invented and marketed. In the twenty-first century what comes closer to the Universal Exhibitions of the nineteenth century than the Olympics, themselves revived and reinvented in 1894? And Kapoor's sculpture will provide visitors almost exactly what Eiffel's tower had bestowed upon them—the opportunity to climb stairs to see a city as a wonder of the world.

**223**
Abdoulah Wade, Pierre Goudiaby,
African Renaissance, 2010
164 feet, bronze
Dakar, Senegal
Photo: SEYLLOU/Getty Images

**224**
Peter Bollinger, Doug Michels, Cybele Rowe
Spirit of Houston, planned 2000
555 feet, stainless steel
Photo: Spirit of Houston website, no longer available

**225**
Anish Kapoor
Orbit Tower, 2012
377 feet, steel
Olympic Park, London
Photo: Getty Images

**226**
Ian Ritchie Architects
Dublin Spire (officially, Monument of Light), 2003
398 feet, stainless steel
Dublin, Ireland
Photo: Chris Jackson/Getty Images

**227**
Renzo Piano
Shard (London Bridge Tower), 2012
1016 feet, steel, concrete, glass
London
Photo: Getty Images

Kapoor's statue has been completed in time. The designers of *Spirit of Houston* could ignore exigencies, the Olympic Committee in London could not. And facing a fixed and important deadline, planners were wise to consider the case of the Dublin Spire (fig. 226), a millennial monument planned with the pragmatism responsible for the success of Eiffel Tower. But even the spare Dublin Spire was not completed until 2003, three years after its much publicized deadline.[25] Kapoor was nonetheless wise to have taken the Eiffel Tower as a model. His design converts the tower into five giant rings, the logo of the Olympics, twisted into a convoluted spiral. Bold engineering combines a logo, ferris wheel, roller coaster, and viewing tower into an amusement park extravaganza.

377 feet tall, Kapoor's homage to the Eiffel Tower is diminutive—it is not even half as high as the tower. But another new structure in London, also designed in dialogue with the Paris icon, achieves an increase in height albeit of a restrained sort: the Eiffel Tower rises to 1,000 feet, the Shard to 1,016 feet (fig. 227). If you imagine the tower covered with sheets of glass, you will have the Shard, a skyscraper near London's Transport Station. Eiffel's accomplishment was erecting the tower without any vestige of the sheathing that veils the armature within the Statue of Liberty and the framework of nearly all nineteenth-century buildings. The architect of the Shard Renzo Piano is famous for collaborating with Richard Rogers on the Pompidou Center and, since that 1977 success, for museums, airports, and similar large projects, many of which incorporate glass curtain walls. Though another Piano skyscraper, the New York Times Tower, outstrips the Shard—as do its counterparts in Shanghai, Tapei, and Dubai. The website *the-shard.com* claims that this "vertical city" is "the tallest building in Western Europe" and "the capital's highest viewing gallery offering 360° views." The statement concludes:

> Well-connected and comprehensively serviced by central London's transport infrastructure, facilities and amenities, the Shard is a timeless reminder of the power of imagination to inspire change.

Reminder, the Shard certainly is: a reminder of the history of competing colossi recounted in this book, a reminder of the simplistic equation of height with human progress, a reminder of the dreary sameness, not "imaginative" innovation, of the hyperbole, a reminder too of the hubris of building glass skyscrapers to assert capitalist power in the age of terrorist threat. To call a glass skyscraper the Shard after 9/11 is to remind us of the infinite number of shards of glass that an act of violence could scatter across the city of London.

Man-made enormity was originally an expression of power and unassailable authority; it now verges on kitsch and hallucination, even humiliation. Empty skyscrapers attest to bankruptcy rather than wealth; citizens newly indebted to North Korea castigate a colossal statue in Senegal; shifting ground threatens a World War II memorial in Volgograd; digital grotesqueries proliferate online. Colossi erode; they can be miniaturized. To seek status on the basis of size alone is an exercise doomed to failure. It always was.

The grandiosity of the nineteenth-century monuments discussed in this book continues to exert an appeal. Just as the size of the Suez and Panama Canals has become anachronistic, so too has the size of the Statue of Liberty and Eiffel Tower. Though both are still big, even dizzying to climb, compared to Dubai's colossus, they are very small. Souvenirs.

1 **African Renaissance**, 2010, Senegal, Africa, **164 feet**.

2 **Motherland Calls**, 1967, Volgograd, Russia, **278 feet** to top of sword.

3 **Statue of Liberty**, 1886, New York, NY, **305 feet** pedestal base to top of torch. Photo: Corbis.

4 **Motherland**, 1981, Kiev, Ukraine, **335 feet** with pedestal.

5 **Anish Kapoor**, **Orbit Tower**, 2012, London, UK, **377 feet**.

6 **Dublin Spire**, 2003, Dublin, Ireland, **398 feet**.

7 **Spring Temple Buddha**, 2002, Lushan County, Henan, China, **420 feet** including, 66-foot lotus throne.

8 **Great Pyramid of Giza**, 2638-1613 B.C., Giza, Egypt, **481 feet**. Photo: Corbis.

9 **Spirit of Houston**, 2000 (design), Houston, Texas, **550 feet**.

10 **Eiffel Tower**, 1889, Paris, France, **1000 feet**. Photo: Getty Images.

11 **Shard**, 2012, London, UK, **1016 feet**.

12 **Empire State Building**, 1931, New York, NY, **1250 feet**. Photo: Getty Images.

13 **World Trade Center**, 1972, 1973, New York, NY, **1368 feet** (WTC 1), **1362 feet** (WTC 2). Photo: Getty Images.

14 **Shanghai World Financial Center**, 2008, Shanghai, China, **1614 feet**.

15 **Taipei 101**, 2004, Taipei, Taiwan, **1667 feet**.

16 **Burj Khalifa**, 2010, Dubai, United Arab Emirates, **2700 feet**.

1 2 3 4 5 6 7 8 9 10 11

2700
2600
2500
2400
2300
2200
2100
2000
1900
1800
1700
1600
1500
1400
1300
1200
1100
1000
900
800
700
600
500
400
300
200
12
13
14
15
16

# Notes

## Introduction

1. Evan Thomas, "Four Lives and the Day that Changed America," *Newsweek*, 31 December 2001, p. 43.
2. On the Rue du Caire, see Timothy Mitchell, "Exhibiting Egypt," in *Colonizing Egypt* (Berkeley and Los Angeles: University of California Press, 1991), pp. 1–33; Zeynep Çelik, *Displaying the Orient* (Berkeley and Los Angeles: University of California Press, 1991), pp. 75–78.
3. Eugène Melchior de Vogüé, "À travers l'Exposition, III: Le Palais de Force," *Revue des deux mondes* (1 August 1889), pp. 703–4.
4. Jules Verne, *Paris in the Twentieth Century*, trans. Richard Howard (New York: Random House, 1996), p. 165. The novel was written in 1863 and set in 1960. It was first published in French in 1994.
5. Ibid., p. 90.
6. Ibid., pp. 132, 135–36.
7. Look, for instance, at Allan Sekula's film *The Lottery of the Sea*, which I saw as a film in progress at the Maritime Modernity Conference, Center for Study of the Novel, organized by Margaret Cohen, April 2005.
8. Neil Smith, *American Empire: Roosevelt's Geographer and the Prelude to Globalization* (Berkeley and Los Angeles: University of California Press, 2003), p. 15.
9. Ibid.
10. *Cruel Tales*, trans. Robert Baldick (London: Oxford University Press, 1963), pp. 41–45; here pp. 41–42, 45. Although published as a book in 1883, *Cruel Tales* began to appear in serial form in 1867.
11. Albert C. Smith, *Architectural Model as Machine: A New View of Models from Antiquity to the Present Day* (Oxford: Architectural Press, 2004), p. xxx, n. 8: "The word scale derives from Latin *scalae* which means ladder, currently can mean to climb. A scale can be a mechanism that provides an understandable balance between a known and an unknown."
12. See, for example, Elliott Colla, "The Measure of Egypt," *Postcolonial Studies* 7, no. 3 (Fall 2004), pp. 271–93; Andro Linklater, *Measuring America: How an Untamed Wilderness Shaped the United States and Fulfilled the Promise of Democracy* (New York: Walker & Co., 2002); Witold Kula, *Measures and Men*, trans. R. Szreter (Princeton, N.J.: Princeton University Press, 1986).
13. Charles Moore and Gerald Allen, *Dimensions: Space, Shape, & Scale in Architecture* (New York: Architectural Record Books, 1976), p. 17. Emphasis in original.
14. See, for example, Donald J. Koberg, "The Experience of Scale: A Handbook of Apparent Sizes and How They Can Be Used in the Design of Effective Space," unpublished manuscript, Department of Architecture, College of Environmental Design, University of California, Berkeley, 1961: "scale is no more than or no less than, apparent size."
16. Immanuel Kant, "Analytic of the Sublime," *Critique of Judgement*, trans. James Creed Meredith (1911 and 1928; reprint, Oxford: Clarendon Press, 1991), pp. 100–101.
16. Of course, numerous canonical texts examine the impact of urban transformation, technological innovation, and industrialization. (The works by Sigfried Giedion and Walter Benjamin are but two famous examples.) Even art historians exclusively focused on painting cannot discuss late nineteenth-century French art without addressing
the dramatic reshaping of Paris by Baron Haussmann.
17. Verne, *Paris in the Twentieth Century*, p. 138.

## Chapter 1: Egypt's Size

I have been living with the *Description de l'Égypte* for a very long time. Preliminary aspects of this argument were presented as an Aga Khan Guest Lecture, Massachusetts Institute of Technology, April 2002; and as a Keynote Lecture, Graduate Symposium, "Expanding the Visual Field: Manifestations of Cultural Ex(Change)," University of Southern California, April 2002. These talks were then revised as a text entitled "Colossal Egypt on Paper," 2002. My student Adam Cramer built on that essay to write a brilliant honor's thesis on the role of mathematics during the Napoleonic period and specifically in the *Description de l'Égypte*.

1. Pierre Jacotin, "Mémoire sur la construction de la carte," in *La description de l'Égypte ou Recueil des observations et des recherches qui ont été faites en Égypte pendant l'expédition de l'armée française, publié par les ordres de Sa Majesté l'empereur Napoléon le Grand* [later dedicated "au Roi"], 26 volumes (including plates and texts) (Paris: Impr. Impériale [later royale], 1809–1822; 2nd ed., Paris: C. L. F. Panckouke, 1821–1829), *État moderne*, vol. 2, 1822, p. 2.
2. Anne Godlewska, "The Napoleonic Survey of Egypt: A Masterpiece of Cartographic Compilation and Early Nineteenth-Century Fieldwork," *Cartographica* 25, nos. 1–2, monograph 38–39 (Spring/Summer 1988), p. 10; S. C. Burchell, *Building the Suez Canal* (New York: Harper & Row, 1966), p. 32. A canal linking the Red Sea and the Nile had been cut approximately 3,500 years earlier in the reign of the legendary pharaoh Sesostris. The aim had not been the union of the Mediterranean and Red Seas but merely the facilitation of trade and communication between Cairo and Suez. The canal was extended under Roman rule but was ultimately left to silt up in the eighth century.
3. J. Christopher Herold, *Bonaparte in Egypt* (London: Hamilton, 1963), p. 20.
4. "[Bonaparte] found himself momentarily separated from the troops, directing his horse to the right and to the left in this sea of sand; it was then that he perceived the first of the two walls of the opposing embankments; he cried: "Monge, Monge, we are in the canal"; the engineers then recognized its vestiges from Suez to Bubaste." Edmé-François Jomard, *Souvenirs sur Gaspard Monge et ses rapports avec Napoléon* (Paris: Thunot, 1853), p. 48.
5. There is some dispute here; Gillispie, for example, states that there was one archaeologist and one student of archaeology. Charles C. Gillispie, ed., *Monuments of Egypt: The Napoleonic Edition* (Princeton: Princeton University Press, 1987), p. 5.
6. Edward Said, *Orientalism* (New York: Vintage Books, 1979).
7. On the *Description of Egypt*, see Said, *Orientalism*, pp. 84–87; Gillispie, *Monuments of Egypt*; David Prochaska, "Art of Colonialism, Colonialism in Art: The *Description de l'Égypte (1809–1828)*," *L'Esprit Créateur* 34, no. 2 (1994), pp. 69–91; Charles C. Gillipsie, "Aspects scientifiques de l'Expédition d'Égypte (1798–1801)," in *L'Expédition d'Égypte: 1798–1801*, by Henry Laurens et al. (Paris: Armand Colin, 1989), pp. 371–96; Terence M. Russell, ed., *The Napoleonic Survey of Egypt: The Monuments and Customs of Egypt*, 2 vols. (Aldershot: Ashgate, 2001). The most probing and informative recent work is the collection of essays in *L'expédition d'Égypte, une entreprise des lumières 1798–1801: Actes du colloque international, 8–10 June 1998*, ed. Patrice Bret (Paris: Académie des Sciences, 1999). See also Michael W. Albin, "Napoleon's *Description de l'Égypte*: Problems of Corporate Authorship," *Publishing History* 8 (1980), pp. 65–85. For illustrations, see the indispensable paperback edition by Taschen, the only publication to reproduce all plates. Generally, books publish the plates of antiquities, excluding maps, but even these are not

reproduced in their entirety. Wonderful preliminary drawings are published in Fernand Beaucour, ed., *The Discovery of Egypt*, trans. Bambi Ballard (Paris: Flammarion, 1990). Other plates and drawings are now available online in the collection of the Bibliothèque Nationale.

8. On mapping in the *Description de l'Égypte*, see Godlewska, "The Napoleonic Survey of Egypt"; Anne Godlewska, "Map, Text and Image: The Mentality of Conquerors: A New Look at the *Description de l'Égypte*," *Transactions of the Institute of British Geographers* 20, no. 1 (1995), pp. 5–28; Anne Godlewska, "Napoleon's Geographers: Imperialists and Soldiers of Modernity," in *Geography and Empire*, ed. Anne Godlewska and Neil Smith (Oxford: Blackwell, 1994); Anne Godlewska, "Traditions, Crisis, and New Paradigms in the Rise of the Modern French Discipline of Geography 1760–1850," *Annals of the Association of American Geographers* 79, no. 2 (June 1989), pp. 192–213; Ghislaine Alleaume, "Entre l'inventaire du territoire et la construction de la mémoire: L'oeuvre cartographique de l'expédition d'Égypte," in Bret, *L'expédition d'Égypte, une enterprise des lumières*, pp. 279–94; Josef W. Konvitz, *Cartography in France, 1660–1848: Science, Engineering, and Statecraft* (Chicago: University of Chicago Press, 1987).
9. Alois Riegl, "The Modern Cult of Monumentality: Its Character and Its Origin," trans. Kurt W. Forster and Diane Ghirardo, *Oppositions* 25 (Fall 1982), pp. 21–51.
10. See Lorraine Daston, "Objectivity and the Escape from Perspective," *Social Studies of Science* 22 (1992), p. 609: "Certain forms of quantification have come to be allied with objectivity not because they necessarily mirror reality more accurately, but because they serve the ideal of communicability, especially across the barriers of distance and distrust. A perspectival objectivity was the ethos of the interchangeable and therefore featureless observer—unmarked by nationality, by sensory dullness or acuity, by training or tradition; by quirky apparatus, by colourful writing style, or by any other idiosyncrasy that might interfere with the communication, comparison and accumulation of results.... Subjectivity became synonymous with the individual and solitude; objectivity, with the collective and conviviality."
11. See Edwin T. Layton Jr., "Escape from the Jail of Shape: Dimensionality and Engineering Science," in *Technological Development and Science in the Industrial Age*, ed. Peter Kroes and Martijn Bakker (Dordrecht: Kluwer Academic Publishers, 1992), pp. 35–68.
12. André Dutertre (1753–1842) was the first draftsman of the commission; he returned to France in 1801.
13. Jean Baptiste Prosper Jollois (1776–1842) was an ordinary engineer in Egypt and a student at École Polytechnique and École des Ponts et Chaussées. René Édouard Devilliers [de Villiers du Terrage] (1780–1855), geographer, first served as a geometer and then as an engineer of bridges and roads. See also René Édouard de Villiers du Terrage, *Journal et souvenirs sur l'Expédition d'Égypte (1798–1801)* (Paris: E. Plon, Nourrit, 1899). Both Jollois and Villiers became members of the commission responsible for the publication of the *Description*. See Jean Tranié and J. C. Carmigniani, *Bonaparte: La campagne d'Égypte* (Paris: Pygmalion, 1988), pp. 286, 290.
14. Edmé-François Jomard (1777–1862) was a graduate of the École Polytechnique and engineer-geographer; he became secretary in charge of the editing of the *Description* and directed its engraving for twenty years.
15. Madeleine Pinault Sorensen, "Du dessin d'artiste ou d'ingénieur au dessin archéologique," in Bret, *L'expédition d'Égypte, une enterprise des lumières*, pp. 157–76. Sorensen describes Dutertre as a remarkable landscapist who saw as a painter, while the engineers, including Jomard, saw landscape in a more dry, linear manner. But, she adds, Dutertre also could draw as an archaeologist when called upon to do so; p. 170 n. 47. See also the essay by Anna Piussi, "Les menottes d'or du patronage napoléonien: Le frontispice de la *Description de l'Égypte*. Hommage à Dutertre, Balzac et Cécile," in Bret, *L'expédition d'Égypte, une enterprise des lumières*, pp. 307–25. Regretting that so little is known about Dutertre, Piussi has reconstructed key facts of his career. To his contemporaries, Dutertre was known essentially for his copies of masters of the Renaissance. See Joachim Le Breton, *Rapports à l'Empereur sur le progress des science, des letters et des arts depuis 1789*, ed. Udolpho van de Sandt (1808; reprint, Paris: Beli, 1989), p. 140. Piussi, "Les menottes d'or du patronage napoléonien," p. 314, argues as follows: The original contract of the society in charge of the publication of the *Description de l'Égypte* [no date but before 1802] placed Dutertre in charge of engravings, but by February 1802 this responsibility was given to Conté. On 28 June 1802 he resigned, and the archives of the *Description* reveal two years of contention with the committee. Ultimately realizing he had few ways to exploit his enormous portfolio from Egypt, he rejoined the *Description*'s cooperators on 28 April 1804. At the Salon of 1804, he exhibited two portraits of generals and two drawings that were probably destined for the *Description*, thereby violating the formal interdiction against diffusing materials for the *Description* in advance of its publication. Piussi stresses that Napoleon, far from encouraging public knowledge of the expedition, prevented it by patronizing a publication that exercised exclusive control over the art of its contributors.
16. See André Dutertre, "Projet d'une école de dessin, lu par le citoyen Dutertre, dans la séance de l'Institut du 6 vendémiaire an 7," *Décade Égyptienne* no. 1, An VII [1799], pp. 103–4; and reprinted in *Mémoires sur l'Égypte, publiés pendant les campagnes du générale Bonaparte, dans les années VI et VII* (Paris: P. Didot l'aîné, An VIII [1800]), vol. 1, pp. 137–38. Dutertre's emphasis (like Neveu's) was the study of human body, but his proposal for a drawing program began with broader claims about the "general utility of drawing," an art that was "a truly demonstrative language." Among his claims, he argued that drawing "conserves the monuments that time consumes."
17. Godlewska, "The Napoleonic Survey of Egypt," p. 99. She also claims Dutertre authored a map at the Service historique de l'armée de terre, Vincennes; p. 32.
18. Konvitz, *Cartography in France,1660–1848*, p. 135. On French engineers and engineering education during the ancien régime, see Antoine Picon, *French Architects and Engineers in the Age of Enlightenment*, trans. Martin Thom (Cambridge: Cambridge University Press, 1992); Ken Alder, *Engineering the Revolution: Arms and Enlightenment in France, 1763–1815* (Princeton: Princeton University Press, 1997). See also Bruno Belhoste, Antoine Picon, and Joël Sakarovitch, "Les exercises dans les écoles d'ingénieurs sous l'Ancien Regime et la Révolution," *Histoire de l'Education* 46 (1990), pp. 53–109, which argues that under the ancien régime, the École Royale des Ponts et Chaussées conceived of the engineer artist, who was still close to the architect, while the École Royale du Génie de Mézières defined the engineer-geometer, who was concerned with the folding or bending of space by the rules of their art. By contrast, training the engineer-savant was the goal of the École Centrale des Travaux Publics, founded in 1794 and renamed the École Polytechnique.
19. M. G. Pinet, "Notice historique sur l'enseignement du dessin à l'École Polytechnique," *Journal de l'École Polytechnique* 13, series 2 (1909), pp. 115–80.
20. "Instruction du général Meunier, 2 janvier 1799. Connoissances à exiger des élèves qui se destinent au service d'*ingénieurs* géographes artistes aux armées attachés au département de la Guerre," in Patrice Bret, "Le Dépôt général de la Guerre et la formation scientifique des ingénieurs-géographes militaires en France (1789–1830)," *Annals of Science* 48, no. 2 (1991), p. 142.
21. Ibid.
22. Nicolas-François-Antoine de Chastillon, "Traité des ombres dans le dessin géométral de Chastillon," [1763], Archives du Génie, Vincennes. Cited in Janis Langins, *Conserving the Enlightenment: French Military Engineering from Vauban to the Revolution* (Cambridge: MIT Press, 2004), p. 240; Bruno Belhoste, "Du dessin de l'ingénieur à la géométrie descriptive: L'Enseignement de Chastillon à l'Ecole royale du genie de Mézières," *In Extenso: Recherches à l'École d'Architecture Paris-Villemin 13* (1990), p. 115.
23. On engineering students' drawing exercises, other than geometry, see Antoine Picon, *L'art de l'ingénieur: Constructeur, entrepreneur, inventeur* (Paris: Centre Georges Pompidou / Le Moniteur, 1997). On descriptive geometry's drawing exercises, see Édouard Glas, "On the Dynamics of Mathematical Change in the Case of Monge and the French Revolution," *Studies in History of Philosophy and Science*, 17, no. 3 (1986), p. 257: "In Monge's geometry,... geometrical figures and bodies are no longer treated as forms by themselves, as isolated cases to be distinguished in mathematical proofs. Geometry is no longer defined as the study of measures and congruences, but of universal interconnections between the points of spatial configurations." See also Alder, *Engineering the Revolution*, pp. 139–40. On Monge, see also Peter Booker, "Gaspard Monge and his Effect on Engineering Drawing and Technical Education," *Transactions of the Newcomen Society* 34 (1961–62), pp. 15–36. Jomard, *Souvenirs sur Gaspard Monge*; Lorraine Daston, "Physicalist Tradition in Early Nineteenth-Century French Geometry," *Studies in the History and Philosophy of Science* 17 (1986), pp. 269–95; B. [Barnabé] Brisson, *Note historique sur Gaspard Monge* (Paris: Plancher, 1818); Charles Dupin, *Essai historique sur les services et les travaux scientifiques de Gaspard Monge* (Paris: Bachelier, 1819); François Pairault, *Gaspard Monge: Le fondateur de Polytechnique* (Paris: Tallandier, 2000).
24. Gaspard Monge, *An Elementary Treatise on Descriptive Geometry, with a Theory of Shadows and of Perspective: Extracted from the French of G. Monge*, trans. J. F Heather (London: J. Weale, 1851), p. 1.
25. Joel Sakarovitch, "La construction du géométral, ou comment dessiner l'espace," *Cahiers de la Recherché Architecturale* 40 (1997), pp. 9–18.
26. Robin Evans, *The Projective Cast: Architecture and Its Three Geometries* (Cambridge: MIT Press, 1995).
27. Alder, *Engineering the Revolution, p. 141.* "What Latour's analysis slights is the degree to which the authority of these pictures derives from the self-discipline necessary to make one. Before engineers can use pictures of this sort to command workers, the drawings themselves must be highly ordered entities. Students spent years learning the self-restraint that enabled them to picture only certain carefully defined characteristics of objects." Emphasis in original.
28. Ibid., p. 145.
29. Ibid. Alder is referring to Theodore Porter's "Objectivity and Authority: How French Engineers Reduced Public Utility to Numbers," *Poetics Today* 12, no. 2 (1991), pp. 245–65.
30. As Adam Cramer summarizes, "French engineering as practiced by students and graduates of École Polytechnique used number and calculation—features inextricably linked to real objects, to practical utility—to justify civic projects in the name of public value and efficiency. Mathematics, in its specificity to the physical contingencies of a bridge, had a special political func-

tion: to allow 'the public interest to be served without encouraging the corps' business to become a matter of public debate." "The very utilitarian demand that had turned engineers into civil servants, employing a mathematical language 'credible to the public but not, on the whole, comprehensible to it,' tore engineering out of public debate and put it into the hands of, essentially, a secret society able to 'fend off political controversy.'" Adam Cramer, "Pyramids in Egypt, Pyramids on Paper: The Cultural Mathematics of the Description of Egypt" (honor's thesis, University of California, Berkeley, May 2005), p. 255. Godlewska argues that the makers of the *Description* employed number and measurement prominently to create a knowledge based on the"uncritical repetition of apparent factuality" thereby "sublimating ephemeral and chaotic Egypt into the 'eternal and immutable.'" "Mathematical procedure became, so to speak, the ritual of thinking.... If something could be represented with precision, detail, or accuracy, it clearly had the value of truth. The ultimate in truth was reproducibility or what Horkheimer and Adorno would call 'tautology.' This is reflected in Fourier's praise of the drawings and maps of monuments produced by the expedition's engineers: '...one could use them to construct edifices identical to those that we have described.'" Godlewska, "Map, Text and Image," pp. 6–9.

31. Alder, *Engineering the Revolution, p. 67.*
32. Monge, *An Elementary Treatise on Descriptive Geometry*, pp. 22–23.
33. Sorensen, "Du dessin d'artiste ou d'ingénieur au dessin archéologique." See also Albin,"Napoleon's *Description de l'Égypte.*"
34. Konvitz, *Cartography in France, 1660–1848, p. 93:* "To convey the appearance of mountains, military engineers relied upon artistic techniques—lines, colors, and shading. They even combined oblique and horizontal perspectives on the same map. L. N. Lespinasse, in his treatise on coloring military reconnaissance maps [1818], perceived a conflict between geometric accuracy and topographic verisimilitude: the former was a function of carefully recorded measurements and calculations, the latter a function of the mapper's ability to see and draw."
35. Ibid., p. 140. In 1795 Prony established the École de Géographie independently of other reforms; by 1799, when measurement reform was complete and real work could begin, there was no budget to do so.
36. The army "n'avait presque aucune connaissance du pays qu'elle avait à parcourir à travers le désert." Alleaume, "Entre l'inventaire du territoire et la construction de la mémoire," p. 280.
37. Edward S. Casey, *Representing Place: Landscape Paintings and Maps* (Minneapolis: University of Minnesota Press, 2002), p. 255.
38. Andro Linklater, *Measuring America: How an Untamed Wilderness Shaped the United States and Fulfilled the Promise of Democracy* (New York: Walker & Co., 2002), p. 69. The basis for the decimal system of weight was the weight of a cubic measure of water. "The idea that the earth might serve as a scientific basis for a system of measures had first been put forward by the French astronomer and cartographer Jean Picard in 1671."
39. Casey, *Representing Place, p. 255.*
40. Konvitz, *Cartography in France, 1660–1848*, pp. 46–47; John Noble Wilford, *The Mapmakers,* rev. ed. (1981; New York: Vintage, *2001),* p. 254. See also Linklater, who disputes the validity of the arguments against the pendulum: "What makes that month of April 1790 so extraordinary is that it marks the moment when, after 10,000 years of traditional measurement, the decision to look for a new, scientific basis was taken simultaneously in not two but three different capitals [London, Paris, and New York]." Linklater, *Measuring America*, pp. 122–23, p. 102. See also Jean Dhombres, "L'esprit de géométrie en Égypte: Monge et Fourier et Jomard: De la science conquérante à la science positivée," in Bret, *L'expédition d'Égypte, une enterprise des lumières*, p. 329: "Like the meter, the pyramid is a double monument, as much built in defiance of time, as much as a manual of geometry." See also Maurice Crosland, "The Paris Congress on Definitive Standards (1798–1799): The First International Scientific Congress?" *Isis* 60 (1969), pp. 226–31.
41. Sorensen, "Du dessin d'artiste ou d'ingénieur au dessin archéologique."
42. This is the emphasis of Prochaska, "Art of Colonialism, Colonialism in Art." See also Villiers du Terrage, *Journal et souvenirs*, p. 265, who recounts an incident when Jollois, who had been delayed because of flooding, was reprimanded by Le Père for disobedience. Menou wrote, "I exhort you to end all these little intrigues...which better belong to the inhabitants of boudoirs than to the virile and proud Republicans who resemble the Spartans who knew only order, fatherland and the public good." To which the engineer responded, "Young and independent as we were, we did not feel defeated."
43. Gillispie, *Monuments of Egypt, p. 7.*
44. Godlewska, "Map, Text and Image," pp. 11–12: "In numerous places in the *Description* the maps were described as 'truth,' precisely because they were based on measurement and, in contrast to the landscape sketches, on a measured grid that spanned the entire country. Preoccupation with mathematical rigour blurs the distinction between sketch and map.... Many of these landscape sketches in their final engraved form even included cartographic-style index numbers for quick consultation using the plate legends. The plate legends also gave the plates a distinctly cartographic flavor by explaining precisely where each view was taken from in relation to a large number of other views and especially in relation to the accompanying maps and plans." The monuments surrounded by landscape were carefully measured; Jomard deemed the measurements so accurate that he relied on them in arguments.
45. Matthew H. Edney, "Reconsidering Enlightenment Geography and Map Making: Reconnaissance, Mapping, Archive," in *Geography and Enlightenment*, ed. David N. Livingstone and Charles W. J. Withers (Chicago: University of Chicago Press, 1999), p. 170. He cites Alasdair C. MacIntyre, *Three Rival Versions of Moral Enquiry: Encyclopaedia, Genealogy, and Tradition: Being Gifford Lectures Delivered in the University of Edinburgh in 1988* (London: Duckworth, 1990), p. 172.
46. Godlewska, "Map, Text and Image."
47. Stephen Kern, *The Culture of Time and Space 1880–1918* (Cambridge: Harvard University Press, 1983), p. 134. Terms for basic units of measurement such as "foot" and "pace" reveal anatomical origins, and thus "notions of space are rooted in our physiological organism."
48. Linklater, *Measuring America*, p. 113.
49. Ibid., p. 91.
50. Ibid.
51. Ibid., p. 239. "The foreignness of the metric system went deeper than names. It took uniformity to a degree that no layperson could immediately comprehend.... The metric system forced people to separate the measure from the activity altogether and deal with an abstract unit that, as Kula observed, 'would be equally applicable totextiles, wooden planks, field strips and even to the road to Paris.' What underlay the popular dislike of the metric system was a very modern anxiety, the sense of alienation from the natural world." See also Kula, *Measures and Men.*
52. Monge, *An Elementary Treatise on Descriptive Geometry*, p. 106: "The visible portion of an object is separated from that which is hid from view, by a line called the apparent outline. The perspective of the apparent outline is the sketch which, on the picture, envelopes the image of the object to be represented; it is therefore, important, in general, to determine accurately the apparent outline of an object...."

53. This point has been made by Casey, *Representing Place*, p. 173: "a cartographic vision…is achieved by the device of projections that, along with rectilinear grids and geometric shapes, are abstractive in relation to the uneven surface of the earth. [These devices] no longer share [the earth's] raw irregularities. These means are at once spatial, presentational, and symbolic."
54. Monge, *An Elementary Treatise on Descriptive Geometry*, p. 19.
55. Wilford, *The Mapmakers*, p. 37. A map projects "spherical coordinates to a plane surface in a systematic manner. The grids (or graticules) of parallels and meridians are squeezed or stretched or otherwise distorted for a sphere cannot be flattened without some distortion. Each projection, therefore, is a compromise between correct shape and correct size." Note that Ptolemy had also addressed the challenges posed by drawing the round earth on flat paper. A globe is the only possible medium for showing all geographical relationships in true perspective; but, as Ptolemy knew, globes had serious drawbacks: they lacked portability and to show details at a legible scale, they would be taller than skyscrapers. Ibid., p. 36.
56. Godlewska, "Map, Text and Image," p. 45.
57. Elliott Colla, "The Measure of Egypt," *Postcolonial Studies* 7, no. 3 (Fall 2004), pp. 271–93. "For Bonaparte, the measure of the pyramid was not merely an issue of curiosity: to know the height of the object would help deduce the elevation of the Red Sea in relation to the Mediterranean—a useful calculation for the canal proposed" (p. 275).
58. Wilford, *The Mapmakers*, p. 115.
59. Bret, "Le physicien, la pyramide et l'obélisque," p. 141.
60. C. F. [Constantin-François] Volney, *Voyage en Égypte et en Syrie* (*1787*), reprinted in *Œuvres*, 3 vols. (Paris: Fayard, 1998), vol. 3, pp. 193–94.
61. Aristotle, *Poetics*, section 1, part 7; Edmund Burke, *A Philosophical Enquiry into the Origin of Our Ideas of the Sublime and the Beautiful*, ed. James T. Boulton (1757; reprint, Notre Dame: University of Notre Dame Press, 1958); Immanuel Kant, "Analytic of the Sublime," *Critique of Judgement*, trans. James Creed Meredith (1911 and 1928; reprint, Oxford: Clarendon Press, 1991), pp. 90–134; Whitney Davis, "Opticality and Rhetoricity in Paul de Man's 'Historical Materialism,'" in *Replications: Archaeology, Art History, Psychoanalysis* (University Park: Pennsylvania State University Press, 1996); Paul De Man, "Phenomenality and Materiality in Kant," in *Hermeneutics: Questions and Prospects*, ed. Gary Schapiro and Alan Sica (Amherst: University of Massachusetts Press, 1984), pp. 121–46; Jacques Derrida, "The Colossal," in *The Truth in Painting*, trans. Geoff Bennington and Ian McLeod (Chicago: University of Chicago Press, 1987), pp. 119–47.
62. "Description générale de Memphis et des pyramides," *Description de l'Égypte*, vol. 5, chap. 18, p. 597; translated in Russell, *The Napoleonic Survey of Egypt*, vol. 2, p 377.
63. Jomard, "Remarques et recherches sur les Pyramides d'Égypte," in *Description de l'Égypte*, vol. 9, pp. 495–96.
64. Ibid.
65. *Description de l'Égypte, Antiquités*, vol. 4, plate 72.
66. "The general aspect of these monuments gives rise to a striking observation: their summits, seen from far away, produce the same general effect as the summits of high mountains of pyramidal form which pierce and cut the sky. The more one approaches the more this effect diminishes." Ibid.
67. See Elliott Colla, "Hooked on Pharaonics: Literature and the Appropriation of Ancient Egypt" (Ph.D. diss., University of California, Berkeley, 2000), pp. 80–85.
68. Jomard, *La Description de l'Égypte,* cited in Russell, *The Napoleonic Survey of Egypt*, vol. 2, p. 378. He proposed, for example, that the "King's chamber might not necessarily have been a tomb, but a metric monument, designed to embody and perpetuate a system of measures."
69. Dhombres, "L'esprit de géométrie en Égypte," p. 340: "And informed by the contemporary French will to conserve for eternity the traces that permitted the determination of the meter, [Jomard] adds that the Egyptians also gave the monumental pyramid the function of avoiding the outrages of time." Regarding Jomard's drawing of interior pyramid, Dhombres argues (p. 340): "It was not only the numerical precision that struck him but even more the simplicity of the numbers of the measurements. From this simplicity seemed to follow the existence of a code…. Jomard gives the impression of having decoded the pyramid…. [but] Every series of numerical data regarding the pyramid risks in effect being put in relation to another series, for example an astronomical series. A system of numbers [numerisme] can prove nothing: it is enigmatic by nature."
70. Colla, "Hooked on Pharaonics," pp. 60–65.
71. Kant, "Analytic of the Sublime," pp. 90–134.
72. Ibid., p. 99: "Comprehension (comprehensio aesthetica): with advance of apprehension comprehension becomes more difficult at every step and so attains its maximum, and this is the aesthetically greatest fundamental measure for the estimation of magnitude; the parts first apprehended begin to disappear from the imagination as this advances to apprehension of yet others, as much, then, is lost at one end as is gained at the other, and for comprehension we get a maximum which the imagination cannot exceed."
73. Ibid., pp. 99–100.
74. Note that Jomard repeated the same argument; "Description des Pyramides du Nord ou Pyramides de Gyzeh," *Description* de *l'Égypte*, vol. 5, p. 597. For a translation, see Russell, *The Napoleonic Survey of Egypt*, vol. 2, p. 377.
75. Monge, *An Elementary Treatise on Descriptive Geometry*, p. 123.
76. Ibid., pp. 1–3. Cramer, "Pyramids in Egypt, Pyramids on Paper," pp. 8–9, summarizes: "Monge's text, in the Euclidean manner, begins at the level of basic postulate, synthetically defining all possible projections, indeed all space itself, as bodies determined by points alone."
77. Claude-Étienne Savary, *Letters on Egypt* (1787; London: n.p., 1798), p. 220.
78. Jomard, "Description des Pyramides du Nord ou Pyramides de Gyzeh," *Description de l'Égypte*, vol. 5, p. 634; for a translation, see Russell, *The Napoleonic Survey of Egypt*, vol. 2, pp. 392, 394.
79. The Queen's Chamber, for example, was only cleaned out in the early nineteenth century by Giovanni Battista Caviglia. See Miroslav Verner, *The Pyramids: The Mystery, Culture, and Science of Egypt's Great Monuments*, trans. Steven Rendall (New York: Grove, 2001), p. 190. Of course discoveries continued to be made; for instance, in 1954, Egyptian archaeologists discovered buried boats in two pits on the pyramid's south side; ibid., p. 194.
80. *Description de l'Égypte, contenant plusieurs remarques curieuses sur la geographie ancienne et moderne de ce pais, sur ces monumens anciens, sur les murs… Composée sur les memoires de m. de Maillet… par M. l'abbe Le Mascrier…* (Paris:Chez L. Genneau et J. Rollin, fils, 1735).

## Chapter 2: Suez's Statue

The invaluable research of graduate assistant Amy Freund made this chapter possible. I also thank Bartholdi expert Régis Hueber, Curator at the Musée Bartholdi, for providing access to his archives and Christian Kempf for his professional generosity.

1. Zachary Karabell, *Parting the Desert: The Creation of the Suez Canal* (New York: A. A. Knopf, 2003), p. 27. On the Saint-Simonians and the Suez Canal, see also Georges Taboulet, "Aux origines du canal de Suez: Le conflit entre Ferdinand de Lesseps et les Saint-Simoniens," *Revue Historique* (October–December 1968); and Bernard Jouve, *L'épopée saint-simonienne: Saint-Simon, Enfantin et leur disciple Alexis Petit de Suez au pays de George Sand* (Paris: Guénégaud, 2001).
2. *Œuvres de Saint-Simon et d'Enfantin, publiées par les membres du Conseil institué par Enfantin (1865–1878;* reprint, Aalen: Otto Zeller, 1963*)*, vol. 9, pp. 213–14.
3. See Denise Brahimi, "L'inspiration saint-simonienne dans *La Description de l'Égypte*," in *Les saint-simoniens et l'Orient: Vers la modernité*, ed. Magali Morsy (Aix-en-Provence: Edisud, 1989), pp.19–28. On the Saint-Simonians, see Antoine Picon, *Les saint simoniens: Raison, imaginaire et utopie* (Paris: Belin, 2002); Sébastien Charléty, *Histoire du saint-simonisme (1825–1864)* (Paris: Paul Harmattan, 1931); Frank E. Manuel, *The New World of Henri Saint-Simon* (Cambridge: Harvard University Press, 1956); E. S. Mason, "Saint-Simonism and the Rationalisation of Industry," *Quarterly Journal of Economics* 45 (1930–31), pp. 640–83; G. Pinet, "L'École Polytechnique et les saint-simoniens," *Revue de Paris* 3 (May–June 1894), pp. 73–96; Philippe Régnier, "Aux origines de l'idée politique industrielle: Les saint-simoniens," *Culture Technique* 26 (December1992), pp. 116–21. On the Saint-Simonians in Egypt, see especially Philippe Régnier, *Les saint-simoniens en Égypte, 1833–1851* (Cairo: Banque de l'Union Européenne / Amin Fakhry Abdelnour, 1989); and also Morsy, *Les saint-simoniens et l'Orient*.
4. Emile Pereire cited in John C. Eckalar, "The Saint-Simonians in Industry and Economic Development, *American Journal of Economics and Sociology* 38, no. 1 (January 1979), p. 87.
5. Karabell, *Parting the Desert*, p. *35*.
6. Enfantin, 1833, *Œuvres de Saint-Simon et d'Enfantin*, vol.9, pp. 56–57; Régnier, *Les saint-simoniens en Égypte*, p. 27.
7. *Œuvres de Saint-Simon et d'Enfantin*, vol. 9, p. 213.
8. Karabell, *Parting the Desert*, p. 37; Régnier, *Les saint-simoniens en Égypte*, p. 83.
9. Enfantin to Arlès; postscript of 21 février 1836; *Œuvres de Saint-Simon et d'Enfantin*, vol. 10, pp. 151–52.
10. Enfantin, November 1840; cited in Georges Taboulet, "Aux origines du canal de Suez: Le conflit entre Ferdinand de Lesseps et les Saint-Simoniens," *Revue Historique* (October–December 1968), p. 362.
11. Enfantin, 28 June 1845, *Œuvres de Saint-Simon et d'Enfantin*, vol. 12, p. 12.
12. Barbara Johnson, "Erasing Panama, Mallarmé and the Text of History," in *A World of Difference* (Baltimore: Johns Hopkins University Press, 1987), p. 60.
13. "…éclipsé, subalternisé, escamoté, volé même." Cited in Taboulet, "Aux origines du canal de Suez," p. 363.
14. Ibid., p. 366.
15. Ghislaine Alleaume, "Linant de Bellefonds (1799–1883) et le saint-simonisme en Égypte," in Morsy, *Les saint-simoniens et l'Orient*, pp. 113–32.
16. On Linant see Régnier, *Les saint-simoniens en Égypte*, pp. 76–78.
17. Annie Rey-Goldseiguer, "Le projet industriel de Paulin Talabot," in Morsy, *Les saint simoniens et l'Orient*, pp. 97–111.
18. Karabell, *Parting the Desert*, pp. 38–39.
19. Ferdinand de Lesseps, *Souvenirs de quarante ans* (Paris: Nouvelle Revue), pp. 25–27; Cited in Johnson, "Erasing Panama," p. 62.
20. Karabell, *Parting the Desert*, p. 74. Lesseps, *Diary*, 15 November 1854, in *Lettres 1854–1856*, p. 17.
21. Ghislain de Diesbach, *Ferdinand de Lesseps* (Paris: Perrin, 1998), pp. 147–48.

22. On Bartholdi's journey of 1855–56, see the catalogues to three key exhibitions curated by Régis Hueber at the Musée Bartholdi, Colmar: *D'un album* de voyage: *Auguste Bartholdi en Égypte (1855–1856)* (Colmar: Musée Bartholdi, 1990); *Au Yemen en 1856: Photographies et dessins d'Auguste Bartholdi* (Colmar: Musée Bartholdi, 1994); *Dahabieh, Almées et Palmiers: 52 dessins du premier voyage en Orient 1855–56 d'Auguste Bartholdi (*Colmar: Musée Bartholdi, 1998). Also see Régis Hueber, "Les Salons d'Amilcar: Notes sur les dessins et tableaux orientalistes d'Auguste Bartholdi," *Annuaire de la Société d'Histoire et d'Archéologie de Colmar* (1993), pp. 75–137. On Bartholdi's photography in Egypt, see the fine essays by Christian Kempf, "Bartholdi et le calotype," in *D'un album de voyage*, pp. 15–23; and by Claire Bustarret, "Du Nil au Yémen: Bartholdi photographe," *Histoire de l'Art* 7 (October 1989), pp. 35–52. See also Pierre Provoyeur, "Artistic Problems," in *Liberty: The French-American Statue in Art and History*, exhibition catalogue, New York Public Library (New York: Harper and Row, 1986), pp. 78–99. The latter catalogue is an excellent resource concerning Bartholdi.
23. Régis Hueber, "A Thousand Miles up the Nile," in *D'un album de voyage*, p. 25. On the Suez Canal, see Tom F. Peters, *Building the Nineteenth Century* (Cambridge: MIT Press, 1996), pp.178–202; J. Charles-Roux, *L'isthme et le canal de Suez*, 2 vols. (Paris: Hachette, 1901).
24. Cited in Kempf, "Bartholdi et le calotype," in *D'un album de voyage*; p. 45 n. 5. Paris, Archives Nationales, Fonds F 17 2935 B.
25. Léon Belly to his mother, Cairo, 7 July 1856, Archives Municipales de Saint-Omer, Ms. 1159; cited in Hueber, *Dahabieh*, Almées *et Palmiers*, p. 7. On Belly, see Conrad de Mandach, "Léon Belly (1827–1877)," *Gazette des Beaux-Arts* 55ième Année, vol. 9 (1913), no. 667, pp. 73–84 and no. 668, pp. 143–57.
26. Hueber, "A Thousand Miles up the Nile."
27. Anne Middleton Wagner, *Jean- Baptiste Carpeaux: Sculptor of the Second Empire* (New Haven: Yale University Press, 1986).
28. See especially Jacques De Caso, "Serial Sculpture in Nineteenth-Century France," in *Metamorphoses in Nineteenth-Century Sculpture*, ed. Jeanne L. Wasserman (Cambridge: Fogg Museum, Harvard University Press, 1975), pp. 1–27.
29. Salon of 1857, *View of Monfalout on the Banks of the Nile*; Salon of 1861, *Café on the Banks of the Nile*; Salon of 1864, *Children Are Everywhere the Same*; and *Chadoufs: Irrigation Machines on the Banks of the Nile*; Salon of 1865, *Mosque of Djirdjeh*.
30. *The Lyre of the Berbers*, a two-figure group, was exhibited at the Salon of 1857 under Bartholdi's name.
31. Other scholars have discerned this genealogy; see for example, Pierre Provoyeur, "Artistic Problems," p. 92, who states that the watercolors and maquettes for the two projects "provide visible proof of a line of descent." See also Pierre Vidal, *Frédéric-Auguste Bartholdi: Par la main, par l'esprit* (Paris: Les Créations du Pélican, 2000), p. 47. The term *fellah* was current in France from the seventeenth century and generally connotes Egyptian peasant; it derives from the Arabic word *fă llăh* (Maghrebian Arabic: *fe̥lla¯h*), meaning cultivator. For the way the *Description de l'Égypte* reported the wrongful oppression of the fellah, see Brahimi, "L'Inspiration Saint-Simonienne dans *La Description de l'Égypte*," pp. 22–23.
32. Frédéric-Auguste Bartholdi, *The Statue of Liberty Enlightening the World* (1885; New York: New York Bound, 1984), p. 37.
33. Pierre Provoyeur, "Artistic Problems," p. 92.
34. In 1787 Volney argued that the original Arab conquerors, the first of Egypt's four races, were perpetuated in the fellaheen, who conserved their original physiognomy. Volney, *Voyage en Syrie et en Égypte* (3rd ed., 1799; reprint, Paris: Fayard, 1998), p. 62.
35. Christine Peltre, *Orientalism in Art*, trans. John Goodman (New York: Abbeville Press, 1998), p. 158.
36. See for example statues by Louis Kley, *Egyptian Woman Getting Water*, Salon of 1861, and by Didier Debut, *Small Girl Fellah*, Salon of 1868. See paintings, for example, by Léon Belly, *Female Fellaheen on the Banks of the Nile*, Salon of 1863; Léon Bonnat, *A Female Fellah and Her Infant Son*, Salon of 1870; Gérôme, *Fellah Women Getting Water*, Salon of 1870.
37. On Cordier's "mannequins" and statues of female fellaheen, see *Charles Cordier, 1827–1905: L'autre et l'ailleurs*, exhibition catalogue, Paris, Musée d'Orsay (Paris: Éditions de La Martinière, 2004), pp. 72–77, 166–68, 214–16; Georges Douin, *Histoire du règne du Khédive Ismaïl: L'Apogée 1867–1873*, 2 vols. (Rome: Stampata nell Ìstituto poligrafico dello stato per la Reale società di geografia d'Egitto 1934), vol. 2, p. 16; Charles Edmond [Chojecki], *L'Égypte à l'Exposition universelle de 1867* (Paris: Dentu, 1867), p. 238.
38. Edmond About, *Le fellah: Souvenirs d'Égypte* (Paris: Dentu,1867), p. 154.
39. Alexander Schölch, *Egypt for Egyptians! The Socio-Political Crisis in Egypt 1878–1882* (London: Ithaca Press, 1981), pp. 18–20.
40. When it was first published in *Revue des deux-mondes* between February and April 1869, its title was *Ahmed le fellah*. Jean-Marie Carré, *Voyageurs et écrivains français en Égypte* (Cairo: Institut français d'archéologie orientale, 1956), vol. 2, p. 267; Marseilles, Archives départementales et al., *L'Orient des provençaux dans l'histoire*, exhibition catalogue (Marseilles: l'Imprimerie Aubanel, 1984), p. 382. About had been sent by the French government to study reforms demanded by the viceroy, but once arrived, he accepted approximately 25,000 francs from Ismaïl to write the novel.
41. Edmond About, *Le fellah:* Souvenirs d'Égypte, 2nd ed. (Paris: Librairie de L. Hachette, 1870), p. 222.
42. Théophile Gautier, *Voyage en Égypte*, ed. Paolo Tortonese (1869; reprint Paris, La Boîte à Documents, 1991), pp. 47–49.
43. Alfred Assollant, "La femme fellah de M. Landelle," in *L'Exposition Universelle de 1867 illustrée: Publication Internationale autorisée par la Commission Impériale*, ed. François Ducuing, 2 vols. (Paris: 106 rue Richelieu, 1867), vol. 2, pp. 115–16.
44. Edward Said, *Orientalism* (New York: Random House, 1978), pp. 108–9.
45. Colmar, Musée Bartholdi. Letter to Emile Jacob, 26 January 1856; cited partly in Hueber, "A Thousand Miles up the Nile," *D'un album de voyage*, pp. 43–44.
46. Gautier, *Voyage en Égypte*, p. 47.
47. Rey-Goldseiguer, "Le projet industriel de Paulin Talabot," pp. 88, 94, 136.
48. Ibid., p. 178.
49. Fonds Enfantin, Paris, Arsénal: An undated letter says, "J'ai vu [illegible] parmi des amis de Gérôme le peintre de forts aimables jeunes qui [illegible] donne des excellentes nouvelles de la famille [S—— illegible]." The letter is addressed to "mon bon Pere Lambert." Charles Lambert was the founder of the École Polytechnique of Cairo and principal Saint-Simonien from 1833 to 1851. On Lambert, see Régnier, *Les saint-simoniens en Égypte*, pp. 108–10.
50. Fonds Enfantin, Paris, Arsénal. Fonds Enfantin, Paris, Arsénal: "Le Général me fait faire dans ce moment des tableaux de les batailles remportées par lui en Syrie—et il attend l'achèvement de ce travail avec [tant?] d'impatience que je ne le quitte qu'à regret. Depuis quelques temps il s'établie en Égypte un [coin…?] qui nous amène des artistes de tous les genres et au quantité après Monsr Belly [sont?] venu Jerome, Deshais, Bartoldy nous attendons [Ziem Bida?]… l'année prochaine Théophile Gautier. Je vers sur notre [deser?] un [rosee?] consolatrice—j'ai trouvé parmi ces messieurs

des joies bien douces—[& au?] [Zende?] de la Patrée le milieu dans lequel je me [?] vivre Monsr Jerome chevalier de la légion d'honneur et peintre d'histoire très distingué et Monsr [Pereire?] son ami et son élève vous remettra [illegible] cette lettre."

51. Régis Hueber, "La Reine de Saba craint les chambres obscures: Essai d'un itinéraire Bartholdien en Arabie du Sud," in *Au Yemen en 1856: Photographies et dessins d'Auguste Bartholdi* (Colmar: Musée Bartholdi, 1994), p. 66 n. 39.
52. On Duvéyrier, lawyer-businessman-playwright and close ally of Enfantin, see Régnier, *Les saint-simoniens en Égypte*, p. 26.
53. *Œuvres de Saint-Simon et d'Enfantin*, vol. 8, pp. 65–93.
54. Régnier, *Les saint-simoniens en Égypte*, pp. 38–39: "These deified *women*, true idols, associate a sort of Phrygian bonnet and the pike of the sans-culottes with the gigantic statue of Athena dressed by Phidias in the Parthenon. But the presence of a pyramid in the background of the first drawing...also indicates eighteenth-century egyptomania, expanded especially by Illuminists and Freemasons. The iconography of the Revolution furnishes many examples of this bizarre syncretism which crystallizes more than once the name and the image of the goddess Isis."
55. Colmar, Musée Bartholdi. Journal entry for 11 April 1869; letter of 15 April 1869.
56. On Lesseps' lectures, see Frédéric Le Play, *Commission impériale: Rapport sur l'Exposition universelle de 1867 à Paris: Précis des opérations et liste des collaborateurs avec un appendice sur l'avenir des expositions* (Paris: Imprimerie impériale, 1869), p. 113. On the Egyptian pavilions, see Edmond, *L'Égypte à l'Exposition universelle de 1867* and Zeynep Çelik, *Displaying the Orient: Architecture of Islam at Nineteenth-Century World's Fairs* (Berkeley and Los Angeles: University of California Press, 1991), pp. 57–63; 111–16.
57. André Raymond, *Cairo*, trans. Willard Wood (Cambridge: Harvard University Press, 2000), p. 313. Ismaïl was in Paris from 1846 to 1849.
58. Ibid., p. 311.
59. *L'Égypte à l'Exposition universelle de 1867* (Paris, 1867); cited in Régnier, *Les Saint-Simoniens en Égypte*, p. 172.
60. *L'Exposition universelle de 1867 illustrée*, vol. 1, p. 58. Douin, *Histoire du règne du Khédive Ismaïl: l'apogée 1867–1873*, II, p. 15.
61. Ferdinand de Lesseps, *Souvenirs de quarante ans dediés à mes enfants* (Paris: Nouvelle Revue, 1887), p. 336.
62. Peters, *Building the Nineteenth Century*, pp. 185–86.
63. Berchère, *Le désert de Suez*, pp. 78–79.
64. S. C. Burchell, *Building the Suez Canal* (New York: American Heritage Publishing Company, 1966), p. 121.
65. *L'Exposition universelle de 1867 illustrée*, vol. 1, p. 116.
66. Berchère, *Le désert de Suez*, p. 115.
67. See for example Edwin De Leon, *The Khedive's Egypt, or The Old House of Bondage under New Masters* (New York: Harper & Brothers, 1878), pp. 225–28.
68. Berchère, *Le désert de Suez*, pp. 196–98.
69. About, *Le fellah*, p. 302.
70. Fr. Ducuing, "Les visites souveraines: Ismaïl Pacha," *L'Exposition universelle de 1867 illustrée*, vol. 1, p 374.
71. Cited in Kempf, "Bartholdi et le calotype," in *D'un album de voyage*; p. 45 n. 5. Archives Nationales, Fonds F 17 2935 B.
72. Dominique François Arago, "Report," reprinted in Alan Trachtenberg, ed., *Classic Essays on Photography* (Stony Creek, Conn.: Leete's Island Books, 1980), p. 17; for the original French see "Rapport à la Chambre des députés, 3 juillet 1839," in André Rouillé, ed., *La photographie en France: textes & controverses: une anthologie 1816*–1871 (Paris: Macula, 1989), pp. 36–43. Arago continues by arguing that photography would also assist mapping: "Since the invention follows the laws of geometry, it will be possible to reestablish with the aid of a small number of given factors the exact size of the highest points of the most inaccessible structures."
73. Ibid.
74. *Souvenirs littéraires* (Paris: Hachette, 1882–83), I, pp. 422–3; cited in Elizabeth Anne McCauley, "The Photographic Adventure of Maxime Du Camp," *Library Chronicle of the University of Texas at Austin* 19 (1982), p. 22.
75. Cited in Jacques Noiray, *Le romancier et la machine: L'image de la machine dans le roman français (1850–1900)*, 2 vols. (Paris, Corti, 1982), vol. 2, p. 247.
76. "Songs of Matter" in *Modern Songs*, 1855; cited in Julia Ballerini, "Photography conscripted: Horace Vernet, Gerard de Nerval and Maxime du Camp in Egypt" (Ph.D. diss., City University of New York, 1987), p. 209.
77. Bartholdi, *The Statue of Liberty Enlightening the World*, pp. 35–37.
78. Geraldine A. Johnson, ed., *Sculpture and Photography: Envisioning the Third Dimension* (Cambridge: Cambridge University Press, 1998), p. 4.
79. Colmar, Musée Bartholdi. Letter to Emile Jacob, 26 January 1856.
80. See Kempf, "Bartholdi et le calotype," in *D'un album de voyage*, p. 22: "Completely abandoning the project of photographing human types, whom he could not make understand the necessity of not moving because of the slowness of the calotype [process], he distanced himself further from the terms of his mission in devoting hardly more than a fifth of his photographs to the 'principal monuments of the traveled countries.'" Kempf also emphasizes that only one fifth of Bartholdi's pictures are devoted to monuments; most are picturesque views of houses and cafes and so on. Some of these served as settings or compositions for his paintings. See also Ballerini, "Photography Conscripted," pp. 280–81: "In the 1850s... exposure times were still slow. They were not the fifteen minutes of Goupil-Fesquet, but in the case of DuCamp, about two minutes.... In the work of some photographers of the 1850s and 1860s, the human forms that populate the prints are half-consumed in blurs of emulsion. The photographs by Frédéric-Auguste Bartholdi... working in Egypt 1855–6, contain many examples of such a photographically consumed race of man. The same holds true of Louis de Clercq working in Syria, Palestine and Egypt in 1859–60."
81. Jane R. Becker, "Auguste Rodin and Photography: Extending the Sculptural Idiom," in *The Artist and the Camera: Degas to Picasso*, ed. Dorothy Kosinski (Dallas: Dallas Museum of Art, 1999), p. 91.
82. Édouard Papet, "Le moulage sur nature au service de la science," in *À fleur de peau: Le moulage sur nature au XIXe siècle*, exhibition catalogue, Paris, Musée d'Orsay (Paris: Réunion des Musées Nationaux, 2002), p. 90. See also Anne Roquebert, "La sculpture ethnographique au XIXe siècle, objet de mission ou oeuvre de musée?" in *La sculpture ethnographique, de la "Vénus hottentote" à la "Tehura" de Gauguin*, exhibition catalogue, Paris, Musée d'Orsay (Paris: Réunion des Musées Nationaux, 1994), pp. 5–32; and Jules Dumont d'Urville, *Voyage au pôle Sud et dans l'Océanie sur les corvettes "l'Astrolabe" et "la Zélée," exécutée par ordre du roi pendant les années 1837–1838–1839–1840, sous le commandement de M. J. Dumont d'Urville* (Paris: Gide, 1841–46). On his expedition, Jules Dumont d'Urville took along Alexandre Pierre Marie Dumoutier (1797–1871), artist and member of the Société Phrénologique, who produced many stunning casts.
83. Papet, "Le moulage sur nature au service de la science," p. 90. Emphasis added.
84. Paris, Grand Palais, *La sculpture française au XIXe siècle*, exhibition catalogue (Paris: Réunion des Musées Nationaux, 1986), p. 67: "Terme ambigu, moulage peut désigner soit une opération, étape presque obligatoire dans la fabrication d'une sculpture, soit par extension l'objet qui résulte de cette opération. Moulage indique alors qu'il ne s'agit plus d'un original mais d'une répétition dont le nombre d'exemplaires est illimité." Or see Emile Littré, *Dictionnaire de la langue française* (London: Hachette, 1875): "Moulé, moulée: 1. Jeté en moule. Un buste moulé."
85. Roland Barthes, *Camera Lucida: Reflections on Photography*, trans. Richard Howard (New York: Hill and Wang, 1981), pp. 10–11.
86. Bartholdi's description of photography as a form of casting was certainly informed by scientists' prevalent linking of the two as different means to document various kinds of specimens, including racial types. See Christine Barthe, "Des modèles et des normes, allers-retours entre photographies, et sculptures ethnographiques," and Edouard Papet, "Le moulage sur nature ethnographique au XIXe siècle," in Paris, Musée d'Orsay, *Charles Cordier, 1827–1905*, pp. 113–28; see also Christine Barthe, "'Les éléments de l'observation': Des daguerréotypes pour l'anthropologie," in *Le Daguerréotype français: Un objet photographique*, exhibition catalogue, Paris, Musée d'Orsay (Paris: Réunion des Musées Nationaux, 2003), pp. 73–86; and Papet, "Le moulage sur nature au service de la science." Hélène Pinet has emphasized the shared terminology of sculpture and photography; for example, proofs or "tirages" were used for prints as well as casts which "gave both practices an industrial character." See "'Montrer est la question vitale': Rodin and photography," in Johnson, *Sculpture and* Photography, p. 70.
87. See Maxime Du Camp, *Le Nil, Égypte et Nubie* (1852; 4th ed., Paris: Hachette, 1877); cited in Gustave Flaubert, *Flaubert in Egypt*, trans. and ed. Francis Steegmuller (London: Bodley Head, 1972; reprint New York: Penguin, 1996), pp. 101–2. On Du Camp, see the scholarship of Julia Ballerini: "Photography Conscripted"; "The Invisibility of Hadj-Ishmael: Maxime Du Camp's 1850 Photographs of Egypt," in *The Body Imaged*, ed. Kathleen Adler and Marcia Pointon (Cambridge: Cambridge University Press, 1993), pp. 147–60; "Rewriting the Nubian Figure in the Photograph: Maxime Du Camp's 'Cultural Hypochondria,'" in *Colonialist Photography: Imag(in)ing Race and Place*, ed. Eleanor Hight and Gary D. Sampson (London: Routledge, 2002), pp. 30–50.
88. Flaubert's fictive, disgruntled female dancer complained: "The tent is closed—the fellaheen are around [it]—and like a sentinel from Istanbul your dragoman with a gray beard stands at the door. Like the bullet leaves a rifle, like the arrow leaves the bow, like the vulture who soars and like the hatred after the insult, you rush forward, carrying under your left arm something square in a black veil. Why do you look in this box that your panting sailors carry on their neck?... But me, I am afraid when through the window of the harem, through its bars of wood, I catch sight of you in the distance, imprisoning [your] head in a black shroud. It seems to me that you will decapitate yourself in there." See Gustave Flaubert, *Manuscrit autographe*, posthumously published; cited in Jean-Marie Carré, *Voyageurs et écrivains français en Égypte*, 2 vols. (Cairo: Impr. de l'Institut français d'archéologie orientale, 1956), vol. 2, pp. 122–23; see also *Œuvres complètes de Flaubert, Voyages* (Paris: Société des Belles-Lettres, 1948), vol. 2, p. 65.
89. Henry Cammas and André Lefèvre, *La vallée du Nil: Impressions et photographies* (Paris, 1862), p. 191.
90. Félix Nadar, *Le Paris souter-rain:1861, des os et des eaux* (1900; reprint Paris: Caisse nationale des monuments historiques et des sites, 1982), p. 29. See also Shelley Rice, *Parisian Views* (Cambridge: MIT Press, 1997); and Allan Sekula, "Photography between Labour and Capital," in *Mining Photographs and Other Pictures, 1948–1968: A Selection from the Negative Archives of Shedden Studio, Glace Bay, Cape Breton,*

photographs by Leslie Shedden, ed. Benjamin Buchloh and Robert Wilkie (Halifax, Canada: Press of the Nova Scotia College of Art and Design and the University College of Cape Breton, 1983), pp. 223–26.

91. Colmar, Musée Bartholdi. Letter of 10 April 1856.
92. "I am bothered by my models; one lies down, the other rises or turns her back to me when I am drawing her side." Berchère, *Le désert de Suez*, p. 103.
93. Mandach, "Léon Belly," p. 150 (original emphasis).
94. Charles S. Peirce, "Logic as Semiotic: The Theory of Signs," in *The Philosophy of Peirce: Selected Writings*, ed. Justus Buchler (New York: Harcourt, Brace and Company, 1940), p. 106: "Photographs, especially instantaneous photographs, are very instructive, because we know that they are in certain respects exactly like the objects they represent. But this resemblance is due to the photographs having been produced under such circumstances that they were physically forced to correspond point by point to nature."
95. Ballerini, "Photography Conscripted," p. 281.
96. "It is the artist who is truthful and it is photography which lies, for in reality, time does not stop, and if the artist succeeds in producing the impression of a movement which takes several moments for accomplishment, his work is certainly much less conventional than the scientific image, where time is abruptly suspended." Rodin, *Rodin on Art and Artists: Conversations with Paul Gsell*, trans. Romilly Fredden (New York: Dover, 1983), p. 54; published first as *Rodin, L'Art*, ed. Paul Gsell (Paris, Editions Grassette and Fasquelle, 1911); cited in Becker, "Auguste Rodin and Photography," p. 92. In "My Testament" Rodin wrote: "Mere exactitude, of which photography and moulage [life casting] are the lowest forms, does not inspire feelings." In a January 1889 letter to the mayor of Calais, he stated: "Many cast from nature, that is to say, replace an art work with a photograph. It is quick but it is not art." Ibid., p. 91.
97. Pierre Provoyeur, "Bartholdi and the Colossal Tradition," in *Liberty: The French-American Statue in Art and History*, exhibition catalogue, New York Public Library (New York: Harper and Row, 1986), p. 66.
98. Ibid.
99. Provoyeur has argued that Bartholdi was uncomfortable with the Papacy; ibid., pp. 66–67. The sculptor may also have known, as Marvin Trachtenberg has argued, the 1852 sculpture competition at the École des Beaux-Arts for a lighthouse which included entries with female figures although none were simple standing figures; instead, most were half woman, half architecture; see his *The Statue of Liberty* (New York: Penguin Books, 1986), p. 51.
100. Colmar, Musée Bartholdi. Letter of 23 March 1869. Partly cited in Régis Hueber, ed., *Auguste Bartholdi: Desseins... dessins. Esquisses préparatoires d'un statuaire*, exhibition catalogue (Colmar, Musée Bartholdi, 1995), p. 41: "Je vais me consacrer entièrement à mon affaire d'Égypte, celle-ci a l'avantage de se montrer franchement par son côté impossible; mais au moins je [n'—pose qu'—] du voyage. Je prends tous les points d'appui possibles, j'en ai d'excellents, mais avec cela il y a un côté de loterie et il faut un jeu de chance. Je ferai tout ce que je pourrai pour saisir l'occasion—son unique mêche et si j'échoua, c'est qu'il n'y aura pas mêche. J'ai fait montrer mon projet à l'Empereur et à l'Impératrice. Il paraît que tout le monde en a été enchanté; mais ils se bornent à faire des vœux pour mon succès... si peu que ce soit, cela me permettra de dire qu'ils ont des vœux, sans être démenti. J'aurai également l'appui de M. de Nieuwerkerke. Jusqu'à la fin de la semaine, j'aurai recueilli tout ce que je puis avoir. Après cela, j'irai aborder le taureau par les cornes."
101. Colmar, Musée Bartholdi. Letters or entries of 5 April 1869; 15 April 1869. "Je l'ai vu, lui ai parlé et comme je m'y attendrais il m'a jeté pas mal d'eau froide sur mon enthousiasme." "Je ne trouve personne chez Lesseps toujours accueil superficiel quoique aimable."
102. Colmar, Musée Bartholdi. Letter of 8 April 1869.
103. Colmar, Musée Bartholdi. Letter of 11 April 1869. "Toujours est-il que je suis en ce moment chez M. de Lesseps à Ismaïlia au milieu de l'Isthme. J'ai fait comme s'il eût été très dévoué à mes projets; il est très aimable avec moi, son hospitalité est de plus gracieuses. Je ne puis lui reprocher qu'une chose, c'est de ne guère me soutenir dans mon entreprise. Je [lui pardonne?], quoique en général on préfère ses affaires à celles des autres, mais il faut penser combien il est occupé par sa grande œuvre. Mon projet n'étant qu'un détail très accessoire il n'a pas envie de se dépenser de ce côté. Toutefois il me témoigne beaucoup d'aimabilité et de sympathie comme quelqu'un qui dirait: Tâches de réussir et j'en serai enchanté."
104. Colmar, Musée Bartholdi. Letter of 23 March 1869. Partly cited in *Dessins*, p. 41. "Ferdinand de Lesseps, familier de la Cour, est vraisemblablement responsable de la tiédeur impériale. Le projet de Bartholdi ne peut que lui déplaire. A la veille d'inaugurer 'son' canal, il n'entend pas que quiconque puisse détourner l'attention (et l'argent) d'Ismaïl, vers quoi que ce soit que lui, de Lesseps, n'eût prévu, décidé, réalisé. Gageons qu'il s'employa, tant en France qu'en Égypte, à s'aborder l'insolent projet."
105. Cited in Taboulet, "Aux origines du canal de Suez," p. 363.
106. "Souvenir à mon ancien ami Auguste Bartholdi." Cited in Colmar, Musée Bartholdi, *Au Yemen en 1856*, p. 63 n. 15.
107. Colmar, Musée Bartholdi. Letter of 8 April 1869; partly cited in *Dessins*, p. 42. "Après avoir attendu deux heures arrive le médecin du vice-roi et il m'introduit. J'entre dans des appartements d'un aspect tout Européen, le seul caractère particulier consiste en un divan qui fait le [tour] de la moitié de la chambre. Il y avait dans le salon, M. Mariette, le docteur Burguières et [des] domestiques. Après quelques généralités, je présente au vice-roi mes dessins et la statuette. Il regarde avec intérêt, je lui donne des explications, il me dit qu'il aimerait mieux voir l'appareil lumineux porté sur la tête à la manière des femmes fellahs. Je lui réponds que ce serait plus facile, afin de ne pas le contrarier (cependant ce serait moins bien). Je lui demande la permission de lui laisser mes dessins et de le revoir à son voyage à Paris dans un mois, et sur un petit salut me retire. Voilà le résultat de mes entreprises. Ce n'est pas grand comme tu vois; cependant c'est quelque chose. De plus dans les travaux qui se font au Caire, je vois beaucoup de choses à faire et je tâcherai de me procurer un peu de besogne, en cas d'échec de mon projet. Ainsi mon voyage ne restera pas sans porter quelques fruits. Pour le moment il est fini. Dans l'après-midi je fis quelques visites... au Cabinet du vice-roi. Je ne trouve personne..."
108. According to De Leon, Ismaïl Pasha spent £200,000 during his regime on lighthouses on the Red Sea and the Mediterranean. De Leon, *The Khedive's Egypt*, p. 366.
109. In 1914, for instance, a French artist was commissioned to make a bronze statue of the nationalist leader Mustafa Kamil. On the pedestal, a seated peasant woman is confined within a large square; she was meant to represent Egypt under British occupation. In 1928, Mahmud Mukhtar completed *The Awakening of Egypt*, a large granite sculpture in which a peasant woman is unveiling herself as her hand rests on a Sphinx. Fraught throughout this period was the relationship among veiling, nationalism, and modernity. See Beth Baron, "Nationalist Iconography: Egypt as a Woman," in *Rethinking Nationalism in the Arab Middle East*, ed. James Jankowski and Israel Gershoni (New York: Columbia University Press, 1997), pp. 112–15.
110. Jeanine Durand-Révillon, "La galerie anthropologique du Muséum national d'histoire naturelle et Charles-Henri-Joseph Cordier," in *La sculpture ethnographique*, p. 62.

111. Ibid.

112. Régnier, *Les saint-simoniens en Égypte*, p. 172. See also Jean-Jacques Luthi, *La vie quotidienne en Égypte au temps des khédives* (Paris: Harmattan, 1998), p. 66; Luthi also points out that, contrary to common assumptions, there were no major objections to such sculptures on the part of Muslims as "they had come to distinguish an idol from a work of art."

113. Edmond, *L'Égypte à l'Exposition universelle de 1867*, p. 238.

114. Add to this Ismaïl's interest in the equally slick, flirtatious art of Gérôme as evidenced in a letter of 1868 to the artist by his secretary. Hélène Lafont- Couturier, "Mr. Gérôme works for Goupil," *Gérôme & Goupil: Art et entreprise* (Paris: Editions de la Réunion des Musées nationaux, 2000), pp. 28–29.

115. The thesis about photography is Bustarret's in "Du Nil au Yémen."

116. "Salon of 1841," *Revue de Paris*, ser. 3, 28 (1841), p.155; cited in Wagner, *Jean-Baptiste Carpeaux*, p. 18.

117. Ibid.

118. The anxiety was, of course, pervasive: Rodin, to choose only one of the most prominent instances, criticized his age "as one of engineers and manufacturers, not artists." Auguste Rodin, *Art: Conversations with Paul Gsell*, 1911, trans. Jacques De Caso and Patricia B. Sanders (Berkeley and Los Angeles: University of California Press, 1984), p. 4. He also lamented that "science" and "mechanics" tended to "replace the work of the human mind with the work of a machine," yielding "the death of art." Auguste Rodin, *Rodin: The Man and His Art, with Leaves from His Notebook*, trans. S. K. Star (New York: Century, 1918), p. 206.

119. Colmar, Musée Bartholdi. Letter of 17 April 1869: "Excursion à Schalouff.... Nous allons faire une tour dans la rade, voir les jetées et les grands travaux par lesquels on s'est avancé d'une lieu sur la mer. Les jetées m'intéressent particulièrement et je regarde tout ce qui peut avoir quelque valeur pour mon projet de phare; malgré mes faibles débuts et le peu d'appui et d'encouragement que j'ai trouvé, je n'ai pas encore donné ma démission, à cet égard. Il est malheureux qu'avec les idées modernes, l'art et la poésie paraissent des superfluités; car vraiment je [conçois] peu d'œuvres d'art qui se présenter-aient dans ces conditions plus saisissantes que celle-ci. Nous verrons, il ne faut pas encore en désespérer."

120. The fine arts were reduced in importance, that is, relative to the earlier Universal Exhibition of 1855. See Patricia Mainardi, *Art and Politics of the Second Empire: The Universal Expositions of 1855 and 1867* (New Haven: Yale University Press, 1987), p. 132.

121. *Le Temps*, 12 April 1867; cited in ibid., p. 133.

122. Du Camp, *Le Nil, Égypte et Nubie*, p. 148; cited in Véronique Magri, *Le discours sur l'autre: A travers quatre récits de voyage en Orient* (Paris: Honoré Champion Editeur, 1995), p. 89.

## Chapter 3: Liberty's Surface

A version of this chapter was presented at Yale University in 2005. I thank students and other members of that audience for their questions. I especially appreciated the suggestions of Edward Cooke, David Joselit, and Christopher Wood.

1. Christian Kempf, "Bartholdi et le calotype," in *D'un album de voyage: Auguste Bartholdi en Égypte (1855–1856)*, exhibition catalogue (Colmar: Musée Bartholdi, 1990), pp. 15–23. Bartholdi's mother noted in her personal journal, Sunday, 30 July 1854: "Auguste est allé prendre une leçon de photographie." That very month he was also trying to raise money to cast Rapp. We do not know with whom he studied; perhaps with Le Gray, Charles Nègre, or Charles Marville, who made a striking picture of Liberty's head at the Gaget and Gauthier atelier. He owned photographs by these photographers, Disderi, and LeSecq, as well as photographs published by Blanquart-Evrard. The latter published many views of architecture and landscape between 1851 and 1855, including Maxime Du Camp's pictures of Egypt. Bartholdi took his camera on family picnics and took photographs of family and friends during the late summer and fall of 1854. Ibid., pp. 16–17. Kempf also tells us that Bartholdi only exceptionally retouched photographic negatives: a few skies and a few underexposed faces.

2. Cited in Colmar, Musée Bartholdi, *Le Rapp (1852–1856): Premier monument public de Bartholdi (1834–1904)*, exhibition catalogue (Colmar: Musée Bartholdi, 2000), p. 46.

3. See chapter 2, note 86.

4. See Darcy Grimaldo Grigsby, "Eroded Stone, Petrified Flesh and the Sphinx of Race," *Parallax* 43 (April 2007), pp. 21–40. Vivant Denon, *Voyage dans la basse et la haute Égypte* (1802; reprint, Paris: Pygmalion, 1990), p. 267.

5. Pierre Provoyeur, "Bartholdi and the Colossal Tradition," in *Liberty: The French-American Statue in Art and History*, exhibition catalogue, New York Public Library (New York: Harper and Row, 1986), p. 64.

6. Eugène Lesbazeilles, *Les colosses anciens et modernes* (Paris: Hachette, 1876), pp. 4–5.

7. Ibid.

8. Charles Moreau-Vauthier, *Gérôme, peintre et sculpteur: L'Homme et l'artiste, d'après sa correspondance, ses notes, les souvenirs de ses élèves et de ses amis* (Paris: Hachette, 1906), pp. 119–20.

9. Lesbazeilles, *Les colosses anciens et modernes*, pp. 35–36.

10. Colmar, Musée Bartholdi, letters of 26 January 1856 and 10 April 1856.

11. Charles Sanders Peirce, "Logic as Semiotic: The Theory of Signs," in *The Philosophy of Peirce: Selected Writings*, ed. Justus Buchler (New York: Harcourt, Brace and Company, 1940), p. 106. Peirce calls indices the class of signs "by physical connection."

12. Georges Didi-Hubermann, "L'air et l'empreinte," in *À fleur de peau: Le moulage sur nature au XIXe siècle*, ed. Edouard Papet, exhibition catalogue, Paris, Musee d'Orsay (Paris: Réunion des Musées Nationaux, 2001), p. 53. "The contact occurs without air...[T]he intimacy of the cast from nature is therefore a suffocating intimacy; without visibility nor circulation of air."

13. But, in the life cast, no unwrapping can ever retrieve the body again. The living body is gone. While calotypes are indices of the optical, casts after nature are the product of contact between solids. The skin of the cast is the interface between one solid, the body, and another, the plaster.

14. On the relationship of cast and photograph see also Rosalind Krauss, "X Marks the Spot," in Yves-Alain Bois and Rosalind E. Krauss, *Formless: A User's Guide* (Cambridge: MIT Press, 1997), pp. 214–19: "For the concern was no longer with the tectonics of industrial production, but with its logic, which is that of serialization, the multiple and replication. And although casting is a paradigm of any process of reduplication, of spinning out masses of copies from a single matrix or mold, it was the photographic rather than the cast form of the duplicate that increasingly took hold of the art world's imagination. For the photograph brought with it the simulacral notion of the mirage, of a reality that had been engulfed within its own technology of imitation, a fall into a hall of mirrors, a disappearance into a labyrinth in which original and copy are indistinguishable." Note that while the photograph collapses the distinction between the original and the copy, the copy and referent/object (the thing itself) remain distinguishable.

15. Théophile Gautier, "Photosculpture," *Moniteur Universel* no. 4, 4 January 1864, pp. 1–2. On Gautier's *Le pied de momie*, 1840, and *Le roman de la momie*, 1857, see Christine Majeune-Girodias, *Le roman de la momie* (Paris: Ellipses, 2000).

16. Denon, *Voyage dans la basse et la haute Égypte*, p. 267.

17. Albert speaking in Gautier's *Mademoiselle de Maupin* (Paris: Garnier-Flammarion, 1966), p. 252; partly cited in Anne Schmack, "Surface et profondeur dans 'Mademoiselle de Maupin,'" *Orbis Litterarum* 36 (1981), p. 34.

18. Gautier, "Photosculpture." Wolfgang Drost, "La photosculpture entre art industriel et artisinat: La réussite de François Willème (1830–1905)," *Gazette des Beaux-Arts* (October 1985), pp. 113–29; Robert A. Sobieszek, "Sculpture as the Sum of Its Profiles: François Willème and Photosculpture in France, 1859–1868," *Art Bulletin* 62, no. 4 (1980), pp. 617–30. Pierre Larousse, *Grand dictionnaire universel du XIXe siècle* (Paris, 1866–1879).

19. Gautier, "Photosculpture," p. 1.

20. Ibid.

21. On the Statue of Liberty see Marvin Trachtenberg, *The Statue of Liberty*, rev. ed. (New York: Penguin Books, 1986); New York Public Library, *Liberty: The French-American Statue in Art and History*; Frédéric-Auguste Bartholdi, *The Statue of Liberty Enlightening the World* (New York: The New York Trust, 1885); Bertrand Lemoine, *La statue de la liberté / The Statue of Liberty* (Bruxelles: Mardaga, 1986).

22. On seriality in sculptural production, see the invaluable essay by Jacques De Caso, "Serial Sculpture in Nineteenth-Century France," in *Metamorphoses in Nineteenth-Century Sculpture*, ed. Jeanne L. Wasserman (Cambridge: Fogg Museum, Harvard University Press, 1975), pp. 1–27.

23. Lawrence Alloway, *Topics in American Art since 1945* (New York: W. W. Norton, 1975), p. 247; cited in Anne Cannon Palumbo and Ann Uhry Abrams, "Proliferation of the Image," in New York Public Library, *Liberty: The French-American Statue in Art and History*, p. 231. Palumbo and Abrams emphasize that long before the statue was made, thousands knew what it looked like because of images in the press and journals. They add, "Modern technology and mass production made possible the manufacture of inexpensive three-dimensional replicas as well."

24. Bartholdi, *The Statue of Liberty Enlightening the World*, p. 51.

25. *Morning News* (Paris), 11 May 1884, p. 1.

26. Ibid. Bartholdi, *The Statue of Liberty Enlightening the World*, pp. 43–52. See also J. B. Gauthier, "La statue colossale: La liberté éclairant le monde," *La plomberie au XIX siècle* (Paris, 1885), pp. 18–21.

27. Gauthier, "La statue colossale," p. 20.

28. Ibid.

29. Bartholdi's hollow end product should be distinguished from the hollowness of bronze sculpture; that procedure replicated a lost- wax original, a solid form, which was never subject to labor from the inside. For an introduction to the history of bronze casting, see Nicholas Penny, *The Materials of Sculpture* (New Haven: Yale University Press, 1993), pp. 219–56.

30. Peirce, "Logic as Semiotic," pp. 102–3: "An *Index* is a sign which refers to the Object that it denotes by virtue of being really affected by that Object.... In so far as the Index is affected by the Object, it necessarily has some Quality in common with the Object...it is not the mere resemblance of its Object, even in these respects which makes it a sign, but it is the actual modification of it by the Object." "A *Symbol* is a sign which refers to the Object that it denotes by virtue of a law, usually an association of general ideas, which operates to cause the Symbol to be interpreted as referring to that Object. It is thus itself a general type or law.... As such it acts through a Replica. Not only is it general itself, but the Object to which it refers is of a general nature."

31. See for example the version of Bartholdi's *Album des travaux de construction de la statue colossale de la Libertó, destinée au port de New-York. Hommage respectueux de l'auteur et des constructeurs* (Paris, 1883) at the Library of Congress. The thirteen mounted

photographs (65 1/2 x 50 cm) were bound and inscribed to "His Majesty the Czar." The copy includes the signature of Bartoldi as well as Gaget, Gauthier & cie.

32. See the introduction to Immanuel Kant, "Analytic of the Sublime," in *Critique of Judgement*, trans. James Creed Meredith (1911 and 1928; reprint, Oxford: Clarendon Press, 1991), pp. 100–101.
33. Bartholdi, *The Statue of Liberty Enlightening the World*, p. 52.
34. Lemoine, *La statue de la liberté / The Statue of Liberty*, pp. 40–41.
35. The lighthouse was designed by the engineer Léonce Reynaud for Roches-Douvres.
36. Wyn Wachhorst, *Thomas Alva Edison: an American Myth* (Cambridge: MIT Press, 1981). On Edison in Paris in 1889, see Andre Millard, *Edison and the Business of Innovation* (Baltimore: Johns Hopkins University Press, 1990), pp. 118–21.
37. "The Phonograph," *Scientific American*, 30 March 1878, p. 193. Italics in original.
38. "Inventor Edison's Last. A Wonderful Machine that will be of Immense Value for Various Purposes. Promising that it shall utter words which 'may be heard distinctly four miles away,'" *World* (New York), 20 March 1878.
39. On light see Shelley Wood Cordulack, "A Franco-American Battle of Beams: Electricity and the Selling of Modernity," *Journal of Design History* 18 (2005), pp. 147–66.
40. "The Phonograph," *Scientific American*, 30 March 1878, p. 193: "He proposes to construct a tube which shall be shaped like the interior of the human mouth, and which shall be supplied with teeth somewhat similar to those employed in the *vox humana* organ-stop."
41. Gaby Wood, *Edison's Eve: A Magical History of the Quest for Mechanical Life* (New York: Knopf, 2002), pp. 158–59. Sent to Europe in 1889 to research part suppliers and markets, Edison's assistant wrote him: "An almost universal objection was made to the weight and dimensions.... Is it not possible to reduce the size to conform to their ideas?"
42. A. W. Raitt, *The Life of Villiers de L'Isle-Adam* (Oxford: Clarendon Press, 1981), p. 235. February 1876: "Villiers became involved in negotiations with the Franco-American Committee which was at the time collecting money for the erection of the Statue of Liberty. On 25 February Oswald announced that Villiers, with typical generosity, had offered to donate the takings of the first night and of the best night thereafter," p. 165; pp. 181–82. Raitt footnotes several unpublished letters from Committee to Villiers at Fonds Bollery, Bibliothèque Municipale, La Rochelle.
43. *L'Eve nouvelle*, the first version of *L'Eve future* appeared serially in *Le Gaulois*, 4–18 September 1880. The almost complete novel appeared in *L'Étoile Française* from 14 December 1880 to 4 February 1881. A definitive version of *L'Eve future* was published in *La Vie Moderne* 18 July 1885 to 27 March 1886. Finally it was published as a book in 1886, although a few details were changed. In *Le romancier et la machine: L'image de la machine dans le roman français (1850–1900)*, 2 vols. (Paris: Corti, 1982), Jacques Noiray argues that Villiers was also inspired by the proliferation of articles at the Universal Exhibition of 1878 and also the vulgarization of two revolutionary inventions: the telephone and the phonograph. We have no evidence that Villiers visited the exhibition but it seems highly likely that he did; ibid., vol. 2, p. 281. See also Alain Néry, *Les idées politiques et sociales de Villiers de L'Isle-Adam* (Paris: Diffusion Université Culture, 1984), p. 153.
44. Villiers de L'Isle-Adam, *Tomorrow's Eve*, trans. Robert Martin Adams (Chicago: University of Illinois Press, 2001), pp. 17–18.
45. Ibid., p. 75.
46. See the excellent essay by Alex Potts, "Dolls and Things: The Reification and Disintegration of Sculpture in Rodin and Rilke," in *Sight and Insight: Essays on Art and Culture in Honour of E. H. Gombrich at 85*, ed. John Onians (London: Phaidon, 1994), pp. 355–78. Potts argues that in modern visual aesthetics, the status of sculpture has a tendency to hover uneasily between highly charged object of fantasy and mere physical object/commodity.
47. Villiers de L'Isle-Adam, *Tomorrow's Eve*, p. 84.
48. Ibid., p. 125.
49. Noiray, *Le romancier et la machine*, vol. 2, p. 327.
50. Villiers de L'Isle-Adam, *Tomorrow's Eve*, pp. 204, 207; see also p. 76, which describes how the coffin's interior was molded to her female form. Lying in her casket "she fastened tightly about her body several wide bands of silk..."
51. See, for example, Bernardin de Saint-Pierre, *Paul and Virginie* (1788). On the drowned woman, see also Elisabeth Bronfen, "Femininity—Missing in Action," in *Over Her Dead Body: Death, Femininity and the Aesthetic* (New York: Routledge, 1992), pp. 205–24.
52. Raitt, *The Life of Villiers de L'Isle-Adam*. See Villiers de L'Isle-Adam, *Corréspondance générale de Villiers de L'Isle Adam et documents inédits*, 2 vols. (Paris: Mercure de France, 1962), vol. 2, pp. 288, 289, 295. Villiers de L'Isle-Adam, *Nouvelles reliques*, ed. P. G. Castex and J. M. Bellefroid (Paris: Corti, 1968), p. 40.
53. Villiers de L'Isle-Adam, *Corréspondance générale*, vol. 2, p. 289, 30 June 1889 to Mallarmé.
54. Ibid., p. 295, 10 August 1889, Mallarmé to Villiers.
55. E. de Rougemont, *Villiers de l'Isle-Adam: Biographie et bibliographie* (Paris: Mercure de France, 1910), p. 336, Verlaine to F. A. Cazals.
56. Thanks to Wood, *Edison's Eve*, p. 145, we know about "a letter of 1910 from the Villiers de l'Isle-Adam 'committee' in Paris, thanking the inventor for his donation of $25."
57. See for example, "The Phonograph," *Scientific American*, 30 March 1878, p. 193: "If we lived in 1678 instead of 1878 the life of Mr. Edison would not be worth a moment's purchase; in fact, he would have been resolved into carbonic acid, hydrogen, and his other constituent gases long ago in the flames set apart for earthly communers with his satanic majesty." Wachhorst, *Thomas Alva Edison*, p. 19, argues that Edison's Wizard image arose not in response to the filament light bulb but to the phonograph. A reporter from the New York *Daily Graphic* visited Edison in 1878 after the appearance of phonograph and published his own comment "Aren't you a good deal of a wizard, Mr. Edison?" The image stuck.
58. For Eiffel's own use of the word "pyramid," often "pyramid in iron," see Fonds Eiffel, Musée d'Orsay ARO 1981–1255, ARO 1981–1259.

### Chapter 4: Eiffel's Emptiness

This chapter and the next began as an article, "Geometry/ Labor = Volume/Mass?" *October* 106 (Fall 2003), pp. 3–34. It was funded by an Andrew W. Mellon New Directions Fellowship and a U.C. Berkeley Townsend Center Initiative Grant for Associate Professors. I would like to thank Professor Kathleen James-Chakraborty, architectural historian, for her suggestions as well as the engineers at the University of California, Berkeley, who have generously attempted to teach me the basics of structural engineering: Professor Gregory Fenves, Sebastien Payen, and especially Charles Chadwell, whose tutoring was essential. I am also indebted to my graduate research assistant Amy Freund and undergraduate research apprentices Adam Cramer and Elizabeth Benjamin. Adam Cramer also elucidated principles of mathematics and was wonderfully imaginative about the implications of my work. Audiences at the University of Southern

California and at the Aga Khan program at MIT have assisted me with their stimulating queries, especially Todd Olson, Vanessa Schwartz, Deborah Silverman, Nancy Troy, Nasser Rabat, Erika Naginski, and Heghnar Watenpaugh. All translations are mine unless otherwise indicated.

1. During the Third Republic 280 engineers served in the Parlement; see Bruno Marnot, *Les ingénieurs au Parlement sous la IIIe République* (Paris: CNRS Editions, 2000).
2. On Freycinet, see Theodore Zeldin, *France, 1848–1945*, 2 vols. (Oxford: Clarendon Press, 1973–77), vol. 1, pp. 589–90, 595, 627, 631–38, 646.
3. Charles de Freycinet, *La question d'Égypte* (Paris: Calmann-Lévy, 1905).
4. Charles de Freycinet, *De l'expérience en géométrie* (Paris: Gauthier-Villars, 1903), pp. 13–17.
5. Gaspard Monge, *An Elementary Treatise on Descriptive Geometry, with a Theory of Shadows and of Perspective: Extracted from the French of G. Monge.*, trans. J. F. Heather (London: J. Weale, 1851), pp. 1, 3. Adam Cramer, "Pyramids in Egypt, Pyramids on Paper: The Cultural Mathematics of the *Description of Egypt*," undergraduate honor's thesis, University of California, Berkeley, May 2005, pp. 8–9. "The student first learns how to project a mere point orthogonally onto two perpendicular planes. Then the student is taught to use the dual projections of two points to determine the dual projections of a line. Finally, Monge describes how the student can determine planes by finding the lines of their limiting edges. This method of definition is logical, built not on empirical somatic experience but rather on rational constructions. Monge's method takes as its object not a real, visible, quantifiable thing in the real world of sensory experience, but rather logic itself."
6. On Aristotle's Metaphysics, see B. A. Rosenfeld, *A History of Non-Euclidean Geometry: Evolution of the Concept of a Geometric Space*, trans. Abe Shenitzer (New York: Springer-Verlag, 1988), p. 111; on Auguste Comte, *Cours de philosophie positive* (Paris, 1830–1842), see ibid., pp. 199–200; see also the discussion of the Austrian physicist Ernst Mach's work of 1905 in ibid., pp. 201–2.
7. The 1779 competition, for example, required determining the number of workers employed to make "un remblai de 96 toises," knowing that if there were eight or more, each makes at least one toise. Hydraulic and mechanical problems were reduced to geometry and algebra. Bruno Belhoste, Antoine Picon, and Joël Sakarovitch, "Les exercises dans les écoles d'ingénieurs sous l'Ancien Regime et la Révolution," *Histoire de l'Education* 46 (1990), p. 62. The goal of the École du Génie de Mézières was to form military engineers able to solve problems of defense and attack; its curriculum focused on the building fortifications, but also on "the transport of enormous masses of earth." René Taton, *L'Œuvre scientifique de Monge* (Paris: Presses Universitaires de France, 1951), p. 193.
8. Monge presented his memoir to the academy on 27 January and 7 February 1776; it was then published in the academy's volume of 1781. Taton, *L'Œuvre scientifique de Monge*, p. 194. See also Belhoste, Picon, and Sakarovitch, "Les exercises dans les écoles d'ingénieurs sous l'Ancien Regime et la Révolution," p. 62. Gaspard Monge, "Mémoire sur la théorie des déblais et remblais," in *Histoire de l'Académie Royale des sciences, Année M. DCCLXXXI avec les Mémoires de Mathématique et de Physique, pour la meme Année, Tirés des Registres de cette Académie* (Paris: Imprimerie Royale, 1784), pp. 666–704.
9. Monge, "Mémoire sur la théorie des déblais et remblais," pp. 699–700.
10. Ibid., 704.
11. Peters, *Building the Nineteenth Century*, pp. 185–88.
12. English translation in ibid., p. 201.
13. Ibid., p. 193.
14. Lavalley "understood building as a linear concatenation of events, not as a matrix of parallel occurrences through which a builder had to weave a critical path." Ibid., p. 192. "Cheap labor, the distance from machine manufacturers and energy sources in France, and long supply lines originally made the engineers choose the simplest possible technology for the canal. But the situation was different in the second construction phase, where deadlines had become critical." Ibid. p. 198.
15. Pierre Provoyeur, "Artistic Problems," in *Liberty: The French-American Statue in Art and History*, exhibition catalogue, New York Public Library (New York: Harper and Row, 1986), pp. 78–99.
16. On Bartholdi's first trip to the United States see Janet Headley, "Voyage of Discovery: Bartholdi's First American Visit (1871)," in New York Public Library, *Liberty: The French-American Statue*, pp. 100–105. On his second trip in 1876 at the time of the Philadelphia exhibition, see Janet Headley, "Bartholdi's Second American Visit: The Philadelphia Exhibition (1876)," in New York Public Library, *Liberty: The French-American Statue*, pp. 140–47.
17. Long Branch, N.J., 15 July 1871; cited in New York Public Library, *Liberty: The French-American Statue*, p. 102.
18. Chicago, 16 August 1871. Bartholdi Papers, Rodman Gilder, translator. New York Public Library.
19. New York, 24 June 24 1871. Bartholdi Papers, Rodman Gilder, translator. New York Public Library.
20. Frédéric-Auguste Bartholdi, Membre du Jury International, *Exposition Internationale de Philadelphie en 1876, Section Française: Rapport sur les Arts Décoratifs* (Paris Impr. Nationale, 1877), p. 15. See also his statement, p. 6: "In sum, luxury, comfort, questions of art, the desire to acquire and to generalize the sentiment of the beautiful, are very recent needs, and only influence production once there are parts of the American society who can live outside the burning preoccupations of business."
21. The Statue of Liberty was inaugurated in Paris on 21 May 1884 and in New York City on 4 July 1885; the Washington Monument was dedicated on 21 February 1885 and opened to the public on 9 October 1888.
22. In 1863 Jules Verne had made a similar claim when he described the modern Parisienne subjected by "the Angel of Geometry, formerly so lavish with his most alluring curves,... to all the rigors of straight lines and acute angles. The Frenchwoman has become Americanized." Jules Verne, *Paris in the Twentieth Century*, trans. Richard Howard (New York: Random House, 1996), p. 142. The unpublished novel was written in 1863 and set in 1960.
23. Letter to his mother, 21 July 1871. Bartholdi Papers, Rodman Gilder, translator. New York Public Library.
24. This has been pointed out by Bertrand Lemoine, *La statue de la liberté /The Statue of Liberty* (Bruxelles: Mardaga,1986), p. 38.
25. Frédéric Auguste Bartholdi, *The Statue of Liberty Enlightening the World* (New York: New York Trust, 1885), p. 42.
26. "For an effect of great size to be produced it must be simple enough to strike us at a glance, that is, as an ensemble.... We must force ourselves to embrace the idea of an expanse, and too many small divisions, far from augmenting, diminishes that power in us." Quatremère de Quincy cited in Lemoine, *La statue de la liberté / The Statue of Liberty*, p. 32.
27. Eugène Lesbazeilles, *Les Colosses anciens et modernes* (Paris: Hachette, 1876), p. 13.
28. Bartholdi, *The Statue of Liberty Enlightening the World*, p. 42: "I may cite for example the principle of great simplicity in the movement and in the exterior lines. The gesture ought to be made plain by the profile to all the senses. The details of the lines ought not to arrest the eye. The breaks in the lines should be bold, and such as are suggested by the general design. Beside the work should be as far as possible filled out, and should not present black spots or exaggerated recesses. The surfaces should be broad and simple, defined by a bold and clear design, accentuated in the important places. The enlargement of the details or their multiplicity is to be feared. By exaggerating the forms, in order to render them more clearly visible, or by enriching them with details, we would destroy the proportion of the work. Finally, the model, like the design, should have a summarized character, such as one would give to a rapid sketch."
29. See Pierre Provoyeur, "Technological and Industrial Challenges," New York Public Library, *Liberty: The French-American Statue*, pp. 106–19; see also pp. 97–98.
30. *De l'expérience en Géométrie*, pp. 13–17.
31. Appreciate the foundry's conditional phrase cited in the last chapter: "if, by some means, one could have reunited the pieces." J. B. Gauthier, "La statue colossale: La Liberté éclairant le monde," *La Plomberie au XIX siècle* (Paris: Impr. De Chaix, 1885), pp. 18–21.
32. Daniel Bermond, *Gustave Eiffel* (Paris: Perrin, 2002), p. 71. The École was born of the Saint-Simonian movement; its goal was to prepare youth for the era of factories.
33. Ibid., p. 72.
34. Here I paraphrase Bermond, who characterizes Eiffel as "une intelligence toute pratique"; ibid., p. 101. Eiffel's first employment, beginning in 1856, was with a fellow graduate of the École Centrale. Only six years older than Eiffel, Charles Nepveu was a "constructor of steam-driven machines, tools, forges, boilers, sheet metal, fixed and rolling materials for locomotives." A utopian industrialist informed by Saint-Simonian thinking, Nepveu was extremely talented. In 1848, at the age of 22, he had written *Essai sur l'organisation du travail* (Essay on the Organization of Work), in which he called for the association of "capitalists" and workers, a minimum wage, and insurance for workers. Nepveu thought big, and he and Eiffel hit it off. Both wished to differentiate themselves from the crowd of engineers; both were entrepreneurial and innovative. Eiffel remained loyal to his patron even after Nepveu suffered a breakdown and temporarily disappeared, having written suicide notes, one of which included a request on behalf of his talented protegé. After his return, his own business in shambles, Nepveu arranged for Eiffel to work for a railway company. See ibid., pp. 84–90.
35. Ibid., pp. 94, 101.
36. Ibid., p. 102.
37. Edwin T. Layton Jr., "Escape from the Jail of Shape: Dimensionality and Engineering Science," in *Technological Development and Science in the Industrial Age*, ed. Peter Kroes and Martijn Bakker (Netherlands: Kluwer Academic Publishers, 1992), pp. 35–68. See also Barbara Rose, "Blow Up: The Problem of Scale in Sculpture," *Art in America* 56 (1968), pp. 80–91.
38. Layton, "Escape from the Jail of Shape."
39. J. E. Gordon, *Structures: Or, Why Things Don't Fall Down* (New York: Da Capo Press, 1978), p. 192. Gordon adds that "we can neglect the square-cube law with most masonry buildings because... the stresses in masonry are so low that we can afford to go on scaling them up almost indefinitely." Thus the Colossi of Memnos and the Egyptian pyramids ill prepared Bartholdi to take seriously this structural problem of dimension.
40. Bernard Marrey, *La vie & l'œuvre extraordinaires de Monsieur Gustave Eiffel, ingénieur...* (Paris: Graphite, 1984), p. 61.
41. Reproduced in Paris, Musée d'Orsay, *Catalogue sommaire illustré du fonds Eiffel* (Paris: Réunion des Musées Nationaux, 1989), p. 19.
42. In his 1881 *Graphical Determination of Forces in Engineering Structures*, for instance, "Chalmers emphasized

the underlying geometric concept of engineering designs, remarking that structures are geometric forms whose forces, governed by the law of statics, act along geometric lines. Of the engineer he said, accordingly, 'it is natural that he strove to follow a train of geometric thought.'" T. M. (Thomas Malcolm) Charlton, *A History of Theory of Structures in the Nineteenth Century* (Cambridge: Cambridge University Press, 1982), p. 58.

43. The sides of a polygon of forces "represent in magnitude and direction a system of concurrent forces in equilibrium;" "it was not long after the adoption of the metal framework including trusses for structures that powerful graphical methods of analysis were developed on the basis of the triangle and polygon of forces." Ibid., pp. 59–60.
44. Bartholdi, *The Statue of Liberty Enlightens the World*, p. 52.
45. Henri Loyrette, *Gustave Eiffel* (Paris: Payot, 1986), p. 36; Bermond, *Gustave Eiffel*, p. 137.
46. Paris, Musée d'Orsay, Fonds Eiffel ARO 1981–1155 (Personal letters). Letter from Eiffel to "cher papa, Alexandria 5 mai 1865" [in this letter he also refers to the assassination of Lincoln; Bermond's footnote is wrong]. This seems to be the only letter from Egypt. "J'ai fait en effet ma très bien et intéressant voyage soit dans l'isthme soit en [Caire?] où je suis resté quelques jours [et] vois les [——] et notamment les pyramides et le [Sérapeuse?] de Memphis. J'ai recueilli quelques notes sur le Canal que je publierai probablement à mon retour."
47. Paris, Musée d'Orsay, Fonds Eiffel ARO 1981–1208 (includes marginal drawings on some pages and also full-page cross sections of the canal). "Note sur une visite du Canal du Suez faite en Avril 1865," p. 11: "The cube of *déblais* removed was 4,350,00, a little more than half the earth to be removed dry. The daily work of each man varied between one and two cubic meters and the price of the *déblais* did not surpass .70, inclusive of the payment of the *corvées*, provisions, water, and general costs of supervision." "Le cube des déblais enlevés a été de 4 350 000, soit un peu plus de la moitié des terres à enlever à sec.... Le travail journalier de chaque homme a varié entre 1 et 2 mètres cubes et le prix du déblais n'a pas dépassé 0.70 y compris, paiement des corvées, vivres approvisionnement d'eau et frais généraux de direction."
48. Ibid.
49. Ibid. "Quelle que soit la confiance que nous soyons habitués à avoir sur la supériorité des machines relativement au travail de l'homme on ne peut s'empêchera la vue de ces grands travaux si rapidement et si économiquement faits, de regrettez qu'ils ne soient pas continuer de la même façon dont ils ont été si bien commencé."
50. The hundreds of celebratory letters and poems sent to Eiffel in 1889 include dozens of references to Egypt's pyramids. See the following twenty-four texts, primarily poems, in the Fonds Eiffel, Musée d'Orsay ARO 1981–1313: "La Vallée du Nil du haut de la Tour Eiffel, Lire: Vision d'Abou Naddar," inscribed À Monsieur Eiffel, which appeared in the journal, *L'Égypte aux Égyptiens, Directeur & Redacteur en Chef: J. Sanua Abou Naddara*, 6, rue Geoffroy-Marie, 6, Paris, 12ème année, no. 8, 15 août 1888; *L'Égypte aux Égyptiens, Directeur & Redacteur en Chef: J. Sanua Abou Naddara*, 12ème année, no. 4, 29 avril 1888; *L'Égypte aux Égyptiens, Directeur & Redacteur en Chef: J. Sanua Abou Naddara*, 13e année, no. 7, 26 juillet 1889; "Un jeune poète de Batignolles," signed T.? R. Lacroix (Batignolles), avril 1889; "La tour Eiffel, La France: Monologue by Herve Le Biguais," Xbre 1889; "À Monsieur Eiffel from E. Besson, 'ouvrier menuiser,'" 19 août 1887; "Athénais Bonnard"; "À l'illustre Eiffel: Hommage d'admiration: Ascension de la Tour Eiffel (en rêve)," Julia Beaumont, 1890, published, p. 8; Raoul Bonnery, "La Tour Eiffel: À François Coppée, le jour de ses 300 mètres"; Emile Bordet, "À la tour du centenaire," handwritten but also published in *Le Trouvère*, 6e année, no. 52, 1 octobre 1888, pp. 91–95; Guillaume Deroure, "À la Tour Eiffel," 1889; A/ Faqueux, "À La Tour Eiffel," 1889; À Gaillac, "À Monsieur Eiffel: Hommage de l'admiration," 11 février 1889; H. Le Coq, "La Tour Eiffel"; L. Lemaire. "La Tour de 300 mètres: à M. G. Eiffel," août 1889; Gustave Moulay, "Enthousiasme," 29 août 1889; Potin, "À Monsieur Eiffel," mai 1889; Jules Florentin Ruel, "La Tour de l'ingénieur Eiffel" with letter, received 27 août 1889 addressed to Monsieur l'Ingénieur: Saint-Roman, "Poésie en 350 vers sur La Tour Eiffel L'Exposition: Comparaisons, Descriptions du Colosse avec les sensations diverses que produisent les divers étages," Paris, E. Mayer et Cie, 1889: Cte de Tarade, "La Tour Eiffel," 19 août 1889; C. Touche, "Au pied de la Tour," 15 septembre 1889; André Valter, "La Tour Eiffel," 21 avril 1889; A. Victor, "La Tour Eiffel: Chant Patritique,"
24 mai 1889 (published); F. Moury, "Devant la Tour Eiffel," n.d., inscribed to Eiffel.
51. Reproduced in Loyrette, *Gustave Eiffel*, p. 11.
52. Fonds Eiffel, Musée d'Orsay, ARO 1981–1286; cited in Bermond, *Gustave Eiffel*, p. 277.
53. Barthes, *The Eiffel Tower and Other Mythologies*, trans. Richard Howard (New York: Hill and Wang, 1979), p. 7 (original emphasis): "The Tower is *nothing*, it achieves a kind of zero degree of the monument; it participates in no rite, in no cult, not even in Art; you cannot visit the Tower as a museum: there is nothing to see *inside* the Tower." Michel Serres, *Statues* (Paris: Edition Bourin, 1987), pp. 128–29: "Three hundred meters that were not dedicated to the glory of a god, did not celebrate any victory or productive invention, three stories with no traditional, religious, military or economic function. Apart from its symbolic use without any shining torches or heads, it is foolish yet wise, given the time when its engineer planned it. As transparent as it is devoid of meaning, its emptiness shows through its useless, derisory crossbars.... Without having any other meaning it exists solely for the purpose of being there. Static, built to stay erect, posed...empty, translucent, almost theoretic, entirely explicit without any mystery or secret, perfectly metric, more formula than form, it exposes certain static theorems."
54. Michael Baxandall, "The Historical Object, Benjamin Baker's Forth Bridge," in *Patterns of Intention: On the Historical Explanation of Pictures* (New Haven: Yale University Press, 1985), pp. 12–40.
55. A not quite complete series of Durandelle's photographs is in the Fonds Eiffel at the Musée d'Orsay; small reproductions are published in Paris, Musée d'Orsay, *Catalogue sommaire illustré du fonds Eiffel*, pp. 95–101. On Durandelle, see Elvire Perego, "Delmaet et Durandelle ou la rectitude des lignes," *Photographies* 5 (July 1984), pp. 54–73, 122–25. See also Henri Loyrette, "Ingénieurs et photographes," *Photographies* 5 (July 1984), pp. 12–18, translation in English, "Ingeniors [*sic*] and Photographers," pp. 122–25.
56. See the photographs in the Fonds Eiffel, Musée d'Orsay PHO 1981-118-25, 26. Durandelle, mounted photos on cardboard printed with the title "Exposition Universelle de 1889. État d'avancement des travaux de la tour. G, Eiffel, Ingénieur et Constructeur." The series includes 58 images; Fonds Eiffel, Musée d'Orsay PHO 1981-118-1-58.
57. Fonds Eiffel, Musée d'Orsay PHO 1981-118-46 ff.
58. Fonds Eiffel, Musée d'Orsay PHO 1981-118-38-41, 43.
59. Fonds Eiffel, Musée d'Orsay PHO 1981-126-1-10. Small reproductions are published in Paris, Musée d'Orsay, *Catalogue sommaire illustré du fonds Eiffel*, pp. 112–13.
60. "L'Architecture en fer," in *Le Musée des Scien ces* (11 February 1857), pp. 321–23; cited in Loyrette, "Ingénieurs et photographes," pp. 12–14, translation in English, "Ingeniors [*sic*] and Photographers," p. 125.
61. Sigfried Giedion, *Space, Time and Architecture: The Growth of a New Tradition*, 5th ed. (Cambridge: Harvard University Press, 1990), p. 220.

62. Loyrette, "Ingeniors [*sic*] and Photographers," p. 123.
63. "Petition des artistes addressee à Alphand publiée dans Le Temps, le 14 février 1887," Paris, Musée d'Orsay, 1889: *La Tour Eiffel et l'Exposition universelle* (Paris: Editions de la Réunion des Musées Nationaux, 1989), pp. 28–29; reproduced in Frédéric Seitz, *La Tour Eiffel: Cent ans de sollicitude* (Paris: Editions Belin-Herscher, 2001), pp. 20–21. For the English translation, see *The Eiffel Tower: A Tour de Force. Its Centennial Exhibition*, ed. Phillip Dennis Cate, exhibition catalogue, New York, The Grolier Club (New York: Grolier Club, 1989), p. 31. Among the signatories were the painters Gérôme, Meissonier, and Bouguereau, and the architect of the Opera House, Charles Garnier.
64. Delacroix was responding to the Universal Exhibition of 1855. "La vue de toutes ces machines m'attriste profondément: Je n'aime pas cette matière qui a l'air de faire, toute seule et abandonnée à elle-même, des choses dignes d'admiration." Cited in Jacques Noiray, *Le romancier et la machine: L'image de la machine dans le roman français* (1850–1900), 2 vols. (Paris: Corti, 1982), vol. 1, p. 247. My general argument is indebted to Loyrette, "Ingénieurs et photographes."
65. Vicomte de Vogüé, *Revue des Deux Mondes*, 1 July 1889, pp. 194–95. Cited in part in Bermond, *Gustave Eiffel*, p. 292. On Vogüé, see Jennifer L. Shaw, *Dream States: Puvis de Chevannes, Modernism, and the Fantasy of France* (New Haven: Yale University Press), 2002, pp. 119–21, 165–75.
66. Emile Cheysson, *L'Économie sociale: L'Exposition universelle de 1889: Communication faite au Congrès d'économie sociale, le 13 juin 1889* (Paris: n.p., 1889), p. 5.
67. See Bernard Kalaora and Antoine Savoye, *Les Inventeurs oubliés: Le Play et ses continuateurs aux origines des sciences sociales* (Paris: Champ Vallon, 1989), p. 175; Paul Rabinow, *French Modern: Norms and Forms of the Social Environment* (Cambridge: MIT Press, 1989), pp. 170–78.
68. J. Christopher Jones, *Design Methods: Seeds of Human Futures* (London: Wiley-Interscience, 1970), cited in Ken Baynes and Francis Pugh, *The Art of the Engineer* (Woodstock, New York: Overlook Press, 1981), p. 11.
69. Ibid.
70. François Poncetton, *Eiffel, le magicien du fer* (Paris: Éditions de la Tournelle, 1939), p. 186; also see Bertrand Lemoine, *La tour de Monsieur Eiffel* (Paris: Découvertes Gallimard, 1989), p. 38.
71. Thomas Nagel, *The View from Nowhere* (New York: Oxford University Press, 1986), cited in Lorraine Daston, "Objectivity and the Escape from Perspective," *Social Studies of Science* 22 (1992), p. 599. See also Ken Alder, *Engineering the Revolution: Arms and Enlightenment in France*, 1763–1815 (Princeton: Princeton University Press, 1997), esp. pp. 127–62, 292–318. As Molly Nesbit has argued, education reforms during the Third Republic included mandatory drawing education for all children, both perspective drawing of what they saw and orthographic drawing of what they knew. Nesbit has importantly elucidated the gender implications of this program in "Ready-Made Originals: The Duchamp Model," *October* 37 (Summer 1986), pp. 53–64, and in "The Language of Industry," in *The Definitively Unfinished Marcel Duchamp*, ed. Thierry de Duve (Cambridge: MIT Press, 1991), pp. 351–84.
72. David P. Billington, *The Tower and the Bridge: The New Art of Structural Engineering* (Princeton: Princeton University Press, 1983), p. 65.
73. Peters, *Building the Nineteenth Century*, pp. 265–66.
74. Joseph Gallant, "The Shape of the Eiffel Tower," *American Journal of Physics* 70, no. 2 (February 2002), pp. 160–62.
75. The work of geometer Carl Culmann was disseminated in France by Maurice Lévy in his *La statique graphique et ses applications aux constructions* (Paris, 1874), as well as by Eiffel's employee, the engineer Maurice Koechlin, who was trained by Culmann. See Charlton, *A History of Theory of Structures*, pp. 170–71; Maurice Koechlin, *Les applications de la statique graphique* (Paris, 1889).
76. Conversation with Professor Gregory Fenves, 3 March 2003. Not many structures do this; exceptional are suspension bridges, the Eiffel Tower, and Chicago's Hancock Tower.
77. Gustave Eiffel, *La tour de trois cent mètres*, 2 vols. (Paris: Société des Imprimeries Lemercier, 1900), cited in Gallant, "The Shape of the Eiffel Tower."
78. "Eiffel's use of wrought iron in an open-lattice design produced such an extremely light structure that the Tower has approximately the same weight as the air that surrounds it. The mass of the air in a box just large enough to enclose the Tower 125² meters² x 312 meters is 6.28 million kilograms, which is 86.0% of the Tower's 7.30 million kilograms." Gallant, "The Shape of the Eiffel Tower."
79. See, for instance, Zeldin, *France, 1848–1945*, vol. 1, pp. 198–284, 640–788; Michelle Perrot, *Workers on Strike: France, 1871–1890*, trans. Chris Turner (Leamington Spa: Berg, 1987).
80. *Le Temps*, 14 February 1887; cited in Seitz, *La Tour Eiffel*, pp. 21–22; incompletely cited in Lemoine, *La tour de Monsieur Eiffel*, p. 100.
81. Auguste Rodin, *Art: Conversations with Paul Grell, 1911*, trans. Jacques De Caso and Patricia B. Sanders (Berkeley and Los Angeles: University of California Press, 1984), p. 4.
82. Auguste Rodin, *Rodin: The Man and His Art, with Leaves from his Notebook*, ed. Judith Cladel, trans. S. K. Star (New York: Century, 1918), p. 206.
83. Frederick Lawton, *The Life and Work of Auguste Rodin* (London: T. Fisher Unwin, 1906), p. 116.
84. Marcelle Tirel, *The Last Years of Rodin* (London: A. M. Philpot, 1925), pp. 112–13. Tirel was Rodin's secretary. See also *The New York Times*, 25 August 1907, p. C3, which announces the fundraising campaign in Europe and America organized by Armand Dayot.
85. Lawton, *The Life and Work of Auguste Rodin*, p. 117.
86. Tirel, *The Last Years of Rodin*, p. 113.
87. Charles Ricketts, "Dalou," *Burlington Magazine* 7 (1905), pp. 348–54; here p. 354.
88. Andre Millard, *Edison and the Business of Innovation* (Baltimore: Johns Hopkins University Press, 1990), pp. 120–21: "The exhibit for the Paris Exposition was a major project for the laboratory. In December 1888 work began on the design for the display, which was constructed in the machine shops and Phonograph Works. It was then crated up and shipped to Europe, accompanied by some of Edison's laboratory staff under the leadership of William Hammer, a master of electrical promotion who had successfully installed lighting displays at numerous exhibitions. Edison's electrical exhibit was one of the centerpieces of the exhibition. It featured thousands of electric light bulbs, a complete electric power station, and several electric signs and displays. It took up an acre of fair grounds."
89. Neil Baldwin, *Edison: Inventing the Century* (New York: Hyperion, 1995). Among the visitors to the Eiffel Tower was Bartholdi, who signed the guest book: "Hommage à M. Eiffel avec l'expression des souvenirs reconnaissants de la statue de la Liberté qui lui doit son ossature de fer." (Homage to M. Eiffel with the expression of my grateful memories of the Statue of Liberty which owes to him its iron skeleton.) Cited in Bermond, *Gustave Eiffel*, p. 303.
90. Wyn Wachhorst, *Thomas Alva Edison: An American Myth* (Cambridge: MIT Press, 1981).
91. The event of 25 April 1876 at Garnier's new Opera House included a concert by Rossini. Gounod was commissioned to compose for 600–800 male singers. But the event did not succeed and it also failed as a fundraiser. The press criticized the music as "tedious:" not even the "actress 'in a white tunic and a crown of raw gold, carrying the American flag' who depicted aspects of liberty in the charade... could draw a crowd." Catherine Hodeir, "The French Campaign," in New York Public Library, Liberty. *The French-American Statue*, p. 127.
92. Musée d'Orsay, Fonds Eiffel, ARO 1981-1296.
93. "With Mr. Edison on the Eiffel Tower," *Scientific American*, 14 September 1889, p. 166.
94. Jacques Noiray, *Le romancier et la machine*, vol. 2, p. 281. See also *La Nature* 29, no. 9 (1877), p. 276.
95. "With Mr. Edison on the Eiffel Tower," *Scientific American*, 14 September 1889, p. 166.
96. Ibid. The citation in Baldwin, *Edison: Inventing the Century*, p. 206, excises a sentence.
97. Lesseps, *Souvenirs*, p. 476.
98. Ibid.
99. Logan Marshall, *The Story of the Panama Canal: The Wonderful Account of the Gigantic Undertaking Commenced by the French, and Brought to Triumphant Completion by the United States* (N.p.: L. T. Myers, 1913), p. 101.
100. David McCullough, *The Path between the Seas: The Creation of the Panama Canal, 1870–1914* (New York: Simon and Schuster, 1977), p. 188. This is the best general history of the making of the Panama Canal.
101. Michael L. Conniff, *Black Labor on a White Canal* (Pittsburgh: University of Pittsburgh Press, 1985).
102. On Panama's geological specificity, see McCullough, *The Path Between the Seas.*, pp. 167–68.
103. Ibid.
104. Barbara Johnson, "Erasing Panama: Mallarmé and the Text of History," in *A World of Difference* (Baltimore: Johns Hopkins University Press, 1987), pp. 57–67; Johnson offers full texts in English translation in appendices of Stéphane Mallarmé's "News in Brief," pp. 201–3; and his poem "Or," p. 204.
105. See Bartholdi, *The Statue of Liberty Enlightening the World*, p. 58. During the 1884 presentation in Paris of the Statue of Liberty to the United States, "M. de Lesseps, after an allusion to the Panama Canal, 'which is the work of the citizens of the two Republics,' thanked M. Bartholdi...." See also Diesbach, *Ferdinand de Lesseps*, p. 367.
106. Bermond, *Gustave Eiffel*, p. 350.
107. See Paris, Musée d'Orsay, *1889: La Tour Eiffel et l'Exposition universelle* (Paris: Editions de la Réunion des Musées Nationaux, 1989), pp. 119–21.
108. Cited in Bermond, *Gustave Eiffel*, pp. 351, 356.
109. Mallarmé, "News in Brief," in Johnson, *A World of Difference*, p. 201.
110. Mallarmé, "Or," in Johnson, *A World of Difference*, p. 204.
111. The global stock market crash of fall 2008 was replete with images of the flow of capital become frozen; the goal was to "liquefy" the market so that cash and credit would "flow" once again.
112. On the Panama scandal, see Jean-Yves Mollier, *Le scandale de Panama* (Paris: Fayard, 1991); Bermond, *Gustave Eiffel*, pp. 345–70.
113. See Richard Thomson, "Camille Pissarro, 'Turpitudes Sociales,' and the Universal Exhibition of 1889," *Arts Magazine* 56, no. 8 (April 1982), pp. 82–88.
114. One worker fell to his death; another was injured and died three days later from gangrene. Bermond, *Gustave Eiffel*, pp. 296–97.
115. Jean Juarès, *Petite République*, 21 October 1901, "Truth or Fiction?" reprinted and translated in *Studies in Socialism*, trans. Mildred Minturn (1906; reprint New York: Kraus Reprint Co., 1970).

## Chapter 5: Panama's Cut

Aspects of this argument have been presented at Stanford University's Center for the Novel; Yale University; the University of Michigan, Ann Arbor; University of California, Berkeley; and University of Colorado, Boulder. I thank members of these audiences for their suggestions, especially Margaret Cohen, Jennifer Roberts, Caroline Arscott, Susan Siegfried, Steven Edwards, and T. J. Clark.

1. For example, on a German map of 1507, "the two continents [North and South America] are separated by a strait at Panama, though a secondary map... has them joined at the Isthmus of Panama." John Noble Wilford, *The Mapmakers* (1981; reprint, New York: Vintage, 2001), pp. 83–84.
2. Théophile Gautier, *Voyage en Égypte*, ed. Paolo Tortonese (1869; reprint Paris: La Boîte à Documents, 1991), pp. 151–52.
3. See, for example, Ralph Emmett Avery, *Greatest Engineering Feat in the World: Panama* (New York: Leslie-Judge Company, 1915).
4. Lucien N. B. (Lucien Napoléon Bonaparte) Wyse, *Le canal de Panama, l'isthme américain: Explorations, comparaison des traces étudiés, négociations, état des travaux* (Paris: Hachette et cie, 1886).
5. There are relatively few French representations of the making of the Panama Canal. This is surprising, given Lesseps' propensity to publicize and self-aggrandize. A few photographers recorded stages of construction. Several series are available at the BN Cabinet des Cartes. On Panama's jungle, see Stephen Frenkel, "Jungle Stories: North American Representations of Tropical Panama," *Geographical Review* 86, no. 3 (July 1996), pp. 317–33. Frenkel argues that while "the jungle may have a precise botanical meaning... it also encompasses much of what was mythical or negative about the tropics." p. 327. Frenkel quotes Candace Slater, "Amazonia as Edenic Narrative," in *Uncommon Ground: Toward Reinventing Nature*, ed. William Cronon (New York: W. W. *Norton*, 1995), p. 118: "[T]he jungle is an emphatically non-paradisal space. A figurative as well as literal maze (of housing laws, for instance), it is also a place of ruthless struggle for survival ('Man, its a real jungle out there,' one may say with a grimace). Rife with disease ('jungle fever') and decay ('jungle rot'), it is home to beasts and unsavory characters such as hoboes and tramps."
6. Barbara Johnson, "Erasing Panama: Mallarmé and the Text of History," in *A World of Difference* (Baltimore: Johns Hopkins University Press, 1987), pp. 57–67. See also Denis William Brogan, *France under the Republic: The Development of Modern France (1870–1939)* (New York: Harper & Brothers, 1940), p. 269: "Lesseps, it should be remembered, was not a professional engineer, but, in the original sense, of the word, an *entrepreneur.* One of his chief technical assistants, M. Bunau-Varilla, has described how politely and incredulously Lesseps listened to technical objections. 'He saw in them obviously only another of those engineers' ideas that had hampered him so much at Suez, and which he had got over by letting Nature and common sense have their way.'" Cited in Johnson, "Erasing Panama," p. 63.
7. David McCullough, *The Path between the Seas: The Creation of the Panama Canal, 1870–1914* (New York: Simon and Schuster, 1977), pp. 553.
8. The *Scientific American* article appeared on 14 September 1889; the Panama Canal Company had declared bankruptcy 14 December 1888; that is, nine months earlier.
9. Victor Gillam, "A Thing Well Begun Is Half Done," *Judge*, 7 October 1899, p. 240–41. Washington, D.C., Library of Congress.
10. John Major, *Prize Possession: The United States and the Panama Canal, 1903–1979* (Cambridge: Cambridge University Press, 1993), pp. 34–63; Tulio Halperín Donghi, *The Contemporary History of Latin America*, trans. John Charles Chasteen (Durham, Duke University Press, 1993), pp. 164–65. See also Michael LaRosa and German R. Mejia, eds., *The United States Discovers Panama: The Writings of Soldiers, Scholars, Scientists, and Scoundrels, 1850–1905* (Lanham, Md.: Rowman and Littlefield, 2004).
11. Cited in McCullough, *The Path between the Seas*, p. 384; Major, *Prize Possession*, p. 63.
12. Tom F. Peters, *Building the Nineteenth Century* (Cambridge: MIT Press, 1996), p. 281.
13. Victor Fournel, *Paris nouveau et Paris future* (1865), cited in Françoise Choay, *The Modern City: Planning in the Nineteenth Century* (New York: G. Braziller, 1969), p. 14; David Harvey, *Paris: Capital of Modernity* (New York: Routledge, 2003), p. 101.
14. Wolfgang Schivelbusch, *The Railway Journey: The Industrialization of Time and Space in the Nineteenth Century* (Berkeley and Los Angeles: University of California Press, 1977), p. 97.
15. Ibid., p. 96.
16. *Scientific American*, 26 November 1910.
17. Dynamite was patented in 1867 by Alfred Nobel, who at the end of his life founded the Nobel Peace Prize.
18. Herbert Alleyne, who arrived in the Canal Zone 15 June 1908; George Peters (Dominican), and Amos Parks (Barbados), Canal Zone Library Museum, "Isthmian Historical Society Competition for the Best True Stories of Life and Work on the Isthmus of Panama during the Construction of the Panama Canal," 1963, box 25, folder 3.
19. Albert Banister (St. Lucia). Ibid.
20. Slides still occur today. See for example Maximiliano De Puy, Manuel Barrelier, José F. Garcia, Carlos A. Reyes, and Robert Schuster, "Landslides on the Panama Canal—Recent Activity in the Gaillard Cut," *Geological Society of America Conference Paper* no. 38–7 (2002): "In 1991, the Panama Canal Commission (now the Panama Canal Authority) embarked on the U.S. $1 billion Canal Improvement Program, which included the second widening of the Gaillard Cut to permit two-way passage of Panamax-size ships. Excavation works for the Cut Widening Program (CWP) were completed in December 2001. As in the first widening, this second widening effort also brought a resurgence of landslide activity: several landslides occurred, both first-time slides and reactivations. These slides were triggered by various factors, such as improper excavation sequences, unpredictably high groundwater levels, and previously undetected geologic conditions. This increase in landslide activity is still in progress and is expected to continue as a result of the new Channel Deepening Program for the Gaillard Cut that began in January 2002." Available on the website of the Geological Society of America, http://gsa.confex. com/gsa/2002AM/ finalprogram/ index.html.
21. Frank Morton Todd, *The Story of the Exposition: Being the Official History of the International Celebration Held at San Francisco in 1915 to Commemorate the Discovery of the Pacific Ocean and the Construction of the Panama Canal*, 5 vols. (New York: G. P. Putnam's Sons, 1921), vol. 2, p. 43.
22. Brown continues: "But it simultaneously concretizes labor, rearticulating what Marx called the 'many-sided play of the muscles' that is lost within a mechanized labor system. Above all, it occults the mechanical achievement by refiguring the decade-long canal construction as the gesture of the individual, who is *whole* without being *part* of a labor, technological, or military force—without being a 'tool of the government.'" On the Hercules poster, entitled "The Thirteenth Labor of Hercules," see Bill Brown, "Science Fiction, the World's Fair, and the Prosthetics of Empire, 1910–1915," in *Cultures of United States Imperialism*, ed. Amy Kaplan

and Donald E. Pease (Durham, Duke University Press, 1993). Brown argues that Hercules is "a transcendental hero who emblematizes power.... And while colossal women (like Liberty, Columbia, and the Republic) typically symbolize the American nation, the male colossus now symbolizes the mechanical, international triumph." "This [imperialist] body emerges during a transition from the theatricalization of the American male that took place during the Spanish-American War—epitomized by Roosevelt's Rough Riders—to the theatricalization of American machinery in WWI.... This body emerges when American technology, as epitomized by the Panama Canal, appears as the new mechanical mode of American international triumph, when Roosevelt is famously photographed not on top of a horse but sitting at the controls of the Bucyrus shovel at Pedro Miguel, the startlingly white American in control of, but miniaturized by, the gargantuan, dark prosthetic machine."

23. Other than his own publications, there is a very scanty literature on Van Ingen (1858–1955). Most informative is a brief essay by Charles De Kay, "William B. Van Ingen, Mural Painter," *Architectural Record* (January– June 1903), pp. 322–34; his obituary in the *New York Times*, 7 February 1955, p. 21; Russell Sturgis, "Mr. Van Ingen's Lunettes in the Harrisburg State House," *Scribner's Magazine* 41, no. 4 (April 1907), pp. 509–12.
24. De Kay, "William B. Van Ingen, Mural Painter," p. 326.
25. Ibid., p. 329.
26. See also "Reflections of a Mural Painter," *Art World* 2 (July 1917), pp. 352–54.
27. According to an article published after Van Ingen's death in 1955, he made charcoal sketches; "Miraflores Locks Mural by W. B. Van Ingen, Administration Building, Balboa Heights, Canal Zone," *American Artist* 24 (November 1960), p. 10. Unfortunately, I have not been able to locate any preparatory studies.
28. "He was assisted by C. T. Berry and Ira Ramsen." Ibid. His studio was located on 58 West 57th Street. For the making of the murals see William B. Van Ingen, "The Making of a Series of Murals at Panama," *Art World* 3 (October 1917), pp. 17–19; "Art Notes," *New York Times*, 6 November 1914. The murals were restored in February 1960 by Frederic Taubes, a specialist in paint technology and also a contributing editor to *American Artist*. Taubes stated, "I found an assured, authoritative brushwork, attesting to the consummate skill of Mr. Van Ingen." For the restoration of Van Ingen's paintings, see "Miraflores Locks Mural by W. B. Van Ingen: Administration Building, Balboa Heights, Canal Zone," *American Artist* 24 (November 1960), p. 10. See also Panama Canal Company Records, Panama Canal Company, Washington, D.C., and Balboa, Republic of Panama. File 7220–A. Murals in the Administration Building; Albert B. Newman, "Restoring the Panama Mural Paintings," *Journal of Chemical Education* 7 (April 1930), reprinted in *Cooper Union Bulletin* 2 (April 1930), pp. 873–81.
29. Van Ingen, "The Making of a Series of Murals at Panama," *Art World* (October 1917), vol. 3, pp. 17–19.
30. Ibid., p. 17.
31. Ibid. See also "Art Notes," *New York Times*, 6 November 1914 (emphasis added): "M. Van Ingen had the practically impossible task of the impression produced on his mind of vastness, and of order in apparent confusion, of tremendous activity, of complicated construction, of definite lines and masses and colors, and of over-powering noise.... To get all this on canvas would mean a power of synthesis such as no modern artist has yet shown. Moreover, it probably was not quite synthesis that was wanted for the Administration Building, but *record of conditions necessarily of short duration. The water has covered all this scaffolding erected in opposition to the angry defiance of nature.*" "The making of the Culebra Cut was shown in a canvas about 90 feet long, which is now at the Isthmus. A sketch of it is at the Lotos Club."
32. Immanuel Kant, "Analytic of the Sublime," in *Critique of Judgement*, trans. James Creed Meredith (1911 and 1928; reprint, Oxford: Clarendon Press, 1991), pp. 90–134. See also chapter 1 here.
33. Oliver Wendell Holmes, "The Stereoscope and the Stereograph," *Atlantic Monthly* 3 (1859), pp. 738–48, reprinted in *Photography in Print: Writings from 1816 to the Present*, ed. Vicki Goldberg (Albuquerque: University of New Mexico Press, 1988), p. 112. Between 1859 and 1863, Oliver Wendell Holmes, Harvard savant, published three articles in the *Atlantic Monthly*. Oliver Wendell Holmes, "Doings of the Sunbeam," *Atlantic Monthly* 12 (July 1863), p. 8. This essay was written in 1862.
34. Holmes, "The Stereoscope and the Stereograph." Emphasis in original.
35. Alan Trachtenberg, *Reading American Photographs: Images as History: Mathew Brady to Walker Evans* (New York: Hill and Wang, 1989), pp. 16–19; Allan Sekula, "Photography between Labour and Capital," in *Mining Photographs and Other Pictures, 1948–1968: A Selection from the Negative Archives of Shedden Studio, Glace Bay, Cape Breton, photographs by Leslie Shedden*, ed. Benjamin Buchloh and Robert Wilkie (Halifax, N.S.: Press of the Nova Scotia College of Art and Design and the University College of Cape Breton, 1983), pp. 193–268, p. 220.
36. The great period of growth the stereograph industry was from the late 1880s through 1914; Earle, *Points of View*, p. 18.
37. *Oliver Wendell Holmes on the Stereoscope and Stereograph* (New York: Underwood and Underwood, 1898).
38. More patents were taken out for stereoscopes between 1903 and 1905 than at any other time; Earle, *Points of View*, p. 76.
39. John Waldsmith, *Stereo Views: An Illustrated History and Price Guide* (Radnor, Penn.: Wallace-Homestead, 1991), p. 181. On the marketing of stereoviews, see Howard S. Becker, "Stereographs: Local, National, and International Art Worlds," in Earle, *Points of View*, p. 93: "The large scale migration of imagery coincided with highly organized merchandising schemes, designed to move the output of industrialized producers." Denis Cosgrove, "Landscape and the European Sense of Sight—Eyeing Nature," in *Handbook of Cultural Geography* (London: Sage, 2003), p. 250: "Sight in the modern world is increasingly prosthetic, directed and experienced through a vast array of mechanical aids to vision which radically extend the capacities of the unassisted eye: lenses, cameras, light projectors, screens and scopes."
40. For "dream-traveling," see *The Living Age*, 30 July 1904, pp. 310–14; cited in Earle, *Points of View*, p. 76. "Cases are known where women in very humble life have spent their pence in the collection of picture-cards.... What means is there, other than the dream-travelling which is engendered by the picture post-card...to know that far from England there are places of rare beauty and of very living interest?" The role of the booming media and photography in transmitting images of the West to a mass public has been discussed by John Rennie Short, *Representing the Republic: Mapping the United States, 1600–1900* (London: Reaktion, 2001), p. 197.
41. Earle, *Points of View*, p. 19.
42. Becker, "Stereographs," pp. 91–92: Early stereography then consisted of regional practitioners producing for limited audiences.... In a short time, however, these local operators, professional and amateur, were replaced by large companies which provided thousands of views to their customers.... Large companies introduced assembly line methods of production and various kinds of mechanization so they could produce enormous numbers of stereocards. They further revolutionized the distribution of views by marketing them in a series, with as many as a hundred cards covering a single subject."
43. Dennis Longwell, "Panama Canal Photographs by Ernest 'Red' Hallen," *Art Journal* 36, no. 2 (Winter 1976–77), pp. 123–25, concerning an exhibition at the Museum of Modern Art, New York City. The best collection of Hallen's photographs is at West Point, where Goethals's copies reside. Hallen took photographs in Panama from 1907 until his retirement from government service in 1937.
44. Susan Schulten, *The Geographical Imagination in America*, 1880–1950 (Chicago: University of Chicago Press, 2001), p. 252 n. 46.
45. *Scientific American*, 3 June 1905; 17 July 1909 (two-page spreads of panoramic photos at Gatun Dam that make it seem horizontal); 6 February 1909 (includes a two-page spread of a panoramic photograph of Culebra Cut); 26 November 1910; 20 April 1912; 8 July 1912 (about slides at the Culebra Cut) ; 9 November 1912; 10 May 1913 (about slides at the Culebra Cut); 14 June 1913.
46. Schulten has illuminated how the institutionalization of the discipline of geography in the United States was connected to the history of the Panama Canal; *The Geographical Imagination in America*, p. 76: "At the University of Pennsylvania, geography originated as a byproduct of the government's efforts to build an isthmian canal in Latin America. Two economists, asked to predict the canal's implications for trade, realized that such questions demanded geographic research. As a result, Emory Johnson and his student J. Russell Smith, founded the Department of Geography within the University's Wharton School of Finance." J. Russell Smith had come to geography from economics after work with the Isthmian Canal Commission in 1900. After World War I he would begin Columbia University's Geography Department, also within a School of Business; ibid., p. 83. See also Virginia M. Rowley, *J. Russell Smith: Geographer, Educator, and Conservationist* (Philadelphia: University of Pennsylvania Press, 1964); for his Panama Canal report, pp. 21–23.
47. Schulten, *The Geographical Imagination in America*, p. 83.
48. Earle, *Points of View*, p. 19. "The American stereograph was a commercially successful medium because it entered society predisposed to what it offered."
49. David Brewster, "Account of a Binocular Camera, and of a Method of Obtaining Drawings of Full Length and Colossal Statues, and of Living Bodies, which can be Exhibited as solids by the Stereoscope," *Transactions of the Royal Scottish Society of Arts* 3 (Edinburgh: R. Grant, 1851), pp. 259–64, reprinted Nicholas J. Wade, ed., *Brewster and Wheatstone on Vision* (London: Academic Press, 1983), pp. 218–21. "Stereoscopic Journeys," *Eclectic Magazine of Foreign Literature, Science, and Art* (New York) (April 1857), pp. 560–61. For secondary sources, see Robert J. Silverman, "The Stereoscope and Photographic Depiction in the Nineteenth Century," *Technology and Culture* 34, no. 4 (October 1993), pp. 729–56; Nancy M. West, "Fantasy, Photography, and the Marketplace: Oliver Wendell Holmes and the Stereoscope," *Nineteenth-Century Contexts* 19 (1996) pp. 231–58; Laura Burd Schiavo, "From Phantom Image to Perfect Vision: Physiological Optics, Commercial Photography, and the Popularization of the Stereoscope," in *New Media*, 1740–1915, ed. Lisa Gitelman and Geoffrey B. Pingree (Cambridge: MIT Press, 2003), pp. 113–37; Rosalind Krauss, "Photography's Discursive Spaces: Landscape/View," *Art Journal* 42 (Winter 1982); Michel Freziot, "Surface and Depth," in *Paris in 3-D: From Stereoscopy to Virtual Reality, 1850–2000*, in association with the Musée Carnavalet, Museum of the History of

Paris (Paris: Booth-Clibborn Editions, 2000), pp. 30–35; Jacques Ninio, "Three Dimensional Perception," in *Paris in 3-D*, pp. 17–22; Jonathan Crary, *Techniques of the Observer: On Vision and Modernity in the Nineteenth Century* (Cambridge: MIT Press, 1992); for an illuminating criticism of Crary's *Techniques of the Observer*, see David Phillips, "Modern Vision," *Oxford Art Journal* 16, no. 1 (1993), pp. 129–38.

50. Wheatstone, "Contributions to the Physiology of Vision —Part the First: On some Remarkable, and hitherto Unobserved, Phenomena of Binocular Vision," *Philosophical Transactions of the Royal Society* 128 (London 1838), pp. 371–94; reprinted in Wade, *Brewster and Wheatstone on Vision*, p. 70.
51. On size constancy, see Edwin G. Boring, "Size-Constancy in a Picture," *American Journal of Psychology* 77, no. 3 (September 1964), pp. 494–98; C. Oliver Weber and Natalie Bicknell, "The Size Constancy Phenomenon in Stereoscopic Space," *American Journal of Psychology* 47, no. 3 (July 1935), pp. 436–48; Stanley Coren, "A Size-Contrast Illusion without Physical Size Differences," *American Journal of Psychology* 84, no. 4 (December 1971), pp. 565–66.
52. Weber and Bicknell, "The Size Constancy Phenomenon in Stereoscopic Space," p. 436.
53. Ibid., pp. 436–37.
54. Edmund Burke, *A Philosophical Enquiry into the Origin of Our Ideas of the Sublime and the Beautiful*, ed. James T. Boulton (1757; reprint, Notre Dame: University of Notre Dame Press, 1958), part 2, section 7, "Vastness," p. 72.
55. Holmes, "The Stereoscope and the Stereograph," p. 110. "The very things which an artist would leave out or render imperfectly, the photograph takes infinite care with, and so makes its illusions perfect. What is the picture of a drum without the marks on its head...?"
56. In 1858 Warren De la Rue made the first stereograph of the moon; he knew he would face criticism. In his own defense, he reiterated Sir John Herschel's opinion that "the view is such as would be seen by *a giant with eyes thousands of miles apart:* after all, the stereoscope affords such a view as we should get if we possessed a perfect model of the moon and placed it at a suitable distance from the eyes, and we may be well satisfied to possess such a means of extending our knowledge respecting the moon, by thus availing ourselves of the giant eyes of science." Silverman, "The Stereoscope and Photographic Depiction in the Nineteenth Century," pp. 750–53.
57. *Joseph Pennell's Pictures of the Panama Canal: Reproductions of a Series of Lithographs Made by Him on the Isthmus of Panama January–March 1812* (London: Heninemann, 1913).
58. Other painters of the finished canal include E. J. Read, whose watercolors illustrate *Panama and the Canal in Pictures and Prose* by Willis J. Abbot (London: Syndicate, 1913); also Jonas Lie, *Culebra Cut*, Detroit Institute of the Arts. Many of Read's oil and watercolor paintings, made between 1913 and 1914, are at the Canal Zone Library Museum, Panama.
59. Joseph Pennell, "Is Photography among the Fine Arts?" (1897), excerpted in Goldberg, *Photography in Print*, pp. 210–13; here pp. 211–12.
60. Ibid, p. 212.
61. For example, *Paradise Rocks—Study at Paradise, Newport, Rhode Island*, 1884; The Metropolitan Museum of Art, New York City. "This picture is his earliest landscape known to have been based on a specific photograph—a commercial stereograph view that he owned, which descended in his family." The Metropolitan Museum also has one of the watercolors La Farge made in 1887 and 1888, after a trip to Japan, that are based on photographs. The drawings were then made into wood engravings for use as magazine illustrations.
62. Longwell, "Panama Canal Photographs by Ernest 'Red' Hallen."
63. David E. Nye, *American Technological Sublime* (Cambridge: MIT Press, 1994).
64. Van Ingen, *Exhibition of Mural Paintings by Mr. William B. Van Ingen to be Placed in the Rotunda of the Administration Building on the Panama Canal Zone*, November 7, 1914, p. 2 (unpaginated) (New York), 1914.
65. *Joseph Pennell's Pictures of the Panama Canal*, p. 14. "I did not go to Panama to study engineering—which I know nothing about; or social problems—which I had not time to master; or Central American politics— which we are in for; but to draw the Canal as it is...." Interestingly, he adds "The dam, to me, was too big and too vague to draw."
66. Van Ingen, "The Making of a Series of Murals at Panama," p. 19.
67. Frederic J. Haskin, *The Panama Canal* (Garden City: Doubleday, Page & Co., 1914), p. 24.
68. "To go to the Culebra is as if one were privileged to watch the building of the Pyramids." Frank Morton Todd, *The Story of the Exposition*, vol. 1, pp. 22–23.
69. Jonathan Crary, "Géricault, the Panorama, and Sites of Reality in the Early Nineteenth Century," *Grey Room* 9 (Fall 2002), p. 21: "[T]he related impression of completeness, of an inexhaustible inclusion of the real, is achieved through the novel 360-degree format of the image. Like the name itself, the setup of the panorama presumes to present a total view, characterized by a seemingly self-evident wholeness. [...The] adjective panoramic in the nineteenth century [...suggested] a full 360-degree view that has no obstructions, nothing blocking an optical appropriation of it."
70. On the greater popularity in the United States of moving panoramas which were also more transportable, see Stephan Oettermann, *The Panorama: History of a Mass Medium*, trans. Deborah Lucas Schneider (New York: Zone Books, 1997), p. 323. On panoramas, see also Angela Miller, "Space as Destiny: The Panorama Vogue in Mid-Nineteenth-Century America," in Irving Lavin, ed., *World Art: Themes of Unity in Diversity: Acts of the XXVIth International Congress of the History of Art* (University Park: Pennsylvania State University Press, 1989), pp. 739–42; Ralph Hyde, *Panoramania! The Art and Entertainment of the "All-Embracing" View* (London: Trefoil in association with the Barbican Art Gallery, 1988), pp. 125–30; Crary, "Géricault, the Panorama, and Sites of Reality in the Early Nineteenth Century"; Bernard Comment, *The Painted Panorama*, trans. Anne-Marie Glasheen (New York: Harry Abrams, 1999); François Robichon, "Le Panorama, spectacle de l'histoire," *Le Mouvement Social* 131 (April– June 1985), pp. 65–86; Oliver Grau, *Virtual Art: From Illusion to Immersion*, trans. Gloria Custance (Cambridge: MIT Press, 2003).
71. De Kay, "William B. Van Ingen, Mural Painter," pp. 327–28.
72. My emphasis. Julia Ballerini, "Photography Conscripted: Horace Vernet, Gérard de Nerval and Maxime Du Camp in Egypt" (Ph.D. dissertation, CUNY, 1987), p. 219.
73. De Kay, "William B. Van Ingen, Mural Painter," pp. 323–24.
74. "Art Notes," *New York Times*, 6 November 1914, p. 10.
75. In a different context, Kevin Hetherington discusses the problem of disposal in *Capitalism's Eye: Cultural Spaces of the Commodity* (New York: Routledge, 2007); see especially chap. 7, "Disposal and the Display Case," pp. 157–79. Hetherington is expanding on the work of Rolland Munro: "Munro suggests that dirt or pollution can never be fully disposed of.... Munro recognizes that representational stability, associated with acts of disposal, is never ultimately achieved as a form of closure. The idea that societies develop conduits of disposal that are themselves fluid and uncertain is a useful one here. Yet rather than see the rubbish bin as the archetypal conduit of disposal, I suggest the door is a better example. Not

only do doors allow traffic in both directions when open, they can also be closed to keep things outside/ inside, present/absent, at least temporarily and provisionally."

76. Frank Morton Todd, *The Story of the Exposition*, vol. 3, p. 94.
77. Ibid., vol.5, p.85.
78. Ibid.
79. Goethals' letter is cited in Ehring Morison, ed. *The Letters of Theodore Roosevelt* (Cambridge: Harvard University Press, 1954) vol.5, p.xvii; and McCullough, *The Path Between the Seas*, pp.510, 512.
80. Van Ingen, "The Making of a Series of Murals at Panama."

### Chapter 6: Toyland

This chapter is indebted to the stimulating conversation and research of Erica Lee, model maker and thinker. Formerly a student of architecture and now a graduate student of history, Erica is an exceptionally creative interlocutor.

1. Karl Marx, *Capital, A Critique of Political Economy*, trans. David McLellan (Oxford: Oxford University Press, 1999) vol. 1, chapter 15, section 1, p. 238. On Marx and the machine, see Nathan Rosenberg, "Marx as a Student of Technology," in *Inside the Black Box: Technology and Economics* (Cambridge: Cambridge University Press, 1982), pp. 34–51; Donald Mackenzie, "Marx and the Machine," *Technology and Culture* 25 (1984), pp. 473–502.
2. See chapter 4. Cited in Jacques Noiray, *Le romancier et la machine: L'image de la machine dans le roman français (1850– 1900)*, 2 vols. (Paris: Corti, 1982), vol. 1, p. 247.
3. The word *model* stems from the Latin term *modellus*, the diminutive of the Latin *modulus*, a diminutive of modus, which means to measure. Albert C. Smith asserts that "The word model also relates to the word 'modest' through the Latin modus. 'Modest' means having a limited and not exaggerated estimate of one's ability or worth, or lacking in vanity or conceit, or not bold or self-assertive.... Modest also means not in excess... quite similar to the word 'moderate' which means characterized by an avoidance of extremes in behavior." Smith also draws attention to the prophetic role of models; they predict a future. *Architectural Model as Machine: A New View of Models from Antiquity to the Present Day* (Oxford: Architectural Press, 2004), p. 68. On models, see also Karen Moon, *Modeling Messages: The Architect and the Model* (New York: Monacelli Press, 2005); Jasper Halfmann and Clod Zillich, "Reality and Reduced Model," *Studio International* 193, no. 986 (March–April 1977).
4. Erica Lee, communication to author, June 2008.
5. Smith, *Architectural Model as Machine*. The Italian Renaissance architect Alberti insisted that models should include neither color nor ornament, partly because he wanted to ensure that the patron was attentive to the architect's craft not the model maker's. Ibid., p. 28.
6. Marx, *Capital*, chapter 1, section 4, "The Fetishism of Commodities and the Secret thereof," pp. 43, 47.
7. See for example, a subscription card: "Statue of 'Liberty Enlightening the World.' The Committee in charge of the construction of the base and pedestal for the reception of this great work, in order to raise funds for its completion, have prepared a miniature Statuette, six inches in height, the Statue bronzed, Pedestal nickel-silvered, which they are now delivering to subscribers throughout the United States at One Dollar Each. This attractive souvenir and Mantel or Desk ornament is a perfect facsimile of the model furnished by the artist. The Statuette, in same metal, twelve inches high, at Five Dollars Each, delivered. The designs of Statue and Pedestal are protected by U.S. Patents, and the models can only be furnished by this Committee. RICHARD BUTLER, Secretary. American Committee of the Statue of Liberty. 33 Mercer Street, New York."
8. New York Public Library, *Liberty: The French-American Statue in Art and History*, exhibition catalogue (New York: Harper and Row, 1986), p. 109.
9. Beverly Gordon calls this category of souvenir "piece-of-the-rock souvenirs." Beverly Gordon, "Souvenir: Message of the Extraordinary," *Journal of Popular Culture* 20, no. 3 (Winter 1986), p. 141.
10. Patent Design No. 11,023 dated 18 February 1879. The date of the patent was inscribed on the six- and twelve-inch models. These models are reproduced in *Liberty: The French-American Statue*, p. 109.
11. Ibid.
12. The Bartholdi and Butler papers at the New York Public Library contain repeated, sometimes desperate, requests from Bartholdi for Butler to resolve his conflicts with different producers of models.
13. See Jacques De Caso, "Serial Sculpture in Nineteenth-Century France," in *Metamorphoses in Nineteenth-Century Sculpture*, ed. Jeanne L. Wasserman (Cambridge: Fogg Museum / Harvard University Press, 1975), pp. 1–27; see also Anne Middleton Wagner, *Jean-Baptiste Carpeaux: Sculptor of the Second Empire* (New Haven: Yale University Press, 1986). On 6 December 1885, the *New York Times* reported that "Various parties have infringed [Bartholdi's] patents" and noted that an injunction had been granted to prevent unauthorized manufacture of imitations of the statue. In 1883 a copyright had been granted to a Hermann Follmer to produce a model of *Liberty*, about which Bartholdi complained in a letter to Richard Butler dated 28 July 1883. The New York Public Library holds all letters by Bartholdi to Butler. Cited in Edward L. Kallop Jr., with the assistance of Catherine Hodeir, "Models and Reductions of Liberty," in *Liberty: The French-American Statue*, pp. 224–29. I have depended on this key source by Kallop. See also Anne Cannon Palumbo and Ann Uhry Abrams, "Proliferation of the Image," in *Liberty: The French-American Statue*, pp. 230–65.
14. Kallop, "Models and Reductions of Liberty," p. 225. Avoiron et cie, specialists in "imitation bronze" (zinc), had the contract with Bartholdi from 1878 to 1886, when Bartholdi unsuccessfully attempted to shift to an American manufacture. The Avoiron reproductions were inscribed with copyright dates.
15. According to Kallop, only five reproductions by Thiébaut Frères exist today, one of which served as part of the enlargement process for the thirty-six-foot replica dedicated on 4 July 1889 on the Ile de Cygnes in Paris. Ibid.
16. Contract dated 22 November 1887. Jean-Pierre Spilmont and Michel Friedman, *Mémoires de la Tour Eiffel* (Paris: Grasset, 1983), p. 125.
17. The Conseil's ruling on 9 March 1889 added that Eiffel, as a "concessionaire," "could only exercise the restrictive rights enumerated in the act of concession, among which the exclusive right of reproduction of the tower does not figure." Avis du Conseil d'État, séance du 9 mars 1889, *Bulletin officiel de l'Exposition de 1889*, no. 122 (16 March 1889).
18. Spilmont and Friedman, *Mémoires de la Tour Eiffel*, p. 160. Frédéric Seitz, *La Tour Eiffel: Cent ans de sollicitude* (Paris: Belin-Herscher, 2001), p. 93.
19. Spilmont and Friedman, *Mémoires de la Tour Eiffel*, pp. 158–59.
20. Robert Morris, "Size Matters," *Critical Inquiry* 26, no. 3 (Spring 2000), pp. 474–87. Morris cites Burke's distinction between the beautiful and the sublime ("Only big signs have a shot at masculine sublime metaphors."). On miniatures, see chapter 7, "Miniature," in Gaston Bachelard, *The Poetics of Space*, trans. Maria Jolas (1958; reprint, Boston: Beacon Press, 1968), pp. 148–72; Susan Stewart, *On Longing: Narratives of the Miniature, the Gigantic, the Souvenir, the Collection* (Durham, N.C.: Duke University Press, 1993); Claude Lévi-Strauss, *The Savage Mind* (Chicago: University of Chicago Press, 1962), pp. 23–25; John Mack, *The Art of Small Things* (Cambridge: Harvard University Press, 2007).
21. Morris, "Size Matters"; Edmund Burke, *A Philosophical Enquiry into the Origin of Our Ideas of the Sublime and the Beautiful*, ed. James T. Boulton (1757; reprint, Notre Dame: University of Notre Dame Press, 1958).
22. Lévi-Strauss, *The Savage Mind*, pp. 23–24.
23. Rosemarie Blettner, cited in Philippe Boudon, "L'Amérique c'est grand, ou 'How big is big?'" in *Américanisme et modernité: L'idéal américain dans l'architecture*, ed. J. L. Cohen and H. Damisch (Paris: Flammarion, 1993), pp. 25–36.
24. Lévi-Strauss, *The Savage Mind*, p. 24.
25. On souvenirs, see Britt Salvesen, "'The Most Magnificent, Useful and Interesting Souvenir': Representations of the International Exhibition of 1862," *Visual Resources* 13, no. 1 (1997) pp. 1–32; Thomas Richards, *The Commodity Culture of Victorian England: Advertising and Spectacle, 1851–1914* (Stanford, Calif.: Stanford University Press, 1990); Paul Greenhalgh, *Ephemeral Vistas: The Expositions Universelles, Great Exhibitions, and World's Fairs, 1851–1939* (Manchester: Manchester University Press, 1988); and Stewart, *On Longing*; Amy F. Ogata, "Viewing Souvenirs: Peepshows and the International Expositions," *Journal of Design History* 15, no. 2 (2002), pp. 69–82; Gordon, "Souvenir: Message of the Extraordinary," pp. 135–36. Michael Hitchcock, introduction to *Souvenirs: The Material Culture of Tourism*, ed. Michael Hitchcock and Ken Teague (Aldershot: Ashgate, 2000), p. 13. Michael Hitchcock briefly mentions alterations of scale in souvenirs: "Souvenirs, though often based on traditional art forms, are often miniaturized to suit the needs of long distance, especially airborne, travelers.... But there is a counter trend in which ordinary-sized functional items (e.g. combs, spoons, knives) are enlarged. These items might otherwise be insufficiently attractive in their normal state to spark the interest of potential customers and 'gigantism' might be regarded as a crude kind of value-added."
26. Paul Bluysen, *Paris en 1889: Souvenirs et croquis de l'Exposition* (Paris: n.p., 1890).
27. Stewart, *On Longing*, pp. 47–60.
28. Monique Mosser, "Models of French Architecture in the Age of Enlightenment," *Daidalos* (15 December 1981), p. 73, refers to the "symbolic—relatively magic—implications of the reducing process." "It creates, as it were, a concentrated picture, the quintessence of the monument in small format."
29. Bachelard, *The Poetics of Space*, pp. 154–55. See especially chapter 7, "Miniature."
30. Walter Benjamin, "The Work of Art in the Age of Mechanical Reproduction," in *Illuminations* (New York: Schocken Books, 1969).
31. Geraldine A. Johnson, ed., *Sculpture and Photography: Envisioning the Third Dimension* (Cambridge University Press, 1998), p. 4.
32. David Brewster, "Account of a Binocular Camera, and of a Method of Obtaining Drawings of Full Length and Colossal Statues, and of Living Bodies, which can be Exhibited as solids by the Stereoscope," *Transactions of the Royal Scottish Society of Arts* 3 (1851), pp. 259–64, reprinted in *Brewster and Wheatstone on Vision*, ed. Nicholas J. Wade (London: Academic Press, 1983), pp. 218–21. Brewster explains that for an object to appear in relief, we need information about the sides of the object normally eclipsed when the object is seen at a great distance. If, however, we distance the two lenses from one another, this information can be recovered in order to enhance our sense of the colossal object's three-dimensionality: "As it is

the outer parts or surfaces of a large statue that are invisible, its great outline and largest parts must be best seen in the reduced copy; and consequently, its relief or third dimension in space, must be much greater in the reduced copy."

33. Robert J. Silverman, "The Stereoscope and Photographic Depiction in the Nineteenth century," *Technology and Culture* 34, no. 4 (October 1993), p. 748.
34. "Artistes contre la tour Eiffel," *Le Temps*, 1887, p. 2; English translation in *The Eiffel Tower: A Tour de Force*, exhibition catalogue, ed. Phillip Dennis Cate (New York: Grolier Club, 1989), p. 31.
35. J. K. Huysmans, "Le Fer," in *Certains* (Paris: Tresse & Stock, 1889), pp. 175–77.
36. The series was published in 1902 but it was based on drawings and photographs made between 1887 and 1892. On Rivière, see Armond Fields, *Henri Rivière* (Salt Lake City: Gibbs M. Smith, 1983); Paris, Musée d'Orsay, *Henri Rivière, graveur et photographe*, exhibition catalogue (Paris: Ed. de la Réunion des Musées Nationaux, 1988); Mariel Oberthür, *Henri Rivière: Connu, méconnu* (Semur-en-Auxois: Editions Spiralinthe, 2004).
37. Roland Barthes, *The Eiffel Tower and Other Mythologies*, trans. Richard Howard (New York: Hill and Wang, 1979), p. 3.
38. Stephan Oettermann, *The Panorama: History of a Mass Medium* (New York: Zone Books, 1997), p. 171.
39. Erica Lee, communication to author, spring 2008.
40. Anonymous letter to Eiffel, 1889, Paris, Musée d'Orsay, Fonds Eiffel, ARO 1981–1313 Letters to Eiffel.
41. Anonymous letter to Eiffel, September 1889, Paris, Musée d'Orsay, Fonds Eiffel, ARO 1981–1313 Letters to Eiffel.
42. Hugues le Roux, "Une ascension de la Tour Eiffel," *L'Exposition de Paris*, no. 8 (1 April 1889), pp. 55–59. Translated in Cate, *The Eiffel Tower: A Tour de Force*, p. 48.
43. Ibid., p. 47.
44. Bluysen, *Paris en 1889*.
45. William B. Van Ingen, "The Making of a Series of Murals at Panama," *Art World* 3 (October 1917), pp. 17–19.
46. Stephen Frenkel, "Jungle Stories: North American Representations of Tropical Panama," *Geographical Review* 86, no. 3 (July 1996), pp. 317–33. One contemporary celebrated "the zeal and taste of their mistresses," women who made "veritable gardens of beauty—miniature representatives of the jungle." Joseph Bucklin Bishop, *The Panama Gateway* (New York: Charles Scribner's Sons, 1913), p. 311, cited in Frenkel, "Jungle Stories," p. 330.
47. Panama Canal Commission, Documents at the National Archives Record Center, Greenbelt, Md. (28 D 311921): "A park-like effect has been aimed at, with open vistas, to the avoidance of the close confusion of the jungle into which native vegetation lapses when left alone or indiscriminately cultivated"; cited in Frenkel, "Jungle Stories," p. 330.
48. Frank Morton Todd, *The Story of the Exposition: Being the Official History of the International Celebration Held at San Francisco in 1915 to Commemorate the Discovery of the Pacific Ocean and the Construction of the Panama Canal*, 5 vols. (New York: G. P. Putnam's Sons, 1921), vol. 5, pp. 161–62.
49. Bill Brown, "Science Fiction, the World's Fair, and the Prosthetics of Empire, 1910–1915," in *Cultures of United States Imperialism*, ed. Amy Kaplan and Donald E. Pease (Durham, N.C.: Duke University Press, 1993), p. 142.
50. Todd, *The Story of the Exposition*, vol. 2, p. 151.
51. Panama-Pacific International Exposition Company, *The Panama Canal at San Francisco* (San Francisco: Panama Canal Exhibition Co., 1915), p. 4.
52. Ibid.
53. Ibid, p. 5.
54. Ibid.
55. Ibid., p. 3.
56. Todd, *The Story of the Exposition*, vol. 2, p. 150.
57. Letter by "F. C. Boggs, Chief of the Washington Office, Panama Canal" writing from "San Francisco, Cal., Feb. 26, 1915 [to] The Panama Canal Exhibition Company, San Francisco, California." Published in Panama-Pacific International Exposition Company, *The Panama Canal at San Francisco*, p. 3.
58. Panama-Pacific International Exposition Company, *The Panama Canal at San Francisco*, p. 3.
59. Todd, *The Story of the Exposition*, vol. 2, p. 151.
60. Panama-Pacific International Exposition Company, *The Panama Canal at San Francisco*, p. 6.
61. Literary scholar Bill Brown has called the effect a "prefiguration of aerial cinematography." "Science Fiction, the World's Fair, and the Prosthetics of Empire," p. 142.
62. Panama-Pacific International Exposition Company, *The Panama Canal at San Francisco*, p. 8.
63. While *The Pony Engine* was published in 1910 and another briefer version was published in 1906 as *Anyone Can*, the most famous publication of this story appeared in 1930 by "Watty Piper."
64. Ralph E. Avery, *The Greatest Engineering Feat in the World at Panama* (New York: Leslie-Judge Company, 1915), p. 376.

### Coda

1. "Panama Canal-Panamax," GlobalSecuity.org website http://www.globalsecurity.org/military/ facility/panama-canal-panamax.htm
2. I saw Alan Sekula's *The Lottery of the Sea* as a film-in-progress at the Maritime Modernity Conference, Center for Study of the Novel, organized by Margaret Cohen, April 2005.
3. The world's largest supertanker was built in 1979 at the Oppama Shipyard of Sumitomo Heavy Industries, Ltd. as the *Seawise Giant*. This ship was built with a capacity of 564,763 DWT, a length overall of 458.45 metres (1,504.1 ft) and a draft of 24.611 metres (80.74 ft). It had 46 tanks, 31,541 square metres (339,500 sq ft) of deck, and was too large to pass through the English Channel. *Seawise Giant* was renamed *Happy Giant* in 1989 and *Jahre Viking* in 1991. From 1979 to 2004, it was owned by Loki Stream, at which point it was bought by First Olsen Tankers, renamed *Knock Nevis*, and converted into a permanently moored storage tanker. In 2009 it was sold to an Indian Breaker Company, and renamed *Mont*. It was subsequently beached and is awaiting scrapping.
4. Panama Canal Authority (ACP), *Proposal for the Expansion of the Panama Canal. Third Set of Locks Project*, April 24, 2006, p. 19.
5. Ibid., pp. 22–23.
6. Ibid., p. 37. "This program consists of: (1) implementation of an enhanced locks lighting system; (2) construction of two tie-up stations in Gaillard Cut; (3) Gaillard Cut widening from 192 to 218 m (from 630' to 715'); (4) improvements to the tugboats fleet; (5) implementation of the carousel lockage system in Gatun locks; (6) development of an improved vessel scheduling system; (7) deepening of Gatun Lake navigational channels from 11.3 to 10.4 meters (from 37' to 34') PLD; (8) modification of all locks structures to allow an additional draft of about 0.30m (1'); (9) deepening of the Pacific and Atlantic entrances; and, (10) construction of a new spillway in Gatun, for flood control."
7. Howard W. French, "In World Skyscraper Race, It Isn't Lonely at the Top," *The New York Times*, May 8, 2007.
8. Ibid.
9. Geraldine Bedell, "Burj Khalifa—a bleak symbol of Dubai's era of bling," *The Observer*, January 10, 2010. The subtitle reads: "Dubai's stunning 828m skyscraper is an ideal monument for an era of credit-fuelled over-consumption—irresponsible and unsustainable."
10. Paul Goldberger, "Castle in the Air. Dubai reaches for the sky," *The New Yorker*, March 30, 2010. It was "designed by the architect Adrian Smith and the engineer William Baker, both of Skidmore, Owings

& Merrill. (Smith left the firm during construction, and Baker and his colleagues George Efstathiou and Eric Tomich saw the project through to completion.) Skidmore has built plenty of iconic skyscrapers before."

11. Ibid.
12. Goldberger draws attention to the building's complex shape—like the curvaceous, irregular footprint of the Statue of Liberty, a statue made into a building. See Greg Lynn's discussion of the Statue of Liberty in relation to his own architectural project for a 1991 Chicago competition which attempted to maintain "an interior structure that is provisional rather than essential." Lynn is attracted to the ways the Statue of Liberty blown up large and made into a building with an engineered interior produced a novel, unforeseen architecture: "The effects of the colossal scale [in the Statue of Liberty with Eiffel's armature] then, are visible not only in the enlargement of the singular body, but more important, in the unpredicted local relationships of disparate building systems.... The elements that negotiate between the trusses and the draped body could not be predicted within either the architectural or the sculptural discourse." "Multiplicitous and Inorganic Bodies," *Assemblage* 19, December 1992, pp. 32–49; here pp. 40–42; reprinted in *Folds, Bodies & Blobs: Collected Essays*, Brussels: La Lettre volée, 1998, pp. 33–62.
13. Bedell, "Burj Khalifa—a bleak symbol of Dubai's era of bling," just its air-conditioning system uses the amount of energy required to melt 12,500 tons of ice a day.
14. Michael Sheridan, "Visitors trapped in Dubai's Burj Khalifa tower days before building closed," *New York Daily News*, February 10, 2010.
15. See the BBC investigation, "The Dark Side of the Dubai Dream," by Lila Allen, April 6, 2009. Laborers have been reported to have earned as little as UK£2.84 a day. Allen reports that the workers lived in abysmal overcrowded shanty towns and they often were not paid; sometimes their passports were confiscated. [http://news.bbc.co.uk/2/hi/ uk_news/magazine/7985361.stm]
16. Andy Hoffman, "Dubai's Burj Khalifa: Built out of opulence; named for its savior," *Globe and Mail*, January 4, 2010.
17. According to the Panama Canal Authority (ACP) Press Release of March 12, 2010, the recognition was awarded by *Latin Lawyer Magazine*.
18. Jim Krane, (New York: St. Martin's Press), 2009.
19. Stéphane Mallarmé, "News in Brief," in Barbara Johnson, *A World of Difference* (Baltimore: Johns Hopkins University Press, 1987), trans. Barbara Johnson, pp. 201–3.
20. Two hundred steps, symbolizing the 200 days of the Battle of Stalingrad, lead from the bottom of the hill to the monument. The principal sculptor was Yevgeny Vuchetich.
21. "Leisure/Tourism: Maitreya Project: The Maitreya Project, India". *Aros Architects website*. Aros Architects. http://www. arosltd.com/projects.php?id=3. Retrieved 2008–03–04.
22. [http://www.endex.com/gf/buildings/liberty/worldstatues/spirit/ spirit.htm]
23. "Anish Kapoor's tangled tower at the heart of London 2012" Mark Brown, *The Guardian*, March 31, 2010.
24. Andrew Hough, *Telegraph*, October 25, 2009.
25. Dublin's "needle" of steel stands at the site where a statue of Admiral Nelson, perched on a giant column, stood before the IRA blew it up in 1966. A controversial figurative work was thus replaced by an abstract piece without any allusions to British imperial power, yet the new monument is much mocked in Dublin. And female connotation returns to denigrate it: one of its many nicknames, as a cab driver told me, is stiletto in the ghetto.

# Index

Numbers in bold refer to pages with illustrations

## L



## M



## N



## O



## P

## Q



## R



## S



## T



## U



## V



## W



## Y

## Acknowledgments

*Colossal* began in 2001 as a short talk at a College Art Association session, "Naming the 'Modern' in Nineteenth-Century Art," chaired by Hollis Clayson and Martha Ward. Since then, this book has benefited from the opportunity to present stages of my thinking to many different audiences, thanks to Erika Naginski and Nasser Rabbat at MIT; David Joselit, Ed Cooke, and Tim Barringer at Yale; Kathleen James-Chakraborty at U.C. Berkeley's School of Architecture; Dror Wahrman at University of Indiana, Bloomington; Margaret Cohen at Stanford University; Susan Siegfried at University of Michigan, Ann Arbor; Nancy Troy and Jonathan Reynolds at University of Southern California; Natalia Brizuela at U.C. Berkeley's Spanish Department; and the graduate students who asked me to give lectures at Northwestern University, the University of British Columbia, and Columbia University.

This book would not have been realized without Andrew W. Mellon New Directions Fellowships in 2002–03 and 2008–09 that funded my interrogations of the history of engineering. Ralph Hexter, when Dean of Letters and Science, consistently supported my project and helped me win the Mellon Fellowship. In addition, my research was funded by a Graham Foundation for Advanced Studies in the Fine Arts Grant and a Townsend Center Initiative Grant for Associate Professors which facilitated my conversations with Kathleen James-Chakraborty, formerly Professor of Architecture at Berkeley. A Furthermore Grant in Publishing, A Program of the J. M. Kaplan Fund, generously subvented the costs of producing *Colossal*.

Gregory Fenves, Professor of Engineering at UC Berkeley, allowed me to audit one of his courses, and Charles Chadwell, while a graduate student, tutored me in engineering. Professor J. David Rogers, Karl F. Hasselman Chair, Geological Sciences & Engineering University of Missouri-Rolla, answered questions about landslides at the Panama Canal, the subject of his ongoing research. Joseph Masheck shared his knowledge of Robert Smithson's Panama Canal project. David Weingarten of Ace Architects permitted me to photograph miniatures in his outstanding collection. My cousin Danilo Newell took me to see Van Ingen's murals in Panama.

As always, Todd Olson has been my invaluable interlocutor. Anne Wagner read my entire manuscript at an early stage and made significant suggestions. Tim Clark read chapter 5 and encouraged me to tackle key issues more forthrightly. Thomas Crow has long supported my work; *Colossal* is no exception. U.C. Berkeley graduate students were essential to *Colossal*'s preparation. Amy Freund photographed the archives at Colmar, including Bartholdi's correspondence. Jessica Dandona tracked down photographs in France and the United States; and helped with French translations. Kailani Polzak organized the book's illustrations and handled the technological challenges of digital images. Visiting the Statue of Liberty with Jessica May was also important.

Another source of invaluable assistance for this wide-ranging project was U.C. Berkeley's Undergraduate Research Assistantship Program (URAP) which enables students to conduct research for professors. I thank especially Adam Cramer and Erica Lee for our imaginative discussions. Lee also negotiated the photographing of Van Ingen's paintings by the Panama Canal Authority. Katie Eitzen conducted research and arranged to have her father photograph Van Ingen's paintings for research purposes. J. Nahry Tak efficiently contacted institutions and persons. Thanks as well to Dasha Ortenberg, Justine Suzanne Jones, Suge Lee, Ceci Moss, Caitlin Rocklen, and Jacob Rodriguez.

I am indebted to Gloria Kury for her support of *Colossal*; she has been a remarkably far-sighted, generous, and creative editor whose sustained interest in the colossal details of my book long passed my own. Her stubborn insistence that I revisit key parts of my argument and also write a coda has made *Colossal* a better book. Copyeditor Sara Lickey was thorough and sensitive in her work. Geoff Kaplan helped convert my manuscript into a book. Its design posed exceptional challenges that Diane Jaroch handled with consummate skill and intelligence. I thank all for their playful relationship to the ever more anachronistic object that is the book. Madelaine Dusseau and Chelsea Weathers were essential members of the team. Over the last five years Julie Wolf, the photographer for the History of Art Department at U.C. Berkeley, photographed numerous objects for *Colossal*.

Writing a book, I have the opportunity to thank loving friends and family who have supported me in so many ways during these last, often difficult years: my stalwart sister Lynne Grigsby, my step-father Peter Walters and his wife Andrea; my oldest friend Trish Reed who told me to make this book bigger when I needed to hear that advice; my cousins in Panama, Danilo, Jorge, and Henry Newell and their families; my dear friends, Maureen Beck and Stephen Schachter; Jan Leigh and Michael Fahy; Jack Rosenberg; Francesca Rose and her parents Tom and Carol Rose; Anna Seidler; Helen and Joel Isaacson; Timiza Wagner; David Sheidlower; Roger Hankins; Michael Miller; Erika Naginski; Huey Copeland; Christina Kiaer; Masumi Iriye and David O'Brien; Linda Fitzgerald; my excellent doctor Jeffrey Wolfe at UCSF; and my colleagues in History of Art at U.C. Berkeley for making possible what I needed most. I remember also those whom I have lost: Michele Amrich, Sarah Sheidlower, and Chris Meyer.

Finally this book is for my essential Todd, Gregoria and Pierre: "You are so vivid I could see you in the sky."